Urban Life and Urban Landscape Series

Domesticating the Street

The Reform

of Public Space

in Hartford,

1850–1930

Peter C. Baldwin

 Ohio State University Press, *Columbus*

An earlier version of chapter 3 appeared in the *Journal of Urban History* 23 (September 1997): 709–38.

Library of Congress Cataloging-in-Publication Data

Baldwin, Peter C., 1962–
    Domesticating the street : the reform of public space in Hartford, 1850–1930 / Peter C. Baldwin.
        p.   cm.
    Includes bibliographical references.
    ISBN 0-8142-0824-X (cloth : alk. paper). — ISBN 0-8142-5026-2 (pbk. : alk. paper)
    1. City planning—Connecticut—Hartford—History.   2. Public spaces—Connecticut—Hartford—History.   I. Title.
    HT168.H29B35   1999
    307.1′216′097463—dc21   99-28008
                                                CIP

Text and jacket design by Carrie Nelson House.
Type set in Electra by G & S Typesetters.
Printed by McNaughton & Gunn.

The paper used in this publication meets the minimum requirements of the American National Standard for Information Sciences—Permanence of Paper for Printed Library Materials. ANSI Z39.48–1992.

9 8 7 6 5 4 3 2 1

Contents

List of Illustrations   vi

Acknowledgments   viii

Introduction: The View from State House Square   1

1   Horace Bushnell and the Origins of Segregated Space   11   *parks*

2   Purifying the City   34   *dirt, billboards, ?*

3   The Fight against the Vice District   64   *prostitution - pastors, suffrage*

4   Saving the Newsies   93   *girls and boys restrictions*

5   Segregating the Parks   116   *Parker*

6   "The Children Are Off the Streets"   147   *girl / boy*

7   Expressmen and Peddlers   177   *dispersing the poor markets*

8   Creating a Traffic System   201   *technology, prestige - teaching peds to cross correctly*

9   City Plans   230

10   Of Hartford Seen in a Different Light   261

Notes   267

Index   349

Illustrations

Main Street at State House Square, mid-1920s   2
Horace Bushnell   13
Site of Bushnell Park   21
Central Hartford, 1854   23
Seth Marsh's 1858 plan for Bushnell Park   27
Hartford, 1895   36
Main Street, 1899   41
Charles Street, 1906   43
Washington Street   46
Dotha Bushnell Hillyer   49
Signs on a building on Main Street, ca. 1900   61
Part of the East Side, 1909   67
The River House, ca. 1900   68
Gold Street before clearance, 1890s   72
Emily S. G. Holcombe, 1900   73
Katharine Houghton Hepburn, ca. 1914   82
Fusco's saloon, ca. 1913   85
Boys scavenging, 1918   96
A young newsboy selling papers downtown, 1909   97
Newsboys entering a saloon, 1909   99
Newsgirls in an alley, 1909   109
George A. Parker, 1912   136
Elizabeth Park rose garden, 1921   138
Outdoor dancing at Colt Park, 1918   143
The Boys' Reading Room, 1876   150
Children playing in State Street, 1906   155

Playing in a puddle, 1913   156
Children's garden at Colt Park, 1914   162
Playground at Pope Park   167
View of City Hall Square, ca. 1900   179
State House Square before Thanksgiving, 1876   186
Selling chickens on Charles Street, ca. 1910   190
Kosher chicken butcher, Charles Street, 1910   191
Roads out of Hartford, 1911   209
Main Street, 1905   216
Traffic at the isle of safety, State Street, 1924   221
Carrère and Hastings plan for Hartford, 1912   245

Acknowledgments

For the successful completion of this book, I am obliged to the many people who have given me suggestions, comments, criticisms, and words of encouragement.

The idea for such a study evolved from discussions about city life with Randy Burgess, when we worked for the *Hartford Courant*. As a graduate student at Brown University, I further developed the idea as a result of my discussions about the historiography of public space with Howard Chudacoff, and my reading in Latin American urban history with Thomas Skidmore. John L. Thomas forced me to focus the idea into a feasible research project.

In my research, I relied on help from archivists, librarians, and other staff at the following institutions: the Connecticut State Library, the Hartford Public Library, the Connecticut Historical Society, Trinity College and Watkinson libraries, the Hartford Town and City Clerk's office, the Stowe-Day Library, the Library of Congress, the Center for Oral History at the University of Connecticut, the Jewish Historical Society of Greater Hartford, Hartford Seminary, the Capitol Region Council of Churches, the Christian Conference of Connecticut, the Catholic Archdiocese of Hartford, the Automobile Club of Hartford, the American Automobile Association, the University of Connecticut Archives, Schlesinger Library at Radcliffe College, and Brown University's Rockefeller, Hay, and Sciences libraries. I owe special thanks to Mark Jones of the Connecticut State Library and Penny Rusnak of the Hartford Public Library.

My argument has been clarified and strengthened thanks to comments from many people. Howard Chudacoff, John L. Thomas, and David Meyer read and commented on drafts of the manuscript in its earlier version as a dissertation. Many other people made helpful suggestions about the research or commented on parts of the manuscript. Among these are Dona Brown, Randy Burgess, Chrissy Cortina, Ray Douglas, Clay McShane, Zane Miller, Adam Nelson, Susan Pennybacker, Laura Prieto, Sarah Purcell, Ed Rafferty, Bruce Stave, and the anonymous readers at the *Journal of Urban History* and the Ohio State University Press. My thanks also to Barbara Hanrahan, Ruth Melville, Nancy Woodington, and everyone else at the Ohio State University Press.

This book is dedicated to my parents, Frank and Blythe Baldwin.

Introduction

The View from State House Square

Filled with the honking of horns and the smell of exhaust, Hartford's State House Square in 1930 was both the traffic-choked heart of a modern city and a public space rich in history. It had been the city's symbolic and functional center for nearly three hundred years, ever since the Puritans had arrived from Massachusetts, built their meeting house, and held their markets there. A few blocks to the east of the square flowed the Connecticut River, which for the city's first two centuries carried trading ships bound for distant seaports. To the north and west—along Main, Asylum, and Pratt streets—sparkled the display windows of the department stores and specialty shops that made downtown Hartford a metropolitan retail center. Theaters, restaurants, shops, banks, and office buildings lined the sides of the square, and over its southern edge loomed some of the insurance towers that were so crucial to the city's modern economy.

The Old State House stood inside the square overlooking the adjoining post office. An elegant brick and brownstone building topped with a

Main Street at State House Square, looking south, mid-1920s. Although some pedestrians can be seen walking through traffic to reach the trolleys, most confined themselves to the sidewalks and crosswalks, allowing the streets to efficiently process traffic reaching the square from throughout the metropolitan area. (Glenn Weaver, *Hartford: An Illustrated History of Connecticut's Capital*)

cupola and a small gilded dome, the Old State House had housed Connecticut's legislature for most of the first century of statehood, had heard New Englanders debate disunion in 1814, and had served as city hall from 1879 to 1915. It survived as a visible link to the past in a city enthusiastically striving to be up-to-date. The Old State House owed its continued existence in part to the efforts of early twentieth-century reformers, who fought to block demolition after the building ceased to be useful for city offices. The reformers argued that the Old State House was a monument to the history of the city and the state by virtue of its having witnessed many important events, and because of its position "on a spot where the public have congregated since the very beginning of the colony." [1]

The symbolic building had been saved, yet the function of the square had been radically transformed in the decades leading up to 1930. Though the square remained the center of the city's business district, it had lost much of its importance as an all-purpose public space—while becoming ever more vital as a transportation node. In the late nineteenth century, when it was known as City Hall Square, swarms of noisy children cried the day's headlines there as they thrust newspapers at passersby. Expressmen parked their horse-drawn wagons and passed the time quarreling with each other and loudly admiring female pedestrians. Farmers flocked to the square before holidays to sell their turkeys and geese. Prostitutes loitered there at night and escorted their customers to the otherwise respectable hotels nearby.

Thanks in part to the same reformers who had saved the Old State House, the square by 1930 had become a more orderly, though no less busy, place. Responding to reformers' demands, the city government sharply restricted who could sell newspapers (and how they could sell them), forced the expressmen out of the square and then off the streets entirely, limited peddling and set up public markets to rid the streets of peddlers, and cracked down on prostitutes, forcing them to operate more covertly and scattering them to far-flung sections of town. City officials set up playgrounds to keep children occupied in their own neighborhoods and even arrested some children who insisted on roller-skating in the square. By the late 1920s the square was dominated by motorized vehicles. At rush hour, more than a hundred streetcars an hour shuttled through Central Row (on the south side of the square), while nearly as many clattered in each direction along Main Street (on the west side); typically, several streetcars could be seen waiting for a berth at the trolley stops. Only a mechanical system of traffic lights—and the near absence of competing street activities—kept the trolleys, cars, and trucks flowing through the square and allowed disciplined herds of pedestrians to cross the streets safely. [2]

The transformation of State House Square in the late nineteenth and early twentieth centuries may seem to suggest an early example of what urban critics have called "the death of the street" as a multifunctional public space. Critics like Jane Jacobs, William H. Whyte, James Holston, James Howard Kunstler, and Mike Davis have placed much of the blame for the decline of street life on the automobile-oriented urban redevelopment following World War II. This development, they argue, has disregarded the value of lingering in the spaces that connect home and work. "To reduce contact with untouchables, urban redevelopment has converted once vital pedestrian streets into traffic sewers," Davis has written. Several historical studies of street life reflect this sense of decline, generally pinpointing the change in the late nineteenth and early twentieth centuries. Historians have argued that changes in pavements and public policy allowed the streets to become overwhelmed with traffic to the exclusion of other activities.[3]

Yet by examining the history of public space in Hartford, we can see that these arguments, which focus on the transformation of downtown streets in metropolitan centers, may not apply to American urban streets in general. It is true that automobile traffic overwhelmed Hartford's major thoroughfares, but social and commercial activities survived and evolved in certain other streets, both in slums and in residential neighborhoods. It would be a mistake to dismiss the persistence of these activities as a sign that the transformation of public space was initially incomplete: The activities are still present as we near the end of the first century of the automobile age. "The street" has not died—but streets have changed, some more than others.

Throughout the fifty-year period ending in 1930 the streets around State House Square were far from typical of those in Hartford. Their changing function is scarcely proof of any citywide triumph of vehicular traffic. We can understand the transformation of public space only by considering these streets in their relation to the rest of the city. The reason that State House Square attracted so much traffic is that it served as the hub of the metropolitan transportation system that developed in the late nineteenth century. Trolley lines and later automobile routes converged on the square from all over Hartford and the surrounding suburbs. The transportation system introduced striking differences in the functions of different streets and stimulated a differentiation of private land use by neighborhood, which in turn produced further changes in the streets. The efficient operation of the transportation system depended in part on the relocation of competing activities to other streets or to new spaces designed for specific purposes. Peddling was forced off the thoroughfares and into the slums and the Hucksters' Market. Recreational activities were pushed into parks, playgrounds, and side streets. City officials increasingly viewed the streets as forming a branching system of arteries and trunk lines, using terms drawn from anatomy and railroads. They made physical improvements in some streets that further concentrated traffic along certain routes and further displaced competing uses. Side streets, however, were kept relatively quiet; they were neither transformed into transportation routes nor annihilated as public spaces.

The development of the transportation system was part of a larger trend toward segregating the use of urban space. Public space lost its original status as undifferentiated land that was free from the restrictions accompanying private ownership and relatively open to all people and activities. The reforms of the late nineteenth and early twentieth centuries produced instead a citywide system of land use that encompassed both private and public property and assigned specific functions to each of the myriad components of the city. Public space was broken into various and more restricted public spaces.

This new, articulated system of urban land use could not have developed as it did without the rise of widespread trolley and automobile travel. Nevertheless, this system was more a result of human efforts than a by-product of transportation technology. Even before mass use of the automobile, Hartford reformers in the late nineteenth and early twentieth centuries had worked both to create alternative spaces for social and commercial activities and to regulate activities in the streets. The reformers were guided not so much by a conscious desire to clear the way for traffic as by a belief that a proper urban environment nurtured individual refinement and social harmony. The roots of this belief lay deep in the city's past. The Hartford theologian Horace Bushnell had theorized in the 1840s that the female-dominated, middle-class home had a powerful influence on character, an influence he sought to extend to exterior, public space in the 1850s as he created a landscaped park and recommended objectives for city planning. Reformers in the 1890s and 1900s; including Bushnell's daughter, Dotha Hillyer, revived such ideas as they attempted to spread the interrelated concepts of femininity and gentility to the disorderly and male-dominated downtown. They fought with some success, for example, to clean up the streets and to suppress public advertising. The greatest victory in this crusade to purify the city came when radical suffragists, trumpeting their womanly duty to defend the health and morals of their families, put an end to the city's vice district.

The fight against the vice district revealed a philosophical schism among Hartford reformers. One strain of reform sought to purify the entire city in order to spread gentility to everyone. Another conceded that such universal reform was impossible, trying instead to preserve or create the desired atmosphere in certain carefully segregated spaces. A controversy among reformers over whether the street could be made safe enough for young girls to sell newspapers, or whether the dangers to feminine virtue were irrepressible, demonstrated this split. In this case the more pessimistic side prevailed, the newsgirls were ordered off the streets, and the trend in Hartford reform turned toward segregating rather than purifying public space. Segregating space was easier than trying to purify it. Instead of fighting to impose a single vision on the entire city, reformers could focus their efforts where they had the greatest chance for success — and beat a strategic retreat where they faced determined opposition or insurmountable obstacles.

This latter reform tendency evolved in symbiotic relation with the development of the transportation system. Reformers seeking to beautify certain streets or other public spaces, for example, increasingly justified their efforts on the grounds of efficiency, while motorists learned to couch their arguments for efficient traffic flow in terms of public safety. In the 1920s, just as the reform impulse was fading away, the power of the automobile began gathering momentum on its own. Schemes for major street improvements were based almost exclusively on efficient transportation, which was understood to benefit the city economically. Appropriating the reformists' concept of dividing urban space and turning that concept to nonreformist ends, business-minded city officials openly defended zoning as a way to protect real estate investments.

Given that the local reform tradition was rooted in values associated with women and the home, it is not surprising that the conflicts among reformers reflected tensions within that cluster of values. On the one hand, reformers who sought to purify public space drew on a cultural understanding of "woman's sphere" as a set of concerns that could be extended throughout society. These reformers tended to be women, particularly women with at least some desire for a broader female role in society; through their reform campaigns, they created a new feminine role in politics. On the other hand, the reformers who settled for protecting morality and refinement within specific places defined woman's sphere as a space physically removed from a threatening outside world. Such reformers, usually men, extended this idea of separation to the segregation of public space. The distinction, however, was never clear-cut; the competing impulses to purify and to segregate space were two broad philosophical persuasions, not the gender-based ideologies of rival camps of reformers. Women and men could be found on each side of the divide; some individuals even supported both types of reform.[4]

In seeking to explain the evolution of a new system of public space, I emphasize the ideas and efforts of conscious human actors. My study traces a local tradition of environmental reform from its origins in theology through its elaboration and division in the early twentieth century to its perversion into economic utilitarianism in the 1920s. The reformers' efforts, together with the growth in traffic, produced an interwoven system of public and private space whose numerous parts took on specific functions. As the impulse to purify space was superseded in the 1910s by the competing impulse to segregate space, altruistic reform campaigns increasingly complemented practical-minded efforts to clear major routes for traffic. Ultimately the quest for traffic efficiency subordinated environmental reform altogether.

In tracing these reform campaigns, I argue that ideas have a powerful role in shaping cities, a role comparable to — perhaps even exceeding — the effects of technology. I do not ignore technological change, mass immigration, industrialization, or other factors whose effects on public space have been incontrovertibly documented by decades of historical research. As Hartford reformers well knew, technological, demographic, and economic change presented city dwellers with new problems and new possibilities, but these changes did not dictate a single urban form.

Human beings had to determine how to respond to the changes, and their choices were shaped not merely by the logic of necessity, but by their beliefs and by their morals.

In any discussion of reform politics, it is important to look beneath the rhetoric to discern how the proposed reforms might advance the reformers' selfish interests. Campaigns to reform the use of public space were seldom examples of pure altruism. Competing interest groups struggled for power over this highly visible and symbolic terrain, and their struggle had an important effect on the resulting system of public space.[5] In Hartford the result was not a simple triumph of one group over another. Working-class resistance to middle-class reform campaigns had a major influence in strengthening the trend toward segregation.

Nevertheless, Hartford's streets were more than just a battleground in a war for social and political power. Though the reform campaigns were rooted in middle-class, Protestant values, particularly values associated with women, they were not intended as mere assertions of class or gender interests. Guided by a sense of Christian stewardship and of personal responsibility for the public good, the reformers sought to mold a city where harmony meant more than the exercise of one group's hegemony. Even the exception proves the rule: Suffragists, who in their fight to cleanse Hartford explicitly demanded greater power for women, sincerely defended their effort as a way to reunite the city around a shared morality. The suffragists were inspired by an evangelical urge to universalize women's culture and an eagerness to participate in creating a politics of selflessness, more than by an ambition to build the power of women as an antagonistic interest group. Other reformers acknowledged the durability of competing group interests and needs. Nevertheless, while they proposed reforms that accommodated and even encouraged the segregation of public space, reformers hoped that their measures would help society transcend its conflicts and balance diversity with unity. The city and its people would be held together by orderly systems of public space that would preserve a sense of shared public interest. That these reforms accelerated the slide toward a deeply divided city was an unintended consequence of a reform impulse rooted in very different hopes. In particular, the reformers never intended their innovations to be commandeered for the purposes of private wealth, as they were in the 1920s.

From Horace Bushnell to Dotha Hillyer and George Parker, Hartford's reformers believed that public space could be a nurturing home rather than a social battleground. In the face of powerful countervailing trends toward conflict, they hoped to make the city a place that shaped and reproduced harmonious social relations. "The city," wrote Parker, "should mother its children."[6] We need to listen to these reformers carefully and to take their words seriously, without losing sight of the unfortunate trends to which their reforms ultimately contributed.

1

Horace Bushnell and the Origins of Segregated Space

Deep in the night, the riverside town of Hartford was roused by the ringing of church bells. The sleepy people who stumbled outdoors found the streets lit by the frightening glow of fire from the direction of Trinity Church, the Roman Catholic church on Talcott Street. By the time the night watchmen had discovered the fire and called out the volunteer fire companies, the flames had spread so rapidly through the old wooden building that nothing could be done to save it. The blaze soon leapt to the roof of the parsonage next door, and the firemen busied themselves by drowning it with streams of water to prevent the rest of the city from catching fire.

The Trinity Church fire, which broke out between midnight and 1 A.M. on May 11, 1853, was a blow to the growing Irish Catholic community of Hartford. Though they had built an expensive brownstone cathedral less than two years before, the Catholics still used the old church for weekday services, for Sunday school, and for the day school that served some four hundred boys and girls. Just as important, the disaster

11

was further proof that Hartford had lost any semblance of small-town unity. Everyone knew the fire was no accident. It was widely believed to be the work of anti-Catholic arsonists acting out through terrorism and destruction the nativist hatred that had been building up for the past twenty years.[1]

The Rev. Horace Bushnell, the Congregationalist pastor who lived a few blocks away on Winthrop Street,[2] must have been appalled by the torching of Trinity Church. True, Bushnell had been an early and outspoken enemy of Catholicism, but by the early 1850s he saw greater danger in the fragmentation of American society than in any Papist plot. National unity had been shattered by the issue of slavery, rich and poor were separated by widening class divisions, and religious factionalism divided even the town where he made his home. In this light, the burning of a church could only seem another sign of approaching anarchy.

This fear of the collapse of community lay behind the ambitious civic project that Bushnell publicly launched later in 1853. In an attempt to bring back what he fondly recalled as the harmony of his rural youth, he persuaded the authorities and citizens of Hartford to create a landscaped park in the heart of the city. Though hostility and estrangement might thrive in the hurried, complicated new urban environment, Bushnell hoped the park would be a place where all could come together in peace and happiness. The park would unite people and spread kind feelings throughout the city, just as the middle-class Protestant home did for the family on a smaller scale. Bushnell extended these ideas the following year in a treatise on city planning in which he proposed urban vistas that would create the feeling — and thence the reality — that the city was a coherent unit. There was an inherent but unacknowledged tension within Bushnell's ideas. While he hoped to reunite a divided people by reforming the urban environment, a crucial part of this reform would involve segregating the use of public space — creating a park, a space distinct from the surrounding city, where more refined behavior and values would prevail. This tension emerged more clearly a generation later, as Hartford reformers divided over whether to spread middle-class values throughout the entire urban environment or to concentrate on saving certain carefully segregated spaces.

Horace Bushnell (*Tenth Anniversary Commemorative Booklet, Horace Bushnell Memorial Hall*)

The Pastor from Arcadia

The city-planning work that consumed much of Bushnell's energy in 1853 and 1854 followed a decade of intense creativity in which he wrote the books and sermons that made him one of the most prominent American theologians.[3] During that period, he also lamented the growing divisions within American society and reflected on the preindustrial life whose final years he had glimpsed during his childhood. While welcoming the urban growth and industrialization that were radically transforming New England, Bushnell longed to recapture the values of what he remembered as the "Puritan Arcadia." Bushnell's revision of Congregational theology, his ambivalence about industrial capitalism, and his distrust of the individualistic ethos of Jacksonian America led him to emphasize the importance of the home and of social unity. On this intellectual foundation he built his ideas of city planning.

Bushnell, who was born in 1802 in the Litchfield County hills of northwestern Connecticut, grew up working on the family farm and in his father's wool-carding mill. He attended college, attempted careers in teaching and journalism, returned to Yale to study law, and finally entered Yale Divinity School in 1831. After completing his studies he received a call in 1833 to the North Congregational Church of Hartford, his first and only pastorate, in which he served until poor health forced him to resign in 1859. Whether or not Bushnell deliberately chose his words to appeal to the merchants who dominated his fractious congregation, his sermons and other writings celebrated material progress and sought to reconcile Calvinism with the new romantic aesthetic of the urban middle classes.[4]

His central work was the one he first published in 1847 as *Discourses on Christian Nurture*. Originally presented as two sermons to his congregation in 1846, Bushnell's discourses minimized the value of religious revivals, denying that an individual's entrance into Christianity is best achieved through a cataclysmic conversion experience. Instead, Bushnell argued, the proper goal of Christian education is that "the child . . . grow up a Christian" and feel his moral character blossom under the benign nurturance of his parents. Elevating the importance of emotion and the teachings of the heart, Bushnell argued that the child begins his spiritual development even before he understands language: "At first the child is held as a mere passive lump in the arms, and he opens into conscious life under the soul of the parent streaming into his eyes and ears, through the manners and tones of the nursery. . . . Farther-on, the parents begin to govern him by appeals to the will, expressed in commands, and whatever their requirement may be, he can as little withstand it, as the violet can cool the scorching sun, or the tattered leaf can tame the hurricane."[5]

By emphasizing the religious importance of child rearing, Bushnell shifted the focus of the Christian experience from the individual's interior struggle to the process of socialization, and from a church dominated by men to a home shaped by the influence of women. Further stressing the feminine qualities of true Christian faith, he criticized contemporaries whose piety was a masculine one of "conquest rather than of love. A kind of public piety that is strenuous and fiery on great occasions but wants the beauty of holiness, wants constancy, singleness of aim, loveliness, purity. . . . and—if I may add another term not so immediately religious, but one that carries, by association, a thousand religious qualities—wants domesticity of character."[6]

Bushnell's feminization of religion was in harmony with the romantic ideas of womanhood developing among the American urban middle classes in the 1830s and 1840s. In sentimental fiction and advice literature, as well as in the works of Bushnell and Catharine Beecher, the ideal middle-class woman was defined by the four cardinal virtues of piety, purity, submissiveness, and domesticity. Removed from economic production, sequestered within the home, and relegated to the role of consumer, the true woman was still far from useless. She exerted a subtle yet powerful influence within her domestic sphere. Morally superior to men and protected from the contaminating touch of their worldly struggles, she was ideally suited to uplifting her family members and bringing them to God.[7]

Yet in Bushnell's view, this new feminine role was but a makeshift substitute for the home life of preindustrial New England. In an 1851 address at the Litchfield County centennial celebration, he indulged in a nostalgic evocation of the "Puritan Arcadia," when people were "closer to nature and the simple life of the home." He defined life in early New England as "the Age of Homespun," whose essential characteristic was subsistence production within the family unit—particularly the household production of cloth—and whose central figure was the mother. Social as well as economic life revolved around the home. Neighbors might drop by in the evening to join the family around the fireside and discuss theology while the children played. That way of life had now vanished and would soon fade from memory, Bushnell told his audience. "It was a society back of the world, in the sacred retreats of natural feeling, truth and piety." The worldly influences of textile mills and commercial exchange had ended the Age of Homespun. "This transition from mother and daughter power to water and steam-power is a great one, greater by far than many have as yet begun to conceive—one that is to carry with it a complete revolution of domestic life and social manners."[8]

Woman's new role was just part of the deep socioeconomic change produced by industrialization and free-market capitalism, Bushnell continued. The people of early New England "had no capital, no machinery, no distribution of labor, nothing but wild forest and rock." Economic change had replaced the socially unifying struggle of man against nature with new class divisions and a host of social problems. But it was pointless to be hostile to industrial capitalism. The continued growth of manufacturing was essential for the prosperity of America's cities, and "prosperity, great as its dangers are, is yet the condition of virtue," Bushnell argued in an 1847 sermon. A decaying city became a place of decaying morality, where churches fell into disuse, and drinking, gambling, and whoring raged out of control. If instead people united for the good of their city, economic progress would go hand in hand with "social warmth" and "fellow spirit." Locally funded public-works projects would stimulate local prosperity. Economic self-interest would thus discourage internal social strife in favor of intercity competition. Capitalism did not have to be socially divisive.[9]

Instead of trying to bring back the Puritan Arcadia, Christians should salvage what they could of its values and attack a second cause of the problems in American society: an alarming trend toward individualism that had been initiated by the more radical thinkers of the American Revolution.[10] At issue, as Bushnell explained in *Discourses on Christian Nurture*, was whether society was a collection of separate individuals held together only by rational choice in a social compact. Regrettably, "the state, the church, the family, have ceased to be regarded as such, according to their proper idea, and become mere collections of units. A national life, a church life, a family life, is no longer conceived, or perhaps conceivable by many."

Despite this mistaken way of thinking, the truth was that "all society is organic — the church, the state, the school, the family, — and there is a spirit in each of these organisms peculiar to itself, and more or less hostile, more or less favorable to religious character, and to some extent, at least, sovereign over the individual man."[11]

The Christian home was more than a refuge for the values of the Puritan Arcadia, more than a nursery where children would grow strong enough to resist sin in their adult lives, and more than a daily source of inspiration for men troubled by the worries and temptations of the world. The Christian home was in fact a microcosm of the organic society, the mustard seed from which harmony could grow even in the rough world created by Jefferson and Jackson. Just as the child was shaped by parental influence, so did members of society develop a sense of unity through their daily interactions. Adults as well as children were deeply affected by the "unconscious influence" that they exerted on each other, Bushnell declared in an 1846 sermon with that title. Their sympathetic powers were sensitive to emotions and feelings conveyed unintentionally by those they saw and heard, and through this unconscious influence they became part of the larger society. "Being thus made common to each other voluntarily, you become one mass, one consolidated social body, animated by one life." [12]

This was a comforting thought at a time when Bushnell saw American society so desperately in need of unity. Controversies over slavery repeatedly threatened to tear the nation apart. The Compromise of 1850 only papered them over. Workers no longer lived under the same roof or shared meals with their employers, as the Bushnell family's farmhands had done in New Preston. Instead they were becoming a separate and even antagonistic class. The various religious sects were vying with each other for adherents in an increasingly contentious manner, Bushnell warned:

> Nothing is more undignified, or more opposed to the real object of society, which is to open the heart to man as man, and breed a state of courtesy and mutual regard between those who have different opinions. . . . Nothing could be more fatal to any thing like public spirit, or to any practical unity of force, in behalf of the common interest. We cannot flow together, — no warmth of feeling can be kindled for the public good. Society is divided, even down to the root. We are not people of Hartford, but we are Congregationalists, Episcopalians, Baptists, Methodists. [13]

Bushnell hoped that new, common institutions could extend the nurturing power of the home into the broader society and unite a divided people. Despite a deep hostility toward Catholicism, he called in early 1853 for compromise between Protestants and Catholics in order to ensure that both groups would support the common schools. Unlike Horace Mann, who hoped public schooling would produce a more fluid, egalitarian society, Bushnell hoped simply to prevent social conflict. Public schools, he argued, were needed "for the common training of so many classes and conditions of people. There needs to be some place where, in early childhood, they may be brought together and made acquainted with each other; thus to wear away the sense of distance, otherwise certain to become an established animosity of orders." Even Catholics could be assimilated into American life if they chose. Unfortunately, Bushnell acknowledged, the Catholics seemed stubbornly intent on keeping separate, so the common school alone was not an adequate solution. [14]

By 1853 Bushnell had identified disunity as the central problem of

American society and had developed the intellectual basis for his attempts to restore harmony. The perception of disunity lay behind his major project of that year, the new urban institution that came to be known as Bushnell Park.

A Pleasant Little Town

Bushnell had expressed a desire for a park in Hartford as early as the 1830s, perhaps only a few years after arriving in the city, and he began seriously planning one in 1849 or 1850.[15] The intervening years had marked a momentous change in the character of the city. In the mid-1830s, Hartford was a river port of barely ten thousand people. It was, one man recalled, "a small commercial town . . . dealing in lumber and smelling of molasses and old Jamaica, strongly impressed with a plodding, mercantile, and mechanical character." Located near the head of navigation for seagoing vessels, it quietly prospered from its trade with the rich farming villages of the Connecticut Valley and with port cities up and down the Atlantic seaboard. Small steamboats towing flat-bottomed barges pushed the river trade as far north as Wells River, Vermont, 220 miles away, returning to Hartford with loads of corn, lumber, and wool. In the 1840s, however, railroads and canals undercut the river trade, allowing Boston, Albany, and New York City to rob Hartford of much of its hinterland. Businessmen in the mid-1840s worried that the city was stagnating and that it would soon be eclipsed by such rivals as New Haven and Springfield.[16]

But while river commerce was fading away, manufacturing, banking, and insurance enterprises were prospering, giving Hartford a solid economic foundation for what would be a century of growth. The city had begun in the 1820s and 1830s to develop into a major publishing center, with more than thirty small firms specializing in textbook publishing and subscription publishing. The late 1840s and early 1850s saw the opening of several important manufacturing firms, including gun factories producing Sharp's rifles and Colt's revolvers, which supplemented the existing iron foundry, tanneries, and other industrial plants. Insurance companies and banks were also growing in size and number in the late 1840s and early 1850s, as the prestige of Hartford insurance firms soared after their successful payment of claims from the 1845 New York

City fire. By 1849 the city was visibly prospering again and had built or was building railroad links in all directions. "In the mechanical department, particularly, a striking change has taken place, and now, early and late, the hum of business from hundreds of busy workmen may be heard, where only a few years since every thing wore a quiet and village-like aspect," the *Hartford Daily Courant* reported in 1852. Despite earlier fears of stagnation, Hartford's population had grown to about 18,000 by 1850 and would exceed 29,000 by 1860.[17]

The city's geography was changing as quickly as its economy. The center of economic life was shifting away from the riverfront toward the new downtown business blocks along Main Street and the new manufacturing district that was beginning to form along the Little River, a sluggish stream that flowed into the Connecticut River south of the city center. Housing was also spreading away from the Connecticut River, and a new pattern was becoming apparent: the poor and the working classes were increasingly concentrated in a belt of slums that ran along the wharves south to the Little River and then west along that river. Joining the influx of working-class and poor people were many hundreds of Irish immigrants, whose neighborhood the nativist *Courant* called "Pigville." There were also significant numbers of blacks and Jews (the Jews were numerous enough by 1843 to organize their first congregation). As the prosperity of the older riverfront neighborhoods declined, brothels and gambling saloons opened up. Wealthy families attempted to sequester themselves from the working class and the increasingly obtrusive manufacturing in the central city by building houses in new outlying residential areas: on Asylum Hill to the west of the old city, and in the Charter Oak, South Green, and Washington Street neighborhoods to the south. Unfortunately for those seeking to escape the smells, the noise, and the Irish, a belt of notorious slums lay between the new southern neighborhoods and the central city. The seclusion from urban hubbub that could be felt on a Charter Oak street, therefore, was mitigated by the regular necessity of passing the Little River hovels on the way downtown.[18]

Growth, industrialization, and immigration had produced class and ethnic divisions in Hartford's geography, yet the city had not entirely lost the appearance of a country town. Hartford in the 1850s was still small enough that every part of the city was within walking distance of the countryside. The developed area extended little more than a mile from the steamboat docks at the foot of State Street. Beyond that stretched pastures and farms on all sides. Even within the developed part of the city, backyards and tracts of vacant land broke up the urban appearance. Only the East Side, the declining neighborhood of tightly packed buildings east of Main Street, looked overcrowded. Travelers visiting Hartford noted its rural setting. "The town is beautifully situated in a basin of green hills; the soil is rich, well-wooded, and carefully improved. . . . It is a lovely place," wrote Charles Dickens, who visited in 1842. Anthony Trollope, who visited in 1861 in the midst of a boom produced by Civil War military contracts, called Hartford "a pleasant little town, with English-looking houses, and an English-looking country around it." Though growing, Hartford was certainly not an unrelieved urban landscape. It was obvious, however, that the continuing growth would only add to what was already a twenty-five-minute walk from the riverfront to the countryside and would effectively cut parts of the city off from its rural environs.[19]

The Outdoor Parlor

If urban growth meant the loss of easy access to the countryside, Hartford's people would have no alternative to the meager recreational opportunities within the city. Residents had grumbled for years about the lack of a promenading ground like the New Haven Green. They made do instead with the South Green, a little public square at the south end of Main Street crowded with women pushing baby carriages, and an even smaller and shabbier green at Village and Windsor streets where boys played ball. The opportunity for what would be Hartford's first major park project came in 1849, when the old railroad station, located near Main Street at the end of a short spur, was replaced by a new one on the main line west of downtown. With the opening of the new railroad station at the corner of Asylum Street and Union Place, the old spur fell into disuse except for freight deliveries.[20]

The roughly thirty-acre site surrounding the neglected railroad spur was by all accounts a stinking hole. It was a shallow valley through which flowed the filthy Little River, derisively termed the Hog River, where dead cats and garbage rotted in muddy backwaters. Upon first considering the site, Bushnell was "appalled by the god-forsaken look of the prem-

The site of Bushnell Park. Bushnell described the thirty-acre tract south of the Little River as a "god-forsaken" wasteland, dominated by a garbage dump, the rail line, and the houses of the poor. (*Connecticut Quarterly*, 1895)

ises." A cluster of mill buildings stood at the western end near the railway junctions. "Around the mill," Bushnell recalled, "were grouped eight or ten low tenements, with as many pig-sties, that appeared to have been dropped there by accident. On the north side, into the low bend of the river. . . . all the garbage and truck of the city were dumped as in a Gehenna without fire — shavings, leather-cuttings, cabbage-stumps, rags, hats without tops, old saddles, stove-pipes rusted out." Heading east on the south side of the river, the two converging arms of the spur passed over ground so marshy that the tracks were raised on earthen embankments. A service yard with an engine house, repair shops, a water tank, and a woodshed stood along the tracks, and ashes and cinders were dumped into nearby pits. "There were besides on the premises two old tanneries — one falling to pieces, the other barely managing to stand upon a slant; and on a high clay-bank . . . was a little African Methodist chapel, looking out for prospect on the general litter of the region. And, finally, there was a back-side frontage of filthy tenements, including a soap-works, that ran completely round upon the east and north-east bank of the river, and projected their out-houses over it on brackets and piers."[21]

The area that eventually became the park had at least 222 people living in it in 1850, about three dozen of them African-Americans who clustered around the African Methodist Episcopal Zion church near what was then the corner of Bliss and Elm streets. Many of the other residents were unskilled Irish laborers and their families. In general, inhabitants tended to be poor; many of them rented rather than owned their dwellings.[22] As his description of the area suggests, Bushnell saw such people as scarcely more desirable than the cabbage stumps and ash piles, as he shared the common Yankee middle-class distaste for the Irish and for blacks. Bushnell's description also betrays his continued ambivalence about the productive functions of the nineteenth-century city. Although he regarded urban economic life as a necessary evil, he recoiled from the unsightly reality of it. Uncomfortable both with ethnic minorities and with industrial capitalism, he would seek solutions to urban problems while saying as little as possible about the disagreeable details. Rather than grappling directly with the miseries of the industrializing city, his solutions would involve creating countervailing strongholds of virtue and beauty—first and foremost, the park.[23]

From Bushnell's public comments in 1853, it appears that he began seriously planning a park within a year or so of the opening of the new railroad station. Bushnell later noted that the opening of the station facilitated the park project by making the New Haven Railroad eager to get rid of its old buildings. He may also have been inspired by the proposals being made by 1850 for a park in New York City, although his ideas about public space were developed independently from those of the eventual builder of Central Park, his former parishioner Frederick Law Olmsted.[24]

Bushnell started work on the park project by contacting some of those who owned large parcels of the future park site. He found that the railroad and the mill owners were willing to sell, but the others were not. He then persuaded one of his parishioners who served on the Common Council to support a charter revision letting the city take land by eminent domain. The council and legislature approved the revision, and voters overwhelmingly gave final approval in July 1853.[25] This enabling

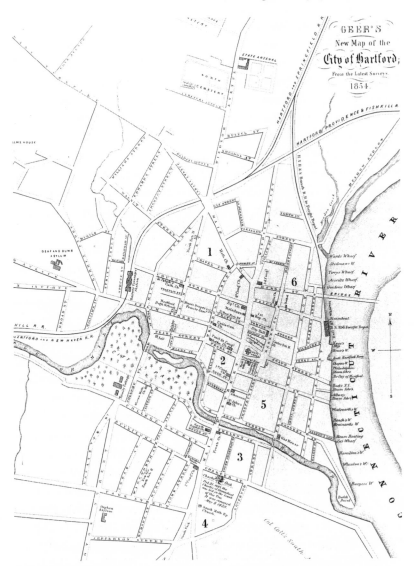

Central Hartford in 1854, showing the park, which had not yet been constructed. (Connecticut State Library)

legislation set off a flurry of competing proposals for park sites in the summer and early fall of 1853. At least five different sites were suggested in outlying parts of the city, mostly by wealthy property owners who would benefit from such an improvement in their neighborhoods.[26]

Certainly it might be cheaper to build a park in the outskirts of town, but Bushnell argued that it was crucial to choose a central site. The site he recommended was near the growing central business district, on land that had been settled since the founding of Hartford. "Common grounds should be internal, not outside of a city," he declared while presenting his proposal at a special Common Council meeting on October 5, 1853 (as paraphrased in the press). "They should be convenient for the mass of the people, who may enjoy their free air. The gentleman of wealth, with his carriage, may drive out and enjoy the beautiful in nature, but those who are not able to do this need a central common. Then if the common is on the outside, it has little to do with the city; but if it is central it gives an air and pleasant aspect to the whole place."[27]

Bushnell said that the park would "add to [Hartford's] health and comfort, but more particularly, act favorably on the taste and manners of the citizens, and, by presenting constantly before the eye a beautiful object, accustom the minds of all to relish beauty, and thus be the means of ennobling and purifying all." The park, in other words, would exert an unconscious influence of its own.[28] Bushnell further told the council that the park was needed "on account of the manners and morals of the people. It was important to bring people together. It has a humanizing influence." A central location was more than a matter of convenience — it was essential to the success of a park in creating civic unity. Evidently uncertain that this reason was persuasive enough, Bushnell tossed in a few others: The park would correct Hartford's inelegant appearance, would give train passengers a favorable first impression, and would raise both property values and the reputation of the city. It would also offer a good site for a new statehouse on its small southern hill, strengthening Hartford's claim to be the proper capital of the state. If the city did not act soon, the land would become a more densely developed slum.[29]

Bushnell's plan for the park embodied some of the ideas that he developed in his later speech on city planning. The main goal was to make the inner part of the park a visual focal point that passersby could see from surrounding streets, and to which they would be drawn. Bushnell proposed that, after clearing away the railroad spur and the buildings, the city should create easy access by building two or three light footbridges over the river and a broad avenue from Main Street into the park's heart. "Little fencing is needed." He proposed placing a fountain in a spot where it could be best seen from the streets. The higher southwestern corner of the park would afford views into picturesque central lowlands. Some grading would be needed, but the natural appearance would be maintained by keeping the existing trees and by using the river as a gently curving northern boundary, perhaps with a drive along the river's edge. Throughout his presentation, Bushnell emphasized the views of the park to be had from the surrounding city, and the views of the city from the park.[30]

After hearing Bushnell's speech and looking at the plan he had prepared, the council set up a committee to study the proposal. The committee members worked closely with Bushnell and allowed him to write their whole report except for the part related to the cost estimates.[31] In the November 14 report, Bushnell linked the park project even more explicitly to his hopes for civic unity:

> Nothing, we are sure, will serve the purpose demanded, but an opening in the heart of the city itself, to which the citizens will naturally flow in their walks and which they will naturally cross in passing on foot from one side or quarter to another . . . a green carpet of ground. . . . a social exchange, where friends will meet and to which they will naturally find their way in their strolls of pleasure and exercise; where high and low, rich and poor will exchange looks and make acquaintance through the eyes; an outdoor parlor, opened for the cultivation of good manners and a right social feeling. It must be a place of life and motion, that will make us more completely conscious of being one people.[32]

Bushnell's choice of metaphor is intriguing: the park was to be "an outdoor parlor," a specialized room in a city that (as he would write a year later) should be viewed as a house. Bushnell's readers would have understood this metaphor as richly evocative of the social atmosphere he desired. The parlor, once found only in the large houses of the very wealthy, was by 1850 becoming common in middle-class homes throughout urban America. Just as the land by the train station might be seen as the front room to Hartford, the parlor was the front room to the home. The parlor was a semipublic place between the openness of the street and the privacy of the back rooms reserved for the family, a place where certain strangers might be admitted as well as old friends. Though the parlor often doubled as a sitting room for the middle-class family, its primary importance was as a social stage. A wide variety of activities took place there, from friendly visits to teas, formal calls, theatricals, small concerts, weddings, and funeral receptions. All these interactions demanded careful attention to etiquette, sometimes to the point of highly stylized ritual. Any emotional conflicts were carefully suppressed. The decor reflected this purpose—the carpeted floors, upholstered chairs, and heavily draped windows softened the harsh lines of the architecture just as the mild conversation prevented or soothed away disagreements. Moreover, the parlor was the place where the family showed its aesthetic taste and cultural sophistication by displaying objets d'art, book collections, souvenirs of travel, and pianos or other musical instruments. In the words of the historian Karen Halttunen, "The parlor was the arena through which the aspiring middle classes worked to establish their claims to social status, to that elusive quality of 'gentility.'" Most important, the parlor was a female-dominated space, the place where the values of domesticity reigned supreme and in which the true woman exerted her influence on society.[33]

These values would not be lost in a parlor floored by a carpet of grass instead of an oriental rug, Bushnell's report indicated. The power of "unconscious influence" would uplift and unify the people who came to the park, just as it improved those within the home. The park not only facilitated random social encounters between friends but also allowed total strangers of different socioeconomic classes to make acquaintance through the nonverbal means that Bushnell believed were even more important than speech. It would be a way for the lower classes to absorb the values and refinements of their betters and to shed their rude ways. The park would be a feminized form of public space, a way of extending female values outside the home.[34] In this respect, the park's function harmonized with the well-established romantic association of women with nature in its tamer and more cultivated forms. Bushnell himself had linked femininity and nature in "The Age of Homespun": "It is the greatness of woman that she is so much like the great powers of nature, back of the noise and clatter of the world's affairs, tempering all things with her benign influence only the more certainly because of her silence, greatest in her beneficence because most remote from ambition, most forgetful of herself and fame."[35]

PROPOSED PARK,
for the
CITY of HARTFORD.
Containing about 30 acres

The 1858 plan for the proposed park by the city surveyor, Seth Marsh. Marsh's plan reflected Bushnell's intention of keeping the park open to its surroundings. Jacob Weidenmann's 1860 plan made more creative use of the spaces but maintained the same openness to the streets. Note Marsh's inclusion of a "State House," which was actually built twenty years later on a site vacated by Trinity College. On this plan, south is up. (*Connecticut Quarterly*, 1895)

Bushnell eventually got the park that he wanted. The project roused some controversy as opponents complained about the cost, the principle of taking land by eminent domain, and the ugliness of the location.[36] But the idea of a park won support from all classes. Factory workers submitted a petition as soon as the first park proposal was made, and the socially prominent poet Lydia H. Sigourney penned an ode to the vision of beauty and harmony. The central location, as one of the park supporters pointed out, made it possible to get voters from all sections of the city to support the proposal. Hartford residents approved the project heartily on January 5, 1854, by a vote of 1,005 to 682.[37]

The people who lived in the park were quietly evicted, but construction was delayed by lack of funds and by flaws in the initial designs. The sickly Bushnell had little to do with the actual construction of the park, although he helped defend the project against opponents who wanted it abandoned. He also served on the committee overseeing the park design. The park was finally completed about 1867. As Bushnell noted in 1869, it was similar to his original plans. The final designs by landscape architect Jacob Weidenmann kept the park partly open to the street by lining its border with widely spaced deciduous trees. The interior, bisected by Bliss Street, was primarily open lawn dotted with irregular clumps of trees and shrubs; there were no dense woods to block the views. A network of paths converged on a central pond, a drive looped around the park's western edge, and a terrace offered views of Asylum Street and the passing trains. Bushnell Park was considerably less isolated from the urban environment than was Central Park, which despite its name was originally on the outskirts of New York. Explaining his own design philosophy in 1871, Olmsted described a park as a place where "people may stroll for an hour, seeing, hearing, and feeling nothing of the bustle and jar of the streets, where they shall, in effect, find the city put far away from them. . . . We want depth of wood enough about [the park] not only for comfort in hot weather, but to completely shut out the city from our landscapes." In the early twentieth century, Hartford park officials sympathized more with Olmsted than Bushnell. Finding openness objectionable, they planted a wall of shrubs and trees along Bushnell Park's northern border.[38]

The most immediate tangible effect of Bushnell's park project was to reconfigure Hartford's class and ethnic boundaries. No longer bordered by slums, the genteel areas south of the Little River now grew quickly, with the construction of elegant town houses on the south side of the park and opulent mansions on Washington Street. Those who located there found a more effective separation from the poor than had previously been possible. Deliberately or not, Bushnell disregarded this effect. He chose to believe that the park's true importance lay in its healing effect on class divisions, as he showed in an 1872 speech proclaiming its success. Not only had the park provided a place of beauty — "one of God's smiles" — but, he claimed, it had unified the classes. "Children of the poor going there have seen the children of higher families of the city, and there has been an associated feeling excited. The rich have seen the condition of the poor and good has come out of this association." Four years later, as Bushnell lay dying, the Common Council voted to name the park after him.[39]

City Planning

In larger issues of city planning, too, Bushnell was guided in the 1850s by the metaphor of house and home. Olmsted would later use this metaphor to justify the functional segregation of the city, arguing that "if a house to be used for many different purposes must have many rooms and passages of various dimensions and variously lighted and furnished, not less must . . . a metropolis be specifically adapted at different points to different ends." In keeping with this philosophy, Olmsted designed suburbs that, like the parks, were both separate from and complementary to the urban environment.[40] Bushnell, in contrast, sought to minimize the divisive aspects of the urban landscape. Instead of reflecting the divisions within industrial urban society, he believed, the urban landscape should be carefully designed to create the illusion of civic unity, in the hope that the illusion might become reality. Bushnell suggested that the entire city should become like a well-constructed and tastefully decorated home that encouraged friendly socializing. The architecture and ornaments of the city, like those of the home, should evoke uplifting associations. Above all, people should feel gathered together within their city, much as family members felt in their home.

Bushnell began considering questions of comprehensive urban design soon after winning voters' approval for the park in 1854, and he announced the formation of a local Society for Public Improvement that autumn. "The great and principal object of the society is to advance the public taste of our citizens in matters relating to the attractiveness and ornament of the city," he wrote in a letter to the *Courant*. The society planned to do this by inviting prominent citizens to present lectures on such topics as "Economy of Taste," "Public Parks," "Public Architecture," "Street Architecture," "Color," and "Trees and Shrubbery." Bushnell himself was scheduled to present a lecture on "Planning of Cities." The society would also meet to discuss specific ways to improve and beautify Hartford, which Bushnell hoped would have the added benefit of making members identify more closely with their city. Before Bushnell could deliver his lecture, his health deteriorated seriously; he was forced to cancel the talk and sail to Cuba in early 1855 to convalesce. Not until 1864 did he have the lecture published in an anthology of his writings on secular topics.[41] Regardless of the ten-year delay in its publication, the essay "City Plans" shows how Bushnell had expanded his ideas about parks into a set of both broad and specific guidelines for urban design, recommendations that were still fresh when they appeared in print.

The first requirement of a good city plan, Bushnell argued in this essay, was that it should remind the inhabitants that they were living together in a city, a separate manmade world discrete from its natural surroundings. As in the walled cities of Europe, the urban environment should create a sense "of being gathered into city life . . . that associates the feeling of art and community." At worst, a city would be like so many in the American West, a grid of straight streets offering views in every direction into the empty countryside. Ideally, a city should be built around a valley, so that its various parts would all look in toward one another. "The center now will be the chief point of show or impression; for everything looks into it, and all the motion of the central crossings will be visible from the surrounding slopes, or summits." The importance of the vista should also guide the siting of public monuments and buildings, symbols of civic identity that should be placed for maximum visibility in open spaces at the convergence of major streets. "The city, in short, will be most perfectly planned, other things being equal, when it makes a world for itself and reveals its ornaments most effectually to itself. Like the inside of a house, it is to be planned for inside show, completeness and beauty."[42]

Bushnell's allusion to home interiors, like his earlier reference to the outdoor parlor, was charged with meaning. Members of the Victorian bourgeoisie self-consciously used interior decorating as a symbolic vocabulary. Objects were selected for their cultural and historical associations, in order both to uplift the character of family members and to display the family's refinement. The eclectic objects displayed in the home—the books and pianos, the engravings of George Washington, the Gothic knickknacks, the busts of Shakespeare, and so forth—were intended to be evocative of aesthetic sensibility and of a morally uplifting past that could guide present aspirations.[43]

Like a house, Bushnell's ideal city would display its history not only in its "ornaments" (its monuments and public buildings) but in its basic architecture—the layout of its streets. "As a house will be most pleasing when it looks as if it grew up with the family, by successive enlargements and room by room. . . . so a city will be most pleasing when the history is told by the plan." In European cities, he explained, history was told by the crowded little streets in the ancient core, by the broad boulevards and parks that replaced what were once city walls, and by the more spacious outlying sections of modern development. In the United States, New Haven displayed its history in the pleasing contrast between the colonial grid at its center and the new neighborhoods along what were once converging country roads. Washington, D.C., on the other hand, showed only a cold and ahistorical design by a single planner.[44]

Bushnell suggested that properly designed vistas would accentuate the appearance of bustling activity and social interaction. "The life and vivacity of the park will be graduated by the general show it makes of the multitudes walking, driving or at play upon it." For that reason it was particularly important to place parks in valleys, where this activity could be seen easily. Similarly, the street plan should heighten the sense of urban closeness. Most streets should be no more than fifty to eighty feet wide, and blocks should be narrow. Otherwise, the city plan "spreads the business and population over too large a surface, introducing magnificent distances where you want the sense of density and a crowding, rapid, all-to-do activity—which is one of the principal attractions of a city." Street layouts should incorporate the contours of the natural topography, not to replace the urban grid with imitations of winding country roads but to improve views within the city and enhance the visibility of the busiest streets. Ideally the skeleton of an irregular street grid would be formed by natural ridges along which would run dignified thoroughfares like New York's Broadway. In most cases, a street climbing to meet a ridgetop route should terminate at that intersection instead of crossing, so that the view up the street would end at an elegant architectural facade instead of in an empty sky. On the other hand, a street that dipped down into a valley should always continue straight through a number of intersecting routes, so that "everything moving in [the hollow], from one end to the other, will be visible at a glance, and a scene of perpetual, ever shifting, vivacity will be maintained." In short, he sought a compact, legible, bustling cityscape.[45]

Utilitarian considerations were of secondary importance to Bushnell, but he did not ignore them. Hidden in the text of the essay is an offhand declaration that "primarily cities are for use — only for show or beauty afterward."[46] The essay touches on the need for major crosstown thoroughfares, for street widths adequate for smooth traffic flow, for an ample sewer system, and for street layouts designed to expose buildings to more sunlight. Yet Bushnell's statement about the primacy of function is undercut by the fact that the bulk of the essay focuses on matters of "show or beauty." Urban planning, he suggested, should aim for higher goals than efficiency and comfort: it should create an environment that would nurture a refined, harmonious society. City planning was not simply a matter of engineering; it demanded both artistic and practical judgment, and it was a matter of great social importance. The rapid creation and growth of cities throughout the United States presented an opportunity for urban design that should not be squandered by leaving the matter in the bungling hands of amateurs and philistines. "We want therefore a city-planning profession, as truly as an architectural, house-planning profession. Every new village, town, city, ought to be contrived as a work of art, and prepared for the new age of ornament to come."[47]

———

In his campaign for the park and his essay on public space, Bushnell pioneered the idea of solving Hartford's social problems by improving its physical environment. In Bushnell Park he had created a new, segregated environment, which, like his idyllic Litchfield County, was a natural place, "back of the world, in the sacred retreats of natural feeling, truth and piety." But unlike later reformers who drew on both his ideas and those of Olmsted, Bushnell did not intend to create a replacement for the social life of the streets. He intended instead to create a place like the home, where kind feelings could be encouraged and then spread to the rest of the city. The sacred retreats of the home and the park were not embattled refuges from a hopelessly corrupt urban environment; they were intended to nurture harmony.

Bushnell saw the segregation of public space as a step toward the more important reunification of an organic society. Suspicious of the dominant currents of romantic reform that sought to perfect America by liberating the potential of the individual, Bushnell based his reform campaign on a concern for community that resonated among later reformers and thinkers more strongly than among his contemporaries.[48] But the Hartford reformers who drew on his and Olmsted's ideas in the late nineteenth and early twentieth centuries found that Bushnell had left a bifurcated legacy. Some of his more optimistic successors sought to spread the feminine values of the park and the home throughout the city and to purify the urban environment in both a physical and moral sense. Drawing on the metaphor of municipal housekeeping and on the rhetoric of maternal nurture, female reformers in the Civic Club, the Daughters of the American Revolution, and the Hartford Equal Franchise League attacked dirty streets and prostitution. But the limited success of their reforms left it obvious that the male world of the streets could not be so thoroughly purified. Unable to reform the entire city at once, moreover, these women came up against the problem that Bushnell had sought to deny in his 1872 celebration of the park's success: the purification of part of the city, though intended as a step toward a broader transformation that would produce "social warmth" and "fellow spirit," might ironically serve the interests of affluent people seeking to buffer themselves from urban unpleasantness.

Other reformers, less inclined to pursue the agonizing quest for social unity, chose the second half of Bushnell's legacy. They unabashedly welcomed the idea of segregating public space, viewing it not as a necessary antidote to the morally troublesome division of society, but as a welcome extension of the logic represented by new middle-class neighborhoods. They understood that the urban environment as a whole could never nurture genteel morality, at least not in a multiethnic industrial city where middle-class Protestants were a shrinking minority. In contrast to Bushnell, this group of reformers accepted both the social divisions created by industrialization and immigration and the fact that competing classes and ethnic groups had different ideas about the use of space. They came to view segregation as the model for a pluralistic society: divided but at peace.

2

Purifying the City

After a quarter century of rapid changes, Hartford seemed to return in the 1870s and 1880s to the moderate growth and social stability for which Horace Bushnell had yearned. The population rose only gradually, by an average of less than a thousand people a year, to reach 53,000 by 1890. Builders erected new houses and commercial buildings without changing the city's basic form. As late as 1890, "Hartford was compact and closely knit, radiating only short distances from post-office square and city hall," reminisced a former newspaper reporter years later. The developed part of the city extended barely two miles from City Hall Square. There were a few clusters of outlying homes, "but there were long stretches of vacant lands where daisies grew and cattle grazed."[1]

The local economy expanded haltingly, weathering a difficult downturn in the 1870s before returning to prosperity. By 1890, Hartford was somewhat more industrialized than in Bushnell's day. On the south side of town stood the enormous Colt's Armory where, under a blue onion dome, workers assembled revolvers and Gatling guns. Sprinkled in and around the downtown were a few dozen smaller factories, producing books, boxes, brass, candy, carriages, chairs, crackers, cutlery, hardware, industrial belting, iron, machinery, pottery, steam boilers, and soap. The emerging center of industry, though, was the "factory district"—a cluster of long, multistory brick buildings along the Park River (formerly the Little River) and the adjacent rail line running southwest from Bushnell Park. Among the major industries there were the Pope Manufacturing Company, the largest American manufacturer of bicycles; the Hartford Machine Screw Company; and the Pratt and Whitney Company, which made machine tools. All told, manufacturers in Hartford employed slightly more than nine thousand men, women, and children in 1890.[2] Adding to the city's economy were the nearby manufacturing villages and towns, mostly created by Hartford capital: Collinsville manufactured axes, New Britain hardware, Thompsonville carpets, Rockville woollen cloth, Willimantic cotton thread, and South Manchester silk. Hartford remained a banking and insurance center as well. The insurance companies had rebounded after suffering heavy losses from the Chicago fire of 1871. They proclaimed their strength by building what one observer called "great granite piles"—ornate, mansard-roofed headquarters that stood out amid the more modest downtown buildings. By 1889 such firms as the Hartford Fire, Phoenix, Aetna, Aetna Life, Connecticut Mutual Life, and Travelers insurance companies had proven that both fire and life insurance companies would continue to compete successfully nationwide. The Hartford insurance industry had "reached a preëminence, which promises to be permanent," boasted the Hartford Board of Trade.[3]

The quiet prosperity produced by Hartford's factories, banks, and insurance companies was readily apparent to any visitor. Spacious homes lined the tree-shaded avenues, lending credence to the claim that Hartford was for its size the richest city in the United States. Some of this wealth had trickled down to the skilled workforce that manned the factories, helping keep peace in Hartford during a turbulent period in American labor history. "Honest work makes faithful workmen. . . . While labor troubles have visited many places during the last few years, causing great waste of capital and bitterness of feeling, Hartford has wholly escaped the contagion," claimed the Board of Trade. "In our large establishments the relations between employers and employees are notably cordial, and any rash agitator who should attempt to disturb the

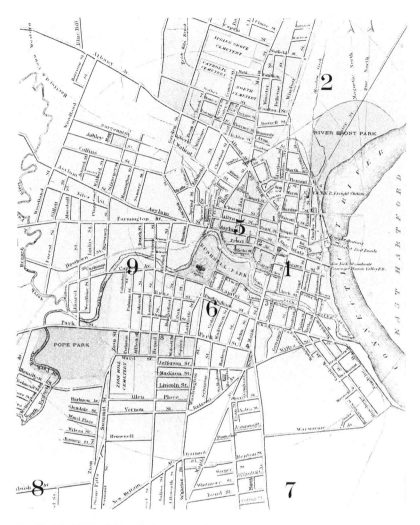

Hartford in 1895. Although the city was beginning to grow quickly, there was still unplatted land within two miles of City Hall Square, in what are now the Barry Square and Upper Albany neighborhoods, as well as in the North and South Meadows. (Connecticut State Library)

harmony would be treated by all with contempt." Organized labor was quite weak despite the efforts of Hartford's Central Labor Union, which helped form a Connecticut branch of the American Federation of Labor in 1887. Strikes were infrequent, and the open shop prevailed until the 1930s.[4]

"Whatever the eighties may have been elsewhere, in Hartford they were a placid era," recalled Henry Perkins, a man who had grown up then in the last middle-class enclave on the East Side. Money was flowing steadily into the city, and the years ahead promised more of the same:

Everyone felt confident of the future when Hartford would be larger and richer, but still the same pleasant place we loved, without any radical alteration in its character or mode of living. . . . The future might hold more leisure, larger houses, more servants, better horses. There might be more expensive parties, more trips abroad, but life would all be cut from the same pattern, a pattern which made for contentment and a sense of security among the prosperous. Alas for the placid eighties![5]

The placid era of the 1870s and 1880s did not end with any violent disturbance, but instead with a powerful surge of growth that transformed Hartford at least as radically as had the first phase of industrialization. The 1890s began a forty-year period of frantic land development. Factories and commercial businesses expanded rapidly, and thousands of new immigrants poured into the city from southern and eastern Europe. The resulting changes in the spatial and social landscape made Bushnell's ideas about urban space seem obsolete. How could such a large and diverse population be brought together? Of what use was the "outdoor parlor" if the population was too scattered to reach it, and if the immigrants preferred to huddle in their ghettos anyway? How could the values of the park be said to extend outside its borders, if the squalor of the streets grew worse and worse?

Faced with what they saw as a new urban crisis, another generation of reformers experimented with ways to reform the use of urban space. Working mainly through voluntary organizations, the Hartford reformers of the 1890s and the early twentieth century drew inspiration both from local reform precedents and from new ideas being developed by reformers throughout the nation. This was a period of enormous reform activity in the United States, as socially conscious men and women, primarily from the middle and upper classes, set out to remedy a host of problems at the local, state, and national levels. Some of these "progressive" reformers, as they came to be called, sought to aid the urban working classes by setting up settlement houses and agitating for cleaner streets, better housing, and government regulation of working conditions. Others sought to improve morality by agitating for the prohibition of alcohol and the suppression of prostitution. Still others sought greater democracy by reforming the electoral process and smashing monopoly, or — conversely — sought greater efficiency by expanding the power of "experts" to direct government policy and economic life scientifically.[6]

Some scholars claim to have discovered a common thread running through this tangle of reform activity. Though progressive reform was neither a coherent movement nor a coherent ideology, they argue, it can be seen as a general persuasion, a nebulous cluster of ideas prevalent among some members of the educated, urban middle class in the 1890s, 1900s, and 1910s. The progressive frame of mind was based on a Protestant sense of social responsibility. Progressives thought they had a moral duty to improve society and to help form an enlightened, altruistic leadership. A second characteristic of progressive thought was a belief that people were shaped mainly by their environment and their experiences, and therefore that they could be improved. As time passed, the progressives argued more and more strongly that the way to do this was through what some of them called "social efficiency," which meant using science, bureaucracy, and trained experts to create modern systems of organization. Their goal was to create a harmonious social order, which would take the place of what the progressives believed was a disappearing sense of local community.[7]

In some respects, progressive reform harmonized with the local tradition of environmental reform initiated by Horace Bushnell, particularly in its emphasis on social responsibility and on the unconscious influence of the environment. Nevertheless, Bushnell had understood reform in more deeply religious and gendered terms, had taken little interest in concepts of efficiency, and continued to cherish the face-to-face interactions of the local community. Though progressive reform was so diverse that some could always be found who sympathized with Bushnell's thought, many Hartford reformers ultimately drifted away from his vision of unity in search of newer, rationalized systems of social order — systems that relied in part on a revaluation of "segregation." The contradictions in progressive thought helped sunder the two halves of Bushnell's reform legacy.

Hartford reformers of the Progressive Era leaned at first toward a purer version of the local reform tradition, unadulterated by thoughts of efficiency and system-building. Believing as strongly as Bushnell in the influence of a feminized environment on individual character, they focused their efforts on spreading the characteristics of the home and the park throughout the city. At first reformers refused to accept the division of Hartford into areas of cleanliness and filth, beauty and ugliness, order and chaos, virtue and vice. They believed that it was not enough to influence people indirectly through the healing experience of the park; the crusade for gentility had to be extended into the downtown streets and slums. From the mid-1890s through the early 1910s, reformers sought to uplift Hartford by fighting for cleaner streets, better housing, and the suppression of prostitution. Enlisting intermittent support from politicians of both parties at a time when Republicans and Democrats traded control of city hall nearly every two years,[8] they achieved some notable victories. They found, however, that their success was limited by the refusal of working-class men and other Hartford residents to be uplifted.

A City Divided

"Beginning in 1889, every year saw the enlargement of old and the building of new [manufacturing] shops," reported the Board of Trade in 1895. "During the interval a few scattered establishments on [the] Park River have grown into an almost continuous line, reaching out into what only six years ago were vacant, unattractive meadows."[9] Existing manufacturers expanded their plants; the Pope Manufacturing Company moved into automobile production in 1897 and briefly became the largest American car manufacturer. By 1900 about 12,000 members of Hartford's population of 80,000 worked for manufacturers. Still ahead was the construction of three of Hartford's largest industrial complexes — the Underwood and Royal typewriter factories and the Hartford Rubber Works, all in the factory district. By 1919, after an astonishing boom produced by World War I, Hartford manufacturers employed nearly 31,000 people in a city of about 138,000. That total subsided in the postwar slump — fewer than 29,000 were so employed on the eve of the Great Depression, but the city's population reached 164,000 in 1930.[10]

Growth introduced jarring new contrasts into the landscape. The author of an 1897 book on the beauty of Hartford gloried in the sylvan hush of the fine neighborhoods, but evoked lurid, even infernal images in describing the industrial area. The writer took the reader into the factory district at sunset, heading west down Capitol Avenue.

Across [Capitol Avenue] drift transfigured volumes of smoke from railway and furnace, and as we proceed to a lower level we lose the breadth of sky and meet hundreds and hundreds of men and women coming from the long buildings, high and low, which, with their dependencies of dwelling and shop, form a community by itself. The heavy smoke from an incoming train puffs up through bridge railings on our right, the vivid flame from a tall chimney glows more fervidly and cuts the softness of the coming dusk, and we enter upon the streets where many kinds of the wheels and cogs of civilization are turned out by the hundred thousand. Block after block of machine shops and offices line the way, shadowed with iron beams, noisy with the sound of whirring wheels earlier in the day, and filled then with men busy in countless activities, now, for the most part, growing silent, for they have let forth their laborers into the crowded street, though in some of them the brilliant lights speak of later hours. Many of these buildings are of recent erection, many are dingy with the smoke and wear of years. To the left extend new streets of picturesque houses which owe their existence to these industries, and beyond them is a bit of woodland which is to form part of a new park.[11]

Great changes and stark contrasts were also visible in the central city. One observer in 1899 marveled at the city's transformation and described how a former resident returning after a long absence would barely recognize the place:

When he left Hartford, soon after the Civil War, there were two lines of street cars . . . drawn by horses. Now there are twenty-one trolley lines centering on the north side of City Hall Square. And on this particular Saturday afternoon there was a hurry and bustle about the square that would have done credit to a much larger city than Hartford. He found . . . elegant modern buildings erected for banking, insurance, dry goods and other kinds of business, not only about the

Main Street in 1899, looking south from Talcott Street. Although the city was small, the downtown impressed observers with its bustling energy and growing wealth. This view shows part of the city's retail center, which, thanks to the trolleys, served a wide metropolitan area. (*Municipal Register*, 1899)

'Square' but also on Main, Pearl, Pratt, Asylum and Trumbull streets. Tall business blocks, fitted with every modern appliance, have been erected within the past two years, where formerly stood old landmarks.[12]

The downtown was becoming a place of vast wealth, where millions of dollars flowed as abstractions through the big financial institutions or clinked as gold and silver in the cashboxes of merchants. Even in the 1890s, the stores along Main and Asylum streets were drawing crowds of shoppers, who at Christmastime jostled one another on the sidewalks and at the counters in their eagerness to spend their money.[13]

Yet poverty lurked nearby in the tightly-packed tenements of the East Side, the flood-prone, riverfront area where nearly a quarter of the city's population lived. Hartford had, for its size, the worst housing conditions of any American city, reported Robert W. DeForest and Lawrence Veiller in a nationwide study done in 1903. Slumlords had cut dilapidated old houses into multiple apartments and had built new tenement houses along the streets and in rear courtyards. Some of the new buildings followed the plan of the New York "dumb-bell" tenements, with small air shafts. Truly wretched conditions were limited to the East Side slum, but this slum bordered so closely on downtown office buildings and department stores that the middle class could easily see the squalor. An observer on the Main Street bridge over the Park River could catch what one offended writer described as "a certain glimpse of muddy river, over which hang, in diverse juts and angles, old, decrepit galleries, shiftless and unkempt, from which float many-colored garments of departing usefulness, and which extend on either side until they shut in the silver line of the Connecticut." [14]

"Shiftless and unkempt"—the phrase ostensibly described the housing, but hinted also at the character of its inhabitants, who seemed to many Hartford residents to be a threatening breed of aliens. Hartford's Yankees had long since learned to live with some foreigners in their midst. The alarm that had greeted the Irish immigration of the 1840s was now a fading memory, for the children of the immigrants had made great strides toward respectability by finding skilled industrial work or even entering the middle class. The more recent German and Scandinavian immigrants had also taken valuable places in the skilled work force of which Hartford was so proud. In 1880, 25 percent of Hartford's people were foreign-born, most of them from Ireland, Germany, and England. The relative proportion of the foreign-born population remained remarkably stable, rising only to 32 percent in 1910, but its composition changed with the heavy influx of immigrants from Italy, Russia, and Poland after 1890. To Hartford's Yankees these newer immigrants were more disturbing than the established groups. Moreover, the new immigrants swelled the city's population with their children, until by 1920 only 29 percent of Hartford's people were native-born whites of native-born parents. The immigrants clustered especially in the East Side and in the Clay Hill and Arsenal neighborhoods north of downtown. Winthrop Street, where Bushnell had once lived, was now part of this growing immigrant neighborhood. The whole East Side, the area first settled by the Puritans, now seemed to be foreign territory. [15]

The East Side soon began dividing into ethnic enclaves as a result of the new waves of immigration. Though people of various ethnic groups could be found on each block and often within each building, the north-

Charles Street, 1906, looking north from Kilbourn. Charles Street, which was located on the East Side, was home to many Italian immigrants. (Connecticut State Library)

ern section of the neighborhood became dominated by Jews, the central section by Italians, and the southern section by Poles. A small Chinese area developed on State Street in the central section. Each enclave had shops serving its dominant ethnic group. In the Italian section, recalled an old resident years later,

> pushcarts had lined its gutters, and around them vendors, customers and pilferers had vied loudly with each other. Sidewalks in front of the stores spilled over with crates of fruit imported from Sicily and baskets of rare greens and chestnuts and boxes of snails peeking out from their beds of sawdust. The windows of the numerous grocery stores were always filled with hanging provolone cheeses, clusters of pepperoni sausages, prosciutti, Genoa salame [sic], and many other cold meats wrapped in colorful foils . . . [the air was filled with] the aromatic odors of frying garlic, frying peppers, and simmering tomato sauces.[16]

Traditional Yankee restrictions on behavior were weaker on the East Side, especially in the Italian and Polish sections, where even the rule of law was more tenuous. Voices were louder, disputes more public and violent, and drinking less discreet. Police made frequent arrests for brawling and especially for drunkenness. They were often confronted by angry resistance from the accused and from neighbors. The atmosphere reflected not simply the different cultures of the immigrants, but especially the fact that the East Side served as Hartford's skid row and red-light district. "How long can you be in the neighborhood of the corner of Front and State without seeing as least one drunkard?" asked John J. McCook, a Trinity College professor who studied tramps. "I have counted a dozen within a few minutes — staggering along from saloon to saloon, dropping in half helplessness upon the steps to fall into a drunken torpor, that was disturbed only by the restlessness of reviving thirst or the petulance of swarming flies or the solicitude of the proprietor, or the rude hand of the passing policeman." Knots of men loitered on street corners in front of the numerous saloons, occasionally forcing passersby to step off the curb and sometimes even beating up police officers who ordered them to disperse. Streetwalkers could be seen soliciting customers at night. Public drinking took place even on Sunday.[17]

The streetcar system ensured that the Yankee middle class became well aware of the diversity in the landscape. Passengers could ride quickly from one section of town to another, watching through the window as slums, prestigious homes, factories, and parks flickered by in a series of clashing images. Streetcars, which had been running in Hartford since 1863, had begun switching from horse to electric power in 1888 and completed the change four years later, greatly increasing the speed of travel.[18]

Though the experience of riding the trolley heightened the passenger's perception of a chaotic landscape, the trolley system was actually beginning to create a new spatial order. In the 1890s the trolley system made central Hartford the hub of a metropolitan region. Rails radiated from downtown to surrounding towns and villages, drawing them more fully into Hartford's orbit. Trolleys to Unionville and Manchester did a booming business in summer and fall, taking thousands of city people on excursions to commercial picnic grounds where they could relax in the shade, feel the cool breezes, and listen to band music.[19] More important, the trolleys brought people from outlying towns into Hartford to shop and to work. "The great stores and industrial enterprises of the city are assuming aspects altogether metropolitan," as a result of the trolleys, wrote Mayor William F. Henney in 1905. Suburban and country people made up much of the customer base needed to build such department stores as G. Fox and Company; Sage Allen and Company; Wise, Smith and Company; and Brown, Thomson and Company. "Hartford is today realizing the dream of its founders — of becoming the trading and shopping center of the Connecticut valley," Henney wrote. "The street railway company . . . has done so much to develop the city."[20]

Perhaps the most dramatic effect of the trolley on Hartford's landscape after 1890 was its influence on the growth of residential areas. The electrification and extension of Hartford's streetcar lines in the 1890s encouraged the creation of new neighborhoods of multifamily housing. For the next forty years, the street grid spread inexorably toward the city line and beyond, into West Hartford, Bloomfield, and Wethersfield. Broad swaths of land north, south, and southwest of the central city filled up with clapboard "triple deckers," red brick "perfect sixes" and — by the 1910s and 1920s — large apartment blocks near the trolley lines. By the 1920s these areas, which housed the families of skilled workmen and low-level office workers, formed buffers between the swarming slums by the riverfront and the secluded neighborhoods of the affluent.[21] Beyond this broken ring of multifamily houses rose such new, middle-class neighborhoods as the West End, Blue Hills, and Fairfield Avenue. This reconfiguration of land use took many decades. The middle class in the 1890s deserted Prospect Street, its last toehold in the center of the city, but lingered in the Charter Oak and South Green neighborhoods until after World War I. Asylum Hill remained prestigious despite its proximity to downtown and its ample trolley service.[22]

Compared with the startling juxtapositions of slum and downtown, factory district and residential neighborhood, the evolving spatial order of the streetcar city was at first too subtle to be understood. Squalor and industrial grime were never far from the best neighborhoods in the 1890s and 1900s. At the eastern edge of the factory district, the Billings and Spencer forge belched smoke a mere four blocks upwind of Washington Street, a broad avenue lined with mansions. The shady streets of Asylum Hill were even closer to the factory district. Katharine Houghton Hepburn, an affluent reformer who lived on Hawthorn Street, found it impossible to ignore the presence of the workers at the nearest factories.

Washington Street. In the late nineteenth century this elm-lined avenue was known as "Governors' Row." (Connecticut State Library)

Distressed by their lack of a comfortable place to eat lunch, she invited workers to picnic on her lawn one day, but she realized from the mess they made that neighborly kindness had limits.[23]

Dirt, poverty, and disorder were inescapable in the new Hartford of the 1890s and 1900s. The landscape seemed to proclaim the waning authority of the Yankee middle class.[24] Urban space was increasingly dominated by activities beyond the influence of either the traditional commercial elite or the new professionals and managers who owed their status to the growing banks and insurance companies. Still, the Yankee middle class could see two examples of how its interrelated concepts of gentility and femininity could be extended to public space. One example, of course, was Bushnell Park. The other was taking shape within the semipublic space of the corporate office.

In Hartford, as in other financial centers in the decades around 1900, the insurance and banking industries were hiring numerous female clerical workers and were creating work environments that conformed in some ways to ideas of decorum and gender relations derived from the home. Within the corporation, women were segregated spatially and assigned subordinate, service roles that supposedly reflected their special skills in caring for others. At the Aetna Life Insurance Company, for example, President Morgan G. Bulkeley was so uneasy about the presence of women in offices that he tried to shield them from public view. Nevertheless, the new female presence forced modifications in the culture and atmosphere of the workplace as a whole. The presence of women employees was thought to encourage cooperation, tranquility, refinement, cleanliness, and self-control. In this way, traditional definitions of femininity contributed to a new office environment that mingled aspects of both public and private space. Like public space, the corporate office both brought together people with no familial or social ties and was subject to incursion by at least some complete strangers. But like private space, it was privately owned, it carefully screened out unsuitable visitors and — most important — it promoted a code of behavior different from that of the streets.[25]

Hartford reformers in the 1890s and 1900s, therefore, could take comfort from the fact that middle-class domestic values had been extended successfully to some public and semipublic spaces. Some members of the Yankee middle class — particularly corporate executives, professionals, and their wives — attempted in the decades around 1900 to make the entire city conform to these values.

Municipal Housekeeping

One of the leaders of this cause was the daughter of Horace Bushnell. Dotha Bushnell Hillyer was, with the possible exception of the parks superintendent George A. Parker, the Hartford resident most widely influential in local reform campaigns during the Progressive Era. Hillyer was the youngest of Bushnell's three daughters and was named after his beloved mother. Though affectionate, Bushnell had very high expectations for his children. "I wish you to feel, as you grow up, that you are not doomed to any low or vain calling because you are a woman," he wrote to one of Dotha's sisters in 1845. "I have no son upon whom I can lean, or in whose character and success I can find pleasure. . . . Therefore I desire the more to have daughters whom I can respect, and in whose beautiful and high accomplishments I can find a father's comfort. You cannot be a soldier or a preacher; but I wish, in the best and truest sense, to have you become a woman." A true woman, Bushnell continued, should be modest, intelligent, sincere, graceful, refined, calm, kind, self-less, smiling, charitable, and pious. "Your victory . . . will be a woman's only — the victory of patience, purity and goodness."[26] Her father's femi-nine ideal would guide Dotha's reform activities in her adult years.

In 1879 Dotha married advantageously to a wealthy banker named Appleton R. Hillyer, to whom she bore three children. Appleton Hillyer's father had given the site for the local Young Men's Christian Association, and the son followed this philanthropic example by donating money to found the association's Hillyer Institute, which later developed into a ju-nior college and finally became part of the University of Hartford. Apple-ton and Dotha settled in the 1890s in a big brick house on Elm Street across from Bushnell Park. From their front windows Dotha could look directly over the park her father had created to the gables and conical roofs of the YMCA on the far side — a daily reminder of what good works could accomplish.[27]

A plump, plain woman with her father's sharp beak of a nose, Dotha Hillyer entered energetically into numerous reform campaigns and orga-nizations from the 1890s through the 1910s. Perhaps her greatest reform victories came through her leadership of the Civic Club, in which — after a brief stint as vice president — she served as president from 1898 to 1915 and from 1918 until the club folded in 1920. The Civic Club worked to create cleaner streets, to improve housing conditions, to set up vacation schools, playgrounds, and gardens for slum children, and to support the efforts of other reform organizations. Dotha Hillyer led her club's suc-cessful effort to establish a Hartford Juvenile Commission in 1909 and served as one of the commission's charter members.[28] She was appointed to the Board of Park Commissioners in 1911 as its first female member and served until 1920, though she declined the presidency. She was also active in the Municipal Art Society and in the Newsboys and Newsgirls Committee of the Consumers' League of Hartford.[29] Hillyer provided personal encouragement and major funding for the Hartford Equal Fran-chise League in the 1910s, though she did so secretly, perhaps in def-erence to her father's emphatic denunciation of woman suffrage. Her generous contributions helped numerous other civic and charitable or-

Dotha Bushnell Hillyer. (*Tenth Anniversary Commemorative Booklet, Horace Bushnell Memorial Hall*)

ganizations. She was thus involved either directly or through financial support in nearly every major reform campaign affecting public space in Hartford.[30]

Hillyer struggled to conform to expected ladylike behavior by making her civic activities as discreet and polite as she could. But she refused to play the role of the demure matron, and she would not back down when her work became controversial. "Her alert, vivid personality stimulated and challenged the best in her associates," recalled a fellow member of the Civic Club. "Her quick mind held back its decisions so that others less quick might not be left behind; she was aggressive, but of a quiet restrained type that never aroused antagonism. She gave the impression of great power and of still more in reserve."[31]

Hillyer's Civic Club was one of many women's organizations throughout the United States that became involved in urban reform campaigns at this time. These organizations worked to extend the female role into areas of public policy that touched on a wide variety of traditionally feminine concerns, particularly issues related to children, cleanliness, housing, health, morality, and beauty. Female reformers advocated curricular reforms, better school administration, sanitoriums and public health clinics, sanitary drinking fountains, the hiring of visiting nurses, infant milk stations, pure food laws, improved water systems, public baths, public laundries, improved garbage disposal, smoke and noise regulations, the suppression of vermin, the suppression of prostitution, public education about venereal disease, the supervision of dance halls, the censorship of movies, the construction of parks and playgrounds, improved tenement conditions, the removal of billboards and other eyesores, and the planting of trees. Street cleaning was an issue of particular interest, drawing attention in the 1880s from the Ladies' Health Protective Association in New York and in the 1890s from the Civic Club of Philadelphia, the Women's Municipal League of New York, and the Hull House settlement in Chicago.[32]

Dirty streets disturbed the late-Victorian middle class on two levels. First, the middle class had legitimate, if somewhat confused, fears about the link between dirt and disease. Although by the 1890s most physicians accepted the theory that disease was spread by germs, there lingered a popular association of contagion with dirt itself, particularly with "miasmas"—harmful vapors that were thought to rise from unclean substances. Sanitary reformers guided by these earlier beliefs had achieved some notable successes in improving public health in American cities after the Civil War. Germ theory's practical implications for public health were not immediately clear to health officials, who only in the 1890s began to turn their attention away from the war on miasmas and visible filth.[33]

Second, and more important, dirt had powerful symbolic meanings in the middle-class mind, suggesting a certain moral weakness among those who created or accepted it. Personal cleanliness indicated self-discipline, good character, and self-respect. "The true line to be drawn between pauperism and honest poverty is the clothesline," wrote New York housing reformer Jacob Riis in 1890. "With it begins the effort to be clean that is the first and the best evidence of a desire to be honest." Similarly, a clean home reflected well on the family, and clean streets reflected well on the community. A clean environment was thought to exert a positive influence on health, behavior, and morality, and to encourage personal improvement. Dirt, in short, represented a threat to middle-class values, particularly to values associated with women.[34]

Women reformers felt an obligation to fight dirt because of their traditional roles as homemakers and as defenders of morality. They argued that they could not fulfill their duty to protect their homes and families unless they cleaned up the filth outside their doors. "Women must come to regard the city as their home," declared Mary McDowell, a settlement-house worker in Chicago. "Home must not end with the front door-step."[35] The reformers were reluctant to acknowledge the class-based assumptions that underlay their definition of womanhood and female duty. "When woman reformers talked about the home going forth into the world, they meant the middle-class home going forth into the lower-class world," observes the historian Sheila Rothman. "For all the assumptions that men were the common villains, it was the lower-class male who was, in the end, the most dangerous beast, and the lower-class woman who had to be lifted up to middle-class standards."[36]

Many women's organizations lobbied their cities to follow the example set by the efficient New York Department of Street Cleaning under the leadership of sanitary expert George E. Waring, Jr., in the 1890s. They hoped that if they could impose standards of middle-class cleanliness on the streets, poor people observing the change would be inspired to keep cleaner houses, to improve their personal hygiene, and ultimately to adopt middle-class morality. The reformers sought to enlist the entire populace in the crusade for cleanliness, partly to keep a messy public from undoing the work of the city's street sweepers, and partly because their crusade was really a moral revival. They began educational campaigns to spread their ideas to immigrants, and organized juvenile street-cleaning leagues for the immigrants' children. Children in the leagues were expected not only to stop littering but also to pick up whatever litter they found, to chastise the litterers, to hand out circulars requesting cleanliness, to go from door to door giving advice, and to report to adult supervisors about the conditions they found. The supervisors would then pass this information on to the appropriate city officials.[37]

The Civic Club in Hartford shared the concerns but not always the tactics of its predecessors in other cities. The club was founded in January 1895, by some one hundred prominent women led by Alice Hooker Day, the wife of a local attorney. Hartford women had previously formed a number of charitable and literary societies that represented a tentative claim to a female role outside the home, but the Civic Club more openly asserted women's place in public affairs. Its declared purpose was to "promote a higher public spirit and a better social order in the community in which we live." It took as its first project the improved cleaning of streets, sidewalks, and crosswalks.[38] Unlike its counterparts in other cities, the Civic Club was at first quite reticent about appealing for public support. Apparently club leaders felt that although women occasionally might need to step into the public sphere to fulfill their domestic obligations, they should never mistake this step as an excuse for unladylike political rhetoric. In the 1890s the club did its work quietly and behind the scenes, through discreet persuasion of elected officials. It issued no manifestos and published only a few terse reports.

The club's initial project was certainly needed, for Hartford's streets were very dirty. The street commissioners had put an end to some of the worst nuisances, in the 1880s ordering property owners to stop dumping their ashes and rubbish in the street, and in the 1890s inaugurating daily sweepings of the major downtown streets. The daily cleanings limited the accumulation of rubbish and horse manure, which could otherwise dry into a pestilential dust that blew through homes and stores. But home-makers continued to leave rubbish overflowing from open barrels, shop-keepers swept their trash into the gutter, and pedestrians tossed cigar butts, apple cores, and wastepaper indiscriminately. And the streets outside the downtown area were not nearly so diligently cleaned. "Hartford needs more than anything else streets that are cleaner than ours are," declared Mayor Henry C. Dwight in 1891.[39]

The problem most severely affected the people who lived in the East Side, reported Dr. Edward K. Root, the city's medical inspector, in an 1896 address to the Civic Club:

> People living in the more wholesome localities have little idea of the extent to which the streets are used by the poorer people of our population. The street is the playground of the children, the meeting place . . . for all the inhabitants of the tenements along its sides. Most of the daily shopping, purchasing of food necessities, is transacted on the sidewalks, and in summer weather the inhabitants virtually live in the streets. These people make comparatively little use of parks, no matter how convenient they may be. They are reserved for excursions and half-holidays after the day's work is done and the family has an outing; but all day long, while the wage earner of the family is at work and the mother [is] busy with the housework, the children are

left to run and play on the pavement close to the house within easy call, but subject and exposed to all the filth and miasms and demoralizing influences of the foulness which exists in these quarters.

The filth spread disease among the poor and cost dozens of lives each year, Root claimed.[40]

But Civic Club members were driven more by concern about the symbolic implications of untidiness than by fear of disease, and they did not, therefore, distinguish between filth and litter. To them the problem seemed most severe in the highly visible public spaces of the downtown, the section of the city shared by the broadest range of people. In March 1895 the club sent out letters to seven hundred downtown shopkeepers and property owners, asking them to cooperate in keeping the streets clean. In the same year the club successfully petitioned the city to install trashcans at busy downtown street corners (to reduce littering) and persuaded the Common Council to pass an ordinance against littering. Upon receiving a complaint from Alice Day, the Board of Street Commissioners agreed to have downtown streets swept early on Sunday morning so that churchgoers could be spared the annoyance of seeing the previous day's litter. Day and Hillyer also urged the police to take stronger measures against littering and to see that dead animals were removed more promptly. Sure enough, police that autumn were seen picking up wastepaper and ordering those who knocked over trashcans to clean up after themselves.[41]

Fresh from this success, the club decided to form a citywide children's league to fight littering. This association, the League of Good Order, would require children to swear off littering, to stop others from littering, and to do everything possible to keep the streets and sidewalks clean. The Civic Club had additional waste cans installed outside schools to encourage children to pick up wastepaper in schoolyards. The League of Good Order achieved some success on Asylum Hill, where children in 1896 divided the neighborhood into districts that they patrolled for litter. If the league accomplished anything in the less hospitable sections of Hartford, it is not recorded in surviving accounts of the Civic Club's activities.[42]

The new interest in clean streets spread to the street department itself, which showed a desire to emulate its New York counterpart. The street commissioners ordered new uniforms for street sweepers much like those worn by the "white wings" under Waring's authority. The street department also bought street-cleaning machines to supplement sweeping by hand. The commissioners shared the Civic Club's belief that clean streets depended in part on public cooperation, but they did not work any more energetically than did the club to obtain this support. The commissioners expressed the hope in 1895 that the new public trashcans "may gradually educate our citizens, both young and old, to the desirability of clean streets, and to the fact that a little thoughtfulness on their part, will very materially assist the municipal authorities in their endeavors to this end." By 1903, the street superintendent Philip Hansling, Jr., claimed to have noticed an increase in public conscientiousness. Littering persisted — downtown, in the East Side, and in the outlying residential districts to which limited street cleaning had been extended — but Hansling hoped that the problem would diminish as civic pride continued to grow. Health officials were somewhat less optimistic about the East Side because of the difficulty in changing "the habits of the people."[43]

Another dirty habit of Hartford residents at this time was spitting in public, which was most common among lower- and working-class men. Members of the middle class viewed this practice with disgust both because spitting violated their standards for proper bodily management in public and because they feared it would spread tuberculosis, which was one of the leading causes of death among the poor in Hartford. The Civic Club placed signs in trolleys asking passengers not to spit on the floor, then persuaded the Board of Health to post similar signs in trolleys and along sidewalks. Health inspector Robert J. Farrell proclaimed the campaign a success in 1906. "At the present time one does not see pools of tobacco spits in front of public spaces. The sidewalks of the business section of the city are today more defiled by dogs than by the expectorations of human beings. Education and public sentiment can accomplish a great deal." But later that year the Common Council found it necessary to pass an ordinance against spitting on sidewalks, in trolleys, train stations, and public buildings. The Hartford Evening Post reported that spitting continued anyway, even in front of the police, and that tougher laws were needed. In 1911 the city finally ordered the police to begin enforcing the law seriously, and the nuisance diminished.[44]

like

Fenell?

The public cleanliness campaigns blurred means and ends. Civic Club members and their supporters believed that heightened civic consciousness and restrained behavior would produce cleaner public spaces, and cleaner public spaces would result in a more responsible, refined citizenry. Both the people and their environment needed to be reformed, and both public persuasion and legal coercion were necessary. "Push the good work of keeping saliva from the sidewalk until all droppings from the mouths of public feeders are eliminated," urged McCook at the end of 1906. "But, since uncivilized eating habits die hard, in the meantime have our street inspectors and our police patrols keep an eye to the occasional orange peel and apple core."[45]

"Uncivilized habits" were particularly strong in the slums, the Civic Club found. Club members observed that tenement dwellers were in the habit of dumping trash in the private alleyways between buildings and in whatever open space was left behind a tenement, creating an eyesore and a fire hazard. Voluntary cooperation on the part of the tenement dwellers would have been necessary to eliminate this practice, but the Civic Club did not attempt to obtain such cooperation with even the limited energy that it devoted to the League of Good Order. Club members appealed instead to the fire marshal and to the local fire insurance companies to force property owners to comply.[46]

Unconstrained by the traditional distinction between public and private space, the Civic Club worked in the 1900s and early 1910s to extend its fight against dirt into the interiors of Hartford's tenement houses. The club was alarmed about the "conditions brought about by a rapid influx of foreigners," Hillyer recalled later. Examples of bad housing included "ten families of recent immigrants with their respective lodgers quartered in a fine old mansion that had once sheltered a family whose ancestors . . . had come over in the Mayflower; the evils of overcrowding together with the dangers of primitive yard closets and antiquated plumbing; the almost complete lack of fire escapes; basement and cellar tenements; dark rooms and halls; and filthy yards." The heart of the problem, it seemed, was a breakdown of domestic privacy, decency, and cleanliness brought on by the immigrant invasion.[47]

Hillyer's understanding of the situation was certainly influenced by nativism, but there is no reason to doubt her sincere concern. Guided by a sense of Christian stewardship, she and the other club members worked to educate the better classes about their responsibility. The Civic Club worked in cooperation with the Charity Organization Society, which had been concerned about poor housing conditions as early as 1896 and had discussed "the need of having homes for the poorer people in the hands of those who take philanthropic interest in maintaining good conditions." In 1900 the two organizations cooperated in mounting an exhibition of photographs that exposed the worst conditions in Hartford and other cities and displayed examples of model housing. The emphasis of the exhibit was on the need for enlightened property owners to build what the *Hartford Daily Courant* called "wholesome housing for the workingman . . . at a reasonable profit on the investment." The New York housing reformer Lawrence Veiller, in a speech at the opening of the exhibit, said that Hartford should build small houses for workingmen rather than model tenements, which he believed were not needed in a moderate-sized city.[48]

Interest in workingmen's homes grew but bore little fruit. The few model row houses that were built in the 1890s and 1900s—on Columbia Street and Park Terrace—proved to be too expensive even for skilled workers. They were occupied instead by banking and insurance clerks. George Parker and the City Plan Commission advocated large developments of workingmen's bungalows on the outskirts of town. They felt that the city might even build these. The city as a whole had an interest in building single-family homes, wrote Parker: "Privacy is essential, for the family is the unit of our civilization." The Hartford Home Building Association, organized by the Chamber of Commerce with capital from Hartford's major employers, built dozens of duplexes and single-family houses in the southwest corner of the city in the early 1920s. Nevertheless, these supplemented rather than replaced the ever-increasing numbers of tenements. The housing problem clearly could not be solved by replacing the dirty tenement with a properly domestic alternative in the outskirts.[49]

Meanwhile, the Civic Club continued to fret about the filthiness of housing on the East Side. Even the successful construction of model homes could not excuse conscientious municipal housekeepers from cleaning up the central neighborhoods. The club invited the New York reformer Robert E. Todd to report to it in 1907 on the conditions in Hartford tenements, but the details printed in the *Courant* were evidently not enough to spur a satisfactory cleanup. The club made a stronger push for cleaning the tenements in 1911. By then, a new state law had empowered the city's Board of Health to make landlords correct some of the worst conditions, and the club "decided that the officials could do effective work only if backed by strong public opinion," Hillyer wrote. Once again, however, the club made no attempt to build a mass movement of tenement dwellers; instead, its efforts at public education took the form of calm appeals to public officials. At Veiller's recommendation, the club hired an investigator to gather new information, which was then presented to the board of health. Under pressure from the club, health officials and the prosecutor forced the most notorious slumlord to install modern plumbing for his tenants. Other landlords cooperated more readily in replacing outhouses with indoor toilets. Dozens of dark rooms were opened to light and fresh air. "All this seems to prove that the first step in tenement house reform is to make a thorough and systematic investigation. Next, to lay the facts before the people and arouse public opinion. Lastly, public enthusiasm must not be allowed to die down until the necessary reforms have been accomplished," Hillyer concluded, reciting a procedure that was widely accepted among reformers at the time. The board of health boasted in 1913 that Hartford's tenement conditions were now the best in the state.[50]

The effort to cleanse the tenements led the Civic Club to redouble its crusade for outdoor cleanliness in 1912. This time the focus was on the slums. The club joined with city officials and insurance companies to organize annual spring cleanup weeks. It had the schools distribute handbills to children telling them about the campaign and requesting their help and the help of their families. Participants cleaned up the papers, tin cans, construction debris, manure, dead animals, and other trash that filled the open spaces, and hauled them to the curb to be removed by the city. The Civic Club arranged to have Boy Scout troops help take a survey of the particularly bad conditions that deserved attention. In the 1915 cleanup, the scouts distributed literature from the fire and health departments and inspected the yards of more than ten thousand buildings, taking note of unusually messy ones. Although it is unclear what if anything the scouts and Civic Club could do if property owners refused to cooperate, the survey was taken quite seriously on the East Side and frightened many people into compliance, reported *American City* magazine.

"When the Scouts were seen in the poor section of the city a strenuous cleaning commenced at once. 'Don't report this yard,' one man said. 'Can't you see I'm cleaning?'"[51]

By depending so heavily on children in this latter phase of the cleanup campaign, the Civic Club might seem to have followed the lead of the big-city women's organizations that tried to build a mass movement around municipal housekeeping. The *Courant* declared that the campaigns "have done much to educate the people," and that the East Side was much cleaner as a result. But the cleanliness crusaders were unable or unwilling to enlist full public support, perhaps because they felt restrained by the need to maintain a ladylike distance from the sordid segments of the city they sought to reform. Their public education efforts took place in an unmistakable atmosphere of middle-class coercion. The Boy Scouts on whom they depended were in the 1910s primarily a middle-class, Protestant organization dedicated to building morality, self-control, and a sense of public duty among the next generation of American leaders. In Hartford, admitted one advocate of scouting, the scouts were outnumbered by rougher boys who sneered at them for belonging to "a society for mollycoddles." For such sanctimonious pups to wield authority over the East Side and to enjoy the cooperation of East Side schoolchildren may well have struck Hartford's immigrants as an arrogant display of Yankee power.[52] The cleanliness crusade, however, provoked neither organized opposition nor even the public griping aroused by the later pedestrian safety campaigns. Uncleanliness persisted not as a self-conscious act of defiance, but as a casual refusal to adopt the self-restraint prized by the middle class. No one, it seems, cared to denounce the Civic Club on the grounds either of individual freedom or of class rights. The housing and cleanup campaigns had no more than a limited long-term effect on the East Side, notwithstanding the initial boasts of the board of health. In the words of one man who grew up there in the 1920s, East Siders remained trapped in "those dismal labyrinths of brick, concrete, broken windows, and rubbish-strewn alleys."[53]

Among the organizations supporting the crusade to cleanse Hartford was the Municipal Art Society, founded in 1904 by a diverse group of affluent men and women led by the local artist Charles Noël Flagg. The society drew most of its membership from the social register. It managed to combine a snobbish aestheticism with a sincere interest in such earthy matters as street cleaning and public restrooms. The founders argued that Hartford should develop the refined taste worthy of such a wealthy city and should resist the spirit of commercialism. A prominent member, Mayor William F. Henney, declared in a 1905 speech, "It is full as natural for a man to desire to keep the city of his home in neat and wholesome and happy condition, as to establish and maintain those conditions in the house in which he lives." The society shared a number of members with the Civic Club — most notably its second vice president, Dotha Hillyer.[54]

The Municipal Art Society was part of a loosely organized national reform effort that came to be known as the City Beautiful movement. Local organizations sought to guide the design of public buildings, parks, boulevard systems, and street improvements ranging from pavements to landscaping. Like the women's clubs devoted to municipal housekeeping, the City Beautiful organizations were keenly interested in the effect of the environment on individual character. They hoped in particular to stimulate taste, civic pride, and social tranquility. The movement gradually took an interest in such immediately practical problems as sewers and water systems, refuse collection, and public transportation.[55]

In Hartford, the Municipal Art Society began working for cleaner streets and alleys shortly after its formation, at a time when the Civic Club was busy with other projects. The society complained to the city in 1905 about the dustiness of the streets, persuading officials to sprinkle the streets more frequently and to wash them thoroughly on a regular basis. The society, and later the Commission on the City Plan that it helped create, also advocated the construction of public restrooms. These "houses of comfort" were needed not only as a public convenience but also to stop men from urinating in alleyways. The need was particularly severe in the center of the city, especially "since the trolley lines [had begun] to bring many strangers into the city who arrive at and depart from City Hall Square," reported the Commission on the City Plan in 1911. The city finally built underground public lavatories on the east side of city hall in early 1914. By 1919 more than twenty-five thousand people a week were using the lavatories, and the number rose as Prohibition closed the saloons that had provided the same service.[56]

Ideally, the Municipal Art Society believed, streets should be free not only of dirt but also of eyesores and moral contamination. Like many other City Beautiful organizations, the society was incensed about billboards. "Our conspicuous places, our most beautiful views, even our residence streets are desecrated by glaring advertisements of second rate plays and intoxicating remedies," one of the society's subcommittees complained in 1908. Before the advent of radio and television, downtown street space was the preferred medium for commercial messages. The facades of some downtown buildings were literally covered with signs advertising businesses and the products they sold. Billboards extended the available advertising space as much as a full story above the cornice line. The concentration of these signs in and around the downtown was a frank declaration of one of the main economic functions of that part of the city: retailing. But the heart of the city had symbolic as well as economic importance. If, as Bushnell had argued, people gained an understanding of their city by observing its vistas and "ornaments," then billboards had a frighteningly insidious influence. The advertisements' prominence and blatant hucksterism seemed to prove the Municipal Art Society's contention that commercialism was overwhelming Hartford's finer qualities. The screaming slogans and garish colors suggested that the pursuit of mammon took precedence over refinement, taste, and beauty. And some of the advertisements also suggested a certain moral laxness.[57]

For that reason, local pastors had been among the first to object to the proliferation of billboards. In 1902 the priest and several parishioners of St. Anne's Catholic Church on Park Street protested to the city about the billboard across the street, asking the mayor to prevent any objectionable messages from being put up there. The Hartford Federation of Churches, an organization of Protestant pastors, protested in 1904 about a huge, round billboard that loomed over Exchange Corner at City Hall Square. The sign bore the words, "Highball. That's all," and showed a man mixing a drink. The pastors joined with the Municipal Art Society in stirring up a public outcry against this affront to sobriety, and the landlord decided to order the sign removed when the lease expired.[58]

This symbolic victory did little to slow the increase in advertising—or to raise its moral tone. By 1908 billboards were common along practically every major thoroughfare. There were some 255 billboards in Hartford, totaling 102,530 square feet—roughly the equivalent of a sign ten

Signs on a building on Main Street, ca. 1900. Reformers were troubled by the crass commercialism of outdoor advertising. (Connecticut State Library)

feet high and two miles long. A particularly controversial double-decker billboard stood at Asylum and Hopkins streets near Hartford Public High School. "Children going to and from school . . . look upon frightful deeds of crime committed in the melodramas playing at local theaters; or in other cases behold dashing demoseilles clad in no more than the law requires, often less," reported the *Times* in 1908. Hoping to put an end to such moral dangers, the Municipal Art Society, the Civic Club, the Federation of Churches, the Daughters of the American Revolution, the Landlords and Taxpayers' Association, and nineteen other local organizations joined in forming the United Committees' Association for Billboard Regulation. This umbrella group considered whether to oppose all billboards or whether to ban all pictures, leaving only the text. The reformers believed that banning pictures would weaken the billboards' powers of temptation while putting an end to bad public art. The city engineer, Frederick L. Ford, who supported the movement, declared, "It is simply one detail of a larger tendency to get back to the former days when the streets were clear, the air was pure and the landscape undefiled by unsightly objects."[59]

In practice, however, the association focused on removing billboards from certain prominent locations that were readily visible to middle-class people in the course of their daily activities. The club successfully pressured billboard owners to remove signs visible from Bushnell Park, the most offensive being a row at Pearl and Ford streets on the main route between the elite Washington Street and Asylum Hill neighborhoods. They secured as well the removal of the double-decker billboard on Asylum Street, which was a daily annoyance to those traveling back and forth between downtown and Asylum Hill. A billboard at Woodland Terrace and Albany Avenue, another residential area, was also taken down. The association in 1911 persuaded the Common Council to pass a billboard ordinance, which among other provisions forbade signs "of an immoral or indecent character" and signs "representing vice or crime," and which gave the mayor the power to order the immediate removal of such signs. Nevertheless, billboards continued to clutter the downtown.[60]

Early campaigns to cleanse Hartford of dirt and ugliness had limited effects. Those concerned spoke of the need to reform the city—but cautiously focused their efforts on those neighborhoods where middle-class dominance was already strongest. The Civic Club organized orderly, middle-class children to clean up Asylum Hill and persuaded city officials to improve downtown street sweeping, even though the problem of dirty streets most severely affected the East Side. When the club turned its attention to the slums in the 1910s, it avoided enlisting mass support for tenement house reform, relying in its cleanup campaign on middle-class leadership and intimidation. Club members hoped to clean up the entire city, but their accomplishments were limited by the fact that their values were not enthusiastically shared by the working class and by their own failure to mount a more inclusive campaign. Basing their moral authority on their status as middle-class ladies—with all that that implied in the late-Victorian era—they imposed on themselves a code of decorum too restrictive to allow effective reform work in the slum environment. Meanwhile, the Municipal Art Society's billboard campaign focused largely on areas with a secure middle-class presence. These campaigns thus failed to break down the division of the city into zones of dirt and cleanliness; in fact, they inadvertently heightened the contrast.

To some extent the campaigns furthered the goal of extending into public space the middle-class, feminine values of cleanliness, morality, decorum, and beauty. The work of the Civic Club in particular helped assert a middle-class, female role in issues affecting the use of streets. This work would be pursued more vigorously by the radical suffragists of the Hartford Equal Franchise League, who shared many of Dotha Hillyer's values but were less ambivalent about entering the male world of politics. From 1912 to 1914, suffragists waged a fierce battle to prevent the reopening of Hartford's red-light district, winning the single greatest victory in the crusade to purify the city's public space.

3

The Fight against the Vice District

As the brothels of Hartford's East Side stood dark and empty in the winter of 1912, a few stubborn voices insisted that the red-light district had kept the city morally decent. In a letter to the *Hartford Times*, an observer named A. N. Brooks argued for reopening the area in which prostitution had been officially tolerated until the recent crackdown: "Segregation is the only way to control the social evil. Prostitution is now, has always been, always will be with us. . . . I believe the house of ill fame in a city the size of Hartford is a great protection to hundreds of innocent young girls. . . . Rather than have these vile practices spread around in all parts of the city, I say confine their operations to a certain community. By so doing you will improve the morals of our city."[1]

Rarely before had anyone in Hartford felt obliged to make so public a defense of the vice district, but never before had the district's existence been in such peril. Embarrassed by a sensational trial that had exposed the police department's connivance in the vice trade, the mayor had ordered all the brothels closed on December 29, 1911. Though many people expected the brothels would be allowed to reopen once the furor subsided, an innovative new group of reformers was demanding that the closing be absolute and final. This antiprostitution campaign, led by woman suffragists, differed from earlier, weaker reform efforts by directly attacking the beliefs about the use of public space that allowed prostitution to flourish.

Official toleration of a vice district, the suffragists understood, was an attempt to resolve contradictions posed by the nineteenth-century ideology of separate spheres for middle-class women and men. Women, thought to be more virtuous, belonged in the home. When they ventured into the tumultuous streets of the central city, they were treading on dangerous public territory that was more properly the place of men; no respectable lady should loiter in such a public place. Prostitutes seemed to violate these mores, but as long as they were confined to a red-light district, their transgressions actually affirmed the dominant ideology. The promiscuity of "public women" highlighted the chastity of ladies who stayed in the home; their availability channeled male sexuality away from respectable females; and their presence in the unruly slum contrasted with the quiet decorum of the residential neighborhood.[2]

Three earlier antiprostitution reform efforts in Hartford had not challenge the ideology of separate spheres, thereby failing also to attack the ideas that underlay the existence of the vice district. Women reformers in the late nineteenth century tried to bring prostitutes into "homes," where they could be reintroduced to morality. Another group of civic-minded women sought to purify a disreputable street—without ever attacking the idea of tolerated prostitution. The boldest of the earlier reform efforts took place five years before the suffragists' campaign, when Protestant clergymen united to turn the coercive power of government against sin, although they disagreed whether strict enforcement of vice district boundaries would suffice. All these reformers believed that urban space was necessarily divided into areas of virtue and depravity. They all accepted the division between the pure female environment of the home and the rough world of the male-dominated street, and many defended the coarser-grained image of a city with differing moral regions. The reformers' goals were modest—to rescue repentant individuals and to enforce the borders of the vice district. They sought, above all, to shield as many women as possible from experiencing or even witnessing the operations of the vice trade. The suffragists, in contrast, sought to suppress prostitution even within the red-light district, as part of a larger battle for women's right to the public sphere—both to public space and to public discourse. Their rejection of separate-spheres ideology made possible new tactics that contributed to their ultimate success in keeping the red-light district closed. Despite the suffragists' triumph, however, prostitution remained common in Hartford and spread to other neighborhoods. Their mixed success showed the limits of any attempt to purify the urban environment.

Orderly Houses

"In thirty years of service on the police force," boasted Hartford Police Chief William F. Gunn in 1907, "I have never seen the city freer of gambling and vice than it is today." One experienced local "sporting man" backed up the chief, sadly agreeing that Hartford was cleaner than at any time in his memory.[3] These two men may have exaggerated, but strong evidence indicates that prostitution in Hartford was no more prevalent at the time it was attacked by pastors and suffragists than it had been in the previous two decades. The suffragists' campaign was not a response to any increase in prostitution itself. Rather, it reflected a growing desire to spread the values of genteel femininity throughout the city.

Brothels were reportedly "very numerous" in Hartford in the 1880s, but no careful study of prostitution appears to have been conducted until 1892.[4] In that year, the Charity Organization Society superintendent, George B. Thayer, compiled and privately circulated a report on some aspects of the problem. Thayer counted about twelve "regular houses of prostitution," all but two on the East Side, the riverfront neighborhood of poor immigrants and squalid tenements just east of Main Street. One of the largest and best known was the River House, a four-story brick building with wooden balconies overlooking the Connecticut River. According to a later report, the prostitutes lived and worked on the upper floors of the River House, while boats were stored on the ground floor. Hartford's brothels, unlike those in some other cities, made an attempt at discretion. "These houses, as a rule, are kept in a very quiet, orderly manner," Thayer wrote. "The police are very rarely called there, they have no occasion to go. Every thing is kept quiet without them. It is only the noisey [sic] ones that they raid."[5]

Part of the East Side, 1909. Some slums had been cleared to make room for Connecticut Boulevard and the approaches to the Connecticut River bridge, but the neighborhood was still the mostly densely populated in Hartford. Despite police raids that had closed most of the State Street brothels, prostitution continued to flourish in the side streets. (*Atlas of the City of Hartford*)

Thayer further reported that dozens of individual women at addresses throughout the city occasionally turned tricks in their lodging houses to supplement the low wages they earned at legitimate jobs. Many of these women lived in rooming houses downtown, on such streets as Main, Chapel, and Asylum, or in scattered residential neighborhoods. Working discreetly in their own quarters, they "rarely if ever come under police surveillance." Full-time individual prostitutes, concentrated in certain

The River House, an East Side brothel situated at the foot of Ferry Street, ca. 1900. (Connecticut State Library)

buildings in and around the downtown, were also left in peace by the law. Because of these women, prostitution existed outside the boundaries of the red-light district as well as inside, though it was more difficult to detect outside. The only prostitutes likely to be arrested were streetwalkers, who according to Thayer's estimates numbered well over a hundred. About twenty-five of the prostitutes in Hartford were male homosexuals. All told, Thayer estimated conservatively, there were at least four hundred prostitutes in the city—and probably many more.[6] The vice trade showed remarkable stability for the next twenty years, with a dozen brothels clustering mainly around State Street on the East Side, and disreputable rooming houses remaining there and in the adjacent downtown.[7]

Thayer was appalled by the presence of such vice, but many other Hartford residents did not see it as a disgrace. The *Hartford Daily Courant*, the Republican voice of the local establishment, referred to prostitution arrests in 1880 as being "for trifling offenses."[8] The Hartford police were similarly nonchalant. Their goal was not to close brothels but to preserve public order. Chief Gunn explained in 1907: "We have found that a vigorous policy of raiding these places only scatters them over the city in the better residence districts. It is, and has for years been, the policy of the police department to keep this class of houses concentrated in a narrow district, and if any nuisance or disturbance is created we get after them, but as a rule unless there is some open breach of the peace or disturbance, they have not been molested."[9]

The Hartford Police Court took an indulgent view of vice offenses, often releasing suspects with small fines or no penalties at all. Typically "the fines were paid, and the houses re-opened on the day the cases were disposed of in the police court," according to one report. Fines against self-employed prostitutes were similarly ineffective, according to a later article: "This simply meant that the women were turned out on the streets to earn the money to pay their fines."[10]

The Ladies Meet the Girls

Hartford women's first attempt at antiprostitution reform took the form of rescuing individual prostitutes from sin, and it continued long after the closing of the red-light district. In the late nineteenth and early twentieth centuries this work, which previously had been left to Protestant pastors, was taken up by female-run institutions. Three shelters for prostitutes opened, two run by Protestant reformers and one by Catholic nuns. Leaders of all three saw prostitution as a symptom of women's personal immorality and tried to solve the problem through personal influence. Shelter workers, especially the Protestants, hoped to facilitate prostitutes' conversions by placing them in settings that simulated domesticity and family relations, thus returning them to women's proper sphere.[11]

Similar shelters had opened in Boston and New York in the 1830s,[12] but the first one in Hartford was opened in 1878 by the Woman's Aid Society, which had formed as a result of a local Protestant religious revival that year. The society saw its shelter north of downtown as a place where wayward "girls" could be given a second chance at a Christian upbringing under the maternal authority of respectable middle-class "ladies."[13] The volunteer ladies held Bible readings and Sunday morning devotional services at the "home." At the services, the ladies claimed, "The girls listen with interest to the counsel of their friends, knowing well that they have their best good at heart." The next step in the process of rescue was to instruct the girls in housework and sewing. Finally, the girls were sent to rural homes where other Christian parental figures would "carry on and supplement with the blessing of God, the reformation which we have *only commenced.*"[14]

The ladies formed a visiting committee to make recruiting forays into the jail, almshouse, hospital, and even the dens of iniquity. The society also attempted to extend the mother-daughter relation to girls in the city jail. It joined the Hartford Equal Rights Club in petitioning the city to hire a police matron whose duties would include caring for jailed prostitutes and offering them advice and protection. The Woman's Aid Society opened a room on the East Side one afternoon a week where girls could go to hear music and to be shown the path of repentance.[15]

Much to the ladies' chagrin, most of the girls resisted this personal influence. Woman's Aid Society reports from the 1880s complained repeatedly that prostitutes were unappreciative of all that was done for them. Not only did most fallen women shun the house on Pavilion Street, but even those who came often returned later to their wicked ways. The ladies blamed the power of rum and the weakness of the girls. "Many of them are like children, with no self-control," one report lamented.[16] The Woman's Aid Society continued to shelter two or three dozen women a year throughout the 1880s and 1890s, but it evolved into a home for expectant single mothers rather than a reformatory for prostitutes. The society had always taken in some pregnant women, and it shifted more in this direction after 1891, when the Shelter for Women opened on the East Side.[17]

Like the Woman's Aid Society, the Shelter for Women was run largely by pious middle-class women and held regularly scheduled religious services. In addition to providing a home for prostitutes, the shelter served free meals and provided temporary lodging to homeless women.[18] The shelter seems to have been somewhat more successful than the Woman's Aid Society, perhaps because it treated its clients with slightly less condescension. It drew more prostitutes than expected in its first year and had to move to larger quarters. But the shelter's clientele was not entirely voluntary. Shelter representatives went to the police station every morning and brought back women arrested for their first vice offenses, whom the police usually chose not to bring to trial. Other prostitutes were discharged by the police court judge into the care of the shelter. Police brought some women directly to the shelter instead of arresting them.[19]

Hartford's third shelter for prostitutes — and its largest — was the House of the Good Shepherd. This establishment, which opened in 1902 in the suburban West End of Hartford, was run by the sisters of Our Lady of Charity of the Good Shepherd. In some respects its goals were similar to those of the Woman's Aid Society. Its professed aim was "to provide a shelter for girls and women of dissolute habits, who wish to do penance for their iniquities and to lead a truly Christian life." It also shared much of the Woman's Aid Society's condescension. The girls were never considered the sisters' equals. Those reformed prostitutes who wished to stay under the protection of the order for life could never even become sisters, but instead joined the subordinate class of "Magdalens." Like the Shelter for Women, the House of the Good Shepherd enjoyed a cooperative relationship with law enforcement officials. In addition to admitting some prostitutes who voluntarily surrendered themselves, it received many who were committed by court order.[20]

These three organizations may have helped reform some prostitutes, but they by no means attempted to rid Hartford of prostitution. There were always scores of fallen women who would spurn the helping hand extended to them and jeer at the middle-class morality of their would-be rescuers. Asked whether she would take refuge at the Shelter for Women after her brothel closed in 1911, one woman "said that when she was ready to die she might consider it."[21]

Gold Street

In addition to these attempts to save individual prostitutes, a second significant reform campaign in the late nineteenth century aimed at cleaning up a small neighborhood outside the red-light district. Reformers in the 1890s successfully swept vice and poverty out of Gold Street, which ran west from Main Street to Bushnell Park.

In 1880, the Common Council received a petition from nearby property owners to widen and otherwise improve the street and to demolish the buildings on the north side. The petitioners described Gold Street as

Gold Street in the 1890s, before the demolition of the tenements on the north side (*left*). (Connecticut State Library)

"a narrow, filthy and at times an almost impassable lane; chiefly occupied by stables and negro tenement houses, and houses of ill fame, making a nuisance, in the heart of the city." Clearing away the tenements for a beautiful new street would thus remove a host of problems while improving traffic flow, they argued.[22] The city fathers balked at such a massive undertaking, but the idea did not go away. To the calls for improving traffic and social conditions, reformers in the 1890s added a third reason for initiating such a project: to redeem the surroundings of the Old Burying Ground, where lay the bones of Hartford's earliest settlers. It was bad enough, thought some respectable citizens, that a reeking slum stood between Main Street and the park; it was intolerable that the slum bordered their ancestors' graves. Descendants could not pay their respects without passing gambling dens and tenements, from whose windows prostitutes solicited passersby.[23]

The local Daughters of the American Revolution took up the cause in 1895, led by Emily S. G. Holcombe, the chapter's regent and the wife of a local insurance executive. The direct descendant of one of the first settlers of Hartford, Emily Seymour Goodwin grew up in Brooklyn, mar-

Emily S. G. Holcombe. (*Municipal
Register*, 1900)

ried John M. Holcombe in 1873, and settled on the eastern slope of Asylum Hill. A genial, gracious woman, active in the social life of the local
elite, she helped found the Hartford chapter of the D.A.R. in 1892 and
remained involved for the next two decades in various projects to com-
memorate the colonial history of Connecticut and its capital city. She
was among the original members of the Municipal Art Society, the local City Beautiful organization founded in 1904, and her husband later
served as president. During the society's fight to prevent the demolition
of the Old State House in 1909, Emily Holcombe raised money for the
building's restoration.[24]

In 1895 Holcombe invited the Rev. George Leon Walker to present a
paper to the D.A.R. about the Burying Ground. "How could we leave
such a spot to its present obscurity, ignominy, and neglect?" Walker asked
his audience, the prosperous Yankee women whose families still represented political and economic power in the increasingly diverse city.
"Honored and sacred to the last spoonful of its dust should be all that
remains of that place of tears and of hope laid out by our forefathers." Far
from honoring the sacred soil behind their tenements, he lamented, the
denizens of Gold Street regularly enriched it by flinging the contents of
their chamberpots out their back windows, along with tin cans and old
shoes. The very least the city could do, Walker said, would be to knock

down buildings on the north side of the street and create a sunny front lawn for the cemetery.[25]

Her sense of obligation to her family, Holcombe wrote later, inspired her to get involved in such a public project. She had remembered visiting the Burying Ground with her father, who had pointed out family names on the stones. Saving the graveyard, she thought, would be "an affectionate memorial to an honored father, and the glad fulfillment of what I believed would be his wish." Thus her work would not go beyond feminine norms. Still, Holcombe was concerned about "what opprobrium might result" from even such nonconfrontational trespassing in the male world of public affairs. Only after seeking the advice of "some very wise men" did she set to work in 1896 and 1897 raising part of the cost of demolishing the buildings. Appealing discreetly to prominent local businessmen, editors, clergy, club members, the Hartford public, and far-flung descendants of the dishonored dead, her organization raised what eventually amounted to $35,600. The money of Hartford's better classes accomplished what the city government alone could not. "Like a full tide it flowed in, cleansing, purifying and wiping away the stain of long reproach to our fair city," Holcombe wrote.[26]

Exactly what that stain was, Holcombe forbore to mention. She acknowledged that "moral as well as material filth desecrated the very atmosphere," but she preferred to emphasize the graveyard's glorious future as a source of civic pride.[27] The Common Council gave final approval for the work in October 1898. Demolition of the buildings began the following April, watched resentfully by former tenants. The *Hartford Post* mockingly quoted an elderly black woman in the crowd: "I brung up all ma chillen down hyar . . . and ma ole man died hyar. I didn't never expect to have to move and I was a figurin' on stayin' right hyar till I died. There never was no place so comfortable and handy and it's a too bad to tear down such mighty good buildin's. I don't see no use in such foolishness nohow." But lower-class complaints were easily ignored, and the evicted tenants were left to fend for themselves. Demolition was completed in May. The D.A.R. then set to work restoring the gravestones and arranging for the construction of a fence and an elaborate gateway that created a monument to the importance of Hartford's Yankee establishment. In this way, the space gained a new didactic function, reinforcing rather than subverting the social order.[28]

The Pastors' Crusade

Establishing the shelters and cleaning up the neighborhood around the Old Burying Ground did represent steps toward treating prostitution as a public problem rather than a personal one, but the women reformers were cautious. Though their work addressed one of the more unpleasant effects of women's subordination and brought the reformers themselves into the public sphere, the ladies spoke in terms that affirmed traditional gender norms. Most important, they did not challenge the toleration of a vice district — or the ideology that allowed such a division of public space.

The red-light district was first seriously questioned on other grounds by local pastors in 1907. Antiprostitution reform had been a traditional concern among Protestant pastors in Hartford as in other cities. Clergymen in other cities, particularly New York, were at the fore of late nineteenth-century campaigns to encourage moral purity and to lead semivigilante "preventive societies" against vice. Hartford pastors had been working quietly to rescue prostitutes and place them in private homes long before female reformers opened the first shelter. They organized the City Missionary Society in 1851 and used it to coordinate their previously individual rescue efforts.[29] Clergymen formed the Hartford Federation of Churches in 1900 and set up the federation's "Committee on Public Morals" to battle vice more directly. The committee hired a detective agency in 1906 to help it investigate prostitution in Hartford, presenting its findings to Mayor William F. Henney in a private letter late that year.[30]

The pastors' aversion to publicizing their findings reflected their fear that vice was already too public. Their letter described several interrelated forms of vice that had edged into both semipublic commercial places and the streets. They noted after-hours liquor sales even in a large hotel, as well as "gambling without much effort at concealment" at saloons. They were greatly troubled by lewd behavior in the curtained booths of saloons, theater cafes, and hotels, where prostitutes solicited clients before taking them to "bed houses" or to hotel rooms. The clergymen feared the erosion of boundaries between depravity and virtue. They noted the State Street brothels, but they were more disturbed by the illicit use of seemingly respectable hotels. Furthermore, "the number of women of this class upon our streets is very noticeable. Our agent was accosted by eleven such women on the street in three evenings. . . . Why is it, Mr. Mayor, that vice dares to so flaunt itself in our open streets?" This letter did not demand that the red-light district be closed, calling only for an end to streetwalking and for better enforcement of liquor laws.

The clergymen concluded by arguing that police had forged a deeply troubling alliance with sin. Mistaking the pastors' detectives for sporting men, police had obligingly directed them to gambling halls and bordellos. Moreover,

> In talking with an officer, and a plain clothes man, our agents learned that the houses of prostitution were protected and that the policemen profited by this form of vice. Members of our police department stated to our detectives, that "they made it hot for women who did not cough up and mentioned several instances [*sic*]." Our agent also learned from members of our police force "that in other cities they have a go between who collects the graft, but here we have to go and get it for ourselves."[31]

Months passed, and the city's response seemed lethargic at best. Mayor Henney, a Republican, was a reformist on matters of orderly administration and civic beautification, but he was apparently unwilling to disturb established patterns of law enforcement.[32] On 19 May 1907, the Federation of Churches reluctantly took its cause to the public. Four pastors used their Sunday sermons to inveigh against vice, drawing details from the previous autumn's investigation. Their sermons received extensive coverage in the newspapers the next day.

The clergymen were blunt in their criticism of the police and the vice trade, but ambiguous about whether they wanted prostitution suppressed entirely or simply forced to operate in semiprivate buildings within a narrowly bounded district. The Rev. Harry E. Peabody, the chairman of the public morals committee, called for closing the "vicious resorts." He placed more emphasis, however, on the "hotels and restaurants and saloons not in the restricted district but on our main streets, where vice and crime ply their trade, insolent, aggressive and unrebuked." Peabody said vice posed particular dangers when it ventured outside the district, because young people going to theaters downtown might be unaware of the evil influences surrounding them. He called on public-spirited Christians to see that "vice and crime . . . at least sink back into their dens."[33] City officials took advantage of this waffling and deflected attention from the policy of a tolerated vice district. They narrowed the issue to corruption alone and claimed to be shocked at hearing that gambling and prostitution were aided by police. The Board of Police Commissioners demanded that the ministers produce evidence for such accusations, and the pastors found themselves on the defensive.[34]

Five more pastors spoke out on vice the next Sunday, trying to regain control of the issue by taking a more aggressive stance. The Rev. Elmer A. Dent protested the attempt to distract attention from the immoral conditions. He and the Rev. Henry H. Kelsey directly attacked Chief Gunn's policy toward East Side vice. Kelsey likened tolerating prostitution to tolerating typhoid fever: in both cases, contagion would inevitably spread.[35]

The Rev. Peabody met the next day with Prosecuting Attorney Harrison B. Freeman, Jr., and apparently secured Freeman's agreement to crack down on prostitution. In July, acting on Freeman's warrants, police conducted a Saturday night vice raid in which seventy people were arrested. Nine of the ten brothels raided were on State Street.[36] In police court Freeman declared that he was serious about cleaning up State Street, and would continue to order raids if the brothels reopened. But he did not promise to suppress vice throughout Hartford or even throughout the East Side. He intended, rather, to change the boundaries of the vice district to keep prostitution off the main streets. Referring to changes in the traffic patterns that would follow the completion of the new Connecticut River bridge the next year, Freeman said, "The new boulevard will soon be put through State street, and I am determined that the street shall be cleaned out." The judge then astonished the crowded courtroom by sentencing seven of the ten madams to prison for three months each.[37]

Though shaken, the red-light district survived the 1907 crusade. By 1909, when police conducted another big raid, the results of the vice crusade were obvious: brothels were no longer found on State Street but were quietly flourishing in less heavily traveled parts of the East Side.[38] Yet despite its limited results, the pastors' crusade had decisively redefined prostitution as a menace to everyone. The social evil, they argued, tainted the public spaces of the city, tempted the young, and corrupted the guardians of order. The pastors had also succeeded in directing the power of city government into an area of moral reform previously left to private organizations. Their new approach to the issue raised difficult questions. Should prostitution be controlled by segregating it, or did segregation mean a craven accommodation with the forces of evil? If Hartford was to have "public women," how publicly could they pursue their trade? Was vice considered to be flaunting itself only if it strayed from the East Side?

The clergymen offered confused and contradictory answers to these questions, but underlying their arguments was the common belief that it was impossible to purify all of Hartford. Vice either could be chased from public view into the East Side brothel, or it could be attacked in the brothel at the risk of pushing it into the street. Initially, the public morals committee had merely emphasized *public* morality. The Rev. Peabody, who was the most alarmed about the spread of vice into the main streets, had implied that he would tolerate the existence of prostitution behind closed doors on side streets in the slums. On the other hand, the Rev. Dent, who assailed the idea of any sort of vice district, simultaneously urged respectable people to retreat from public space. The public streets posed too many temptations for young people, he said. The best solution for both men and women was to take refuge in familial privacy. "Mothers, fathers, make your houses homes. Keep the boys and girls off the streets."[39] Thus, while Dent was calling for total war against the brothels, he was implicitly surrendering the regular thoroughfares to the forces of evil.

Dent was troubled by the growth of commercial leisure activities, especially mixed-sex downtown nightlife. Nighttime had once been so closely associated with vice that the term "nightwalker" was a euphemism for "prostitute." But that connection became muddled in Hartford, as in other cities, in the late nineteenth century. Commercial amusements were drawing more and more people into the public spaces of the city at night, partly as a result of increased leisure time and partly because new electric street lighting dispelled some of the darkness. Hartford had begun replacing its old gas lamps with bright new electric streetlights in 1883, completing the change by 1890.[40] The downtown now became a liminal new world after the sun set—neither dark nor light—where it was unclear which moral conditions would prevail. By 1907 it was evident that this confusing new space was drawing disproportionately

large numbers of people in their late adolescence and early adulthood—
an impressionable age before the moral character was set, in Dent's
view. Every evening, young theatergoers would flock downtown to enjoy vaudeville, burlesque, drama, musical comedy, and motion pictures.
The largest theater at this time was Parson's, noted by the pastors for its
scandalous private booths. Dance halls were also becoming popular at
this time. (A later study found that the halls were pickup places for young
working-class men and women, who would indulge in "demoralizing"
new dances before leaving together.) Some dancers and theatergoers lingered downtown afterward in the hotel barrooms and in the numerous
saloons there and on the East Side.[41] Such activities created a libertine
atmosphere, Dent warned in his May 26 sermon. "At midnight . . . the
saloons close and turn out their raft of iniquity upon our streets, a menace to our peace and good name. Hartford has the unenviable reputation
of having an exceptionally large number of well dressed young people
upon its streets at or after midnight. There is an unusual amount of tip-
pling and drunkenness among this class."[42]

Though stated in overwrought terms, Dent's concerns about commercial leisure were not entirely misplaced. As the historian Kathy Peiss has
shown, shopgirls and other working-class women eagerly used the dance
halls and other "cheap amusements" in constructing new gender identi-
ties that clashed with the expectations of their parents and of moralistic
reformers. The freer sexuality fostered in such places often strayed into
the blurry margins of prostitution. Hartford investigators of prostitution
heard in 1913 from several women whose love of commercial entertainment had led them to turn dating into a lucrative profession. "She likes
to go to dances and the theaters and to have pretty things," the investigators noted of one woman. Of another, they wrote: "She does not care for
home life; likes excitement."[43]

Dent was also accurate in linking the influence of commercial leisure
with the growth in female employment. Hartford department stores and
offices were hiring more and more women, freeing them from the constraints of "home life" and giving them the money they needed to go out.
Dent feared most of all for country girls who came to work in the city,
away from the supervision of their families. Women's role in society was
undergoing alarming changes. "No day in the history of our country so
tests the moral stamina as ours. Women crowd into public life and public

employment. They meet and fall before unaccustomed temptations."[44] On the moral map of Hartford, he felt, all the reassuring old boundaries were now frighteningly blurred.

Women on the Streets

While working-class women were challenging bourgeois gender norms by their presence in dance halls, streets, and workplaces, middle-class women were also crowding into public life in threatening new ways. Among these invaders were the militant suffragists of the Hartford Equal Franchise League. Under the leadership of Katharine Houghton Hepburn,[45] these women would wage a successful battle to abolish the red-light district forever. The suffragists followed the pastors' precedent in calling vice a public menace and seeking government action, but they differed in arguing that it was entangled with larger issues of gender inequality and poverty. In place of the Christian impulse behind earlier antivice efforts, the suffragists brought to their work a secular vision of social progress. Segregating the social evil was no solution, they thought, as it merely perpetuated one of the worst forms of women's victimization, and, through the spread of venereal disease, threatened families in better neighborhoods.

Suffragists sought to redefine the feminine role in society without making it approximate the masculine one. They did not want women to follow the shopgirls' example in adopting the easy sexuality common among men.[46] They shared with the shelter leaders a belief in female moral superiority and wanted to end the separation of spheres on terms congenial to ladies.[47] Middle-class women's traditional concern for the health and morality of their families, they thought, demanded that they leave the false security of their homes to clean up public life.[48] In their fight against prostitution and for the vote, Hartford suffragists acted out the new gender roles they desired to establish. They took their struggle to the papers, to the meeting halls, and to the most public part of the public sphere: the city streets. There, fighting a woman's battle on what had been a man's turf, they sought a sweeping victory over the red-light district. Once cleansed of the most flagrant immorality, both private and public space would be safe for respectable ladies and their families — or so the suffragists hoped.

By the time Mayor Edward L. Smith ordered the brothels closed in 1911,[49] Katharine Houghton Hepburn had been concerned about prostitution for several years. Hepburn, born Katharine Martha Houghton in 1878, had grown up outside Buffalo and was the daughter of a prominent businessman. Her father committed suicide when she was fourteen, her mother died of cancer eighteen months later, and Katharine was left in the care of relatives. Aloof, haughty, and secretly insecure, she became a sort of mother to her two younger sisters, insisting against the wishes of her guardians that all three of them receive high-quality schooling, including college educations at Bryn Mawr. She worked briefly as a schoolteacher after her graduation, then married Dr. Thomas N. Hepburn in 1904, settled with him on Hartford's Asylum Hill, and began raising a family. Encouraged by her sister Edith, Katharine Hepburn and her husband both became involved in social reform. Thomas Hepburn shared the growing concern among urologists at this time that men infected with syphilis and gonorrhea were spreading the disease to their innocent wives and unborn children. To many this danger symbolized a threat to the well-being of the family, a threat they associated with the city and the urban masses. Contagion bred in the immigrant slums could easily spread to the most secluded, middle-class home. Thomas Hepburn wrote an article in 1908 attacking regulated prostitution and was a founding member of the Connecticut Society for Social Hygiene in 1910. Katharine Hepburn served briefly in the Woman's Aid Society and then in her husband's organization. She joined the suffrage cause around 1908 and took up the issue of prostitution in her first speech. In 1909, as vice president of the Connecticut Woman Suffrage Association (CWSA), she gave a speech to the membership about venereal disease.[50]

If Hepburn's remarks on prostitution and her speech about venereal disease startled the staid members of the CWSA, she would not have minded. She was at the head of what one of her supporters called a "younger, enthusiastic and militant group" inspired by the aggressive English suffragism of Emmeline Pankhurst. Her Hartford Equal Franchise League, which stood apart from the older Hartford Equal Rights Club, was interested in broad social reform and was not content to ask meekly for the vote. As president of the CWSA in 1910–11 and 1913–17, Hepburn was a dynamic speaker who relished controversy. She resigned the CWSA presidency in 1917 in disgust with the cautious policies of the

Katharine Houghton Hepburn, ca. 1914. Hepburn was active as a suffragist and a campaigner against prostitution, although this photograph emphasizes her role as a mother. (*Souvenir Book of the Municipal Building Dedication*)

parent organization, the National American Woman Suffrage Association, and gave her support to the National Woman's Party of Alice Paul.[51]

Hepburn saw the fight against prostitution as a woman's issue that transcended the class interests of genteel reformers like herself. Her argument on this point was double. On the one hand, she urged the improvement of women's standing in the paid workforce and drew on Progressive Era ideas about the need for an interventionist state. "The ballot for women would raise their political and consequently their economic status, and would so diminish the number of women who are driven into prostitution through unendurably long hours of work and starvation wages." Working-class women needed protective legislation, which they could secure more easily if all women had the vote. Hepburn also acknowledged the oppressive class relations involved in prostitution—many clients were from wealthier backgrounds than the prostitutes. Fragmentary arrest records from 1910, and data from the 1913 *Report of the Hartford Vice Commission*, support her view. The evidence indicates that Hartford prostitutes at this time were typically young, native-born white women from working- or lower-class backgrounds.[52]

On the other hand, along with her concern for working women, Hepburn held to a modified version of the middle-class belief that women were the defenders of the home, the family, and morality. In promotional literature for the CWSA, she chose to be depicted in her maternal role: one photograph shows her surrounded by her children, while another has her seated in a madonna-like pose, gazing down at the baby in her arms.[53] Recounting her antiprostitution campaign in a 1914 speech, she explained that her group had seen the need for women of all classes to accelerate an ongoing redefinition of motherhood and to take a more public role in order to fulfill traditional obligations:

> Many of us were mothers who had little boys that we should some day send out into the city. And I want to ask the women in this audience, "How much chance do you think you will have with your boys even if you have brought them up as most mothers of our generation are doing . . . [even] if you have taught them that the foundation for the double standard of morality is a lie . . . how much chance, I ask you, do you think there is that your point of view will prevail if when the boy goes out into the outside world, into the man's world where the woman's point of view does not count directly, he finds that— from the mayor to the chief of police down to the patrolman on his beat—every one of these public officials knowingly sanctions in certain parts of the city the buying and selling of women at all hours of the day and night? And if you feel that your boy is not safe, how must the mother in the poorer districts feel whose girl is in danger too? How must the mother feel who is trying to bring up her little

daughter against the terrible odds of long hours of labor and low
wages . . . when she realizes that it is in her immediate neighborhood that these houses are 'segregated?'"

Hepburn believed that middle-class constructs of femininity were shared
by all classes. In fact, she added, "The women living in the slums were
the most to be depended on to take a right view of these questions. They
never once told us that the toleration of houses of ill-fame 'protects good
women.' They knew very well that the boys and men—many of them
married men—whom they saw come down to these houses from the better districts, did not carry back protection to the women that they were
supposed to love and cherish, but that they carried back disease and
death." [54] Both strands of Hepburn's argument assumed that women differed from men in fundamental ways. Women had special needs and
moral concerns that were not respected either in male-dominated government or in male-dominated public space. Hepburn's antiprostitution
efforts reflected a broader contemporary rhetoric and ideology that historians have described as "maternalist"—advocating the extension throughout society of the values that mothers were thought to represent within
the home. [55]

Since they believed the issues to be inextricably intertwined, Hepburn and her supporters intended to press forward simultaneously on
both suffrage and antiprostitution work, but like other observers in Hartford in 1912 they could see that a fight against prostitution would not be
easy. When Smith ordered the brothels closed, Hepburn later recalled,
"People began saying 'They will open up in a little while. It was just like
this two years ago and everything opened up again as soon as things
quieted down.'" [56] Smith himself had avoided making extravagant predictions. "No reasonable man will expect that the adoption and enforcement of this policy will accomplish the impossible," he said. "To
be successful it needs the support of public opinion that is strong and
persistent." [57]

Initial indications were that public opinion might not support a determined campaign against tolerated vice. "Some things can be regulated
but not wholly suppressed," asserted the *Times*. The *Times* printed letters from several readers who staunchly defended the segregated district
for keeping prostitutes off the streets and out of the better neighborhoods.

The notorious Fusco's saloon, formerly a brothel, at the corner of Front and Talcott streets, ca. 1913. The Connecticut Woman Suffrage Association took this and other photographs of the East Side to call attention to the problems of vice and poverty. Note the presence of children. (Connecticut State Library)

One writer even proposed licensing brothels and conducting regular medical examinations of the prostitutes.[58]

Local clergymen wrote sermons and press releases in an effort to arouse public sentiment against prostitution, and they helped run a revival campaign to save Hartford's men and boys from sin,[59] but Hepburn and her supporters took a more aggressive approach. The suffragists held a women's meeting on January 8, 1912, to demand that the city form a vice commission to investigate the problem. A similar commission had conducted a widely admired investigation in Chicago in 1910–11, and imitators had followed in Cleveland, Kansas City, and Minneapolis. Such groups soon would prove to be remarkably successful in publicizing and prosecuting the fight against prostitution in cities throughout the country. The Hartford suffragists also began organizing a mass meeting to be held in Parson's Theater later that month. To publicize the event, they printed ten thousand handbills for distribution throughout the city, warning mothers of the dangers that "white slavery" posed to innocent girls. Their emphasis on white slavery reflected a nationwide fear at the time that many prostitutes were literally sexual slaves. Such a view of prostitution appealed to many female reformers throughout America, since it put the full blame on men and bolstered the claim that women were morally superior. Hepburn's group posted billboards with the message, "The White Slave Traffic. What It Is. The Results. What To Do," along with the date and the location of the meeting. By the day of the mass meeting, city officials were still debating whether to push forward with the vice commission, and the *Times* and the *Courant* remained hostile to the suffragists' goals and tactics.[60]

The meeting, which drew a predominantly female audience of about fifteen hundred, was organized as a demonstration of women's power. The hall was decorated with the suffrage colors white, green, and purple. Those entering were ushered to their seats by women "wearing regalia inscribed with the words 'Knowledge is Power,'" Hepburn recalled. The event drew women not only from Asylum Hill but also from the working-class immigrant neighborhoods. One reporter noted a conspicuous number of "young Hebrew girls." Other women had come from distant parts of the state, Hepburn recalled, "a striking demonstration of the solidarity of women when a great moral issue is at stake." Mayor Smith, who had been asked to serve as chairman of the meeting, was clearly uneasy about the atmosphere. "Hysterics never assists us very much," he warned the crowd. He listened to the speeches denouncing vice districts, but stepped down as chairman when the audience voted on a resolution protesting "the cowardly action of certain of our public officers."[61]

The advertising, the mass meeting, and the symbolic vote were just the beginning of an uncompromising assertion of middle-class women's right to enter the public sphere. The Equal Franchise League kept the issues of prostitution and woman suffrage in the public eye throughout the early months of 1912 by holding weekday afternoon rallies on downtown street corners—hitherto places where decent ladies had not gathered. In holding street rallies, the suffragists were following the example not only of Pankhurst, but of Hartford's working-class women. A year earlier, immigrant women had taken to the streets in protest as part of a garment workers' strike; they heckled scabs and picketed in front of Main Street department stores.[62]

Pankhurst and the garment workers were arrested; Hepburn's suffragists were not. The *Hartford Post*, sympathetic to their cause, described one of the rallies this way: "The meeting was an orderly one, there being several hundred men and women present. An officer kept the sidewalk clear sufficiently for those to pass by who wished, but the majority remained to listen to the arguments." At one of the rallies, Hepburn announced that the Equal Franchise League would make prostitution and tenement conditions prominent issues in the municipal election that spring. Just before the election, the suffragists held another mass meeting at which the audience resolved to ask the mayoral candidates to announce their position on enforcing vice laws. The candidates dodged the question, but the one who seemed least sympathetic—Democrat Thomas J. Spellacy—was defeated. Under Republican Mayor Louis R. Cheney, the Hartford Vice Commission was allowed to do its work.[63]

The vice commission's report, completed in 1913, claimed that the closing of the brothels had indeed reduced prostitution in Hartford. Contrary to skeptics' dire predictions, the closing had neither resulted in more streetwalking nor caused increased vice in other neighborhoods. The report recommended stricter laws and enforcement policies, the hiring of female police officers, and the end to all "discrimination in respect to sex or social standing in the efforts to suppress the social evil." The suffragists were pleased with the report and eager to see it disseminated, but city officials had other ideas. They told the city clerk to do his utmost to keep copies of the report out of "improper hands" and to prevent any copies from being sent out of Hartford. Within two days, the five hundred copies had all been handed out, and no more were available.[64] The suffragists smelled a cover-up and hit on an idea to thwart it. They reprinted the report and sold it for 25 cents per copy at the CWSA headquarters on Pratt Street, in the heart of the downtown shopping district. A large sign, conspicuously posted in the show window, drew in passersby. Hepburn wanted everyone in Hartford to read the report, and ordered additional printings when the first one ran out.[65]

The Common Council refused to act on any of the Vice Commission's recommendations,[66] but once again, the suffragists made the issue plainly visible in the street. Pedestrians could not help but notice the enormous sign that filled the CWSA show window that autumn: "Mothers of Hartford: Do You Know How the Following Members of the City Council Who Claim to Represent You Voted in Regard to the Suppression of Commercialized Vice in Your City[?]" The sign listed the names and addresses of the twenty-four councilmen who had voted against keeping the brothels closed. Another sign invited the curious, "Come In and Get a Pamphlet Free." Hepburn expected this to be a very effective pressure tactic, especially once the wives and daughters of the councilmen saw the sign. "People going by would see it, stop short, read the names, and then come in and get a copy of the pamphlet. We distributed thousands of them."[67]

By this point Hepburn sensed victory. Noting in December 1913 that the brothels had stayed closed for nearly two years, she said, "We have broken down the ban against a free discussion of such subjects and by airing and letting the light in on these dark spots have cleansed Hartford." Though the councilmen held their ground, the suffragists campaigned against them in the April 1914 city election. They posted a blacklist, headed "A Disgrace," with the names of seventeen councilmen who were seeking reelection after refusing to support the brothel closings. The suffragists asked mayoral candidates to declare whether they favored the current policy of suppressing vice and whether they favored the recommendations of the Vice Commission. This time the candidates decided they could not ignore the issue. Both men answered that they agreed with the current policy and with most of the Vice Commission's recommendations. Their responses were published in the press.[68]

Although the suffragists were disappointed that fifteen of the blacklisted councilmen were reelected in April, they were cheered by newly elected Mayor Joseph H. Lawler's announcement that he would "insist upon the rigid suppression of vice in all its forms." A Democrat, representing a party dominated locally by immigrant-stock Catholics and Jews, Lawler had been regarded with suspicion by some of the middle-class Protestant reformers. Though the previous Democratic mayor, Edward L. Smith, had been the one to close the brothels, the party was controlled by chairman Thomas Spellacy, who had shown little interest in fighting vice during his own 1912 run for mayor. Lawler, however, represented the more reformist "new line" faction in the local Demo-

suffrage

cratic party; he had won the Democratic nomination only by defeating the "old line" Spellacy in a primary. Antiprostitution was truly a nonpartisan issue in Hartford, supported by some Democrats and opposed by some Republicans, much like other reforms during this period of alternating party rule and internal party conflict. In any case, Lawler's support guaranteed the success of Hepburn's campaign. Hepburn boasted later that year that "continuous agitation has made it impossible to open up the houses again. . . . Women have the weapon of publicity now and it is a powerful one." [69]

The women capped their success with a spectacular suffrage parade on May 2 that featured hundreds of marchers, brass bands, and allegorical floats. "We prepare children for the world. Let us help prepare the world for children," read one banner. In their official parade program, the suffragists declared that they were struggling to adapt women's political role to modern social conditions. "The revolution in women's work makes votes for women a practical necessity," it read. "As women's work has gone out of the home into the factory many women have been forced to follow. . . . The women who are left in the home are trying to bring up their children and to keep their homes free from evil influences both physical and moral. . . . Yet women have no voice in making the laws which for good or for evil so vitally affect their work." The parade was reportedly one of the biggest in Hartford's history. Thousands of spectators thronged the sidewalks along the entire parade route. Suffragists, Hepburn declared, had learned how important it was "to carry their propaganda to men on the street." [70]

The Dispersion of Vice

The suffragists' victory proved to be lasting but hollow. To their satisfaction, the tolerated vice district never reopened, either in the crowded brick blocks of the immigrant East Side or anywhere else. When speculation to the contrary surfaced in 1918, Mayor Richard J. Kinsella emphatically denied it. Later accounts of the Progressive-Era vice campaigns, written in 1925 and 1931, agreed that the period from 1911 to 1914 marked the end of the red-light district. [71]

Similar changes were taking place in cities across the country in response to public pressure, but prostitution itself—though in decline for other reasons—persisted. The historian Barbara Meil Hobson has argued that "turning out the red lights and dismantling the districts merely dispersed the trade and produced a new set of institutions in the prostitution economy."[72] This appears to have been true in Hartford, despite the Vice Commission's denials. The commission's own evidence showed prostitution, after the brothel closings, to be centered in the commercial downtown. In the winter of 1912–13, investigators asked fifty-one prostitutes where they solicited clients. Their answers indicated that half did at least some soliciting on downtown streets. By far the most popular place to meet clients was on Main Street, where twenty-four of the women said they worked. Asylum Street, another major shopping street, was used by eight prostitutes surveyed. Streets on the East Side drew smaller numbers of women: seven for Front, three for Market, and three for State. (Some women probably worked more than one street.) A man craving an encounter with a prostitute no longer had to sneak down the dirty streets of the poor. He could now find sex for sale beside the bright display windows of Hartford's finest shops—one consumer choice among many in a district showcasing the voluptuous pleasure of spending. Nor were other prostitutes working much more privately. With the brothels closed, they had little choice but to solicit in places not specifically reserved for them, such as restaurants, saloons, theaters, and the train station. Most prostitutes took clients to hotel rooms or rooming houses.[73]

Brothelkeepers continued to try to reopen in the old red-light district, especially in 1912 and 1913, and streetwalkers continued to solicit there as well as downtown. But news reports and court records after that suggest that prostitution had lost its geographic focus in the riverfront slum and had become common in all parts of the fringe area surrounding the downtown.[74] In the later 1910s, news reports and court documents pertaining to prostitution arrests increasingly gave addresses in the southern half of the city. There was no apparent center of vice. Arrests were made on a wide range of respectable working- and middle-class streets scattered from just south of downtown to the extreme South End.[75] There were also reports that streetwalking was increasing and that streetwalkers were soliciting motorists and performing sexual acts in automobiles.[76]

Prostitution continued to thrive in Hartford without the protection of a red-light district. From the closing of the brothels through the end of the decade, prostitution-related arrests averaged nearly two hundred a year—roughly the same arrest rate as in the years immediately before the brothels closed. Clearly, Mayor Kinsella was exaggerating when he spoke in 1918 of "the exemplary freedom of our City from all forms of vice." The city was free of vice only in the sense that police no longer granted it a district where it could operate with impunity.[77]

From the shelters for wayward girls to the pastors' crusade, antiprostitution reform in Hartford overtly reaffirmed middle-class gender norms while inadvertently weakening the separation of spheres. In the shelters, middle-class ladies cautiously extended their role as protectors of private morality into a homelike setting for rescuing women from the streets. Emily Holcombe emphasized the familial aspects of the Gold Street project (protecting the graves of ancestors and obeying her father), avoiding any mention of prostitution. Still, her project represented a step by middle-class women into a more public and politicized role and tacitly began to address prostitution's effects on public space. The pastors' crusade raised troubling questions about the practical value and moral implications of a segregated vice district. In their inability to agree on a solution, and the limited results of their work, the pastors accidentally exposed the weakness of separate-spheres ideology: the spatial boundaries between public and private, vice and virtue, were impossible to police.

The suffragists shared some of the values of their predecessors in the shelter organizations. They believed, for example, that women had a moral mission and that middle-class ideas of femininity could be applied to all classes. They enthusiastically embraced some of the tactics that Holcombe and the pastors had so reluctantly adopted: the use of publicity to call attention to their campaign and the enlistment of governmental power in their fight for reform. But the suffragists used these tactics more skillfully and persistently than earlier antiprostitution reformers had, and they sought a more radical transformation of society—a new role for women, with greater access to public space and public discourse. Far more than any of their predecessors, the suffragists challenged the old dichotomy between virtuous female privacy and the wicked male street. They argued that, regardless of whether prostitution stayed on the East Side or ventured into more reputable areas, regardless of whether it was hidden in brothels or paraded in public, its very existence threatened everyone in the city. Through the spread of venereal disease, the social evil could attack the families and even the bodies of respectable middle-class women. The problem demanded that women abandon the illusory shelter of their homes and take to the streets to press their cause. The emergency forced them to take daring steps, but success would allow them to feel at home in public; the street would be made an appropriate place for ladies because it would be morally purified. The entire public sphere would be imbued with the values of genteel femininity.

The suffragists gained greater access to public space, but they failed to transform that space as thoroughly as they had desired. Earlier police predictions came true, as closing the red-light district meant the end of an attempt, however ineffectual, to keep vice away from middle-class citizens who sought to avoid it. Having demolished the crumbling barriers that marked out Hartford's moral geography, middle-class women gained the right to leave the private sphere — only to find the world outside the home as impure as ever. Regardless of what Hepburn said in 1913, Hartford was not cleansed.

4

Saving the Newsies

The sun rose over Hartford each morning on streetcars rattling down country roads and through empty streets toward the department stores and granite office towers downtown. By the time the first ripple of the daily tide of commuters flowed into City Hall Square, an even earlier group of workers was waiting for it: dozens of young newsboys gripping fresh armfuls of papers and clamoring for attention. "Got up at 5:30 in the morning to catch the trolleys coming in from across the river from Manchester and Glastonbury to sell 50 papers to make 50 cents," recalled Anthony Tapogna, an East Side Italian boy whose brother was also a "newsie." Many newsies would return to the sidewalks and streetcars after school, joined by other boys and girls, to peddle afternoon papers to the rush hour crowds. Some would stay late into the evening to make a few extra cents from sales in saloons.[1]

A harried commuter might be grateful for a chance to relax with the news, but a growing number of reformers around the turn of the century saw the presence of these children downtown as a troubling anomaly. By the early 1900s, American educators and reformers were working to construct a new, separate world for children, both inside and outside of school. As a result of child-labor laws, mandatory school attendance, longer school years, age-graded classrooms, and organized recreation programs, children were increasingly segregated from adult activities and grouped with their peers of the same age.[2] Given this trend, it is not surprising that children, whose lives were supposed to revolve around education and age-segregated play, would be considered out of place in the bustling downtown, an adult-dominated place reserved for work and commercial exchange. Children who simply wished to play outdoors could find more convenient places closer to home. When children went downtown, it was often for the same reasons as adults: to attend commercial amusements, to acquire goods, or to make money.

A few moralists might object to the corruption of young movie addicts,[3] but it was the children who worked on the street who truly offended them. Children's role in the street trades had given them a niche in the economic life of the downtown—and a claim to what was otherwise adult turf—but by 1900 reformers were beginning to question the validity of this role. For the first time, child labor in America was being viewed as a major social problem. Child-welfare organizations through most of the nineteenth century had been more concerned about idle and vagrant children than about child laborers, but by the turn of the century they were attacking child labor as a violation of children's sentimental value.[4] Reformers, who now viewed children as sacred, considered their hawking of newspapers on the street almost blasphemous.

Certain reformers in Hartford worked to rescue all children from what they saw as the corrupting influence of the street trades. Their repeated lobbying campaigns from 1895 to 1910 pressured the city government to forbid the sale of newspapers by boys under ten years of age and to put new restrictions on older newsboys. The boys had to obtain licenses, curtail their hours, and behave more courteously. The child-labor reformers' greatest concern, though, was the newsgirls, whose status as both females and children made their selling of newspapers doubly inappropriate. Reformers warned repeatedly that the girls were in danger of losing their chastity and of learning bad manners. After two full decades of work and against determined opposition, including some from other social activists, the child-labor reformers were finally able to push the newsgirls off the street. As a result of the child-labor reform campaigns, downtown streets became more exclusively the property of adults, especially at night. The area of Hartford with the most diverse range of street activities was becoming more narrowly restricted.

Newsies at Work

There were other street jobs available for Hartford children besides selling papers. Boys and girls could also sell chewing gum, postcards, and shoelaces, for example. Many children helped their families by hunting for wood scraps for the cookstove or for metal scraps that could be sold to junk dealers. The scavengers could be seen at work in the streets around town pushing their homemade wagons. They also kept an eye out for cigar and cigarette butts that could be sold to bums or to tobacco recyclers. Messenger services employed boys to deliver telegrams and notes, sometimes late into the night, a job that had an unsavory reputation because it often involved delivering messages to brothels or running errands for prostitutes or their clients. Some boys also shined shoes on the sidewalk or in saloons, though not as many as in some other cities such as New Haven (many of Hartford's shoes were polished instead by adult Italian immigrants who worked in indoor shoeshine parlors and even had their own labor union).[5]

Newsies, however, were by far the most numerous of the children in the street trades in Hartford, as in other cities. It is hard to determine their exact number at any time—possibly no one ever tried to count—but in 1912 the city's Juvenile Commission reported that 583 boys and 37 girls from ages ten through thirteen had been issued licenses and badges. Boys as young as five or six had sold papers a few years previously, before the ordinance prohibiting newsies under ten. Newsies older than thirteen were not required to obtain licenses, so there is no way of telling how numerous they were. But newsies were less likely to be older teenagers, and since most children who were required to get licenses did so, the licensed children probably represented a majority of all Hartford newsies at that time.[6]

Their main reason for working, according to their later recollections and to a 1921 study by the state, was to supplement their immigrant families' income. Their daily contributions ran between 25 cents and a dollar. Three-fourths of Connecticut children in the street trades came from

Boys scavenging for scrap, 1918. Scavenging was one of many ways in which children could make money on the streets. (Hartford Public Library)

families in which both parents were foreign-born, according to the state's study. Although the newsies might keep a few pennies to buy candy or pay their admission to the movies, the overwhelming majority of them gave most of their earnings to their families.[7]

The work was available because of a greatly expanded market for newspapers at this time, especially for afternoon dailies. Nationwide, the late nineteenth-century booms in afternoon newspaper circulation and the newsie population were indirect results of new patterns of urban growth and transportation. The unprecedented geographical expansion of American cities at this time went hand in hand with an increase in the number of commuting workers, many of whom could be persuaded to buy papers to fill their empty time on the streetcar home. Children flocked to meet this need, concentrating at the points where commuters

Lewis Hine's photo of Matro Stavola, age eight, selling newspapers downtown, March 1909. Like many of Hine's photos of Hartford newsies, this depicts its subject as a small figure left unprotected in an adult-dominated urban landscape. (NCLC collection, Library of Congress)

gathered to catch the trolleys, particularly the major stops downtown. In Hartford, two of the best places were Union Station and City Hall Square. The square was especially good because it was the point of convergence for streetcar lines from throughout the metropolitan area.[8]

Despite the large market, selling papers was a demanding job that forced newsies to hustle aggressively for customers. Newsies in Hartford, as elsewhere, were independent entrepreneurs who bought their goods from the newspaper companies or from newsdealers and sold them at a profit. Some staked claims to spots from which they sold to a regular clientele, while others clustered at busy corners and swarmed around potential customers. Eager to make sales, "They stick a paper in a man's face and keep it there for a dozen steps, until he simply has to buy it. They are a persistent crowd, and their persistency seems to win," reported the *Hartford Courant*. The work rewarded assertiveness and nourished a tough-guy subculture of fighting, swearing, and gambling.

"Competition was keen among the paper boys," recalled one of the newsies:

> I became tough and very alert to the slightest semblance of a whistle on the street. This whistle, of course, plays an important part in a paper boy's life. It means business for him, someone is calling him for a paper. I would often find one of those "wise guys" who would whistle just for the sake of seeing the boys prick up their ears and scramble madly in the direction of the false alarm. People who do such a thing are the bitterest and most hated enemies of the vendors. Some of the names that we paper boys would call these persons would make Bacchus blush. But the majority of our customers were fair and even kind. They would usually buy their papers from the boy who approached them first after they had whistled or called him. Naturally enough, there were always a few fistfights among the paper boys during the course of a day's peddling. I enjoyed the excitement, the fights, and the feeling of making money on one's own that a paper boy experiences.[9]

Some of the sneakier newsboys would use the "last paper" ploy to help sell papers late at night. In one example, the smaller of two brothers would enter a saloon looking for sentimental drunks who would buy his "last papers" so he could go home. Having made his sales, he would go back outside to get more papers from his waiting brother, and the two would walk on to the next saloon. "Drunks are me best customers," said the enterprising young Joseph Bishop. The ploy was effective because, while some newsboys stayed out late just to enjoy a sense of freedom, to make more spending money, or to avoid unpleasant home life, others really did feel obliged to work until they had sold enough papers to satisfy their parents. Newsboys who feared being beaten for poor sales might stay out all night, hanging around theaters and then sleeping in alleys.[10]

Around 1890, girls—particularly from poor Jewish immigrant families on the East Side—began selling newspapers in the afternoons and evenings. The newsgirls quickly adopted some of the newsie subculture. "A truthful and intelligent teacher at the Brown School [on the East Side] has been heard to say that she could tell almost invariably when any of her girl pupils had begun selling newspapers," read an anonymous letter

Two brothers preparing to work the "last paper" scam on sentimental drunks, 1909. Hine admitted to posing this shot, a powerful illustration of the supposedly immoral working environment of newsboys. (NCLC collection, Library of Congress)

to the *Courant* in 1895. "The change in manners and morals is so great that it cannot escape notice." The *Courant*, a morning paper that refused to sell to newsgirls, reported that the girls often "are not merely impertinent to people to whom they offer papers but they use vulgar and abusive language if the offer is declined. They quarrel with each other. They stay out far later in the night than they ought." Like the newsboys, some newsgirls who stayed out past 10 P.M. were truly struggling to sell enough papers to satisfy their parents. Others were shamming.[11] In the course of their work newsgirls entered restaurants, offices, and saloons, reported the *Courant*. Although the editors did not need to point it out, the saloon was, except for the brothel, the single most inappropriate place for a young girl. It was an almost exclusively male environment that nurtured values wholly at odds with female domesticity. Worse, the *Courant* editors claimed to have seen newsgirls late at night entering the saloons near newspaper offices on State Street, at the edge of the red-light district: "The girls run into the saloons not merely with impunity but with impudence. One of them was heard boasting recently, as she came out of one of these places, 'he gimme two dollars.' Another in front of one such place . . . announced, 'This is the kinder place I like. I do my business with sports, I do. They come down with the money.' And these are simply illustrations of what is going on every night. Little girls are made hard and coarse and sent on the way of becoming bad women." [12]

Helping the Daughters of Toil

The *Courant's* remarks were part of the debate that had broken out in Hartford over whether to prohibit girls from selling newspapers. The issue first arose in January 1895, when the Common Council began considering whether to regulate newsgirls' hours to get them off the street at night. A committee of councilmen looked into the matter (under pressure from an unspecified group of wealthy women involved in charitable work), and instead decided to ban all girls under sixteen from selling papers at any hour. One councilman pointed out that government was already taking a greater responsibility for protecting children, and that such a measure would be in keeping with recent laws to ban child labor in factories. The councilmen argued that, away from parental supervision, the newsgirls were not only becoming coarse and rude: they were also "exposed to great dangers upon the streets, especially at night, and . . . the tendency is to lead them to immoral lives." The charity workers reportedly feared that newsgirls were even tempted to become prostitutes.[13] But opinion on the subject was sharply divided. Charity leaders, ministers, and politicians differed from one another, as did the two leading newspapers.

Foremost among the defenders of the newsgirls was Mary Hall, a women's rights advocate and founder of a club for poor boys. Born in 1843, Hall grew up in the country town of Marlborough, Connecticut, where her father was a prosperous miller. She received a secondary education at Wesleyan Academy in Wilbraham, Massachusetts, and pursued a career in teaching until she lost her enthusiasm for the work.

She began teaching herself law in the summer of 1877, hoping that her brother Ezra, an attorney, would help her become the first woman lawyer in Connecticut. Though her brother died of a sudden illness that fall, Mary's career was rescued by John Hooker, Ezra's colleague and neighbor in the Nook Farm area of Asylum Hill. Hooker and his wife, Isabella Beecher Hooker, were both active supporters of women's rights, and they encouraged Mary Hall's ambitions. Hall studied law in John Hooker's office, and, thanks in part to his arguments before the state supreme court, was admitted to the bar as Connecticut's first female lawyer in 1882. The right to practice law was, she hoped, "my passport to a field of helpfulness . . . to my sex."[14]

In addition to her work as a lawyer, Hall was drawn into the woman suffrage movement. She formed a close friendship with Frances Ellen Burr, one of Connecticut's pioneer suffragists. Burr and Hall were among the founding officers of the Hartford Equal Rights Club in 1885. In the early 1900s Hall served on the State Board of Charities, where her insistence on making surprise inspections of state institutions made her a controversial figure. "She . . . is always battling for what she believes is right, making herself hated by those who resent her interference," wrote the *Courant*.[15] Hall's greatest accomplishment was founding and leading the Good Will Club, which provided recreation for Hartford's poor and immigrant boys. From its modest beginnings in Hall's law office in 1880, the club expanded into a major Hartford institution—partly because of fundraising assistance from Frances Burr's brother, the *Hartford Times* publisher Alfred E. Burr.[16]

Given the support she received from Alfred Burr, it was certainly in Hall's interests to please him by defending the rights of girls to sell newspapers. Yet her motives for getting involved in the issue were actually much less self-serving. She had watched the first newsgirls enter the business around 1890, had befriended the girls through their brothers at the Good Will Club, and by 1894 knew nearly every one of the *Times'* forty or fifty newsgirls by name. She sent a letter to the editor defending their work as soon as the first criticisms were voiced in 1893. A letter she wrote the following year suggests that Hall felt the newsgirl controversy was an echo of her own struggle to become a lawyer. "It seems to me the old old story—of not giving girls a chance in the world as boys have when you do this," she wrote, criticizing those who would forbid girls to sell newspapers. Instead of taking girls off the streets to save them from immorality, she added, "My remedy would be [to] make the streets clean morally, so clean that a girl who wishes to sell newspapers can do it in safety."[17]

This call to make the streets morally clean was vague, but it deserves closer examination. First, the idea foreshadowed the suffragists' later call for the suppression of prostitution. Second, Hall's idea shows intriguing differences from that of the suffragists. Hepburn and her supporters spoke of mothers' need for a public environment that would let them raise moral children, and they also spoke in abstract political terms of women's right to share public space with men. Hall's remedy, in contrast, aimed at winning for females the use of the streets for commercial purposes without risking the loss of their higher moral status. Given that an essential aspect of separate-spheres ideology was the spatial separation of commerce and morality, Hall's proposal was a radical one. She was issuing a subtle yet profound challenge to conventional beliefs about gender and public space.

For its part, the *Times* hammered away relentlessly at the newsgirl issue in its editorials, articles, and letters columns. The *Times* agreed that newsgirls had no place in saloons, but it insisted on their right to the streets and denied that they were immoral. "These little girls of 9, 10, and 12 years, are quiet and orderly, and many persons buy a paper of them rather than of the boys."[18] If one believes what was printed in the *Times*, selling newspapers taught poor girls the work ethic, gave them uplifting contact with the better classes, provided them with money for warm clothes, and let them help their widowed mothers put bread on the table. Through honest work newsgirls warded off the extreme poverty that might otherwise force them to sell themselves. But the *Times* and its letter writers, despite their florid rhetoric, also directly and creatively engaged the question of the street's influence on feminine morality.[19]

The fact that the newsgirls did their work in plain view actually served to protect them, making their job no more dangerous than a shopgirl's, the *Times* claimed: "The traffic is open — on the streets — all in public. Is it likely that under such circumstances it leads to vice?"[20] In letters to the editor, the Rev. George Leon Walker and the Rev. Cornelius G. Bristol compared the superior moral climate of the streets downtown to the dangers of the alleys, streets, and tenements in the East Side slum, which was the home of several thousand immigrants — as well as of the red-light district. Bristol wrote:

> It ought not to be questioned for a moment whether the morality of Main Street in daylight and early evening is of an inferior quality to that of Front or Commerce streets. If this be an open question, then the common council should direct its attention to the police department rather than to the newsgirls. Any person who believes that the moral condition of these young girls is made worse by three hours of contact with the busy, changing element that moves in the main thoroughfares must be wofully [*sic*] ignorant of the conditions under which those same girls live for the remainder of the time when not within the schoolroom.

Bristol emphasized that he greatly valued female domesticity, but that he was trying to be realistic. "If the prohibition that is proposed would better the morals of these young girls by keeping them in or about the homes from which they come, there ought to be no objection to it. It can do nothing of the kind, for there is little or nothing there with which to better them, and in many cases their 'home' is but a sad parody on that sacred name," he wrote.[21]

The image of the home as a refuge from the street was, in the case of the slums, a false one, the *Times'* letter writers suggested. The dominant division in the moral geography of the city was not between indoor and outdoor space, but between differing neighborhoods. A home in the slums was no better than its surroundings. Even if not itself given over to vice, an apartment in a tenement house failed to provide the insulated environment that could shelter a girl from the wickedness of the outside world — and in any case it failed to keep the girl indoors. As Walker and Bristol pointed out, some parents even sent their children to saloons to buy beer. A female letter writer went so far as to claim that if the newsgirls were banished "back to the cheap lodgings from which they necessarily come and [left] to reflection . . . the so-called genteelly brought up maidens may with impunity while away their time by promenading openly with observed decorum, but on the sly making appointments and

casting doubtful glances at the admiring crowds, before which they lei-
surely parade."[22]

It is unlikely that only a bundle of papers stood between a poor girl
and a life of streetwalking, but the larger point made by these letters is
well taken. Prohibiting girls from selling newspapers would not have returned them to a cloistered childhood in a bourgeois home. The choice
faced by the city council was not whether to save girls from the immoral
influence of the street, but merely whether to force them out of the
downtown, where most sold their newspapers. In the tenement houses
and slum side streets where they lived and played, the girls would be out
of sight and out of mind. Downtown shoppers and businessmen would
no longer be confronted by insistent reminders that middle-class ideals
of domesticity had no place in the lives of the poor.

The *Times* and its letter writers suggested alternative reforms, including an 8 P.M. limit on newspaper sales by children, a 9 P.M. curfew for
all unaccompanied children, and a prohibition on children entering
saloons. One letter, signed "Equal Rights," questioned why newsgirls
should be treated differently from newsboys. This writer proposed that
the city make public space safer for all children by closing the saloons. A
writer calling herself "A Mother" announced that she was one of a group
of thirty mothers who planned "to give one afternoon in a month to
meeting with these daughters of toil and helping them to right views of
life—and I will engage that by the help of books and photographs and
pleasant chat we will so influence these little women that they will not
only help to conserve the morals of our streets, but carry a little light,
perhaps, into the dark places where many of them are now obliged to
make their homes."[23] In short, the *Times'* editorials and letters proposed
to make the downtown street environment safer for children rather than
to segregate the children from it. Fortified by moral influences and working under regulated conditions, the newsgirls would be safe from harm.

Advocates of a ban on newsgirls, however, held their ground. Most of
them stuck to standard arguments about the threats to girlish innocence.
Since the girls persisted on putting themselves in danger, they asserted,
the city government was obliged to "protect the children from themselves and their parents."[24] Young women in the junior department of
the United Workers' Club shared these concerns but addressed the opposing viewpoint more directly. In a letter to the *Courant*, they rebutted

the comparisons made between the effects of the downtown and East Side streets:

> We are told that these girls [the newsgirls] are better off on the business streets than they would be running about Commerce and Charles and North. Granted that, if this business were stopped, they would not stay at home, it is absolutely not true that they would in this case be more exposed to influences that degrade. The danger to this class of girls is not, except in very small degree, from men of their own class. It is from men in the walks of life higher in the social scale than theirs; from men, or from those like them, who now tap the girl of 14 under the chin as they buy a paper, or laughingly encourage them in their childish attempts at flirtation. . . . The flattery and all the rest that goes to make up the fascination of the streets — where will be the end thereof?

In other words, urban danger came not from the presence of lower-class men, but from the mixing of classes. Regardless of what police might do to suppress crime and control hoodlums, no working-class girl would be safe on the streets so long as she did business with more affluent men. This analysis of the problem attacked Hall's remedy at its very root. By redefining interclass contact as a menace rather than a benefit, moreover, these letter writers cast doubt on any hope for a shared public space safe for all. Lest readers mistake them for ignorant prudes, the letter writers established their authority by assuring readers, "We are speaking not as women whose lives are sheltered and who can know nothing definite about the temptations of those of whom we write. We are speaking for a club of working girls."[25]

At a public hearing held by the Common Council in May 1895, the opposing sides agreed on the need to protect young maidenhood but disagreed whether a ban on newspaper sales by girls would realize that goal — or whether it would simply rob poor families of needed income.[26] Neither the faction on the council seeking to ban newsgirls nor the one wishing merely to make them stop work at 8 P.M. was initially able to gain a majority. Finally, in January 1896, the council agreed to prohibit all street sales by girls or boys under fourteen during school hours or after 8 P.M. This decision gave reformers considerably less than they had wanted.[27]

The Hartford reformers revived the issue in early 1905. The Hartford Consumers' League organized a meeting of the leaders of local charities, church organizations, and civic groups to discuss what to do about the newsgirls. Despite Hall's dissenting arguments, a majority of those present voted to direct their efforts toward a state law forbidding such work. Oscar A. Phelps, a member of the Consumers' League and the superintendent of the First Church of Christ's East Side mission, drafted the bill banning the sale of newspapers on public property by girls under eighteen and had it submitted to the legislature.[28] Among other local organizations supporting the bill were the North Street Settlement, the Civic Club, the Motherhood Club, the Central Labor Union, and the Hartford Federation of Churches.[29] At the legislative hearing on the bill, much of the debate repeated what had been said in 1895 — in fact, Walker's old letter to the editor was even read into the record. But the speakers also brought out an issue that had not been explored ten years earlier: the question of whether the reformers were acting on values not shared by the families of the newsgirls.

That issue was inadvertently raised by the inflammatory and ill-advised remarks of a speaker in favor of the bill, the Rev. Dennis Gleason of St. Anthony's Italian Catholic Church. Gleason remarked that even though the Italians of the East Side were poor, they refused to let their girls sell newspapers on the street. "The same principle which keeps the Italian girls off the street keeps the Italian women modest and virtuous, and makes them faithful wives. This principle they learned in their native land, and they brought it with them to this country. That principle includes the idea that women should be retiring, and it makes for the seclusion of women." The Italians, Gleason's words implied, carried an important aspect of middle-class Yankee domesticity to an admirable extreme.

But did feminine virtue truly require seclusion? Those who opposed the bill vehemently disagreed. Among those anxious to challenge Gleason's remarks was Henry M. Mayer, the assistant principal of the Brown School and the Sunday school superintendent at Beth Israel. In his speech against the bill, Mayer said that poor East Side Jewish girls and their families benefited greatly from newspaper sales, and that this was nothing to be ashamed of. The money helped their families keep them — or their older brothers and sisters — in school at an age when they might otherwise be dropping out to work. Mayer said that members of the Jewish community had visited the homes of the newsgirls and heard no reports of the girls being harmed or threatened on the street. "I believe that the virtue of Jewish womanhood and family life has always been proverbial and needs no law of the state to guard it," he concluded.

Charles L. Ames, the principal of the Brown School, cast the issue in terms of class culture instead of ethnic culture. "The whole difficulty attending this move to place such a bill upon our statute books is that the people are thinking and acting from different standpoints," he said. A wealthy man might oppose the idea of girls selling newspapers because he would want to keep his own children off the streets, but an East Side father "sees no harm in his little girl selling papers for a compensation that shall bring comfort to both family and girl." Even if the girl was not actually driven into newspaper selling by desperate poverty, why shouldn't she have a chance to make a few pennies to buy candy or chewing gum?[30]

The bill—which was also opposed by police officials, local judges, two ex-mayors, the labor advocate John F. Gunshanan, Mayor William F. Henney, and of course Mary Hall—died in committee. The committee agreed that the newsgirls were in little danger on the public streets. The reformers had failed again.[31]

Despite this particular failure, however, the issue of children in the street trades was gaining new attention not only in Hartford but across the nation. In the first decade of the twentieth century, Boston, Newark, Washington, and Cincinnati set age restrictions and limited hours on child labor in the street trades, as did the states of New York and Wisconsin.[32] The National Child Labor Committee, a reform organization advocating laws to restrict child labor, began gathering evidence about night messenger work and other street trades.[33]

In Hartford, the anti-newsgirl campaign resumed in 1909 under the leadership of the Consumers' League of Hartford and its parent organization, the Consumers' League of Connecticut, which was interested in the newsgirls as part of its broader effort against child labor and poor working conditions for women. The statewide organization began its active existence in 1907, hiring Mary Cromwell Welles of Newington to oversee its work.[34] Welles appears to have been similar to her somewhat older opponent, Mary Hall, in a number of ways. Born in 1860 in

Newington, a rural area near Hartford, she was part of the first generation of women to attend college in significant numbers. After graduating from Smith in 1883 and studying abroad, she worked as a teacher, then earned a Ph.D. in social welfare at Yale and switched to a career in social reform. Like Hall, she never married and was noted for her determined defense of what she believed to be right. "She was somewhat radical in her views, and perseverance was one of her major qualities," the *Times* editorial read at her death in 1930, with an evident attempt at tact. "Those who are inclined to resist the march of progress possibly found her a bit difficult to deal with." [35]

In support of the 1909 newsgirl campaign by the Connecticut Consumers' League, the National Child Labor Committee's investigative photographer, Lewis Hine, in March 1909 took photographs of several dozen local newsies and messenger boys. Hine's Hartford photographs were obviously intended to illustrate many of the same points that reformers had been making for years. The photographs emphasized the frailty of young children and their vulnerability on the uncaring city streets. A number of the photographs showed children facing the camera with their backs to blank walls, or framed them as small figures in an empty urban landscape. Hine, who acknowledged that he sometimes paid his subjects and even asked them to hold poses, also presented moralistic photographs of newsboys entering a saloon and messenger boys gambling. A disproportionate number of his Hartford newsie photographs were of girls. Hine also depicted groups of smiling newsies, but he indicated his disapproval in captions that emphasized the children's young age. [36]

Hine and a representative of the Child Labor Commission of New England presented the photographs almost immediately at a legislative hearing in which Hartford reformers were arguing once again for restricting children's participation in the street trades. Two bills on the subject had been drafted by the Consumers' League of Hartford. The first proposed regulating the employment of boys under fifteen in street trades. The second would have banned all girls under sixteen from working in the streets, factories, and stores, and all boys under fifteen from working in factories and stores, among other places. The bills, which were presented and debated together, drew strong opposition not only from Hall, Gunshanan, and the *Times*, but also from manufacturers throughout the

One of Hine's photos of Hartford newsgirls. In his captions he emphasized the girls' extreme youth. Here, for instance, he pointed out, "The smallest girl has been selling for 2 years." (NCLC collection, Library of Congress)

state.[37] Both bills were defeated. The following year, Hartford reformers gave up on persuading the legislature and turned their attention back to the city government.[38]

Regulating an Evil

Although the second of the two 1909 bills was hopelessly ambitious, the first represented a promising new direction for reformers. A proposal to regulate children's role in street trades was potentially viable politically where a sweeping prohibition was not. In 1910 Hartford's newly formed Juvenile Commission led a successful fight to regulate the street trades. It persuaded the Common Council to pass an ordinance prohibiting children under ten from selling newspapers on the street and requiring

children between ten and fourteen to get licenses from the superintendent of schools if they wanted to do this work.[39] To head off the school
superintendent's announced intention of denying permits to girls, the
council specified that there be no discrimination on the basis of sex.[40]

The prohibition on newsies under ten was a major step toward the
reformers' old goal of removing children from what they considered a
dangerous environment, but the licensing requirements represented an
interesting detour. Reformers in other cities and states disagreed over the
value of such measures. "In many instances it has been pointed out . . .
that a system of licensing and badging is but a method of legalizing what
is indisputably an evil," wrote Edward N. Clopper of the National Child
Labor Committee in 1912.[41] For reformers to support licensing required
not just a tactical shift but an intellectual one. The street environment,
formerly said to have disastrous effects, now had to be seen as a potentially acceptable place for children — as long as they were under official
supervision.

The desire for greater supervision over newsboys was nothing new. In
1881, the Hartford police had proposed licensing newsboys and bootblacks as a way to force them to behave. Licensing, the police chief said,
would "give the police some authority where they have none now, it
would enable the officers to relieve our merchants and citizens generally
of a great nuisance, and at the same time benefit all boys who behave
themselves." [42]

In the early twentieth century reformers calling for regulating Hartford's street trades described unsupervised newsies both as potential victims and as potential troublemakers. At a 1909 hearing, E. W. Lord of
the Child Labor Commission of New England spoke with alarm on the
subject: "Street trades are open to these young people without any restriction. They are not under the supervision which the young workers in the
factory are receiving — they are their own masters, do as they please and
naturally cultivate an early independence, which is not fitting for a child.
They have then precocity, which is injurious, and they suffer from the
effect of street life." [43] Mary Welles drew a distinction between newsboys
and newsgirls. In the case of the newsgirls, she said, "I am in favor of a
sweeping law prohibiting them on the streets" in order to preserve their
feminine modesty. But "in the case of the boys, the question is entirely
different, it is not the danger period but a period of great restlessness."

Oscar Phelps added that "paper selling should be made a boys' business and superintended as other work is."[44]

After the passage of the 1910 ordinance, reformers and city officials temporarily turned their attention from protecting children to disciplining them. The text of the "Child Street Sales Permit" included a long list of requirements overtly aimed at controlling the newsies' behavior. "The badge and this permit is [sic] lent to you to show that you have a right to sell things in the streets, but you will hold them only as long as you obey the instructions," the text warned. The newsies were told always to wear their badges, which were supposed to be fastened high on the right side of the chest, while selling on the streets. They were never to sell during school hours or after 8 P.M. They were also given the following commandments: "You must always be clean and properly clothed while selling"; "You must attend school regularly"; "You must not beg"; "You must not go into saloons, or saloon entrances, theaters, moving picture houses or street cars to sell"; "You must not annoy people by getting in their way or by shouting, or hanging around entrances to office buildings"; "You must not draw or write anything indecent on walls or sidewalks"; and "You must not fight or call other boys or girls names." The superintendent of schools could revoke the permit of anyone who violated these conditions.[45]

Welles and other members of the Consumers' League of Connecticut conducted surveys to gauge the ordinance's popularity and effectiveness. "One patrolman declared the ordinance 'an awful good thing. It helps us get the boys in line that we couldn't get hold of before,'" Welles reported in early 1912. "A grocer on City Hall Square . . . used to be much annoyed by the newsboys, but now finds everything quiet in front of his store."[46] League members quoted the police chief as saying that the licensing requirements had kept newsies off the streets after 8 P.M., forced them to attend school, and improved their behavior. But the reformers did not lose sight of their earlier goals. One of the most beneficial effects of the badge system, they reported, was that it made it easier to prevent underage children from selling.[47]

The newsies' reactions to the new system were mixed. Girls interviewed by the reformers tended to dislike having to wear a badge. "Not nice for girls to wear it," said thirteen-year-old Yetta Weinstein. "Children call you names, call you ragpickers." Boys, however, tended to like the badge system, though not for the same reasons as reformers. Some liked the fact that the system discouraged fights and brought more order to the selling of newspapers, but just as many praised it for reducing their competition by banning younger children. "Make more money with badges," said one boy.[48]

Reformers soon became dissatisfied with the way the city regulated the newsies. Not all the newsies wore their badges as they were supposed to, and some did not even bother to get a badge, complained members of the Consumers' League of Connecticut and the president of the Council of Jewish Women.[49] In 1913 the Consumers' League and the Hartford Council on Child Welfare unsuccessfully asked the Common Council to hire female inspectors to enforce the licensing system as well as to inspect dance halls and investigate vice. Councilmen, who were annoyed by suffragists' ongoing antiprostitution campaign, explained their refusal by declaring that the inspectors might abuse their powers.[50]

The Removal of the Newsgirls

The regulations, regardless of their success or failure, did not address the problem that reformers had been fighting for nearly two decades. More than thirty girls continued to peddle papers on Hartford's streets. While other reformers were busy fretting about badgeless newsboys, the Council of Jewish Women began in 1912 to resolve the newsgirl problem privately. This council, which was dominated by the more prosperous German Jewish element within Hartford's ethnically divided Jewish community, was eager to get newer Eastern European immigrants to adapt to middle-class American standards. Members visited the homes of the newsgirls and persuaded many of the parents to take the girls off the streets. When persuasion failed, they bribed the parents with gifts and weekly payments to help make up for the loss in income. Within a year, the number of newsgirls had been halved, and by 1914 it had been reduced to seven. But other girls entered the business to replace those who quit, and when the outbreak of World War I increased the demand for news, the number of newsgirls rose to twenty. The Council of Jewish Women realized that its work would be endless.[51]

At the request of the Jewish women's group, Welles presented a petition to the Common Council that October calling for the removal of the newsgirls from the street. A sympathetic alderman proposed an ordinance that would prohibit all girls under sixteen from selling papers and require boys who were fourteen and fifteen to obtain licenses and obey the same rules as younger boys. With a few minor exceptions, the 1914 public hearing was a tedious repetition of the same points that had been made for twenty years. Welles argued that the council had a duty to complete the work of the Council of Jewish Women. Her old nemesis, Mary Hall, repeated her familiar position in favor of allowing newsgirls. According to the *Times*, Hall added that "she was ashamed of parents afraid to trust their daughters and sons on the bright streets of Hartford," implying that an improvement in the moral environment would logically result from the improved electric street lighting recently installed downtown. She further argued that the charity provided by the Jewish women was turning self-reliant poor families into dependent paupers. The reformers' only new cause for hope was that the *Times* had agreed to stop actively opposing a ban on newsgirls, since their small numbers had made them a less important form of labor.[52]

But an unexpected event suddenly tipped the controversy decisively in the reformers' favor. Before the Common Council could vote on the proposal, an eleven-year-old newsgirl was lured into a remote room one evening by a man offering to buy her last three papers if she would follow him to where he could get change. There he raped her and left her infected with venereal disease. To their thinly disguised satisfaction, the advocates of a ban on newsgirls had seen their dire warnings verified at the most opportune possible moment.[53]

Hall made one last attempt to prevent the inevitable. She met with the girl's family, and, with the cooperation of the *Times*, printed an account of her visit in which she discussed the rape as an individual human tragedy, not as generally illustrative of the dangers of the street trades. Her report took the reader to the top floor of a dark Pequot Street tenement house, the home of a Jewish peddler and his nine children. She described how the mother was struggling despite poverty to provide a good home and wholesome food for her children. The mother cared deeply about the children and was grief-stricken over the rape. "This is the first time in twenty-five years, so far as I can remember, that any newsgirl has gone wrong, and all girls should not be deprived of an opportunity to earn some money honestly," Hall wrote. "Girls can't be kept off the street. They have a right to be there at reasonable hours."[54]

Hall's cause was hopeless. Having accepted that the chastity of young girls was a crucial issue in the newsgirl controversy, Hall and her allies now found themselves in an impossible position. The rape had produced such a powerful impression in the city that not a single councilman dared to vote against the ordinance. "Thus has come to an end a practise [*sic*] about which there has been an amazing amount of argument and feeling for the space of 25 years," Welles noted happily. Though it refused to require licenses for fourteen- and fifteen-year-old boys, the council prohibited all girls under sixteen from selling newspapers. By January there was not a single newsgirl to be seen in Hartford.[55]

Child-labor reformers continued to grumble about unruly newsboys and the lax enforcement of the badge requirement, but they had won their battle.[56] As a result of the Common Council's votes in 1910 and 1914, newsboys under ten and newsgirls under sixteen had become a thing of the past. The remaining boys sold papers only under conditions that restricted their hours and constrained their behavior. They had been placed under the parental authority of the police department and the superintendent of schools. Though reformers and city officials had not entirely banished children from the street trades, they had asserted more exclusive adult ownership over the downtown. The newsie ordinances made it clearer than ever that children did not enjoy equal rights to the streets, especially at night.

The campaign to rid the streets of newsgirls triumphed a few months after suffragists finally declared victory over Hartford's red-light district, but the two campaigns had little in common. The campaign against the newsgirls was built on many ideas the suffragists opposed: the desire to sequester females to preserve their chastity; the denial of equal rights in the workforce; the denial of equal access to public space. Whenever the women's-rights argument entered into the newsgirl issue, it was as a protest against proposed reforms. Like Katharine Hepburn in the antiprostitution campaign, Mary Hall and her allies called for making public space safer instead of forcing females into seclusion. The arguments of the anti-newsgirl forces echoed those of the older antiprostitution reformers who had grudgingly accepted the existence of the East Side brothels. As the Rev. Elmer Dent had explained in the pastors' 1907 campaign to mitigate the effects of the vice district, "Keep the boys and girls off the streets!" From this perspective, Hartford's streets could not be cleansed of vice, disease, and danger. The only way to protect the vulnerable was to separate them from threatening influences, preferably by keeping them inside the home.

Reformers seeking to restrict the newsies may have built some of their arguments on fading beliefs about gender, but their ideas about public space proved to be more influential than those of the seemingly more modern advocates of women's rights. While Hepburn and Hall clung to the doomed hope of purifying the urban environment, the street-trade reformers were part of the rising effort to segregate the use of public space. Restrictions on newspaper selling had strengthened the temporal and age-specific dimensions of urban geography, which were further reinforced by the growth of downtown nightlife, by weak intermittent attempts to impose a curfew on children,[57] and by the playground movement. The newsie ordinances added to a differentiation of public space that was developing out of reforms affecting park construction, pushcart peddling, street paving, and pedestrian traffic.

The campaigns to purify public space through municipal housekeeping and antiprostitution reform had rested on the theoretical support provided by Horace Bushnell and by women who wanted to extend their moral authority outside the home. The campaigns to segregate space developed a somewhat different reform ideology, drawing together new ideas of social "efficiency," child development, and—to some extent—cultural pluralism. This ideology was most clearly articulated in reform activity affecting public recreation.

5

Segregating the Parks

The recreation expert, wrote Hartford Parks Superintendent George A. Parker around 1911, performs an essential public service in easing the troubles of every city dweller. The expert "takes in one hand the most wretched and forsaken child in our midst and leads it to the playground and its activities, and with the other hand points the over-burdened banker and business man to the restfulness of the rural park."[1] Guided by human sympathy and scientific method, the expert would work to meet the special needs of everyone. But as Parker described it, the only link between different groups of people at leisure was that they would all be served by the same public recreational system. The urchin and the banker were to be equal—but separate.

From the 1890s through the 1920s, Hartford's park officials worked to build a parks and recreation system based increasingly on segregation of space. In 1890 Hartford had only one major park, whose uses were more narrowly restricted than Horace Bushnell had intended. The park officials and landscape designers who created a vastly expanded park system in the 1890s initially expected the new parks to serve the same function they attributed to Bushnell Park: providing a naturalistic retreat for the aesthetic enjoyment and psychic renewal of city dwellers. Unlike Horace Bushnell, they and the elite Municipal Art Society attempted to make the parks a completely separate world from that of the streets — protected pockets of nature and gentility in a hostile urban environment. Troubled by the failure of this effort and torn by competing demands from different social groups, Parker turned to segregating space within the park system. He greatly expanded the athletic facilities, drawing noisy crowds into certain sections of the parks, while trying to preserve diminished sections of naturalized landscape. Under his leadership, different parks took on special characteristics to conform to the perceived needs of the local inhabitants, and individual parks were carved up into a patchwork of different uses. By the 1910s, Parker was explicitly calling for greater segregation of park visitors on the basis of age, gender, and socioeconomic status. He discarded much of Bushnell's conservative vision of the park as a unifying institution, believing that the clashing interests of different groups made unity impossible — and that unity was in any case less important than the fulfillment of individual needs.

Less and Less a Mere Common

Bushnell had seen no need either for separate spaces within his new park or for special restrictions on its use. His comments suggested that the main purpose of the park was to allow people to stroll about, appreciating natural beauty and feeling a sense of harmony with their neighbors. But he also expected that the park would provide room for pleasure drives, parades, holiday celebrations, invalids' rest, and children's play. Only the drives themselves involved any special facilities, and Bushnell said nothing to suggest that they should be separated from the rest of the park.[2] His desire for unstructured inclusivity was shared by Mayor Henry C. Deming, who said in an 1860 address to the Common Council that the park should be "a pleasant promenade, parade, and play-ground. Nothing in my judgment should be done in the way of decoration to abridge the freedom of its use, nor the equality of its enjoyment by the refined and unrefined, the washed and unwashed. It should not be converted into prim parterres, forbidding familiarity, sensitive at the approach of rude boys and unpolished brogans . . . nor too much space surrendered to drives;—but it should remain an open, free, unprivileged *Common* for the people."[3]

Some of the park commissioners saw no need to keep customary street activities out of Bushnell Park. The western section, the commission reported in 1864, would be ideal for "the general Parade Ground, for the accommodation of the Military, Firemen, and other gatherings of the public, which have of late years so overcrowded Main street." Through the early 1860s, public meetings were held in the park, and ball games were played.[4] But the opinion of city officials was divided. On the one hand, they did not want to seal the park off from its surroundings, but on the other, they did not want it to be overwhelmed by inappropriate activities. Like Bushnell, they wanted the park to be both inclusive and uplifting, both open to the street and clearly distinguished from it. Not everyone could agree what to do if these goals came into conflict. In an 1861 report, the park commissioners expressed concern about the proper use of the park:

> Having expended so much for this object, it was not to be neglected or abused:—it was not to be treated as a common pasture or open field, but in a manner consistent with the wealth and dignity of the City and the true benefits to be derived therefrom. . . . We desire an open breathing place, for amusement and recreation, where the old and young of both sexes, can enjoy themselves rationally and safely, where the great requisites shall be green grass, dry and pleasant walks and enough of trees for shade and ornament.[5]

The commissioners who wrote the report wanted to include a wide range of people but sought to limit their activities to strolling, driving, and contemplating nature. Such restrictions had classist overtones. Driving was obviously limited to those who could afford carriages. The other activities were open to everyone but were based on elite and middle-class ideas of decorum and self-improvement that many working-class people did not share. Working people were welcome in the park as long as they were willing to behave by the standards of their betters.[6]

By the late 1860s the park commission had firmly decided on this as its policy. A subtle tilt had begun as early as 1861, when the commission, on the recommendation of Frederick Law Olmsted, hired the landscape architect Jacob Weidenmann to redesign the park. Like the initial, amateurish design by the city surveyor, Weidenmann's plan accurately reflected Bushnell's concept of a space partially open to the surrounding streets, yet it placed more emphasis on the picturesque qualities of the park's interior. The pathways, instead of merely running through a central intersection on their way across the park, now curved past clumps of greenery and converged obliquely on a pond with a fountain. The new design suggested that the park visitor was expected to linger and enjoy the appearance of the surroundings. The spaces off the paths were not just ambiguous voids that could be used for anything, but were part of an artistic composition. Such a composition had to be protected from the damage done by "ignorant and malicious individuals," Mayor Charles R. Chapman noted in 1866, in a call for more diligent police patrols. The park's ornamental appearance was heightened by the introduction of a statue in 1869, recalled Sherman W. Adams, a later park commission president. "It may be truly said that a change in the treatment and uses of the park was begun, which has more and more developed. It thereafter took on more of the character of a *public garden*, and became less and less a mere common and stamping-ground."[7]

In 1884 Acting Mayor Frank Kellogg refused to allow the Amalgamated Trades Union to hold a mass meeting in the park, explaining that "so beautiful and attractive a Park" had to be preserved from damage. The park commissioners rejected a similar request by a man who wanted to make weekly public addresses from the park terrace, on the grounds that such speeches would annoy people who wanted to admire beautiful landscapes in peace. "Many acts which might be tolerated upon a public highway, or a common, would be out of place here."[8] Politics was apparently as out of place in the park as it would be in the parlor. The rough-and-tumble play of the working classes was also inappropriate. The park, reported the commissioners in 1889, was

> too widely known as a place of beauty and repose, to be subjected to the harsh usage and disturbing element of boisterous frolics, games, plays or scuffles. The lawns have been kept fairly free from the wear

and tear of boot heels of intruders, who care for the Park only for the chance it affords for a scrimmage with sticks, or shillelahs and stones; the outgrowth of the craze for so-called "polo." A large element of those who visit the Park for any kind of sport, is pure hoodlum; that is, it cares nothing for the Park, *as* a Park, at all.[9]

Actually, the working-class residents of Hartford did want a park, but a park of their own. Residents of the Irish working-class area around Avon Street, northeast of the central city, petitioned the city in 1873 to create a park at a site near their homes. But when they learned that the city planned to finance the project by levying assessments on property owners in the neighborhood, they divided. One faction still wanted the park, but another group declared that they did not want it if they had to pay for it. This latter group complained that the entire city had been taxed to pay for Bushnell Park and for improvements to the South Green, while the hardworking people of their neighborhood had been left with the "discomforts of poor streets, poor lights, poor drainage, and no breathing places." If the more "aristocratic" people had been given a park at city expense, the workingmen should not have to pay for theirs. Hartford voters finally approved spending city money in 1875 to build a park between Avon, North Front, and Windsor streets, but city officials refused to undertake the project on the grounds that the ongoing economic depression made it too burdensome on taxpayers. Supporters of the park now claimed that it would benefit the entire city by improving sanitary conditions in that neighborhood and preventing the start of epidemics. "An improvement to that part is a benefit to the *whole* town, the same as an improvement to any part of a house is a benefit to the *whole* house," they argued, but to no avail.[10] Unlike Bushnell Park, the proposed North Front Street Park was too small and too isolated in an outlying slum to be plausibly described as an amenity for the entire city. The use of taxpayers' money for such a project could be successfully defended only if Hartford residents were willing to redefine the public interest to embrace a system of public services, in which the city as a whole would pay equitably for the special needs of each neighborhood. When public funds were tight, as they were in the 1870s, it was easier for public officials to stick to the older belief that neighborhood improvements should be funded by the neighborhood.[11]

The Rain of Parks

Not until the 1890s did Hartford create a park system to provide recreational spaces for every section of town. By that time, trolley service and population growth were spurring a geographic expansion of the city and creating neighborhoods as far as two miles from Bushnell Park. In this sprawling new city, it became considerably less convenient for many people to visit the park. Geographical expansion interfered with what Horace Bushnell had hoped would be the natural flow of every citizen toward a single outdoor parlor, diminishing whatever value the park might have had as a means of unifying the people.[12]

Instead, the Rev. Francis Goodwin and other members of the park commission worked to acquire land that would allow the creation of a citywide park system. Their efforts produced what later park officials and local historians have called the "Rain of Parks," in which five major parks were either given to the city or purchased during 1894 and 1895. The donations were what became Elizabeth Park on the Hartford–West Hartford border; Pope Park, donated by the industrialist Albert Pope and located conveniently close to his Capitol Avenue bicycle factory; and Keney Park, which stretched through the North End and across the city line into Windsor. The city's purchases were Riverside Park, on the Connecticut River northeast of downtown, and Goodwin Park, on the Wethersfield town line. A sixth major addition to the park system was the former estate of the arms manufacturer Samuel Colt, which his widow left to the city in 1905. A broken ring of parks totaling nearly twelve hundred acres now encircled the city—thirty times the acreage of Bushnell Park. The designs for most of the new parks were done by the firm of Olmsted, Olmsted and Eliot, later renamed "Olmsted Brothers," which was led at this time by John C. Olmsted.[13]

Frederick Law Olmsted, John Olmsted's stepfather, had pioneered the idea of a park system in his plans for the Buffalo parks in 1868, and he had assisted in the planning of the more elaborate "Emerald Necklace" around Boston from the 1870s to the 1890s. These new park systems featured scattered parks linked by greenbelts and parkways. Frederick Olmsted and his partner, Calvert Vaux, viewed the Buffalo system as a "comprehensive arrangement for securing refreshment, recreation and health to the people." Multiple parks were needed in scattered locations to ensure that everyone in the growing metropolis had access to parkland. Both in Buffalo and in Boston, Olmsted included some provisions for active recreation, which he carefully separated from the more traditional naturalistic landscapes. To him active recreation was less important than the contemplation of beauty.[14]

John Olmsted designed the Hartford system along similar lines. In a 1901 speech he explained that the newly created parks were "properly called a system of parks because they have been located with due regard to equitable geographical distribution and to take advantage of, and as far as possible to include, specimens of the several types of natural scenery available in the vicinity." Riverside Park was distinguished by its riverfront meadows, Keney Park by its woods, Elizabeth Park by its resemblance to a "gentleman's suburban residence grounds," Bushnell Park by its urban surroundings, Pope Park by its remarkably varied views, and Goodwin Park by its oak-dotted fields. Unlike later designers, John Olmsted said little about how the parks would be used and nothing to suggest that different groups of people would use different parks. He compared the park system instead to the school system, which included scattered facilities but was held together by a "unity of purpose and methods."[15]

Most of the new park designs treated active recreation as secondary. The Olmsted brothers' 1898 design for Pope Park, in the factory district, showed a fanciful romantic landscape with scenic lawns named Hollowmead and Hithermead, as well as wooded areas named Eastbourne Grove, Bankside Grove, and Hillside Ramble. "Winding picturesquely along its northwestern boundary is the Park River [formerly the Little River], its banks adorned with verdant lawns and groves," read a 1900 description of the nearly completed park. "Indeed, the chief charm of Pope Park lies in its abundance of trees and water. Two groves of unusual beauty grace the Park. . . . With their rustic seats and bridges, and welcome shade, they are favorite resorts for picnic parties, and for all seekers after rest and quiet." Nevertheless, the Olmsteds and the park commissioners made some provision for active recreation even within this naturalistic pleasure ground. The Olmsteds' plan for Pope Park expanded on the example of segregated land use set by the modified Bushnell Park, which by that time included a children's play space and areas "set apart as common" where people were allowed to walk on the grass. The Pope

Park plan included a "Little Folks Lawn" and two isolated meadows to be used for baseball. The baseball fields, labeled Nethermead and Thithermead, were separated from the main part of the park by a steep hill and the river, respectively. Park designers and officials had now begun in earnest to divide parkland into contrasting uses.[16]

1898

The park commissioners saw the development of the sixty-three-acre Riverside Park as a chance to create something new and different—a park designed mainly for the active recreation needs of the poor. In his 1894 report, the park commission president, Sherman Adams, had acknowledged, "There are different ideas prevailing as to the use and treatment of the park grounds. Some think of them only as places of recreation, or sport." Rather than trying to suppress active recreation, which would mean fighting a never-ending battle to protect Bushnell Park from disruption and damage, the commission should provide separate parkland for that purpose. Though John Olmsted would not admit it in his 1901 speech, Riverside Park was designed primarily for the inhabitants of the East Side tenement district nearby. Some East Siders were already using the riverfront meadows for sports and other recreation, but the area had an unsavory—even dangerous—reputation. Part of it was occupied by a hobo encampment. Charles E. Gross, the park commission president, wrote in 1897 that Riverside "will never become a show ground—in the sense that Bushnell Park is such—nor call for elaborate treatment. It will be subject to rougher use than parks in general. Indeed, it is already, in part, so used; and is quite satisfactory as a ball-ground." In addition to baseball fields, the new park offered a "Little Folks Lawn" (like Pope Park) and a wading pool, which immediately drew crowds of children. Most of the park, in fact, was taken up with spaces for active recreation. As parts of the park began opening in 1898, it proved to be a huge success. "Riverside Park . . . has given more satisfaction towards the proper fulfillment of its purpose, and has benefited and is appreciated by more people in need and want of such grounds of rest and recreation than any other in the park system," reported Parks Superintendent Theodore Wirth in 1900.[17]

In the early twentieth century, the city built on the examples set by these two projects, creating more and more divisions within parkland like those in the Olmsteds' plan for Pope Park, and making parks assume specialized functions like those of Riverside Park.

Escaping Those Unsightly Noisy Elements

In creating the new parks, the Olmsted firm and the park officials were particularly eager to exclude the sights and sounds of the street. They objected to anything that they believed would interfere with the park experience. They did not object, however, to vehicular travel in the parks—as long as it was for recreational purposes. These concerns led them to seal the new parks off from their surroundings but also to advocate parkways for pleasure driving.

In contrast to Bushnell Park, the new parks were deliberately screened from the surrounding streets by thickly planted borders of trees and bushes. In keeping with the widely accepted design convention that began with New York's Central Park, the Olmsted firm sought to give Hartford park visitors the illusion that they were not in a city at all, but in a forest meadow with trees all around. The Olmsted associate Charles Eliot went so far as to place earthen berms covered with shrubs along the streets that bordered or crossed Keney Park. Parks Superintendent Theodore Wirth included densely planted borders in his plans for Elizabeth and Rocky Ridge parks to "secure for the park the desired privacy," and he extended these ideas to Bushnell Park, where he planted a riverside wall of greenery blocking the view of Asylum and Ford streets near the train station. When a park commission member wrote to complain that the plantings prevented passersby from enjoying the landscape, Wirth explained that this was intentional. Buffers of vegetation, he wrote, "are essential for the purpose for which a park in the city is created, for they hide out from the park those unsightly noisy elements from which a visitor expects to escape." If people on Asylum Street wanted to see Bushnell Park's scenery, they could come inside. Wirth added that "parks are not built as much to be looked at and to be hastely [sic] enjoyed by people passing by them on their daily walks or trips to and from business, as they are to form an attractive, pleasant retreat to all those that wish to escape from the noise, dust and crowded life of our city streets." [18]

Park officials consistently described heavy street traffic as incompatible with parks, but they vacillated in their treatment of purely recreational driving. Adams in 1890 rejected calls for additional driveways in Bushnell Park, explaining that "this area is chiefly valuable for the opportunity it affords for those who are tired of the noise, bustle, and dust of the streets of the city. . . . Hence, the Park is most appreciated by pedestrians, and the passages of teams and vehicles, and proximity of clouds of dust raised by the whirr [sic] of wheels, is offensive in such a place." On the other hand, a carriage ride through a park could be regarded as another way of enjoying the scenery. The Olmsted firm and the park officials included scenic drives that were open to carriages, horseback riders, and automobiles in most of their designs. Despite some problems with speeding motorists and with test drivers for the automobile manufacturing companies, the park commissioners saw no reason to prohibit pleasure driving.[19]

In 1896 park officials and the Olmsted firm began planning ways to link the parks through a system of recreational roadways. They hoped to assemble a long, winding belt of new parkways and existing streets stretching from Keney Park in the north through Elizabeth, Pope, Rocky Ridge, and Goodwin parks and terminating on Wethersfield Avenue near the city's southern border. Like earlier parkways in other cities, those in Hartford would be landscaped greenbelts designed specifically for pleasure driving, in contrast to regular streets' functions of accommodating commercial and streetcar traffic and providing access to private property. Nature lovers could enjoy a series of beautiful and constantly changing views from the seats of moving carriages as they rode in a great arc around Hartford. "Possibly, the two ends of the series of parkways may ultimately be at the right bank of the 'Great River' on the north and south sides of the City, respectively," reported Charles E. Gross, the park commission president at the time.[20]

The parkways offered a new way of unifying Hartford geographically. Bushnell's old dream of bringing everyone together in a central park was clearly obsolete in the sprawling new city, but late nineteenth-century park designers had found a way to mitigate the inherently divisive effect of giving each neighborhood its own park. The parkways would pull the separate parks together and help integrate a city increasingly divided by the housing choices of the affluent, the voluntary clustering of different ethnic groups, and the economically driven concentration of industry and of commerce. Unfortunately, the unity the park system was supposed to create was more theoretical than real. Even if the proposed system had been completed, it would have been experienced by most Hartford residents only as a collection of discrete parts. The image of unity provided by a carriage tour of the system would have been available solely to the elite. Everyone else would have experienced just one park at a time, usually the one nearest home. The components of the park system would thus have further separated the residents of Hartford's different sections, drawing them into contact with their neighbors, but not with people from other parts of the city, as Bushnell had hoped. These ramifications were either not seen or not acknowledged by park officials in the 1890s. The park commission hired the Olmsted firm to design the first links in the chain of parkways (a western section extending from Park Street along the north branch of the Park River to Girard Avenue in the West End, and a southern section reaching from Goodwin Park almost to the Connecticut River), forming a subcommittee under Charles Dudley Warner to oversee the work.[21]

Warner's committee made almost no progress, possibly because of difficulties in acquiring land. The park commission soon abandoned the attempt to create the parkway between Park Street and Farmington Avenue, considering instead how to treat sections of existing streets as parkways. "The Parkways, when using the public highways, are subject to the city's control, but may be beautified and widened and in many ways made different in appearance from the regular city streets," wrote the commission's president, Patrick Garvan, in 1899. For several years officials continued to talk about creating separate parkways, and plans were drawn up for at least two more sections of the original arc. As late as 1901, Wirth still expressed the hope that a parkway between Elizabeth and Keney parks could become "one of the main features of the park system." In 1909 two disconnected sections of this parkway were laid out—Scarborough Street and Westbourne Parkway—but these became nothing more than residential boulevards lined with houses and distinguished from other streets only by their median strips. They fell far short of the original goal of being linear parks clearly distinct from the regular street system. By 1905 Wirth admitted that the creation of real parkways was "very doubtful." Still, he refused to give up on the idea altogether. When controversy broke out over whether to extend a street through Pope Park, he saw an opportunity for a compromise that would create part of the future parkway system.[22]

The Pope Park controversy pitted real estate speculators and working-

class homeowners who sought improved street access against elite reformers who wanted a strict separation between streets and parks. The
issue arose in 1904 when property owners in the Behind the Rocks neighborhood worried that the newly completed park to their north would
interfere with the residential development of their land. They feared that
the park's presence would prevent construction of streets linking their
property with the factories on the other side of the park. Behind the
Rocks was also cut off from the more densely developed neighborhoods
to the east by a line of cliffs, and the Park River bounded it on the west.
These accidents of location and urban development led property owners to claim that they were "bottled up." They held a mass meeting at
the neighborhood school and launched a petition drive to extend Laurel
Street south across the park's central meadow, on the grounds of "public
convenience and necessity." Gathering more than twelve hundred sig-
natures, mostly from residents of the working-class neighborhood, they
persuaded the Board of Street Commissioners to consider the project.[23]

The proposal outraged those who loved natural beauty. John Olmsted
wrote that streets and parks represented incompatible principles, and that
extending Laurel Street would destroy his artistic creation: "For the enjoyment of the views, continuity of the surface of the meadow is obviously of vital importance. Even though one can see across a street, the
street itself and the vehicles passing upon it are incongruous and ugly
circumstances. . . . Much of the benefit of a visit to a park consists in
the escape from the nervous strain due to ordinary city traffic, and to
introduce such traffic into a park necessarily destroys much of the value
of the park."[24]

The Municipal Art Society led the fight against the Laurel Street extension in 1905. "It seems almost a right inherent in every man to have a
place where he can see and walk upon the green grass and breathe to the
utmost the free air untainted by the street smells, and away from the
smoke and dirt and hurry of city life," argued Louis R. Cheney and
George Parker in the society's protest to the street commissioners. "Without the parks the poor man must breathe his air and have his recreation
on the doorstep or on the street."[25]

Evidently worried that they would be seen as snobbish aesthetes with
no concern for their social inferiors, Cheney and Parker did not dwell

on the general incompatibility of streets and parks; instead, they argued more specifically that Pope Park was the special property of the working-man and, as such, was an inappropriate place for any kind of road. "Pope Park is primarily the poor man's park. Every other large park in Hartford has carriage-ways. In Pope Park they were intentionally omitted, it being the purpose of the designers to have one large park devoted to the convenience and pleasure of those who do not own carriages or automobiles. If Keney Park is for driving, then let Pope Park be for those who do not drive." According to Cheney and Parker, workingmen wishing to reach the factory district on Capitol Avenue could simply walk or bicycle on paths across the park. Those who wanted to ride the trolley to the factories would find it just as convenient if the line ran to the west of the park on Bartholomew Avenue. Another trolley line could be built on the east side of the park to ease access to downtown. Instead of building a roadway across the park, the city should simply make improvements to the streets on its periphery.[26] While Olmsted sought only to protect the park from the disruption of the street, Cheney and Parker advanced the idea of segregation in a different way: they declared a need for separating the park space of the rich from that of the poor.

"Would you have the houses of your city all alike? Would you have the rooms in your houses all alike, no matter what purposes they were used for? If not, then do not have your parks alike," Parker wrote in a draft version of the appeal to the street commissioners. Pope Park was an important component in the proper development of that neighborhood, he argued. The working-class Frog Hollow area around Park Street could become "a sub-civic center and . . . a prosperous, happy community," with Pope Park as its most desirable feature. Parker, unlike Wirth and the Olmsteds, had rejected the hopeless quest to make park space unify a fragmenting city. He now embraced division as a positive good and suggested that segregating park space would contribute to a desirable segregation of Hartford, allowing community to be reconstituted on a more localized level. Segregation was in the workingmen's interests—whether they knew it or not.[27] Parker soon took the even more radical step of emphasizing individual fulfillment over community, promoting segregation for that purpose.

Parker's reinterpretation of segregated space dominated later discussion of the park system, but in 1905 the controversy over the Pope Park

roadway continued to be argued mainly in the limited terms of separating
the park from the street. Wirth, speaking at a special meeting of the Municipal Art Society in May, called for a compromise: a curving parkway
following the contours of the land would be built through the park, but
it would not become a "highway" that could be used by trolleys and other
heavy vehicles. "Those who want to go by bicycle can be accommodated
and those who want to go in carriages and automobiles ought to be willing to go a few feet out of the way in order not to destroy the Park," he
explained in a statement written two weeks later. Wirth's proposed compromise satisfied neither side; they clashed at a public hearing in June.
The priest from the neighborhood's Catholic church, who was one of the
leaders of the pro-street faction, argued that a regular street across the
park would save workingmen ten or fifteen minutes in reaching the factory district and other parts of the city.[28]

The street board ultimately agreed on the parkway compromise despite months of bickering over how the street should be laid out. The
narrow, curving parkway provided improved access for traffic from the
factories to the working-class homes in Behind the Rocks, but no trolley
line was allowed. The Municipal Art Society claimed this compromise
as a victory for its adherents, although they had obviously failed in their
attempt to keep all traffic out of the park.[29] After this the defenders of the
parks were more successful in preventing new street crossings. The ubiq-
uitous Dotha Hillyer, for example, in 1913 led a successful protest against
a proposal to extend Trumbull Street south across Bushnell Park.[30]

The advocacy of parkways by the Olmsteds and Wirth shows that they
were not opposed to vehicular traffic per se. Their goal was to preserve
the park as a distinct social environment by sealing it off from the disruptive aspects of the street that would remind visitors of the encircling city.
Parker's quite different ideas about segregated space eventually led him
to reject the Olmsteds' style of park design.

The Evils Which Parks Conceal

Most of Hartford's parks were sealed off from the streets, but the city
leaked in anyway — not just in the form of factory whistles heard in mani-
cured groves, or of ice wagons glimpsed through a hedge, but in the form
of city people. Visitors brought with them the worst aspects of unruly

street culture and posed the deadliest threat to the dream of making the park a separate world.

Park visitors seeking to commune with nature in the late nineteenth and early twentieth centuries often found themselves sharing the experience with drunks and vagrants. The benches at Tunnel Park, a small green at the junction of Albany Avenue and North Main Street, were usually filled with loitering men who sexually harassed female passersby and made themselves obnoxious in other ways as well. The men would sometimes drink there until the early hours of the morning, keeping the neighborhood awake with their singing, their raucous voices, and their foul language. They left the grass strewn with empty whiskey bottles.[31] Tramps also napped on benches in Bushnell Park whenever the patrolman for the area was out of sight. Park officials tried various tactics to control the tramp problem — removing certain benches, reserving others for women and children, increasing police patrols, and forbidding lying on the benches or on the grass. The official hostility to loitering annoyed some legitimate visitors who liked to relax in the park; it also failed to end the tramp nuisance.[32]

Vandalism, too, was a constant problem. Before Bushnell Park was even completed, vandals had repeatedly damaged the trees, shrubs, and turf. Park visitors often littered the walks and pelted the lily pads with sticks and stones. Every skating season brought a plague of hockey players who cut branches from the trees to serve as hockey sticks and left the pond edge "bare and battered."[33] The expansion of the park system gave miscreants a broader field for their activities. Vandalism once directed against the railroad was now turned gleefully against the parks, Parker reported in 1911. Some people, he wrote, "seem to consider it a great joke to overreach a park employee and deface or destroy park property." Pope Park suffered worse than any other. The park foreman kept a log of the almost daily incidents, which included not only the accidental breaking of branches by boys climbing trees, but also an astonishing number of savagely destructive acts. The killing of small animals was common, as groups of boys amused themselves by stoning or otherwise destroying squirrels, frogs, and cats. Other vandals girdled or set fire to trees, smashed the light globes, tore apart the sandboxes, urinated in the drinking cups, and threw bricks at the toolhouse roof to break the slates. One of the most frequent acts of vandalism was the smearing of excrement, sometimes in large quantities, on park buildings and benches. Much of the vandalism took place at night.[34]

Darkness marked a striking change in the character of the parks, paralleling — in greatly exaggerated form — the change that took place on downtown streets. Park officials strove with at least some success to create a sanctuary for public morality during the day, but nightfall brought the triumph of those values they most abhorred. At night the park was even worse than the street. It was not only the resort of drunks, tramps, and vandals; it was also a trysting place for lovers and for prostitutes and their clients. "The evils which parks conceal at night should be considered as well as the good they do in the day-time," Parker wrote in 1906. "They seem to offer favorable opportunities for misbehaving between the sexes, strongly attracting those who do evil. It seems an ideal place for that 'teasing and catting' which precedes immoral acts, with people not already bad. This is often mistaken for courting, which rightfully belongs to young people, but differs from it as light does from darkness." Riverside Park was a particularly popular place for nocturnal outdoor sexuality. In 1915, a few years after the closing of the nearby red-light district, it was described as "a headquarters for commercial prostitution in its lowest and most revolting forms." Furthermore, the park restrooms, which were apparently left unlocked, were the site of homosexual encounters, and some children were reportedly lured there and sexually molested. And even more serious crimes occurred in the parks at night. A park official wrote in February 1908 that a newborn baby had been found dead in a park restroom. "This is the sixth baby that had been found on the parks within the last few years. . . . It seems to be a perfectly safe proposition to destroy a child and then leave them [sic] in the parks for the city to take care of." In a confidential letter detailing such problems in 1915, the park commission president, Charles Welles Gross, urged greater police vigilance "for the protection of the innocent persons who frequent the parks for proper recreation and other lawful purposes and before an unsavory reputation attaches to the parks and to persons using them."[35]

Park officials worried that the vandalism and vice revealed a deeper problem with the park environment that no amount of patrolling could solve. The mayhem encouraged their growing skepticism about the park as a naturalistic refuge from the street. Officials came to believe that the secluded park enabled and even encouraged vicious activities. As a result, they removed much of the Olmsteds' shrubbery from Riverside Park around 1906, "so that the entire territory is easily seen by the patrolman." By 1908 they had begun removing the border plantings at Pope Park for the same reason. Nighttime vandalism and vice had become so extreme that the working-class parks could actually be improved by opening them to the street. The parks department began installing lighting for security reasons around 1910, further diminishing the visible contrast with the streets.[36]

The whole idea of a naturalistic park in a working-class neighborhood was sadly misguided, Parker concluded. The vandalism in Pope Park was evidence that the park was "not fulfilling its mission," he wrote in 1910. "The park is at fault, and I would suggest, that partly as a remedy, but more because it ought to be done that the park may be used, that the grove between the river and Park Terrace be thoroughly lighted, an abundance of seats put in, tables, summer houses, pergolas and some simple games, that it may become useful to the people of this section and win their respect and care." The boys of the neighborhood should not be blamed too harshly for their vandalism. "Much of it is the result of the natural and normal instinct of the growing child. It is natural for them to climb trees, to cut whips and sticks, to get fruit and nuts and to do most of the things that have caused the injury to plant and shrub life." If vandalism had reached serious levels, it was evidence that the park was inadequately serving the instinctual needs of its visitors. "As a machine out of balance causes friction, unnecessary wear and cost to run, and in the end may destroy itself, so play facilities out of balance cause trouble, are costly, and the facilities provided are often destroyed. Generally, when there is discord or destruction in recreation or park work, it is because they are out of balance."[37] More facilities for active recreation in the working-class parks were needed to save the park machinery from a systemic breakdown.

Balancing the Park Machine

Besides vandalism, public pressure for more active recreation also played a role in the redesign of the parks. Park officials had begun to realize the inadequacy of the Olmsteds' plans almost as soon as the new parks were built, when park visitors voted with their feet. Pope Park, despite its location beside a densely-populated neighborhood, drew surprisingly few visitors except to the playgrounds and tennis courts at the northern end. The main section, south of Park Street, was particularly deserted. "Designed on country park lines, it soon proved the undesirability of maintaining such a park in that locality — it was a misfit," Parker recalled later. Riverside Park, on the other hand, was a great popular success. Its success was certainly not a result of the naturalistic landscaping with which the Olmsteds had tried to disguise spaces intended for active recreation, such as uneven borders of woods and scattered trees in the playing fields. "To begin with, these arrangements were fairly satisfactory, but with the introduction of the Vacation Schools and through their progressive and instructive development, it has become quite apparent that some changes in the future will be necessary," wrote Theodore Wirth in 1904, referring to the Civic Club's summer programs for slum children. Landscape beauty was of secondary importance to facilities for active play, and it had to be sacrificed in order to "meet the playful, sporty instinct of the playful, sporty youth." [38]

The Civic Club, which ran a Vacation School in Riverside Park, encouraged Pope Park's transformation into a space for active recreation as well. In 1900 the club proposed building an "out-door gymnasium" in Pope Park and hiring instructors. Though the club itself was an elite women's organization, it eventually attained its goal in 1902 after enlisting the support of members of the immigrant working class. Among those joining the Civic Club in its campaign were members of the Hartford Turnerbund, the local branch of a nationwide German-American movement that emphasized physical culture and ethnic pride. [39] The outdoor gymnasium turned out to be extremely popular among young workers from the nearby factories. It drew large crowds every evening after the factories closed, though workers avoided the classes organized by the instructors. Lights were installed in 1909 to make the gymnasium better conform to the rhythms of industrial society. Parker declared that the outdoor gymnasium and the new playgrounds deterred vandalism by giving young men and boys something to do. [40]

The parks department rapidly developed more spaces for active recreation in the early 1910s, under pressure from park visitors who voiced their preferences in letters, petitions, and statements at public meetings. Baseball players wanted more diamonds, gymnasts wanted another outdoor gym, tennis players wanted more courts, and roller skaters wanted an outdoor rink. By 1914, there were twenty-six baseball diamonds, eighteen tennis courts, nine football gridirons, and two nine-hole golf courses, in addition to facilities for lawn bowls, quoits, and croquet.[41]

Not everyone shared the enthusiasm for sports. In parks claimed by the elite, active recreation and children's games often annoyed the neighbors. "Afternoons regularly, there has been for some days a base-ball game consisting of twenty boys who have injured the shrubbery and worn the turf," in the green at Washington and Lafayette streets, complained Henry Roberts in 1903. "You are well aware that this plot of land was given to the city by the residents adjacent to it. . . . Its desecration is a matter which has incensed very much those who have donated it to the city." On the other hand, neighbors at Sigourney Square, a green in the plebeian part of Asylum Hill, took the opposite side in a crudely written 1913 petition: "We the undersigned residents of Ashley St., May St., Sargent St. and Sigorney St. our homes facing Sigorney Park heartily approve the permitting of the boys of our nieghborhood playing 'macaroni' and other games in the park. It does not annoy us and the boys really ought to have some place besides the street corners to play games on, so we respectfully petition you to give the boys the nescesary permission."[42]

Such differences could lead to conflict when two groups sought incompatible uses for the same park space. In 1913 city officials prepared to open Pope Park to Sunday-afternoon baseball games in order to satisfy a long-standing desire among workers to play ball on their day off. City hall was quickly besieged with angry letters from Protestants in the Parkville neighborhood who resented the immigrant workers living on the opposite side of the park. "The people here, who go to the Park for rest, quiet and June air, will be denied that, if the rabble, which such sports always attract are there. Neither can there be any quiet for the residents within hearing distance. Sports of an athletic nature are unavoidably noisy," wrote a Sisson Avenue couple. The Rev. John E. Zeiter, a Methodist pastor who had urged his congregation to protest, added that "by far the major portion of the best element of the people in this section are opposed to the use of Pope Park on the Sabbath day for athletic sports."[43]

The growth of spaces for active recreation in city parks produced huge increases in attendance from the late 1900s through the 1910s. Recreational facilities drew 521,000 visitors in 1913, and 2.8 million just eight years later—an average of twenty visits per Hartford resident. These increases threatened to transform the character of the outlying parks and produce further conflicts over their use. Elizabeth Park, originally laid out as a public garden in the suburban West End, became by the early 1910s one of the most heavily used parks in the city, with visitors arriving by trolley from distant neighborhoods. Park workers scrambled to accommodate the visitors by removing a tree nursery to create another lawn, turning a sheep pasture into a playfield, clearing out undergrowth in the woods to create picnic groves, and converting the sheep barn into a dressing room for ballplayers and a warming hut for ice skaters. "And yet with all this addition to the usable space, the park is becoming crowded," Parker reported. He decided to expand sports facilities elsewhere to divert crowds from Elizabeth Park.[44]

Parker Embraces Segregation

Struggling to accommodate the pressures on the park system, George A. Parker articulated a clear philosophy for the design of public space. His ideas were shaped by his deep ambivalence about the modern city, which he once described as "the horrible creature."[45] Born in 1853 in rural New Hampshire, Parker had received a spotty education but finally managed to graduate from the Massachusetts Agricultural College. He held a series of jobs superintending country estates and city parks before coming to Hartford in 1896 as superintendent of Keney Park. He served as Hartford's superintendent of parks from 1906 until his retirement in 1926. A solitary, often lonely man, Parker described himself as "slow witted, without personal magnetism and usually disliked." He devoted himself almost obsessively to his work, building a reputation as one of the leading park superintendents in America. In the 1900s and 1910s he held office in numerous local, regional, and national reform organizations.[46]

Parker believed that the modern city lived a parasitic existence, draining the countryside of energy. The city could also devour its young; it threatened to corrupt children and, through the poisonous effects of the saloon, the brothel, and tobacco, to dump them on what he called "the human scrap heap." Yet Parker believed that a determined effort by

Park Superintendent George A. Parker.
(*Hartford in 1912*)

the citizenry could tame the urban monster, suppress its most dangerous sources of immorality, encourage the growth of positive influences, and create "a sin-proof city."[47] Crucial to the success of such a struggle was the role of an enlightened city government in providing off-street recreational space, particularly in parks. He wrote:

> I believe that parks have a message for the city: that they introduce the influence of the country into city conditions, and that this country influence is essential to the development of children into healthy men and women of normal physical, mental and moral strength, and to uphold adult people in a healthy condition. . . . The time has been when cities could depend upon the country to supply their demands for healthy and normal citizens, but with the rapid increase of the percent of those who live under urban conditions, the cities must be able to grow their own men and women from parents born and bred in the city.[48]

In 1908, before making the major changes at Elizabeth Park, Parker had worried that the growth of active recreation was overwhelming the original function of parks, which he described in Bushnellian terms as "the influence they have upon every section of the city, that is, upon the city as a whole, and the unconscious influence they have upon all its people." This influence, he said, "was in danger of being forgotten and largely destroyed in the desire to provide sports, playgrounds and other conveniences for those who want to go to the parks in order to enjoy sports or do stunts." Parker decided that he could solve this problem by sharply dividing the playing fields from the naturalistic landscapes. "Where special sports require special preparations of ground and exclusive privileges, distinct and separate areas should be obtained for them, and not introduced into those park areas which are pre-eminently for pictorial effect or for the recuperation of over-worked brain or strained emotions."[49]

In creating and expanding Elizabeth Park's sports areas, Parker carefully placed them along the streets to serve as a buffer for the inner sanctuary, which included a celebrated rose garden. "The central portion of this park has been kept purely as a beauty spot, but around its borders are the facilities for recreation on the part of those who demand something more than mere beauty — a picnic grove, baseball diamonds, tennis courts, and a bowling green," according to a 1915 article in *Hartford* magazine.[50] In this way Parker was able to accommodate both those who wanted to play ball and those who wanted to sniff the flowers in peace. He had found a way to make active recreation work to separate the bustle of the street from the serene contemplation of beauty.

Building on the idea of Pope Park as the "poor man's park," Parker worked to give each component of Hartford's park system a distinct character. He had first tentatively advanced the idea of a class-specific system of neighborhood parks with urban amenities in a 1903 report to the American Park and Outdoor Art Association. In that report he had declared the need for park officials to provide the facilities — and allow the activities — desired by the neighborhood. He termed this system "communityism." As park superintendent he rejected John Olmsted's idea of administering a park system with a "unity of purpose and methods." Instead, he became a kind of department store manager offering a full line of wares to a fragmented leisure market. Parker told *Hartford* magazine that proper park development required officials to be alert and responsive to the changing desires of park visitors. The widely varying tastes of these visitors meant that specialized spaces were needed. As he put it in his annual report that year, "I believe in a segregation of play activities by sex and age periods with suitable and separate provisions for each, with other provisions made for those to whom recreation means rest for tired

Visitors enjoying the Elizabeth Park rose garden, 1921. The parks department was careful to separate such aesthetic pursuits from the noise of the athletic fields. (Hartford Public Library)

muscles and brains."[51] *Hartford* magazine explained how these ideas had guided the development of the park facilities for different neighborhoods. "Hartford, for instance, has a large proportion of professional men, bankers, brokers, insurance clerks and others primarily engaged in brain work, and for such golf is the one great recreation, with bowling on the green and curling popular for certain sections in season." Goodwin Park in the South End filled the needs of these men and also provided baseball diamonds to accommodate the growing enthusiasm for active recreation among the middle class. Parks in working-class neighborhoods were different: "Colt Park has been developed as the city's great playfield and there it is that the younger element reigns supreme. . . . Pope Park, the center of a great manufacturing district, must also, from the nature of its use, offer diversified means for recreation and it has been developed to a considerable extent along the same line as Colt Park. . . . Riverside Park is, like Pope, the recreation spot for a great number of people, it being peculiarly the property of those who live east of Main Street." Elizabeth and Bushnell parks were "beauty spots," with other uses included as long as they did not interfere with the main function. Finally, "Keney Park is essentially for driving, riding or walking over, letting the influence of its beauty sink into one's heart and mind, as Park Supt. Parker puts it."[52]

By professing such sentiments and claiming that the park system was the result of Horace Bushnell's "prophetic vision," Parker concealed how radically he and like-minded park officials of his era had redefined the purpose of the park. True, he sought to preserve the "unconscious influence" of naturalistic beauty and even saw a need for park space that, as he said, could serve as "a great outdoor living room for the people," but he viewed these as discrete parts of a complex of park functions.[53] While one consumer of leisure might choose to feel the immanence of God in nature, another would be nailing a line drive into right field, and a third would be eating ham sandwiches in the picnic grove. The park system would serve the special needs of each — in splendid isolation. By dividing Hartford's people by recreational preference, age, and class, Parker had not simply revised Bushnell's ideas. He had turned wholly against the spirit of everything Bushnell stood for. Now the parks would keep Hartford's people as divided in their leisure time as they were at work or in their segregated neighborhoods. No longer intended to bring all of Hartford's people into contact with one another, park space reflected the fragmented society of a modern industrial city.

The diverse recreational sites functioned as a coherent system only because of the streetcar — the same force that by encouraging outward development had made scattered parks necessary in the first place. The new parks were quickly connected to the streetcar system, and Goodwin Park, Keney Park, and Elizabeth Park even served as termini for trolley lines. The Hartford Street Railway Company promoted the idea of visiting outlying parks, undoubtedly in order to stimulate ridership.[54] The trolleys therefore filled part of the integrative role that the Olmsteds and Wirth had envisioned for the parkways. Though the greenbelt plan had never been realized, preventing anyone from experiencing the park system as a continuous unit, the trolleys at least allowed all the parks to be reached from anywhere in the city, and many more people could afford trolleys than would ever have been able to indulge in carriage excursions. The trolley system made it possible for individual park visitors to leave the narrow confines of their neighborhood to seek whatever specialized form of amusement was available in any park in the city. It freed individuals from geographic limits and undercut lingering hopes for rebuilding a sense of community on a neighborhood level.

Parker was far more appreciative of the trolley than the Olmsteds had been. "There is no question as to the desirability of having a good car service to the different [park] entrances," he wrote in a 1905 letter offering advice on the design of New Orleans' Audubon Park. "It seems to me that the time will come when the same or similar reasons which justified the introduction of carriage roads and bicycle paths may also justify the introduction of trolley cars" into the parks themselves. The trolley was "the wage-earner's vehicle, and it has as logical a place in large parks as carriage roads have for the rich man to drive on." The trolley could let passengers see "varied scenes of beauty," could distribute them through large parks, and could take them to playing fields and picnic grounds along the tracks.[55]

Despite his willingness to let the city enter the park in the form of sports, streetlights, and perhaps even trolleys (which were never actually extended into Hartford's parks), Parker still felt that city dwellers had a need for nature's healing influence. Yet he understood even the provision of natural influence in terms of a mechanistic system of urban amenities. "My conception of a park system might be compared to a City Water system, or to its system of streets; both are supposed to have direct connection with every home, and I believe a park system should be so connected," he wrote in 1910. "The public parks and squares might be compared to the reservoir of a water system, and the street trees and parkings to the main pipes, the front yard to the house service."[56] Just as Parker's division of the parks into separate spaces was based on an understanding of park visitors as individual consumers, so this metaphor depicted homes as utility customers linked to an infrastructure. In any case, the city was to be united not in any direct, organic sense, but only through the mediation of an elaborate system created by experts.

Parker had created a more complicated definition of park space to replace the simple dualisms of nature and city, contemplation and action. Though at the time he became park superintendent he had contrasted the natural freedom of the parks with the artificial confinement of the streets, he quickly came to see the remaining difference between the two spaces primarily in terms of order and disorder. The purpose of the park was now first and foremost to provide orderly, specially designed recreational environments to suit the needs and personal tastes of the individual. "I believe that public parks with restricted uses can fulfil their mission more effectively than if not under restriction," he wrote in 1910. The freedom enjoyed by park visitors now consisted primarily of being able to choose from an array of recreational options.[57]

Parker, formerly hostile to the city, became in the 1910s bravely insistent on the social benefits that could be achieved by creating and managing orderly systems in recreation, education, traffic, and land use. In this way, he shared many progressive reformers' faith that rationalized administration could solve a wide range of problems. At the national and state levels, this aspect of progressive thought guided efforts for greater government regulation of interstate commerce, monetary policy, food and drugs, and working conditions. At the local level, belief in scientific administration encouraged attempts at greater municipal control of utilities and transit systems, as well as charter revisions that would shift municipal power to professional managers. The desire for bureaucratic order—often curiously intermingled with a secularized form of evangelical zeal—set progressives apart from previous generations of American reformers. Parker, impressed by the new ideas, looked forward to a time when they could cure the ills of the city and restore the promise of civilization. In about 1911 he wrote that American city governments do not yet "seem to manage in a thorough business like way or to use a more modern term 'with scientific efficiency,' but I seem to see through the fog of my ignorance, forms and purposes that are coming, as well as the receding forms which are going. I have great faith in the city. I believe in it. I feel that the future of the world for some centuries to come will be evolved from city conditions."[58]

Viewing parks now as places of order more than as places of nature, Parker in the 1910s opened them to some activities clearly associated with the street and the city. Among these was the creation of a race track to take the place of Washington Street. Once a quiet avenue lined with the homes of the city's elite, Washington Street had been a popular drive at least as far back as the late 1870s, as well as a well-known place for racing. Although the local equestrian enthusiasts had failed to stop the streetcar system from extending tracks across Washington at Park Street, most of the street was completely free of such obstructions. During the

1880s and 1890s, the street was the site of organized winter sleigh races on Saturday afternoons, drawing sleighs from all over Hartford and the surrounding towns. At these "matinees," as they were called, the elite would show off their racing skill and the quality of their horses on the blocks between Park and Buckingham streets, in front of crowds of spectators. Longer races ran from Vernon Street to Capitol Avenue.[59]

In the early twentieth century, however, Washington Street began developing into a major thoroughfare for north-south traffic. Horse lovers requested an off-street speedway reserved for their use and persuaded the park commission in 1908 to build one in Colt Park. When the parks department was unable to find enough inexpensive ashes to make the marshy site suitable, the racing enthusiasts asked that the speedway be built instead at Riverside Park. The commission considered the project so important that it granted the request even though it meant the destruction of two baseball diamonds, much to the annoyance of East Side ballplayers. To symbolize the abandonment of the old racing site, the Hartford Road Drivers' Club held a parade of sleighs from Washington Street to the newly completed speedway on January 1, 1910. Horse races of various sorts continued to be held there until 1918, when a declining interest in horses led the parks department to put the track to other uses, including motorcycling.[60]

In the years following World War I, Hartford's parks offered activities that competed directly with commercial amusements. Ironically, one of the other advocates of this change was Dotha Hillyer, Horace Bushnell's daughter. Hillyer noticed that "dancing on the green" had become a popular activity at the band concerts held in the parks, and she decided to promote this by installing a quarter-acre dance floor at Colt Park. In summer 1918 she urged the park commission to let her do something for the "grown-up boys and girls" who had come to Hartford to work in war-related industries and who needed respectable amusements outside working hours. The recreation director, S. Wales Dixon, supported the idea, saying, "It provides a clean, wholesome place of entertainment with the best of environment." The dance floor opened that same year and was very popular through the 1920s, with as many as two thousand people a night paying admission. Parks officials arranged for a fourteen-member band to play every summer night, weather permitting. They

Outdoor dancing at Colt Park, 1918. The park offered a sanitized version of the
disreputable dance hall. (Hartford Public Library)

sought to create a sanitized version of a dance hall, with no lewd forms
of dance and no "objectionable jazz features" in the music. Two supervisors, a man and a woman, would dance around the floor, discreetly
warning dancers whose behavior was questionable. "As for jazz, we're not
very rigid in our rules in regard to that," said Dixon. "The public likes it
and we aim to please the public."[61]

In summer 1919 the parks department also began showing movies.
Thousands of people flocked to Colt Park to see the first free show and
to hear the accompanying orchestra. Most films were selected for educational value. Examples included government pictures that showed
"scenes connected with farm work and the work of the rangers in the
forests," reported the *Hartford Courant*. The experience of visiting the
parks, once limited to a stroll in natural surroundings, now included
watching nature on film.[62]

Clearly, Parker differed from moral reformers like the Rev. Rockwell
Harmon Potter, who had denounced the evil influence of the street and

had considered commercial entertainment as its extension. Potter had described commercial leisure as the malign antithesis of the park experience. Nannie Melvin, the protective officer of the Woman's Aid Society, argued that Hartford men needed sports in the parks, "free from commercialism," to improve their morals and to stop them from accosting self-respecting girls on the streets. Parker thought it was all just recreation, though of widely varying moral character. "Among other things the recreation of a city consists of resting, reading and visiting in the home, shopping, theatres and places of amusement, saloons, billiard rooms, clubs and places of 'hanging out,' walking the streets, public parks and playgrounds . . . and in a higher sense religious meetings and exercises," Parker wrote in 1911.⁶³

Like a merchant eyeing his competition, Parker calculated streets' recreational functions in 1915 and realized that the people of Hartford spent twice as much leisure time there as in parks.

> The great attractions to human beings are other human beings, and people go with the crowd. The greatest recreation grounds that Hartford has, although it is not known as such, is Main Street, especially since it has been so well lighted. Here are about two miles of streets which have cost Hartford as much as its park system with facades of large and beautiful buildings costing millions of dollars, and bordered with churches, saloons, restaurants, theaters, attractive stores and those things which attract and relieve the monotony of life; and more than all these, there are people, lots of them, on the street. Even though they do not speak in passing, yet as they move in and out among themselves, they gain strength, rest and relief from the monotony of repeating over and over again the daily task. Here is the great melting pot of Hartford. In a lesser [degree], Asylum Street, Park Street, Front Street and Windsor Street serve a similar purpose. In these five great promenades of Hartford twenty million "human hours" of leisure time are spent yearly. They make for its good and for its evil.⁶⁴

This passage seems, at first reading, like a refutation of Frederick Law Olmsted's oft-quoted description of walking through crowded city streets. By watching out for other people and maneuvering to avoid collisions, Olmsted had said in an 1870 speech, "our minds are thus brought into close dealings with other minds without any friendly flowing toward them, but rather a drawing from them."[65] Parker evaluated the walker's experience less negatively, using different criteria. He claimed that passing encounters with other people would restore the work-wearied individual, but he said nothing about whether this encounter would produce social harmony. Unlike Olmsted and Bushnell, he did not see that as a relevant issue. The important thing was to see that each person found wholesome, orderly recreation.

Until Parker redesigned the park system in the 1910s, Hartford's parks had reflected almost exclusively the interests of the elite and the middle class. Bushnell had sought to create civic unity on bourgeois terms — working-class people were welcome in his outdoor parlor in order that they might gain finer sensibilities and relate harmoniously with their superiors. The active recreation the working class desired was forbidden in Bushnell Park in the 1860s and was slighted in the designs for the new parks of the 1890s. Under George A. Parker, however, the park system evolved into a collection of neighborhood parks aimed at serving each area's predominant socioeconomic group. Parks were further subdivided into smaller spaces to satisfy the diverse needs of individual visitors.

Such a change was welcomed and even instigated by the working classes.[66] The segregation of parks and the space within them gave Hartford's working classes a new voice in shaping their own recreational facilities. They transformed certain park spaces to reflect their accustomed use of the streets, uses including vigorous games and even crime and vandalism. As Parker yielded to these pressures, other park uses came to include new activities associated with interior space — no longer merely the genteel space of the "outdoor parlor," but also the plebeian dance halls and movie theaters that had once been derided as coarse, commercial amusements.

By abandoning the attempt at recreational unity, Parker returned to the original idea of inclusion — with a completely changed meaning. Virtually all of Hartford's people could find something in the parks to suit their tastes, and they could enjoy themselves without interference from those with different tastes or different class backgrounds. To some extent, therefore, Parker was right in suggesting that segregation was in the interests of everyone. By keeping disparate groups of people apart, the redesigned park system minimized conflict. It prevented an endless struggle over whose version of proper behavior would prevail, and an equally futile struggle to stifle nonconformity. Parker had given up on Bushnell's hope that the park would be an unstructured natural environment that would bring back the face-to-face relations and harmonious society of an idealized rural past. Personal encounters could have only limited effects in the dispersed, class-segregated city that Hartford had become, and a new model of the social environment was needed. Parker chose the model of rational organization that urban institutions and infrastructure provided, and he accepted the existence of a pluralistic society. In place of the stark spatial antithesis between park and city envisioned by the Olmsteds and by Wirth, Parker created a fine-grained division of space to bring order to a profusion of recreational tastes.

6

"The Children Are Off the Streets"

Arriving in Hartford in the summer of 1923, a nine-year-old Russian Jewish boy found that the fastest way to fit in was to play in the street with the other children. "I became one of 'the boys' in short order," Morton Tonken recalled years later. "The language came very easily to me, especially swearing, and I acquired this part to perfection. I had to learn how to fight, play ball and piggy, gamble with tops, play jack-knife, marbles, and last but not least, how to raid fruit and peanut wagons at night and steal candy from store counters. This was known as having fun and being brave. Any boy not taking part was dubbed a 'sissy' and became virtually ostracized."[1]

Boys in the immigrant wards of the city had for decades enjoyed a rowdy street culture that set them against the adult world. At one end of the range of play were harmless games like ring-o-levio, piggy, pony, hide-and-seek, and marbles — games in which boys claimed the streets and the sidewalks for their own use, to the occasional annoyance of adults. More daring boys would steal rides on streetcars and delivery wagons. But play could easily stray into violence, vandalism, or petty thievery. Boys enjoyed throwing snowballs at peddlers and pedestrians, as well as playing pranks like stretching a rope across a dark street at a night to knock surprised bicyclists to the ground. Some would show their bravery by stoning children of other ethnic groups, starting brawls, swiping food from sidewalk displays, and setting fires.[2]

Unruly street play was not limited to the immigrant working class. Middle-class boys on Prospect Street in the late nineteenth century "romped up and down the street and through all the back yards, which they regarded as public property," remembered one of these boys years later.[3] Yet it was the play of working-class, immigrant children that most alarmed Progressive Era reformers. Growing in numbers as a result of the great waves of European migration, crammed into what reformers believed to be pathological slum environments, and standing apart from the mainstream culture, these children seemed to pose a grave danger to the values of the native-born middle class. Reformers sought some way of taming and Americanizing these children, lest they grow up wholly estranged from mainstream life.[4]

The Progressive Era movement to reform inner-city play was not, however, primarily motivated by nativist fears. It was roused instead by concerns about the effect of the new slum environment in which much of the immigrant working class had settled. Inner-city children and youths were thought to be trapped in congested, manmade environments, where they were battered by a constant volley of sensations. Reformers, influenced by a new understanding, namely, that the growing child passed through discrete, quasi-evolutionary stages, feared that sensory overstimulation could disrupt proper development. Reformers in Hartford and other cities sought to create new alternative environments that would remove children and youth from street influences. They built playgrounds, gymnasiums, and athletic fields in which play could be directed and in which, they hoped, proper child development could take place.[5] Desires for social control and for proper child development merged in a sophisticated campaign to reform the use of urban space.[6]

As the experience of young Morton Tonken suggests, Hartford reformers were ultimately unable to remove children from the street or to replace the influence of children's street culture with their own version of Americanization. And in order to attract children to the playgrounds and parks, they had to give up much of their control over even these spaces. Nevertheless, the playgrounds and new park facilities were a significant addition to the urban playscape — for the first time, areas within the city were specifically designated for children's recreation. The unexpected growth of automobile traffic complemented this trend toward sharper borders in the geography of play. Traffic forced children off major thoroughfares and into alleys and quiet side streets. Public officials and advocates for motorists indirectly encouraged this development by educating children about traffic safety. By the late 1920s, twin forces — the playground movement and traffic — had resulted in the growing segregation of children's play from adults' use of the street.

Boys' Clubs

The effort to reform play in Hartford began with five boys' clubs established in the second half of the nineteenth century. The first four of these clubs, like so many other local efforts at social work at this time, were connected in one way or another with the charitable efforts of the city's Congregational churches. The Dashaway Club of the early 1860s, the Sixth Ward Temperance Society that succeeded it, the Boys' Reading-Room Association, and finally the Boys' Club of the late 1870s, all aimed at instilling Christian morals in the benighted youth of the slums.[7]

Though club leaders rarely discussed how play was affected by the physical characteristics of the city, their judgments about space were clear from their choice of interior settings. Not surprisingly, the clubs' middle-class, predominantly female leadership shared the nineteenth-century belief that the home was morally superior to the street. An attempt was made to give a homelike atmosphere to the clubs' meeting rooms. The teenage boys in the Sixth Ward Temperance Society, for instance, met in a room at the Morgan Street Mission furnished with a piano, books, and pictures to make it look more like a middle-class parlor. As in a parlor, activities included playing games and singing songs, and a premium was placed on encouraging self-control. Similar activities prevailed at the Boys' Reading Room, where, according to the secretary, H. P. Goddard, "The object has been to make the Reading Room as much like a cheerful, pleasant home as possible." Boys at the Reading Room were required to wash their faces, and they were encouraged to

The Boys' Reading Room, a nineteenth-century boys' club. Discipline was a constant problem for those who sought to control children. (*Scribner's Monthly*, November 1876)

bathe in the bathtubs provided. "It is believed that good has been accomplished, by drawing the boys away from liquor-saloons and other questionable resorts, and by making their evenings pass pleasantly in innocent amusements," Goddard continued, adding that the club's influence made the surrounding neighborhood quieter and more peaceful as well. Leaders of these four clubs found, however, that their attempts to convert the boys to the moral standards of the genteel home involved difficult negotiations. If the boys did not find the club enjoyable enough to balance out the tedium of being uplifted, they could simply refuse to return, as seems to have happened with at least the first two of these clubs.[8]

By far the most successful of the five boys' clubs was the Good Will Club, founded and led by Mary Hall, the defender of newsgirls. Supervisors and boys compromised on a recreational environment, one in which the values of the home mingled with those of the street and in which different models of discipline were developed. The Good Will Club had its origins in the Boys' Evening School, as the Boys' Club was called in its final years. Hall began supervising that school three evenings a week in 1879. She also met separately with a few of the boys to read them Horatio Alger stories and give them lessons in geology and other subjects. Hall eventually severed the club's connections with its parent organization altogether and moved its meetings to the building where she had her law office.[9]

By the time Hall organized the Good Will Club, boys' clubs were appearing in other American cities as well, starting with one in New York in 1876. Other clubs also aimed at improving the moral character of the poor and were often sponsored by middle-class Protestant churches and missions. "Common to all was a sense of mission to the poor in which Christian and philanthropic motives intertwined with fear of class strife and social upheaval," writes the historian David MacLeod. Like the clubs in Hartford, clubs in other cities aimed at encouraging self-control and polite behavior. In the early twentieth century, club workers responded to public concerns about mass immigration by playing up the clubs' power to Americanize the children of immigrants.[10]

Like the four earlier clubs in Hartford, the Good Will Club aimed at educating children in manners, morality, personal appearance, and even some academic subjects. Boys had to pledge not to drink, smoke, or swear. In addition to playing games and singing songs, they received lessons in elocution and lectures on history, geology, and oral hygiene. The club later developed a list of rules that governed the boys' manner of entering and leaving the building, their comportment nearby and inside the building, their personal cleanliness, their greeting of supervisors, and their handling of books and games.[11] Unlike its predecessors, the Good Will Club was avowedly secular. Hall promised that Catholics and Jews could join without fear that anyone would try to meddle with their religious beliefs. She made good on that promise by ending a brief affiliation with the Young Men's Christian Association in the mid-1880s, after Catholic parents started pulling their children out of the club.[12]

The leaders of the Good Will Club pinned their hopes for moral reform on the indirect influences of a wholesome environment and constructive activities. In the 1880s the club began offering physical education programs similar to those later provided by the vacation schools. Physical education consisted of regimented exercises that fit in well with the club supervisors' determination to maintain discipline. In contrast to the feminized parlor or schoolroom atmosphere that earlier boys' clubs had struggled to achieve, physical education at the Good Will club had manly — even militaristic — overtones. A young man led all the boys one evening a week in drills with dumbbells and instructed some of them in fencing and boxing. Other boys joined the "Good Will Cadets," in which they drilled in uniform with wooden rifles, learning how to march and maneuver in formation. Many members enrolled in the club's craft and vocational programs. Though club workers insisted on courtesy, they knew that genteel decorum was an impossible goal. "The noise in that vicinity is pretty loud. Put several hundred boys together and they are pretty sure to make themselves heard," Hall said.[13]

By the early 1910s, the Good Will Club had grown into a major institution for supervising the play of boys from the slums. It attracted more than a thousand individuals a year. Its ever-increasing size forced it to move frequently, and the club was shuffled from one cramped space to another until Hall enlisted the support of the *Hartford Times* publisher, Alfred E. Burr, in raising money for a club building. The club bought the former Hartford Female Seminary on Pratt Street in 1889 and stayed there until 1911, when it built an even larger building on the northern edge of downtown.[14] Hall believed strongly that removing boys from bad surroundings was as important as providing good influences. "The Good Will Club was intended to take care of the young people in the ghetto and keep them off the street and keep them from falling into evil ways," recalled Morris N. Cohen, one of the boys who attended the club in the 1910s. Cohen said he was not sure at the time what those evil street influences might be, but the club's message was unmistakable. "All I knew was that they did not want us on the street so we went to a club where we could not get into mischief."[15]

The Good Will Club and its predecessors pioneered much of the work later undertaken by vacation schools and supervised playgrounds.[16] The boys' club supervisors sought to shape the character of working-class boys by gathering them into an uplifting environment in which their leisure time could be directed. Though the Good Will Club based its work on a fundamentally religious concern for instilling morality in the individual, its mission by the early twentieth century explicitly involved saving children from the harmful effects of the urban environment. Hall was not fully converted by the segregationist views of other Progressive

Era reformers; at the Good Will Club, Hall, who in the newsgirl controversies of 1893–1914 had differed from most of the others active on the issue, showed her tolerance for street values by allowing noise levels wholly inappropriate for the parlor. But the overall thrust of her play reform work put her clearly in the camp of those who wanted to rescue children from the street.

The Shortage of Play Space

By the turn of the century, boys in Hartford's inner neighborhoods could find few outdoor places in which their right to play was uncontested. The city's growth was severely limiting children's access to off-street play space. Vacant lots were disappearing, and the densely developed area of the city was expanding. In 1869 the built-up part of the city had covered only the area bounded by Pavilion Street in the north, Sigourney and Broad streets in the west, and Park and Wyllys streets in the south. Much of the North End and the South End was still farmed, as was part of Asylum Hill, and what became Frog Hollow was mostly open land as well. Backyards were still common even in parts of what is now the downtown.[17]

By 1909, however, development had spilled across the western limits of the city and was marching rapidly through both North End and South End. Though the West End was growing into an elite, semisuburban enclave of single-family homes and backyards, the inner neighborhoods were much denser. Frog Hollow was almost entirely built up with freestanding tenement houses on small lots. The characteristic building of the neighborhood—the "perfect six"—left the six tenant families with only a cramped rear yard and a narrow strip of ground between the sidewalk and the house. The East Side, always the densest section of the city, remained that way despite the clearing of a few blocks of housing for the approaches to the new Connecticut River bridge, as new buildings were shoehorned into rear lots. Housing of similar density was also spreading north into the Arsenal neighborhood below Suffield Street. To the west, the expansion of the downtown had spread tightly packed buildings all the way to the eastern slope of Asylum Hill.[18]

Within Bushnell Park in the late nineteenth century, children were allowed to play in a grove of trees west of the Trumbull Street bridge, but were not permitted to play on the lawns.[19] Children in the poor neighborhoods were left to play in the streets, but even their streets afforded less space than those in the outlying areas. Unlike in the semisuburban outskirts, where houses stood alone in grassy yards, the typical street in Hartford's slums resembled many other urban American streets at this time: a trench lined on either side with a solid wall of buildings. Jagged roof lines of two to four stories tall framed broad muddy streets or narrow muddy alleys. Though most of the streets were wide enough to catch sunlight, they looked like closed spaces — long rooms with a dirt floor and a partial ceiling of utility wires. If the street ended in a dead end or at a cross street, an additional wall heightened the look of enclosure. A few alleys, such as Marsh Court, were literally no wider than an ordinary room, and Oriental Alley was so narrow that two tricycles were said to be enough to block the way.[20]

The confined, almost interior quality of these streets limited the games that could be played, while discouraging (but not entirely preventing) such sports as baseball and football, which were popular where children had access to more space. Baseball and football were intended to be played on specially designed fields, or at least in wide-open spaces where play was shaped by rules, not by lack of space. Street games were more readily adaptable to the interferences posed by tight quarters and competing uses of space. In some, such as ring-o-levio or hares-and-hounds, the urban environment was an essential part of the game and added interesting and challenging dimensions. For example, a winning tactic in the chase game of hares-and-hounds was running through a store and out the back—the hares usually made it through quickly enough to avoid interference, but the shopkeeper was roused to anger in time to stop the pursuing hounds.[21]

Though play could continue under difficult physical conditions, it was sometimes overwhelmed by a combination of insufficient space and determined adult interference. Even outside the slums, boys found their play opportunities limited, as a group of boys who lived on the southern edge of Frog Hollow wrote in a 1912 letter to the mayor. They complained that they had been used to playing in a nearby vacant field, "but the officer on this beat puts us out every time we get there, [so] we have decided to play in the street. . . . So last night we were playing on Lincoln

Children playing in State Street, 1906. In the distance is the post office. Some buildings on this section of State Street were brothels. Note the absence of traffic. (Connecticut State Library)

street in front of the home of two boys in our crowd. Hardly had half an hour elapsed before the officer came up and told us to get the devil out of there." The boys claimed, "We are entittled [*sic*] to some place to play," and asked the mayor to do something about it.[22]

City officials had been trying to do something, but apparently not hard enough. In 1891 Mayor Henry C. Dwight had proposed that the city lease or purchase land "for use as playgrounds for the young people of our city. The ordinances of the city forbid the use of the streets for such purposes, and the boys and girls have no place for games of ball, tennis, etc." The park commissioners suggested a three-acre site on North Front Street, but city officials later dropped the matter without explanation.[23] The next year, the local publisher Leverett Brainard proposed that the city establish a public park and playground east of Broad Street between Ward and Jefferson streets, on the edge of the working-class Frog Hollow neighborhood, but he fared no better.[24] The expansion of the city's park system in the mid-1890s provided new play spaces, particularly in Riverside Park, and later in Pope and Colt parks as well. Riverside Park, the closest to the East Side, was planned from the beginning with children

Playing in a puddle, 1913. One of the Connecticut Woman Suffrage Association's disapproving photographs of the East Side. (Connecticut State Library)

in mind; it featured a "Little Folks Lawn" at the entrance to the park and a wading pool nearby.[25]

Children's need for additional play space, however, was not so much the motivation as the pretext for the play reform movements of the late nineteenth and early twentieth centuries. Campaigns to create alternative play environments were based instead on beliefs that in the streets, children learned immoral values, created havoc, failed to develop properly, and blocked traffic. The play reformers consistently hid the conflict between child and adult beneath a sentimental rhetoric of pity. Instead of labeling slum children troublemakers, reformers described them as innocent victims trapped in a corrupting environment. Playing in the street was therefore unacceptable — even if the child preferred it to playing in a park. "No thoughtful person needs any arguments to prove to him that the streets are not a desirable spot for children," wrote the secretary of the Civic Club in 1905:

The most unreflecting, the most selfish person could not pass through the streets of our East side on a blazing July day without wishing to carry the children off to a more suitable spot. They sit on the curbstone and extract strange substances from the mud of the gutter, they play, more or less peacefully, in the path of wagons and horses, they rush in front of electric cars, screaming with delight at the motorman's frantic bell. If they do not lose a limb or contract a fatal disease their constitutions are weakened by this contact with things unclean. And the moral dangers are more hideous than the physical ones.[26]

The Vacation Schools

Civic Club members, inspired by hearing a talk about the "vacation schools" of Cambridge, Massachusetts, took the lead in carrying children off to more suitable spots. In 1897 they decided to set up a similar school to serve Hartford's East Side. According to an account published a few years later, the vacation school project was based on the club members' desire "to provide other influences than those of the streets and alleys of our tenement districts for the children during the long summer vacation." The project was headed by Dotha Bushnell Hillyer, who took a special interest in what she called "the children of the streets" and their recreational needs. "We have three kinds of education, that of the schools, the houses and the streets; that of the streets undoing in a few hours the painstaking labors of the two others," she argued a few years later. To save the children from this malign influence, Hillyer and other Civic Club members arranged for the use of part of the Brown School on the East Side, hired teachers, and took applications from parents who wished to enroll children from six to fourteen years old. The school opened on June 28 for six weeks of half-day sessions, with eighty students chosen from more than seven hundred applicants. Additional students were later admitted, so that the average attendance was about a hundred.[27]

Like the boys' clubs, the vacation school program initially took place indoors, and the organizers found that their work demanded negotiation and compromise. The school tried to simultaneously educate, edify, and entertain the children, who were predominantly poor and of immigrant stock. In the "manual training rooms," boys were taught clay modeling, while girls were given dolls and taught to sew clothes for them. Children also listened to music and to lectures on natural history, sang songs, read books, copied drawings, wrote letters and stories, exercised with dumb-bells, and learned to play organized games. In choosing and managing the games, according to a later account, the teachers took "special care that they should be of such a nature as to instruct [the children] in honesty, self-denial, fair play, and courtesy." As part of the opening exercises on the first day, students bearing flags marched into the school to music, sang "America," and pledged allegiance to the flag. Then the students and a small audience of club members and other interested adults listened as the principal gave a speech on the importance of polite behavior. For the students, reported the *Hartford Courant,* "The vacation school opens up a new life. Instead of spending their play hours through the summer weeks on a hot, dry, and dusty street, they will find amusement that will be instructive as well as pleasant."[28] The school actually was popular with students. Many more wanted to get in than could be accommodated, and a crowd of disappointed children waited around the door for the first two days in the hope of being admitted.[29]

At the end of the term the students wrote letters describing their experience. The letters selected for publication in the *Courant* were apparently those that best expressed the teachers' ideal of the perfect child — one who was well behaved and abjectly grateful for the kindness of the Civic Club. The students who lived up — or down — to these expectations also gave hints in their letters of the reasons children might have wanted to go to the school. They wrote of receiving dolls, singing songs, and especially going on the picnic excursion. No one mentioned the natural history lectures or the pledge of allegiance. Still, the emphasis on etiquette was unforgettable, and some of the students had also had other bits of advice drilled into their heads. "Mrs. Hillyer told us if you want to have houses you should work," wrote little Annie Bishoff. Despite the doses of advice and discipline, the vacation school did provide children with a mildly entertaining change from spending every summer morning playing in the street. Children enjoyed the school on their own terms, though only within the narrow limits set by club members and teachers.[30]

The vacation school program grew quickly over the next few years and spread into outdoor spaces. With charitable donations and financial aid from the city government, the Civic Club expanded the program to include seven hundred children by 1899, opening a supervised outdoor playground at the Brown School. By 1900 about a thousand students were enrolled in three schools, and an equal number of others came to use the three supervised playgrounds. Uncounted others used the playground that the parks department had installed at Riverside Park for the use of the vacation school.[31] Realizing that the vacation schools had grown too big for the club to handle, Civic Club members asked the city to take over. The Common Council agreed in 1901 and voted enough money to keep the program growing.[32]

Public officials supervising the vacation schools described them more explicitly as social engineering tools, perhaps in an effort to defend the use of public funds for such work. The school and playground environments, they wrote, allowed better child development than the hated alternative of the street. In 1901, according to a special committee that was considering how the program should be run, "The main object of vacation schools is to provide the children during the summer months in the congested sections of the city, where the home life is narrow and the dirty public streets offer the only playgrounds, with environments that are pure and healthful, and to bring such children under influences that make for good."[33]

The committee emphasized the vacation aspect of the vacation schools and argued that the character molding practiced there was quite different from that of the regular schools. This difference should become even more pronounced, the committee argued. Already the vacation schools operated in outdoor as well as indoor environments. Indoors, "the children are occupied for three hours of the morning with physical exercises and drills, and instructed in manual work, such as paper-cutting, woodworking, painting, sewing, weaving and other light exercises which train the eye and the hand, and given helpful talks on cleanliness, civic virtues, and patriotism." Outdoors, in the schoolyards and public parks, they were taught to play games. The committee wanted to expand outdoor work to include more games and more nature study, "and the present indoor schools, savoring so strongly of the regular curriculum, [should be] practically abandoned."[34]

The committee desired a sharper division of children's lives into work time (education) and leisure time, paralleling the experience of their immigrant parents as they adapted to the modern industrial city.[35] The disjunction would be strengthened by splitting children's lives between contrasting physical spaces: a summer of recreation in natural surroundings followed by an autumn of study in the urban, interior setting of the schoolhouse. "With a summer spent under such favorable conditions, the children would return to the serious work of the public schools strengthened physically and mentally by their outdoor life, and better prepared for the strain of the new school year." Children spent more and more time outdoors as the program continued to develop under city supervision from 1901 through 1903. The number of playgrounds grew to five in 1901, including one each at Riverside and Pope parks. Students spent two days a week in the schoolroom, two days in the park, and one day on field trips. The new emphasis on providing amusing recreation made the vacation schools more popular among children, and it also won the support of working-class adults. John F. Gunshanan, a working-class social reformer and former semiprofessional baseball player, was among those advocating an extension of the vacation school program. Gunshanan spoke before the Board of Park Commissioners in 1901, successfully requesting help to open a vacation school at Pope Park near the Frog Hollow district and to install swings and sandboxes there.[36]

In 1904 the public school system took over management of the program and temporarily reversed the trend toward fun and games. The school system was brought in when previous vacation school leaders decided that they could not manage such a large program (enrollment had hit a peak of 1,869).[37] The new supervisors shifted the emphasis away from enticing children into healthy, off-street environments, and back toward education. Field trips were cut back, and children now spent three mornings in the classroom and two in the parks. Furthermore, according to the new vacation school principal, Stanley H. Rood, the mornings in the park "were not passed wholly in aimless play on the part of the children, but were treated in as serious a manner as the other days, the teachers being present with their classes, and stipulated periods being given up to athletic games and gymnastic drills for both boys and girls under the direction of capable physical instructors." Though Rood did not admit it, many children appear to have been unenthusiastic about standing in the muggy heat of the Connecticut Valley summer swinging dumbbells in time to a teacher's commands. Attendance, which was voluntary, dropped off on the outdoor mornings, prompting Rood to conclude rather lamely that "the indoor work appears to have a more potent attraction."

The school system was trying to have it both ways: to give the children an invigorating vacation and to extend their schooling through the summer. According to Rood, who during the regular year served as the grammar schools' supervisor of manual training, the purpose of the vacation schools was to take children off the streets and teach them manners, morals, and manual skills. From the children's perspective, however, the vacation schools lured them in by promising a less restricted play environment only to impose new forms of social control and manipulation. Children expressed their displeasure by dropping out. Attendance at the vacation school fell precipitously during the 1904 term, from 1,348 on one of the early days down to a daily average of 876 in the final week.[38]

School officials never admitted their error—but the program did become gradually less authoritarian and more enjoyable in the years after 1904. The program leaders expanded those aspects of the program that were most popular with children and gave children more choice in their activities. Park days in the 1905 session followed no fixed program; children were allowed to devote their time to whatever form of recreation they wanted. Rood noted a marked increase in attendance compared to the 1904 session.[39] Also in 1905, the Civic Club offered children a chance to plant their own flowers and vegetables in small plots at Riverside Park. In doing so, club members repeated their original call for supervised activities that would draw children away from the street and emphasized the healthy effects of a natural environment. The "school gardens" proved extremely popular, were added to the vacation school program the following year, and were expanded to Colt Park. Observing in 1906 that undirected play was the most popular part of vacation school, Rood urged establishing more playgrounds.[40]

The greatest shift came with Rood's resignation or dismissal following the 1906 season and with the subsequent decision of the superintendent of schools to let principals adapt the program to the interests of their students. Eleven playgrounds were in operation by 1911, and the vacation schools themselves were being allowed to wither away. "Two

Children's garden at Colt Park, 1914. (*Annual Report of the Board of Park Commissioners*, 1915)

Vacation Schools, properly speaking, were continued during the month of July . . . but both of these schools were auxiliary to the playground work carried on at these same plants," school officials reported in 1912. By 1913, what had once been called the vacation school program had been rechristened "Recreation Work in Summer." Average daily attendance reached 4,631 in July 1912 and 6,808 a year later. Having focused on luring children off the streets, the vacation schools had become mainly a program to provide play spaces.[41]

George Parker and the City Child

As the emphasis in playground work shifted from education to recreation, the provision of playground facilities drew greater attention. Leadership passed to the city's parks department, whose superintendent, George A. Parker, viewed the situation of city children with great anxiety.

The problems posed by the urban environment were the worst for the children of the slums, Parker believed. Affluent families living in single-family homes with yards could "reproduce in the city, somewhat, the conditions and freedoms of the country." But the children of the working classes were crowded into dense tenement districts, where opportunities for proper play were lacking.[42]

In assessing the problem, Parker employed more sophisticated conceptual tools than had the leaders of the vacation schools. Like his counterparts in recreation work throughout the country, Parker drew on the new ideas of child development being articulated in the late 1890s and 1900s by Granville Stanley Hall and Luther Halsey Gulick. According to Hall, a child psychologist and the president of Clark University, children passed through stages of development that recapitulated the prehistoric cultural evolution of the human race. Gulick, physical education director first for the Young Men's Christian Association International College and later for the New York City public schools, argued that proper physical and moral development required that children act out instinctual drives through age-specific types of play. For instance, track-and-field sports and tag games were appropriate for boys aged seven to twelve, who were driven by pre-savage, individualistic hunting instincts. Adolescent boys, whose development corresponded to that of hunting tribes, needed more complex team sports. Proper development would prepare the boys to play constructive roles in society when they reached adulthood.[43]

Parker feared that city conditions threatened to prevent this natural development. "The environment for many a child in Hartford destroys or weakens these instinctive emotions, and it is Hartford's problem to remove such environments." Unless the city provided decent play spaces, the child would fail to reach the proper stages of development on time and would become "a hoodlum, a tough, a ne'er-do-well." Parker feared that the growth of youth gangs in the tenement districts was evidence of just such retarded development.[44]

In Parker's view, the socializing power of parks and playgrounds was especially needed because of the home's decline as a family workplace. Though fondly recalling the close family life of his rural youth, he observed:

The family no longer works together, the man goes to his place, and the woman altogether too often goes to her work, the children are in school, the young boy and girl [each] to their own particular task, [until?] the coming together again at the evening meal. Formerly the evening was spent together in the house, but the housing conditions are such among too many of our workers that they cannot and will not stay in the house. The man, the boy and the girl usually separate for the evening each to their own amusement, the mother more often stays in the home.

Without guidance or proper home life, the children were loose in the streets, which had taken the place of the open fields of the rural past. There, they were in danger of succumbing to evil influences. "A remedy for all this is recreation, and only through recreation do I see an adequate relief from present city conditions under which 3/4 of the people live." [45] Adding to the urgency was the fact that "Hartford is a city of many nationalities and has become (whether we will it so or not) one of the melting pots out of which is to come a virile race or else the barbaric element will predominate. . . . At the present time there is a deep unrest, a discontent, a tendency toward a dissolution of much that has been considered most worthy to strive for in the past, and the public parks and playgrounds are places where in a large way all classes and conditions of people may come together daily." [46] Wholesome, age-appropriate recreation was the cure for what ailed the modern city, particularly its poor and immigrant neighborhoods. The city government had to support it in order "to prevent the children of the coming generation from destroying the work of the past." [47]

1909

Parker placed even greater expectations on recreational space than had Horace Bushnell. Like Bushnell, he saw parks as bringing salutary aspects of rural life into the unwholesome urban environment, promoting physical health, and exerting an "unconscious influence" that eased social divisions. But Parker saw the city's ills as even more numerous and serious than Bushnell had. As a result of poor housing conditions and the diurnal departure of fathers, children, and even mothers, the home no longer properly nurtured the young. Therefore, "the city should mother its children," and its task would not be easy. Children were not the mere passive lumps that Bushnell had described. They had innate drives whose management was both crucial and highly complicated under the artificial conditions created by the modern city. "Play should be spontaneous, yet often under our abnormal city conditions it has to be taught and directed. When it has to be taught or directed, it is more of the nature of education than play," Parker wrote. If the parks and playgrounds failed to meet the need for play that was both appropriate and enjoyable, the streets were always there, first beckoning the young with a meretricious illusion of freedom, then luring them to their doom. The children's decline might even have permanent, hereditary consequences; in neo-Lamarckian fashion, their lapse would produce a race that was barbaric rather than virile. Park officials, on whom such awesome responsibility was placed, had to find a solution to these problems.[48]

The New Play Environment

Despite the growing national mania among recreation workers for "directed play," Parker had been skeptical about the concept even before his promotion to Parks Superintendent. In a 1906 article he described how he had sat on a park bench one day the previous summer, puzzling over his vague sense of dissatisfaction about a successful field day put on by the vacation schools. "Slowly my attention was attracted to a dozen children, under ten years old, who had escaped from the procession as it marched off the park and had returned to pick flowers and play by themselves." Unsupervised, the children played more enthusiastically and vigorously than they had all day, leading Parker to wonder "if too much direction did not weaken the spirit of the child" and undermine individuality. But Parker did not have full control over the playgrounds, and he continued to allow a wide range of play experiences even in the parks. Children participated in everything from highly regimented drills to the completely unsupervised recreation that one girl called "real play."[49]

The most disciplined play, ironically, took place in the wide open, tree-lined meadows of the parks, where schools in the 1910s staged elaborately choreographed pageants in which hundreds of children danced in formation and waved flags. In contrast to the streets, the park meadows placed almost no physical constraints on play, but teachers more than made up for this. Describing a 1914 event in Keney Park that involved 2,500 children and 4,800 flags, a reporter commented snidely that it "epitomized both the spirit of democracy of our public schools and the trend of the times in organized playing. For nowadays, it is not permitted that the pupil run and jump and shout as he will, for such playing needs no supervision; he must stand thus and so, and move his arms and legs in unison with hundreds of other little arms and legs, thus and so. This is organized playing, running in a groove and supervised by an instructor who comes fresh from a mould."[50]

Children were allowed somewhat more freedom in the bounded, less naturalized playgrounds. A playground in a schoolyard or vacant lot was typically surrounded by fences that kept children from running in and out except through the gate. Even a playground in a park was a clearly demarcated space set apart from its surroundings, an outdoor "room" with sandboxes, slides, and swings for furniture. Whatever its location, the playground's atmosphere was in stark contrast to the slum street, where rowdy behavior, dirt, and brusque police intervention belied the equally interior appearance. Playgrounds were intended to combine the best aspects of interior and exterior space, while streets were thought to combine the worst. Children in the playgrounds were supposed to play harmoniously under the leadership of middle-class women, instead of in constant struggle against shopkeepers and policemen. In these bounded yet open environments, two or three women could supposedly keep an eye on hundreds of children, making it possible to maintain a balance between control and freedom without resorting to the military discipline of the park pageants.[51]

Degrees of discipline varied from one playground to another. Of the eleven playgrounds open in 1912, seven offered directed play, and four offered free play. Parker wanted more free play, which meant that no child was told to participate in a specific game or to use a specific piece of equipment. Children supposedly had the freedom, within limits, to follow their instinctual drives. "Directed play, like the schools, is from the outside in, while free play is from the inside out," Parker wrote in 1919.[52] Yet in practice, the distinction between free and directed play was blurred. Even when the play was "free," the children were often watched by supervisors, most of whom in the 1910s were employees of the school system. Like their counterparts in the boys' clubs, these supervisors sought to keep rough street behavior from contaminating the playground, and enforced a detailed list of rules. They instructed the younger children in the proper use of the slides and swings, prevented anyone from monopolizing equipment, kept order in the waiting lines, stopped boys from teasing girls, and broke up fights. The staff hoped not merely to keep order, but also to teach children to be considerate, to have "dis-

Playground at Pope Park. (Hartford Public Library)

cipline" and — once they were old enough — to join in the spirit of team play. The playgrounds had fixed seasons and hours posted on signs at the gates. Supervisors made the children leave at closing time just as if they were in a store or factory.[53]

The key was not to boss children around, Parker believed, but to provide them with spaces in which they would be eager to pursue wholesome, age-appropriate activities under the guidance of supervisors. "I believe in a segregation of play activities by sex and age periods with suitable and separate provisions for each," Parker wrote in 1915, expanding on the segregationist philosophy he had recently expressed in his redesign of the parks. It was not necessary in every case for each age group to have its own field or playground area, but the groups should be kept apart and occupied at different forms of play. Sharper distinctions were created by age limits at some of the playgrounds. The parks department also built some gender-specific facilities, such as an "outdoor gymnasium" for girls at Pope Park.[54] Through the 1910s and 1920s, the school system and the parks department encouraged the growth of children's athletic competitions, another form of directed play in open fields. The school system organized a public school athletic league in the early 1910s, with competitions between the schools leading up to a general field day in the parks in June. During the summers, the parks department organized games and races in which children from different playgrounds competed. The department also organized baseball leagues, which by 1928 totaled fourteen, with about a hundred teams.[55]

Parker struggled throughout the 1910s and 1920s to increase the number of playgrounds. He received at least some backing from residents of neighborhoods needing play space, but his strongest support came from the Juvenile Commission, a newly created municipal advisory panel that was his brainchild. The Civic Club had secured the legislature's approval for such a commission, which began its work in the spring of 1909 with a reformist membership including Parker, Dotha Bushnell Hillyer, Mary Graham Jones of the Hartford Social Settlement, and the Rev. Rockwell Harmon Potter of the First Congregational Church.[56]

Potter, the commission's chairman, had long been concerned about immoral street influences. During the Hartford Federation of Churches' 1907 antiprostitution crusade, he had preached on the same text that Bushnell had chosen for the chapter on play in *Christian Nurture*: "And the streets of the city shall be full of boys and girls playing in the streets thereof" (Zechariah 8:5). Bushnell had used the verse as the starting point for generalized ruminations on the divine sanction for play and had considered the street as a physical space only in one passage recommending that parents in large towns forbid their children to play there at night without supervision. Potter's sermon, on the other hand, was a convoluted discussion of the effects of the urban environment on children. He urged in one place that city dwellers "make the streets of the city clean for the play of developing life," but in others he equivocated about whether the word "street" should be interpreted literally or taken as a metaphor for public space in general. Potter complained that in the modern city there were not enough places for children to play, hinting that actual streets were not even to be considered for such use. Streets were, instead, places of temptation, where older children were lured into commercial amusements and other vicious pursuits—"Hence the critical and imperative duty of keeping watch and ward over the streets of a city in such wise that the play of these older children shall be safe." Vacation schools offered suitable play spaces for some younger boys and girls, and further development of the park system would help meet the needs of all children, Potter argued.[57]

In early 1912, while suffragists and clergy were fighting to keep the vice district closed, Potter's Juvenile Commission surveyed the need for playgrounds. They decided that, in addition to the six existing playgrounds, seventeen more were needed, a disproportionate number of these in the slums. George Parker argued that the city should provide a playground in every neighborhood with six hundred children under the age of twelve, and in fact, "The city should be prepared to furnish sandboxes and rope swings wherever a neighborhood of thirty or more children ask for them," but he did not specify what constituted a neighborhood. The Juvenile Commission insisted that the need was urgent: "There are about eleven thousand children under ten years old in need of these playgrounds," and only about three thousand were able to use existing playgrounds or other suitable spaces near their homes. The commission was unable to get all the playgrounds it wanted, but added several in the congested area east of Main Street, boosting the total number there to seven and the total in Hartford to eleven.[58]

Parker and the Juvenile Commission continued to try everything they could think of to increase the numbers of playgrounds. Examples were their attempt to lease land from private owners and their use of the Hucksters' Market as a part-time play area. But even with the addition of more school playgrounds in the late 1920s, the total number of playgrounds operated by the parks department and the school system rose only to twenty-seven by 1930.[59] To ease the crowded play conditions, the parks department worked to keep playgrounds open for longer periods of time. Playgrounds had been open only from 9 A.M. to 6 P.M. in 1912, but in 1914 the city opened a night playground at Colt Park that was lit until 10 P.M. Playgrounds were also kept open for more of the year. By 1919 their seasons, which had included only July and August, ran from early spring through the fall. An all-year playground for young children opened at Elizabeth Park in 1914 to supplement the coasting and skating activities popular with older children. By 1919 the city also had three indoor recreation halls. Supervised play was now possible year round and in any weather.[60]

Parker and his allies claimed to see great improvement in those children who chose to play in the playgrounds instead of the streets. The

children not only were learning to play properly but also were less inclined toward delinquency. "Playgrounds, if abundant and properly located, equipped and managed, make the neighborhood more orderly,
clean and better, " Parker wrote in 1912. "A policeman of the east side is
reported as having said, 'the playground has solved the juvenile problem
for us. We have none now, for the children are off the streets.'" This
appears to have been little more than wishful thinking. Parker admitted
later that there were still "thousands of children in Hartford growing up
without a better playground than the street which is the most dangerous
spot judged from every angle — alleys and streets do not turn out the best
product for citizenship, and the officer on the beat has agreed to that
declaration. Three or four city blocks are about the limit of travel for
children who are looking for a playground."[61]

That remained the problem. No matter how beneficial the influence
of playground space, it could not touch the lives of those children who
for whatever reason stayed away. W. J. Hamersley, the secretary of the
juvenile commission, admitted in 1914 that most play still took place in
the street. Boys appear to have been more likely than girls to prefer the
street over the playground. According to parks department attendance
statistics for 1915, significantly more girls than boys visited parks and
playgrounds. The department recorded 144,000 visits by girls aged 5 to
11, compared with 125,000 visits by boys of the same age. Visits by girls
from 12 to 16 years old outnumbered boys' visits 220,000 to 206,000. Only
in the next age category, 17 to 25 years, was the ratio reversed. The figures
do not separate playground from park attendance, but S. Wales Dixon,
Parker's recreation director, noted that the playgrounds drew mostly girls
and that many boys preferred more vigorous games than were played on
playgrounds.[62]

Parker continued to hope that more playgrounds and athletic fields
would end street play, but from 1909 through the early 1910s he considered trying to extend the influence of the playground into the street as
a temporary measure. Parker said in 1909 that the city should hire "a
neighborhood or street worker" to see that "street play might be made
more wholesome and advantageous until playgrounds are provided." He
explained: "If the street is to be the playground for the children, then
is it not logical to make the best use of it as a playground, until such
time as a better one is provided? A 'director of street play' may yet be the

title of some school official. A playground worker for the street would be a novelty, but yet might be useful. If the children have no playgrounds to go to, then let the playground supervisor go to where the children do play."[63]

Elaborating on this idea in 1914, Parker wrote that recreation workers should be given responsibility for play in the entire neighborhood, not just in the playground. Once again, he drew on familial imagery in describing recreation work: "The city should be divided into districts, each with a supervisor of play, to take care of the play . . . in that way we could keep track and be at the service of the people all the time. These people could be employed by the year, and by meeting people all the time, they would become the big brother or sister of that neighborhood. . . . Every recreation employee should have a uniform, so that they would be easily recognized, and they would be known as the Big Brother of the district."[64]

Parker never put this idea into practice. In 1916 he wrote that the department should not try to organize street play "until all protected spots have been equipped and found wanting." His assistant, Dixon, did at least some informal work with street play on the East Side, stopping boys from fighting and teaching them to play piggy instead. But park officials were reported in 1917 to believe that street play was too dangerous unless the street was blocked off, a step that they did not choose to take.[65]

The fact that Parker even considered supervising street play is a sign of how desperate he was to improve play conditions in Hartford. He had emphasized repeatedly that children needed better play environments more than they needed direction from adults. He had hoped that playgrounds, though supervised, would substitute for the freer play spaces of the countryside that had nurtured previous generations of American children. If he had hired street play directors — "Big Brothers," in his unfortunate words — he would have been tacitly accepting that supervision was more important than environment.

The Impact of the Automobile

Parker did not fully achieve his goals. He succeeded in creating new play spaces for Hartford's children but found that these supplemented rather than replaced street play. Even where playgrounds were available, many boys apparently preferred the greater freedom and excitement of the street. But the rapid growth of automobile traffic in the 1910s and 1920s made it far more difficult for play to coexist with adult activities. Ultimately, such traffic became another powerful force for getting children off the streets.

Parker never explicitly stated that he wanted children off the streets in order to ease traffic flow, and there is no reason to doubt his sincere concern for children's well-being. Nevertheless, he viewed the segregation of play as part of a larger differentiation of public space that would make Hartford function as an efficient system. In such a vision, nontransportation street uses were obstacles to be removed and put in their proper places. Segregating the uses of urban space would reduce conflict and benefit everyone, especially in a financial sense. Parker argued that the main goal of city planning was "to give every foot of . . . territory the greatest use and value to its present owner, its future owner and the city as a whole." As other observers would declare in more explicit terms, such utilitarian planning aimed at greater economic efficiency — a cause to which the games of street urchins clearly did not contribute. Parker and like-minded public figures successfully urged the city to improve the streets to speed the flow of traffic, and some of them worked to control pedestrian behavior for the same reason.[66]

These reforms further encouraged the rapid growth in automobile use during the 1910s and 1920s. Horse-drawn traffic had interrupted play less frequently, and horses usually had the sense not to trample the children in their path. "We would run into the dirt covered roads and there we would play our games. Horses and wagons would pass us carefully," recalled Rose Witkower, who grew up on the East Side in the 1890s and 1900s. But the faster and more numerous vehicles of the 1910s and 1920s diminished the advantages of street play by creating constant interruptions and much greater danger. On many streets, children's claim to the space was overwhelmed. Traffic casualties soared in these years, and the vast majority of the victims were on foot. Children — notably in the immigrant wards — were particularly likely to be killed or injured. Of the thirty-one people killed in automobile accidents in Hartford in 1925, fourteen were children. Another 301 children were injured.[67]

Playground advocates continued to couch their arguments in terms of the moral superiority of the playground over the street, but their rhetoric in the 1910s also emphasized the need to get the children away from the physical dangers traffic posed. A 1913 fundraising letter warned that children were playing in the streets "at the risk of their lives." A 1917 article describing the lack of playgrounds in some tenement districts warned that "the children have to play in streets under the horses' hoofs and auto trucks and there are frequent reminders of this in the accidents that happen."[68] The Automobile Club of Hartford, of which Parker was a member, was also firmly opposed to street play, which made driving slower and more stressful. The club's publications initially complained about children as annoying obstacles to traffic, but later spoke in terms of child welfare. A 1919 article in the club's official publication lamented:

> It is unfortunate that in some parts of the city it seems impossible to prevent children from playing in the streets. We realize that in some sections there is not any other place where they can play, but if they could only be taught to understand the danger of running out into the roadway, and that their safety depended upon their playing on the sidewalk, there would be fewer accidents. Only recently one of our members called at the club in regard to boys playing marbles in the streets. This is very dangerous as the boys are so intent on their play that they think of nothing else and are apt to run in front of a team or automobile.[69]

Besides harassing children who played in the street, Hartford police in the early 1910s began trying to educate them about the dangers of traffic. This work was the responsibility of the officers assigned to crossing-guard duty at the schools. The youngest children, who had not yet developed bad habits, proved the most tractable. In a 1913 article, the *Courant* reported that one traffic policeman "finds the very little children, the kindergarten tots, the easiest to look after. They have become educated so that they pause the minute they reach the curb and wait for the signal that it is safe for them to cross. The older children do not always mind as well. They are thinking only of fun and forget there is any such thing as danger." In the middle of Market Street, a moderately busy thoroughfare on the East Side, one boy stood blowing a feather in the air until the officer hustled him out of the way of oncoming cars and trucks. "The boy seemed to resent the interference," the *Courant* reported, evidently viewing his resistance humorously. As this boy was only beginning to learn, adults were taking away children's right to share certain streets.[70]

In a "Safety First" campaign in spring 1914, the Automobile Club of Hartford took traffic safety education directly into the schools, as other organizations were doing in cities nationwide. Members of the club gave speeches at schools throughout the city, telling students about the dangers of street play and urging them to cross only at the corners and only after looking both ways. The club printed placards — to be posted prominently in schools as well as in store windows — with photographs showing dangerous activities to avoid, for example, playing ball in the street. It also printed smaller instructional cards to distribute to every student.[71] By 1920 the state had undertaken similar efforts. The motor vehicle commissioner, Robbins B. Stoeckel, had written a textbook about the dangers of the road and arranged for it to be distributed to public schools throughout Connecticut.[72]

In 1924, Police Chief Garrett J. Farrell reported that police and school officials had worked out a plan for greater cooperation in reducing childhood traffic fatalities. Schoolchildren causing problems for police on crossing-guard duty would be reported to their school principal for disciplinary action. Police would speak in school assemblies about traffic safety and would show a film on the subject. School authorities would monitor children more closely as they left school to ensure that they stayed on the sidewalk until they reached the supervised street crossing. School officials would also meet with a representative of the National Safety Council to discuss ways to incorporate traffic safety training into the regular curriculum. "This plan is working out wonderfully well," Farrell wrote. "Not only is it helping to reduce accidents to the children of to-day, but it is believed that these lessons in safety will be so deeply instilled that they will continue to be effective when the boys and girls of to-day become the men and women of to-morrow." The Juvenile Commission joined the cause in late 1926 after considerable study. The commission undertook a yearlong safety campaign that included providing traffic safety posters and other educational materials to the schools, and broadcasting radio messages warning parents of the dangers of street play.[73]

State officials were cautiously claiming success by 1930. Child traffic fatalities had declined slightly in Connecticut in the late 1920s, reflecting a national trend, despite continuing increases in automobile use.

"Consistently better records are being made by children under 16 years of age in avoiding accidents," according to a report by the state Department of Motor Vehicles. "Child pedestrians, particularly, are increasingly becoming careful, the injury list having decreased steadily since 1927. . . . The safety education being taught in the schools is having effect." [74]

Traffic may have made children more cautious, but it did not force them off the streets. Instead, it had the effect of segregating street use, creating sharply defined borders in the geography of urban play. Though the dangers and frequent interruptions created by motor vehicles in the 1910s and 1920s made play in busy streets impossible, not every street was busy. In the side streets and alleys of Hartford's tenement districts children continued to play on the pavement as well as on the sidewalks. Morris Cohen, who grew up in a poor Jewish neighborhood north of downtown, recalled how traffic affected boys' games in the 1910s: "We used to play some baseball, we played some football, and we learned to play piggy in the streets, not on Windsor Street itself because it was too busy, but we would go to Portland Street, to Pequot Street, or North Street." [75]

———————

Reformers' efforts to shape children's play had evolved from an initial concern with individual sinfulness into an ideologically sophisticated campaign to change the use of urban space. From the boys' clubs through the Vacation Schools and finally the Parks Department, Hartford reformers had increasingly, though haltingly, turned away from overt attempts at moral reform. Instead, Mary Hall, Dotha Bushnell Hillyer, and George Parker placed greater faith in the influence of moral surroundings. All three hoped that play supervisors and improved play spaces could accomplish more—through the indirect influence described by Hillyer's father—than could heavy-handed tactics of the sort attempted by the earliest boys' clubs. Parker carried this trend the furthest. Though he lamented the decline in organic family life, he rejected it utterly as a model for reform. Segregation, not unity, was the answer. Drawing on new ideas of child development, Parker believed that children could be segregated with their peers into age-appropriate facilities and activities much as adults could be appropriately segregated by class and gender. These new play experiences would make unnecessary the earlier methods of control: striving toward the impossible goal of genteel parlor behavior or imposing the military discipline of directed gymnastics and pageantry. In a new environment of scientific nurture safely removed from the street, Parker hoped, the boys would happily let play experts help them meet their instinctual needs.

Parker failed, however, to isolate children in their own special environments. The new segregated play spaces supplemented but did not replace children's play in the street, and not even the murderous force of the automobile was enough to dislodge them. Yet while the reformers fell short of fully achieving their goals, by the end of the 1920s, the geography of urban play had been transformed. Boys no longer treated the city streets in general as their playground but usually resorted to certain selected spaces — quiet side streets and alleyways away from adult traffic, the Goodwill Club, playgrounds, and parks. The play movement in Hartford, like the campaign against the newsgirls, contributed to a partial separation of children's activities from adults' use of the streets.

7

Expressmen and Peddlers

Much to the annoyance of some members of the middle class, street peddling was inescapable throughout the entire city of Hartford in the 1890s. A woman emerging from the post office after mailing a letter would make her way past newsies, bootblacks, and a man sharpening knives. As she continued west through City Hall Square, she would pass a row of expressmen waiting to deliver packages, and might have to endure their catcalls. Once she got home, she might find the quiet of her neighborhood broken by the heavily accented cries of a peddler.[1] To the peddlers, expressmen, street musicians, bootblacks, and newsboys, the streets were a marketplace that gave them opportunities to climb out of poverty. Middle-class reformers and city officials, however, saw street trades as nuisances to be regulated, confined, or suppressed. Changes in consumer habits were helping them, and by the late 1920s the entrepreneurial chaos of the street had been brought under control. Just as newsies had been restricted and regulated, expressmen had been banished from the streets, while produce peddlers had been pushed into the immigrant East Side.

In their fight against adult-dominated street trades, reformers and city officials raised aesthetic objections and complained that such activities interfered with traffic. Though they made similar complaints about both expressmen and peddlers, they achieved different results. Expressmen — who delivered bulky packages, large merchandise and other items — stoutly resisted efforts to ban them from soliciting business on downtown streets, but succumbed when business declined. Produce peddlers were ultimately confined to the East Side slum as a result of official harassment, the construction of an off-street marketplace, and a change in shopping habits. They were able to stay in business there until the 1950s, but they served a dwindling clientele. The segregation of street peddling into a small area of the city left outlying streets somewhat more orderly and more dominated by vehicular traffic. More important, though, was its reinforcement of the growing differentiation of public space.

Expressmen's Last Stand

Expressmen performed an essential service in late nineteenth-century American cities. In addition to such major national companies as Wells Fargo, Adams, and Railway Express, which offered intercity transport of packages and money, numerous smaller express companies provided local delivery. Expressmen delivered not only packages but also large items — furniture, iceboxes, bicycles, pianos — which had been purchased in downtown stores or ordered by mail and which clearly could not be taken home on the streetcar. The expressman would pick up the item at the store, the railroad station, or any other location, bring it to the customer's back door, and put it in its proper place inside the home.[2]

In late nineteenth-century Hartford, most expressmen waited for business at an officially designated stand they shared with hackmen at City Hall Square, not far from the post office. The expressmen would stand with their long wagons backed up to the curb on the State Street and Main Street sides of city hall, horses facing into the street. In 1886 sixteen expressmen owned a single wagon and team each, and nine others owned two or more teams and hired their drivers. In the 1890s the expressmen moved south from State Street to the Central Row side of the square to make more room for the trolley. After that, hacks occupied the space on Main Street, while express wagons stood on Central Row.[3]

View of City Hall Square, ca. 1900. The express wagons, on Central Row at right, are backed up to the south side of the square. Hack drivers are at the left, on Main Street. Expressmen were accused of blocking traffic and using offensive language. (*The City of Hartford and Vicinity*)

Initial complaints about expressmen and hackmen focused on problems of aesthetics and decorum. "The walk across Main Street from the Asylum Street corner, which is the main approach to the post office [behind city hall], and much traveled, is most of the time hemmed in by standing carriages, and travel, especially for ladies, made exceedingly unpleasant," the police commissioners reported in 1889. Businessmen also raised complaints about "hack and expressmen lounging about" at the smaller stand near the railroad station on Union Place.[4]

City officials' handling of a separate dispute in 1898, in which they banished lunch wagons from the streets, showed that they could impose even the harshest of restrictions. The enclosed wooden lunch wagons — basically kitchens on wheels — had been parked on downtown streets, especially at night, when most restaurants were closed. People who worked late or were downtown for pleasure could buy hot dogs, sandwiches, or coffee there instead of eating in a saloon or a restaurant. As the number of lunch wagons increased rapidly in the mid-1890s, the few restaurants open at night complained of unfair competition.

The issue became a matter of public dispute in 1897, when a Common Council subcommittee urged that the city stop licensing lunch wagons on the grounds that they obstructed traffic. Another group of councilmen investigated the matter and rejected the argument that the wagons obstructed traffic, noting that most of the wagons were on well-lit streets at night after traffic had subsided: "We are of the opinion that they cause much less obstruction than do some other private enterprises regularly allowed on the streets, and that the question of obstruction would not now be raised but for the complaint of keepers of regular restaurants." The councilmen agreed with the restaurateurs that the keepers of lunch wagons had an unfair advantage because they did not pay taxes, but concluded that the city could not forbid night lunch wagons while allowing hacks and express wagons to park on City Hall Square during the middle of the day.[5]

After hearing protests from the Board of Street Commissioners, the council secured an opinion from the city attorney that the city lacked the power to license any obstructions to public travel. The rights of traffic took priority over the interests of street trades. The council called a halt to licensing lunch wagons and announced that all existing licenses would be revoked on April 1, 1898. One councilman argued that other New England cities had already succeeded in ridding their streets of lunch wagons and that Hartford should do the same. The owners of lunch wagons who remained in business did so only by parking on privately owned vacant lots. They eventually removed the wheels and turned the wagons into small shacks selling carry-out food.[6]

The expressmen, therefore, were on shaky ground by the late 1890s. Councilmen had drawn parallels between express wagons and lunch wagons and had decided that lunch wagons had no right to street space. The expressmen's own troubles began in autumn 1901, when local businessmen and city hall employees petitioned the Common Council to move the hackmen and expressmen to a new stand away from City Hall Square. The hackmen and expressmen fought back by submitting a counterpetition asking that they be allowed to stay. The counterpetition displayed the influential signature of the president of Aetna Life Insurance, former mayor Morgan G. Bulkeley, followed by those of dozens of more obscure people, including downtown office workers who were probably the hackmen's customers.[7]

But those who favored moving the express stand quickly dominated the debate, while the expressmen's defenders fell silent. The reasons for moving the stand — as presented in newspaper articles, in letters to the editor, and at a public hearing — included concerns about traffic flow, safety, aesthetics, decorum, and proper urban atmosphere. According to one letter writer:

> The hacks occupied about two thirds of the street [Main Street] from the curb line to the street railway track, leaving a narrow channel for teams, and making a very dangerous place for people to alight from the trolley cars, often in front of a fractious horse. Many narrow escapes from being run over have occurred there. The street at this place should be free of obstructions, as it is one of the most congested places on Main Street. Then the effluvia arising from so many horses standing all day and part of the night around City Hall, especially since the streets were asphalted, constitutes a nuisance that should be abated. The view of the City Hall would be greatly improved by the removal of the hacks and express wagons, as at present it reminds one of an overgrown village, where the farmers drive in and hitch their horses to a post.

Another writer objected to the removal of the hacks, which he said performed a valuable public service, but agreed that the expressmen should be forced out. The better expressmen already had offices to which customers could telephone to request express service, argued this writer, so there was no need for a stand on a public street.[8]

Neither the expressmen nor the hackmen had any legal or moral right to use downtown streets as stables, argued one city official anonymously. He suggested that they be dispersed to their own neighborhoods or to several locations around the edge of the downtown — or that they be forced off the streets altogether.[9] Another enemy of the expressmen, Postmaster Edward B. Bennett, argued that Central Row was so badly choked with express wagons that it was difficult to carry mail to and from the post office. Bennett added that the men waiting at the express stands used foul language that offended the female clerks at the post office. Other speakers told of the stench rising from the stand and of the profanity used by quarreling expressmen. One man called the stand a moral nuisance. "I do protest against the stands, on the ground of good citizenship, against the blasphemy and obscenity on the Square," he said. "I have been insulted. Ladies have been insulted." [10]

After submitting their initial petition, the hackmen and expressmen found that they could not count on much support from members of Hartford's middle class. That job fell on their own shoulders and those of their spokesman, the workingmen's advocate John F. Gunshanan, who had once been an expressman himself. Gunshanan and the expressmen dismissed complaints about their behavior, insisting that any problem could be solved by stricter enforcement of city ordinances against profanity. They argued that the centrally located stand was a valuable public convenience and that it had been a Hartford tradition for seventy-five years. They acknowledged that some express companies already had telephones for dispatching expressmen, but they insisted that the stand was still needed because some self-employed expressmen could not afford telephones. They also said that the smell was not so bad as some people claimed. Without solid middle-class support for the expressmen, however, the issue turned into a conflict between affluent defenders of public order and workingmen who were branded as offensive louts. Predictably, the Board of Street Commissioners ordered the express wagons and hacks to vacate the square by May 1, 1902. [11]

May Day, however, found the expressmen and hackmen stubbornly in their usual place. They ignored orders from the superintendent of streets that they move and tried once again to plead their case before the mayor. On May 3, after a police officer ordered them to leave immediately or face arrest, they all pulled away except for one expressman, who parked on the opposite side of Central Row, and one hackman, Herbert W. Arnold, who defiantly kept his carriage backed up to the Main Street curb as usual. Arnold was arrested and released; he returned to the curb along with several other hackmen and expressmen. [12]

City officials wavered and ultimately gave in. Mayor Ignatius A. Sullivan, a newly elected Democrat with strong ties to organized labor, refused to revoke the hackmen's licenses. He said he hoped some way could be found for them to stay, and he questioned whether they were really a nuisance. According to the *Hartford Courant*, Sullivan "thought they were entitled to as much consideration as one of the manufacturing interests." Despite his support for the hackmen, though, Sullivan did not defend the expressmen. There was less public sympathy for the expressmen, who had a reputation for misbehavior. The *Courant* reported the "drunken staggerings" of one expressman and stated, "Frequently when 'hack stand' is referred to as a nuisance, it is not hack stand but express stand that is meant." Expressmen had acknowledged in the past that the rudeness of a few had given them all a bad public image, but they did little to improve their reputation during this dispute. An expressman named Joseph Carlin disrupted a public hearing before the street board by angrily arguing with the board president. Carlin insisted, "We have as good a right to use the streets of this city as any man, and as for me, I am not going to sell my horses and wagons and harnesses just because this board says we must get out." He ended by grabbing his hat and stalking out of the hearing, declaring that the president was "a damned fool and a damned nuisance." The hackmen were better behaved but equally defiant, threatening that if they were not allowed to park they would simply circle around and around City Hall Square, creating traffic jams, while waiting for fares. The city attorney acknowledged several technicalities that left the street board on shaky legal ground if it chose to pursue the matter. The board finally backed down with no word of explanation and let both the hacks and the express wagons stay at City Hall Square.[13]

This success made the expressmen more cooperative when the issue reemerged a few years later. They agreed to a compromise proposed in 1906 by Councilman Charles A. Goodwin, the president of the Municipal Art Society, that would banish express wagons but not hacks. The expressmen agreed to move to a new stand if the Common Council would raise the rates they could charge customers. In the petition they submitted jointly with the City Beautiful advocates, the expressmen declared that they "fully realize[d] the unsuitable nature of the present stand." Yet the compromise solution was frustrated by city officials' inability to find a satisfactory new site for an express stand. Major downtown business interests—including the Hartford Fire Insurance Company, the Charter Oak National Bank, the National Fire Insurance Co., G. F. Heublein and Bro. distillers, the Case, Lockwood and Brainard publishing house, and the Allyn House hotel—united in opposing an express stand proposed for Trumbull Street for fear that it would bring "annoyance and unsanitary conditions." Working-class residents of

Village and Windsor streets north of the downtown succeeded in keeping the express stand out of their own neighborhood by protesting vigorously against the idea at a public hearing.[14]

The deadlock was broken a few years later by a peremptory order from Mayor Edward L. Smith, also a Democrat, but not one so closely wedded to working-class interests as Sullivan had been. Smith had a lawyerly zeal for public order that led him to close the red-light district, and he had come into office in 1910 promising to ease downtown traffic jams. "The growth of the city, the congestion of traffic about the center, and the general use of the automobile have produced a problem that requires much ingenuity in solving to make the solution fair to everyone," he said in his first speech to the Common Council. During Smith's two-year term, the city adopted new traffic rules that included limiting the length of time a vehicle could park and making State Street the first one-way street in Hartford. According to a later account, Smith acted on his own in having the police clear the expressmen from Central Row. The expressmen were banished by his order to the sole remaining stand, on Union Place at the far western edge of the downtown. In contrast to their behavior in 1901–02, the expressmen did not resist. The action left little or no trace in city records and gained little attention from the press.[15]

Expressmen who solicited business on the streets were becoming a marginal part of city life for reasons that went far beyond Hartford politics. Their banishment from City Hall Square came at a time when ever-increasing numbers of middle-class people could order express service by telephone or could transport items across town by private automobile. To make matters worse, the express business throughout the country soon suffered a devastating blow from the federal government. Congress created a national parcel-post system that started operation in 1913, and in that same year authorized the purchase of motor vehicles to deliver packages cheaply and efficiently. As a result, the express business suddenly lost most of its profitability.[16]

The expressmen were in a very weak position by autumn 1915, when property owners and merchants on Union Place petitioned the city to get rid of the "nuisance" posed by the express stand near the train station there. Union Place, once the site of old tenement houses, was developing into a commercial street with large new buildings. The merchants saw the crowd of loitering expressmen and their horses as an unsightly and unsanitary obstacle to business. The Common Council rejected the request, noting that the expressmen had no other stand. The property owners then took their complaints to court and had the good fortune of finding a sympathetic listener in Judge Edward L. Smith, the very man who had forced the expressmen out of City Hall Square. This time Smith ruled that the city had no power to license an obstacle to traffic and ordered the twelve remaining expressmen away from Union Place, closing down the last express stand in the city. Again the expressmen left without a fuss. Though it was Smith's injunction that closed the express stand, wrote the *Courant*, "Modern conveniences have in many ways changed conditions from the days when the express . . . stands were regarded as a necessary part of municipal service." The newspaper favored the change but added wistfully, "Even though there may be an improvement in Union Place by the removal of the expressmen, there will be a sort of lonesomeness for a time at least, because of their absence." [17]

The Growth and Decay of Produce Peddling

Produce peddlers fared better than expressmen, but not by much. Like expressmen, peddlers came under fire for being disruptive and experienced various official attempts to suppress or relocate them. Also like expressmen, they saw their business decline because of changes that could not be blamed on city officials or reformers. Yet by holding onto a clientele in the slums, they managed to survive even when banished to a single marginal street.

Storekeepers dominated the sale of groceries in Hartford in the 1870s and 1880s despite competition from a few peddlers who hawked fresh meat and produce in a dilapidated market house and from farmers who sold turkeys on the street before holidays.[18] The grocers seem to have accepted this competition without much complaint, but they watched with alarm as dozens of additional "transient traders" began peddling produce on streets throughout the city in the 1870s and 1880s. The grocers complained repeatedly through the late nineteenth century about the peddlers' supposed uncleanliness and dishonesty, but their real objection seems to have been that the peddlers were able to undersell storekeepers, minimizing overhead by transacting business in public space rather than in private shops. Many peddlers were serving a specialized

State House Square (later City Hall Square) being used as a poultry market on the day before Thanksgiving. (*Scribner's Monthly*, November 1876)

clientele made up of those poor enough to be willing to save money by eating low-quality food. Though this clientele might not be the most desirable one in the grocer's eye, a matter of principle was at stake. Merchants were not willing to concede even this clientele, especially as the numbers of peddlers continued to climb.[19]

Some peddlers who could afford wagons served the more prosperous people who were settling in semisuburban residential areas. The peddlers continued to do business in these outlying neighborhoods well into the twentieth century. One man who grew up on Asylum Hill recalled a variety of street trades even in that prestigious neighborhood in the years before World War I. "Each summer a German band worked its way down the street stopping periodically to pass the hat for coppers. Similarly, we could expect visits from the organ grinder with his monkey, a hurdy-gurdy, the ragman calling out 'Cash paid for rags,' the eggman, vegetable peddlers and so on."[20] Many vegetable peddlers in the 1910s started their day by hawking the best produce in their wagons in Hartford's wealthier residential neighborhoods, typically following a daily route. They returned to the immigrant slums later in the day to sell off what was left at lower prices.[21]

But most produce peddlers were concentrated in poorer neighborhoods, particularly the East Side, where immigrants were arriving by the thousands in the late nineteenth century. Their reason for working there was not that language barriers forced them to sell to fellow immigrants. Although some of the Jewish and Italian peddlers who dominated the business in the early twentieth century might have preferred to communicate with customers who shared their language, many peddlers learned English or managed to trade with English speakers without knowing the language well. Many Jewish peddlers even traveled out of Hartford to sell dry goods or notions to farming families, who were highly unlikely to speak Yiddish.[22]

A more important reason for selling on the East Side was that it required a smaller capital investment for peddlers, who usually started their business on a shoestring. A peddler could build the pushcart himself or buy it cheaply, but could not cover as large an area as he could have with a horse-drawn wagon.[23] The daily routine of a pushcart peddler was grueling enough when limited to the East Side; few felt inclined to add to their exertions by pushing their unwieldy carts to distant streets. Typically a Jewish or Italian pushcart peddler in the 1910s and 1920s would start work before dawn not far from his East Side apartment, buying his produce after much haggling at the farmers' market on Connecticut Boulevard and the wholesale merchants' establishments on Allyn Street. One Italian immigrant recalled how his father would "get up at 4 o'clock in the morning and buy his produce—his vegetables and fruit and so forth—and bring them back with him and then travel through the east side of Hartford to sell them. And he might have to make one or two trips in the course of the day, pushing that [pushcart] up the hill, the Morgan Street hill, up around the east side, come back, load up again and do it all over again. And that would take him to maybe 11 o'clock at night."[24]

Official harassment gradually became another factor in the concentration of peddling on the East Side in the decades around the turn of the twentieth century. Some members of the middle class had little patience with the cries of vendors hawking their wares in residential streets. Peddlers traveling down the street had to advertise their presence somehow, either by yelling or by knocking on doors, both of which annoyed some people. In 1888 the Common Council passed an ordinance banning peddlers from announcing their presence by the use of any bell, gong, horn, or other noisemaker, or by yelling too loudly. In 1894 the council considered an even more restrictive measure, forbidding peddlers to step onto private property to offer their wares at the door. The *Hartford Times* supported the measure, arguing that "relief . . . from the peddling nuisance would be hailed with gratitude by the housekeepers of Hartford, especially those who live more or less remote from the center of the city." But this time the council backed down in the face of opposition from peddlers. As one councilman observed, "The peddlers of small fruit, etc., . . . are in most cases doing what they can in a small way to obtain support for themselves and their families. Without the right to go upon private premises in a proper manner their means of livelihood would be taken away."[25]

Despite the passage of the 1888 noise ordinance, peddlers continued to cry their wares loudly. According to a 1913 *Courant* article, Hartford residents were often rudely awakened in the morning "by the noisy solo of a leather-lunged peddler driving his decrepit horse down the avenue, and, in a voice loud enough to be heard in Newington, Windsor, or Glastonbury, inviting, entreating, even demanding that you buy vegetables, or ice, or sell him some rags." Particularly annoying, according to the paper, was the fact that the loud cries were often indistinct or heavily accented. "In nine cases out of ten—almost—it is impossible for the woman of the house to tell what the peddler is shouting. Generally it runs something like this: 'Rade-RUMPH, VerenYAH, nice walderMEPS, berararah!'" As this mockery suggests, the hostility of homeowners toward peddlers may have been influenced by a dislike of immigrant intrusion into Yankee neighborhoods.[26]

By crying their wares in outlying residential neighborhoods, peddlers made themselves vulnerable to arrest whenever neighbors chose to complain.[27] Among those complaining were members of the Municipal Art Society, the elite organization that aimed to make Hartford more attractive. "The cries of vendors in the street, and the use of bells, gongs, and whistles to attract attention to one's wares, may help the vendor a little, but are a nuisance to the community and should be suppressed," the chairman of the group's Special Committee on the Suppression of Unnecessary Noises reported in 1908. "Cities . . . where there is a perpetual

carnival of racket are undesirable places of residence for decent people."
It is uncertain whether the Municipal Art Society's complaints had any
effect, but residents of the city's South End were equally annoyed and
persuaded the police to arrest several noisy street vendors in spring 1909.
In response, two hundred Jewish peddlers held a mass meeting that June
to organize the Hebrew Peddlers' Association. In hope of having the law
overturned, the association agreed to hire a lawyer to defend any member
arrested for crying his wares. The law stayed on the books, and peddlers
continued to be arrested occasionally, but the association survived into
the 1930s as a mutual benefit society and as a political organization fighting such dangers as high license fees and tougher noise ordinances.[28] In
addition to problems with the noise ordinance, peddlers occasionally
ran into trouble on licensing technicalities, and Jewish street traders who
worked in Christian neighborhoods on Sundays risked being reported for
violating blue laws.[29]

City officials never actually prohibited peddlers from making retail
sales in outlying neighborhoods, but in 1912 they did force wholesale
trading off the street and into a newly created "Hucksters' Market" on the
East Side, where it remained through the 1920s. In the years before the
market's opening, farmers from the countryside around Hartford would
drive their wagons into the city every summer morning around 5 A.M.,
backing up against the curb on Main Street between Morgan and
Temple streets on the northern edge of downtown. For the next two hours
or so, farmers would sell their produce to the street peddlers who met
them there. Part of the street would be blocked during this time by as
many as 150 wagons, and the sidewalk would be packed with marketing
activity, forcing pedestrians into the roadway. When the crowd dispersed
after 7:30, the sidewalk and street would be left strewn with refuse. Some
local shopkeepers turned the situation to their advantage and did a brisk
business selling breakfasts and drinks to the men. Other merchants and
property owners considered the trading a nuisance and petitioned the
city in 1908 to put an end to it.[30]

The city finally responded by opening the Hucksters' Market on land
that had been cleared during a recent bridge construction project, on
Connecticut Boulevard between Kilbourn and Morgan streets. The marketplace was nothing more than an empty, sand-covered lot, with some
stands available for rental by farmers and feed troughs and water barrels

Selling chickens on Charles Street, ca. 1910. Health officials and middle-class consumers considered such practices offensively dirty. (The Connecticut Historical Society, Hartford)

for horses. As city officials had decided to ban wholesale marketing in the street, on opening day (July 22, 1912) police were stationed at the old marketing place to direct farmers and peddlers to the new market. The Hucksters' Market proved to be too small for the crowd, which spilled out into the East Side streets, but the city immediately began preparing an expansion project, completing it that autumn. By 1920 the number of farmers selling at the market every day averaged three hundred. The market later moved to a larger location, also on the East Side, and remained in business at least through 1930.[31]

The Hucksters' Market also served some limited retail purposes. In addition to the handful of bargain hunters who rose early to meet the farmers each day, many East Side residents came to the Charles Street side of the market on Thursdays to buy eggs and live chickens. Actually, the hen market had been held on Charles Street long before the Hucksters' Market opened, and it appears to have been changed very little by

Kosher chicken butcher, Charles Street, 1910. (The Connecticut Historical Society, Hartford)

being shifted from the street to the marketplace. As before, Jewish and Italian women would gather to inspect the chickens and bargain with the farmers and peddlers, and rabbis would be on hand to perform the ritual slaughter of the birds.[32]

Peddlers accepted the Hucksters' Market only grudgingly. Now that the city forbade street purchases, produce peddlers were denied their earlier right to buy from farmers before they reached the market. Peddlers complained that by prohibiting the practice of "forestalling," the city allowed farmers to command higher prices. Chicken peddlers objected to being charged for the use of stands on the Charles Street side of the market. "We do not derive any benefit from said stand, it being merely a convenience, and having been established with the idea and purpose of providing a place for the transaction of business by peddlers so that they would not be widely scattered in any other part of the city," members of the Hebrew Peddlers' Association insisted in a 1913 petition. Farmers also had to bear the new expense of renting stalls. Though the peddlers claimed the farmers benefited from the Hucksters' Market, at least one farmer wrote to the newspaper to disagree. He complained about being banished to "an out of the way place . . . in the rear of a row of dilapidated buildings," where his sales suffered. The unenthusiastic reaction of the people who traded at the Hucksters' Market underscores the fact that the market was created not to please them but to satisfy the complaints of Main Street property owners. Significantly, the city treated the wholesale produce dealers on Allyn Street much more indulgently than it treated the farmers. These taxpaying property owners were allowed to continue using the sidewalks in front of their businesses for marketing fruit and vegetables to peddlers — even though the activity blocked traffic and inconvenienced pedestrians. Traffic police interfered occasionally by harassing the peddlers who made purchases there, but usually they ignored the situation.[33]

After the successful establishment of the Hucksters' Market, the city began planning an indoor "Public Municipal Market" that would be a center for retail grocery sales, a modern version of the old Market House that had closed in the 1880s. The Common Council had been toying with the idea at least since 1906, but had never committed itself. Starting in 1912, working-class and consumer organizations began pressing for action. The council received letters and petitions from such diverse groups as the Hartford Central Labor Union, the Housewives' League, the Hartford Motherhood Club, and the Socialist Party.[34] From the way it was described by its advocates, the indoor market should have threatened the livelihoods of the food dealers who supplied Hartford's working class, including the pushcart peddlers. Supporters of the market claimed that it would help hold down food prices by "getting rid of the middleman" and allowing food producers to trade directly with consumers. Yet only the beef dealers opposed the market proposal, and other food dealers sent word that they did not see it as a threat. The Republican mayor Louis R. Cheney and other city officials supported the idea, holding a public referendum on the matter in 1914 at which voters decisively approved a proposal to spend $100,000 to build the market.[35]

Despite the vote, the project stalled out for the next several years. In 1917 another Republican mayor, Frank A. Hagarty, questioned whether the market should be built at all, noting that few shoppers went to the early-morning Hucksters' Market even though there was nothing to prevent them from doing so. Hagarty suggested as an alternative that the city designate "sections of certain streets little used for traffic, so that curb markets might be conducted on those streets from about six to eight or nine A.M. daily." The city quickly established one open-air curb market at Ward and Affleck streets in the Frog Hollow neighborhood and another at Bellevue and Pavilion streets, in a densely developed North End neighborhood. Hagarty was a strong advocate of easing traffic flow and thus an unlikely supporter of farmers' markets in the streets, but the two sites chosen were on side streets, not major arteries, and the markets were open only in the early morning. Furthermore, they were a cheap way for Hagarty to sidestep the demands for an indoor market that had been strengthened by high wartime food prices. It was obvious from the beginning that the curb markets were not going to amount to much. On the first day the two markets drew one vendor each, neither of whom was a farmer. The markets survived into 1918 and probably into 1919, but, like wartime markets in other New England cities, appear to have been a short-lived phenomenon.[36]

Representatives of Hartford's working class continued to call for the construction of an indoor public market. At a public hearing on the matter in January 1919, union leaders strongly supported a proposal to build the market over the Park River between Bushnell Park and Main Street, despite opposition from the Municipal Art Society and downtown business interests. The market issue, coinciding as it did with a period of nationwide labor unrest, was charged with class conflict. Union representatives infuriated their opponents by suggesting that they were wealthy aesthetes with no sympathy for the workingman. James T. Manee, president of the Central Labor Union, argued,

> These men who are getting excited over the beauties of the Hog river don't mow their own lawns. I don't care about the aesthetics of Hartford—I want a public market. . . . The voters have been put off time and time again and now we insist on having this market. . . . The organization I represent is interested in getting a reduction in the cost of food. I used to buy crackers for five cents a pack and now they're twelve cents a pack. If the trust says boost eggs four cents a crate the dealer says mark them up four cents a dozen. We're tired of dilly dallying. Hagarty gave us enough of that.

Opponents of the market project reacted angrily. "They have brought in that hateful word 'class!'" Dr. John J. McCook said of the union leaders.

"Men with the mud of other places not yet dry on their shoes have made insinuations about some of us who have lived here more years than they have lived under the sun."[37]

The council rejected the proposal for building the market over the Park River, even though it would have doubled as a parking garage for downtown shoppers. But an alternative plan to build the market on Connecticut Boulevard on the East Side, near the Hucksters' Market, met with the council's approval. Construction began in summer 1919. The new Public Market, complete with refrigerated showcases, opened for business on August 17, 1920, with most of the forty-two stalls rented.[38]

The Public Market was a failure. There were hardly any poor or working-class shoppers to be seen. Philip A. Mason, superintendent of public buildings, reported in December 1921,

> The class of patronage was very different from what had been expected. A very small proportion of the buying has been done by the people of the east side, they apparently preferring to trade with the numerous small stores in that section where credit could be obtained and with which they were familiar. The greatest proportion of patronage has come from persons operating automobiles, and had it not been for this trade the market could not have existed. It is also worthy of note that the type or class of people who were apparently most interested in the establishment of the market, and to whom it would have been natural to look for support, has patronized it only to a negligible extent.

Many of the stalls were vacant, and the market was losing money.[39]

Though Mason did not mention it, the marketmen were not what had been originally expected either. From the time that the Public Market opened, it was obvious that it would fail to encourage direct trade between producer and consumer. The stalls were rented to middlemen, not to farmers. For example, greengrocers in the Public Market bought their produce at wholesale prices in the Hucksters' Market and sold it at retail prices. The marketmen's main advantage over grocers in private shops was merely lower overhead, an advantage that was not enough to keep them in business. Only eight marketmen were still renting stalls in January 1922, when city officials decided to close the market. The remaining marketmen had to vacate by February 1, less than eighteen months after the market had opened, and the building was turned into a school.[40] "Those who shouted loudest for the market have not patronized it sufficiently to keep the stall holders in business," explained the *Hartford Times*, alluding to the city's working class.[41] The Public Market posed no threat to the established middlemen who served Hartford's East Side; working-class neighbors continued to trade with the familiar mom and pop grocers who offered credit or with peddlers who sold cheap produce in the streets without bearing even the cost of a stall rental.

Although the Public Market was an insignificant part of Hartford's grocery trade, the reasons for its failure are worth considering more closely. Its surprising reliance on prosperous shoppers from distant neighborhoods, and its failure to attract the local working class, reflected the fact that grocery shopping habits in American cities were suddenly dividing along class lines. Until the early twentieth century, middle-class housewives and servants would shop frequently at grocery stores, meat markets, and bakeries, and would also buy from peddlers in their neighborhoods. When shopping at a store, they would buy food in quantities that could be carried easily or would arrange to have larger orders delivered.[42] By the 1920s, however, middle-class shopping habits were changing. More and more middle-class people were buying automobiles and using them for grocery shopping trips. Automobile owners now found it easy and economical to buy many grocery items at a time, particularly at the "cash-and-carry" stores that were spreading rapidly. These stores offered lower prices but did not provide credit or delivery, discouraging large purchases by those with limited money and without automobiles. By the mid-1920s, affluent households were also beginning to buy refrigerators, which further encouraged large purchases by allowing storage of larger amounts of perishable food.[43]

Working-class people, who often lacked refrigeration or adequate storage space in their tenements, continued to shop every day. They usually chose stores in the immediate neighborhood that both served other members of their ethnic group and offered credit. Another incentive for daily shopping was that stores in ethnic and working-class neighborhoods doubled as social centers, places where women would go to exchange gossip or news. Grocers in working-class neighborhoods were slower to follow the trend toward brand-name, packaged products, which were changing the appearance of grocery stores for the middle class. Working-class grocery stores continued to sell many of their goods in bulk even into the 1920s. At the customer's direction, the grocer would scoop flour, tea, coffee, and sugar out of bins; pull pickles from barrels; slice cheese or butter from larger hunks; scoop beans, peas, and rice out of burlap sacks; or grab handfuls of crackers and cookies from display cases.[44]

In Hartford as elsewhere, the big, upscale groceries boasted in advertisements about refrigerated display cases and scrupulous cleanliness, while small, working-class grocers were lectured by health inspectors about their supposedly filthy ways of handling unpackaged food. The food inspector, hired in 1907, warned stores throughout the city to stop displaying vegetables, fruit, candy, and cakes outdoors, and to keep the interiors of the shops cleaner. Smaller merchants, particularly on the East Side, had been the ones most notorious for practices like wrapping meat in newspapers, and they remained the dirtiest. "The small stores give us the most trouble and need considerable supervision," the inspector reported in 1911. True, they were changing: "They show a great improvement, noticeably in the matter of clean showcases and milk and butter boxes, as well as clean floors." Nevertheless, outdoor displays of food remained common through the 1920s. The fear of disease had inspired an attempt at cleaning up, but as in the campaigns against unsanitary streets and tenements, and against prostitution, the reformers fell short of purifying the entire city.[45]

As the grocery trade divided more clearly along class lines, street peddlers fell on the working-class side. Peddlers were much slower than grocers to adopt middle-class standards of cleanliness, which were more difficult to maintain on the streets anyway. For example, all Hartford grocers were forbidden in 1908 to ladle milk from large cans into containers brought by customers. The practice continued only among street peddlers, who added to the danger of contamination by periodically pouring the milk from can to can in order to mix up the cream, even on days when dry winds blew dust through the streets. The more numerous produce peddlers were also criticized for uncleanliness by city officials. "The push-cart vendors seem to give the greatest trouble, especially in the hot weather," reported the food inspector in 1910. "They will buy and sell anything, no matter how badly decayed, and it is quite a job to watch them, as they move constantly from place to place." The worst offenders were reportedly those known as "undertakers," who would buy rotting produce from grocers at the end of each day and sell it the next morning on the streets.[46] At a time when grocery stores for the middle class were beginning to move their food displays off the streets, store food in coolers, and adopt ever higher standards of cleanliness, the street peddler appeared dirtier and more old-fashioned in contrast.

Whether primarily because of police harassment or a smaller clientele in middle-class neighborhoods, produce peddlers in the late 1910s and early 1920s were concentrating more and more on fixed locations in the East Side slum. Many peddlers continued to follow daily rounds in more distant working-class neighborhoods into the 1920s, and a considerable part of the population continued to depend on them for their food.[47] Increasingly, though, produce peddling focused on the curbside markets that were growing on Front and Windsor streets, both east of Main. Windsor Street was in a predominantly Jewish neighborhood north of downtown, while Front Street, dominated by Italians, was the main commercial street of the East Side. By 1920, as a photograph of Front Street shows, it had become an outdoor market, with pushcarts lining the curb.[48] Although peddlers had for years been selling vegetables at curbside only after completing their daily rounds, in the 1920s they were increasingly skipping the rounds in order to secure good spots on the two favored streets. According to Morris Davidson, who helped his father sell fruit and vegetables in the period around 1920, "It seemed customary for [Jewish] peddlers to dispense their wares, in the early morning of each day on Windsor Street, then adjourn for evening business to Front Street." Windsor Street was lined for several blocks on its west side with the pushcarts and horse-drawn wagons of Jewish peddlers. Standing by their carts, the peddlers would yell "bananas, oranges, apples" in energetic competition for the attention of pedestrians passing by. Front Street, the main commercial street of the East Side, was an even larger market. The part north of State Street was for a time lined on both sides with Jewish and Italian vendors, who would sometimes quarrel loudly over the best spots. Front Street's atmosphere by the early 1920s was exotic enough to attract adventurers from the western neighborhoods.[49]

The peddlers comprised only half of the sidewalk markets along Front and Windsor streets. Along the other side of the walk were the stores and outdoor displays of shopkeepers, who resented the competition and tried to suppress it. The peddlers' right to use the street for marketing was challenged repeatedly as merchants persuaded police to enforce strict limits on parking. A crackdown in the summer of 1915 was so strict that for a while peddlers were not allowed to park except for the time it took to make a sale. When another crackdown in 1927 forced peddlers to keep moving, Alderman Rocco D. Pallotti defended their interests by attempting to have parts of Windsor Street and four side streets reserved for their use. The other aldermen refused to go along because they expected that shop owners would object, and they called on the police to return to their old practice of not enforcing the law. This decision kept the peddlers at the mercy of the shopkeepers and the police, who exercised their power again in the spring of 1929 by strictly enforcing the parking limits and making some arrests.[50]

Shopkeepers still opposed letting the peddlers park on Front and Windsor streets for even the forty minutes allowed for parked cars; they wanted them pushed off those streets altogether. The council experimented for a few months with setting up curb markets on two side streets as the only places where peddlers could park. It ended the experiment partly because of protests from Pallotti and the East Side Push-Cart Peddlers' Association, but partly also because the shopkeepers changed their minds. To their surprise, the shopkeepers found that the shops and the pushcarts had actually complemented each other; banishing the peddlers hurt businesses on Front and Windsor streets because it meant the loss of customers who had been drawn by the presence of the pushcarts. Shopkeepers on those two streets even signed a petition in fall 1929 calling on the city to let the peddlers return. The council obliged them by expanding the permitted area of street trading to cover the entire East Side, except for the heavily traveled Connecticut Boulevard, but it imposed an unenforced forty-minute parking limit that still left peddlers at the mercy of police. The special status of peddling on the East Side was to some extent written into law, while curb markets in the outlying neighborhoods, which had failed anyway, were legally prohibited.[51]

The peddlers' apparent victory was an ambiguous one. Having concentrated increasingly on the East Side — in response to police harassment and a dwindling number of customers in the outlying neighborhoods — they had managed to preserve their toehold only with the merchants' permission. By the mid-1930s, the numbers of peddlers in Hartford were beginning to decrease except on Front Street. A few continued to serve the outlying neighborhoods at least through the 1930s and 1940s, driving trucks instead of horse-drawn wagons, but by then peddling was an old man's trade. As the old peddlers died, retired, or went into other forms of business, younger men did not replace them. By the 1930s, peddling in the outlying neighborhoods was no longer a step in the journey toward prosperity. Pushcart peddlers had once saved their money to buy horses and wagons, but now many peddlers who had served the outer neighborhoods were selling their horses and spending their entire working days beside their pushcarts at the curb on Front Street, although business was only fair there except in the early morning. Competition for space was fiercer than ever as the remaining peddlers converged on the street. "Every day, another and another!" complained one peddler. Marginalized and struggling, a few peddlers stayed in business until the East Side was leveled in the 1950s for redevelopment. But even by the 1930s, peddling was little more than a bit of local color provided by aging immigrants.[52]

No single cause can be cited for the decline of the street trades in Hartford. Some street trades would probably have disappeared even without any deliberate attempt to suppress them. The use of the telephone diminished the need for expressmen to solicit business on the street, and all express business—whether conducted at the curb or in the office—was badly damaged by the creation of a federal parcel-post service. Pushcart peddlers lost much of their clientele in the middle-class neighborhoods as a result of changing shopping habits made possible by the automobile and the refrigerator, as well as by a greater concern with cleanliness. Still, city officials, businessmen, and reformers contributed by suppressing or containing certain street trades. In the examples considered here, they were driven by a desire to improve public order, to protect taxpaying businesses from competition, and to clear away obstacles to traffic. Complaints about competition predominated in the campaign to force lunch wagons off the street. Local officials and merchants complained about the rude manners and uncleanliness of the expressmen, and about the fact that their wagons choked Central Row. All three of these concerns combined in efforts to restrict the produce peddlers. Residents of outlying neighborhoods and members of the Municipal Art Society objected to the peddlers' noisy cries, intrusions, and failure to keep the Christian sabbath. Businessmen objected to the messiness of wholesale trading on Main Street, while city officials noted the obstructions to traffic.

Complaints about public order, in the case of the street trades as in other aspects of street life, were influenced by a desire to make the streets conform to higher, feminine standards of decorum. The filth and foul language at the express stands were said to be particularly troubling to ladies. This distinction between men's and women's responses was more than just a sexist fiction: women had to keep their skirts from being soiled by horse manure, and they also had to deal with the possibility of sexual harassment as they passed the uncouth expressmen. Yet the distinction also presumed that women, particularly middle-class women, were more sensitive to disorder and needed to be protected from it. For example, the *Times* declared that the relatively privileged housewives in Hartford's outlying neighborhoods were the people most in need of relief from produce peddlers, although these women probably saw and heard fewer peddlers in the course of their day than anyone else in the city.

The produce peddlers' retreat to the East Side, however, allowed them to escape the hostility of middle-class people who might have been inclined to purge the streets of pushcarts. In this way the peddlers avoided the fate of lunch wagon owners and expressmen, whose desire for central locations had brought them into conflict with middle-class shoppers, office workers, and motorists. On the slum streets the peddlers found themselves comfortably isolated from such conflicts. Even the shopkeepers eventually accepted their presence. If the peddlers' standards of behavior were offensive to outsiders, the outsiders could simply stay away.

The segregation of produce peddling was thus a solution acceptable both to the peddlers and to members of the middle class, who were offended by public disorder. It was not a measure that was pushed in any organized way by a reform group, but rather a compromise solution that developed over many years as city officials tried to balance conflicting pressures. That this solution was achieved without being the major focus of reform activity is indicative of one important feature of the larger trend toward the segregation of public space: segregation was far easier than purification.

or fixing other "ills" like poverty

8

Creating a Traffic System

Though its western end cut through the heart of the bustling, smoky factory district, the eastern end of Capitol Avenue was still peaceful at the turn of the century. From its origin at Main Street, it was a residential backwater — a narrow street lined with dignified brownstone row houses and low wrought-iron fences. Climbing the gentle hill westward toward the capitol, the tree-lined avenue passed fine old brick homes divided into respectable lodgings for clerks, machinists, and salesmen.[1] Early every morning, a thin stream of workingmen walked up the avenue from the poorer neighborhoods east and south of Main, the stragglers hurrying to avoid being docked a half-hour's pay for arriving at the factories after the seven o'clock opening. Trolleys served both Main Street and the factory district, but not eastern Capitol Avenue. Their routes looped north through the downtown, causing delays that made a brisk walk up Capitol the best way to work for those running late.[2]

In 1906 an alderman suggested saving workers the walk by laying new trolley tracks to link the lines on Main Street with those on the western section of Capitol Avenue near the factories. The proposal marked the beginning of a decade-long fight over whether the avenue properly belonged to those who lived on it or to those who used it to get across town. In petitions and public hearings through 1914, residents strongly opposed proposals for trolley lines, street widening, and asphalt paving. Trolleys, they argued, "would be a serious detriment to the comfort of residents of said street." They noted that many trees would have to be cut to widen the street enough to accommodate trolley lines and insisted that the beauty of their neighborhood should not be sacrificed for the convenience of people who did not live there. They urged the city to support an alternative plan favored by the trolley company: to improve service in the area by installing an additional set of tracks along Park Street, a parallel street several blocks south. "Park Street is already a trolley street and a business street and Capitol Avenue is not. There is not a store or place of business on this street [Capitol] between Main Street and Washington Street and I think putting the trolley lines here would change the status of the street," argued one neighbor, Anson T. McCook, in 1914.[3]

McCook was right. Trolley lines had already changed the character of many Hartford streets, and asphalt paving was having the same effect. As the city grew rapidly in the late nineteenth and early twentieth centuries, vastly increased amounts of traffic were moving through the streets. Trolley lines and asphalt paving concentrated this traffic along a handful of routes while leaving nearby streets relatively undisturbed. Heavy traffic annoyed some homeowners and encouraged their departure, but the proximity of many potential customers made these streets more attractive for commercial development, and convenient trolley transportation encouraged the building of large apartment houses. With the growth of the suburban periphery and the widespread use of streetcar and automobile, the densely developed thoroughfares were increasingly those radiating outward from the business and industrial centers of Hartford. Decisions taken by city government shaped this differentiated pattern of streets by determining which would be overwhelmed by vehicles and which would remain quiet and residential. These decisions served the function of later zoning regulations, namely, creating a coherent pattern of land use. Starting just after the turn of the century, more and more of these decisions were made consciously. Encouraged first by local reformers and then by city-planning experts, the city government eagerly made physical improvements in the streets, modified traffic regulations, and impelled changes in pedestrian behavior in order to turn the streets into a system for rapid circulation. The eastern section of Capitol Avenue never became a major part of the new system because of a combination of trolley company foot-dragging, neighborhood opposition, and municipal stinginess.[4] Still, the fears of its residents became the realities of many other people who lived along Hartford's streets.

Making Most Excellent Thoroughfares

Hartford's street plan in the late nineteenth century resembled a web spun by a drunken spider. Radiating from the center of the downtown were avenues that had originally been created as colonial-era links with neighboring villages or as turnpikes after independence. As the city's population grew in the nineteenth century, streetcar lines along the avenues allowed the growth of residential neighborhoods outside the original urban core. Developers filled in the spaces between the avenues with haphazard grids of residential streets, most of which were short, narrow, and suitable only for local traffic.[5]

Improvements in street surfaces in the 1860s and 1870s enabled Hartford's streets to handle the traffic of a small industrial city adequately. Because of unusually troublesome soil conditions, Hartford moved more quickly than other cities to cover its dirt streets with water-bound macadam, a semipermanent pavement that consisted of packed layers of small stones. Without such pavement, the thick clayey soil would soften in the spring and become almost like quicksand. After a heavy rain, wheels would sink into deep mud, and pedestrians crossing the street without a stone crosswalk underfoot risked losing a boot. The city at first spread macadam on all kinds of streets alike. By 1885 there were about fifty-five miles of macadamized streets and forty-seven miles of dirt.[6] But this primitive paving, though adequate for quiet side streets, soon became unsatisfactory on certain well-traveled routes in and around the center of the growing city, where heavy wagons tore the macadam apart. People who had to travel such major streets as Asylum Street, State Street, and Farmington Avenue in the 1880s and early 1890s found badly worn surfaces and seasonal dust and mud puddles. Street commissioners spoke of the mud with philosophical resignation: "Commissioners cannot control the elements, and mud and dust will follow rain and heat as surely as night follows day," they reported in 1889.[7]

Such attitudes soon changed. One of Hartford's leading industrialists, Col. Albert A. Pope of Boston, was already taking a great interest in bettering road conditions. Pope, whose Pope Manufacturing Company made Hartford the center of American bicycle production and, briefly, a center for automobile manufacture, led a nationwide "Good Roads" movement in the 1890s. He lectured, wrote articles, supported trade magazines, and lobbied for road improvements. Speaking to a sympathetic audience of Hartford's leading businessmen in 1890, he urged them to work at both the state and local level to "inaugurate a system of streets and highways in this fair town, which shall speedily become a model for every one of your American sister cities."[8] By 1894 Mayor Leverett Brainard noted, "Our citizens are quite generally calling for some improved method [of paving]." Even the street commissioners had to admit that the streets were not good enough. They reported, "Macadam does very well for resident streets, but the city has outgrown it for business streets."[9]

At this time the city had just laid the legal groundwork for better paving. Until the 1890s Hartford had avoided other cities' common practice of leaving decisions about paving — and the cost of doing the work — in the hands of the abutting property owners. Officials usually claimed that paving caused property values to rise along the newly paved street, primarily benefiting abutters. But in Hartford the practice had been successfully opposed by those who argued that streets were a general benefit to public travel and should be paved at public expense; these opponents complained that local assessments constituted an undue burden on working-class property owners.[10] The city government finally adopted the controversial system of local control and local assessments in 1893. Anticipating the installation of costly durable pavements like asphalt, city officials decided that it would be unfair to make all taxpayers pay for improvements that would affect only a few streets. They obtained a charter revision from the state legislature that permitted the city to assess abutting property owners for two-thirds of the cost of installing pavement other than macadam. Such work could be undertaken only if the owners of two-thirds of the affected frontage petitioned for it.[11]

City officials eagerly inspected pavements in Baltimore, Philadelphia, and New York and returned to Hartford with great enthusiasm for asphalt, which members claimed was durable, attractive, sanitary, relatively inexpensive, and ideal for travel. To their disappointment, they found their enthusiasm was not shared by those who would have to bear most of the cost. It was very difficult to get abutting property owners to sign petitions for asphalt paving. Rather than resuming the old practice of having the city pay for street work, officials decided to attack the other side of the problem: the onerous requirement of obtaining abutters' approval. They secured legislation in 1895 that allowed the city to install durable pavement without any petition from the abutters who would pay for it, in addition to any paving done at the abutters' request. In effect the city declared a general public need for well-paved thoroughfares while forcing neighboring property owners to foot the bill. Following the adoption of this law, the city installed asphalt blocks on State Street and Central Row in 1895–96 and laid sheet asphalt on Main and Atheneum streets in 1896–97.[12]

Changing transportation technology in the late nineteenth and early twentieth centuries made better streets a matter of both prestige and necessity. In the first half of the century, the rise of intercity railroad travel had limited the importance of the radial avenues as traffic carriers. By the turn of the century, however, patterns of travel were changing, as George Parker explained in 1904:

> Streets are becoming of ever increasing importance in the functions of a city. A century ago streets and roads were the avenues of long distant [sic] travel as well as for local use, and the age of the stage-coach and the wayside inn and the turnpikes brought them to their greatest glory and importance. But with the advent of [the] railway making the railroad station practically the gateway of the city, streets and roads fell into disuse, except for local travel, and the roads degenerated and became impassable, except in a burdensome way. But with the advent of the bicycle, the trolley car and the motor carriage, roads and streets are again regaining their old time prestige, and the good roads movements are making most excellent thoroughfares and they are fast rivaling the railroad stations as the gateways and forecourts of our cities.[13]

The growing popularity of bicycles also made better pavement a necessity, as bicycles required a smooth, hard street surface. And of course the growing number of automobiles, whose high speeds caused macadam streets to deteriorate rapidly, was even more important. From the late 1890s through the 1920s, city and state officials scrambled to adapt Hartford's ancient roads to what one of them called "the stupendous increases in the traffic they are called upon to bear."[14] Their efforts to pave, widen, and maintain a handful of major thoroughfares encouraged further growth in the volume of traffic and resulted in striking differences in the ways streets were used.

Paving proceeded slowly at first. By 1909 only 8.4 percent of Hartford's streets were paved with "durable pavements," meaning asphalt, concrete, granite, brick, or anything else superior to macadam. Hartford may have been slower than some other American cities in paving its streets, but it was not unique. In most moderate-sized urban areas, the majority of streets lacked durable paving before automobile use became common. Amounts of durable paving varied widely: in the largest cities it typically covered a third or more of the streets. "Hartford is far behind other progressive cities in mileage of improved pavement," complained the city engineer, Roscoe N. Clark.[15]

Streets initially selected for paving were those with the heaviest freight traffic, mainly the major streets in the downtown and factory district. But easing travel was not the only benefit city officials saw in paving. Asphalt streets were easier to clean, a major consideration at a time when large numbers of horses were on the streets. For this reason, the Board of Health in 1903 and 1904 urged paving the East Side streets even though most of them handled little traffic. To show the potential health risks of unpaved streets, the board noted the large amount of time that slum dwellers spent outside their tenements—and also what it considered to be their filthy habits. The board succeeded in getting improved pavement on some of the worst streets and alleys by 1909 and made more progress in the early 1910s.[16]

Whether intended to ease traffic or improve sanitation, paving projects were usually unpopular with the neighbors. Only business owners seemed to welcome them.[17] Homeowners and landlords alike balked at the prospect of assessments that usually exceeded a hundred dollars even for properties with a modest amount of frontage. "The cost of a new pavement would be an excessive tax on the property for which not one cent additional rent could be obtained," complained one landlord. Landlords and residents of Hopkins Street protested a plan that would lay asphalt on what was becoming a route for heavy teams between the factory district and downtown. Two women argued that the asphalt would make the working-class street swelteringly hot and would annoy neighbors with the loud clopping of horses' hoofs. Other opponents emphasized that it would "inflict a great pecuniary hardship upon the people owning property on said street."[18] Homeowners along the avenues soon faced the same prospect of financing paving improvements that would draw more unwanted traffic past their houses. By about 1910 the stress of automobile traffic was crumbling the macadam on the radial avenues — just as the weight of heavy teams and wagons had earlier crumbled it on the commercial streets — and city officials were replacing macadam with asphalt despite neighborhood opposition. Meanwhile, the city continued to maintain macadam surfaces on residential streets.[19]

In maintaining different pavements according to the function of a street, Hartford was following the universal practice of the period. Motorists in every city encountered striking differences in street surfaces at least until the 1920s. Despite a flood of asphalt paving on the main thoroughfares in the 1910s, water-bound macadam, gravel, and dirt surfaces remained common on urban side streets. As late as 1923, small cities often had many more miles of dirt streets than of pavement, and a number of larger cities admitted that most of their pavement was water-bound macadam or gravel. The differences in pavement quality in every American city concentrated traffic on certain streets. "It has been found invariably true that wherever a road is improved, it is quickly sought by motor traffic," noted an article published by American City Magazine. Experts like Frank S. Besson of the Army Corps of Engineers urged that cities plan the paving and width of each street to match its specific function. Noting the need for economy in street improvements, Besson recommended paving residential streets with asphalt only as increased traffic made maintenance of the inferior surface prohibitively expensive. The recommended practice was thus both to respond reactively to a developing traffic pattern and to try actively to shape that pattern through improving the pavement on certain streets.[20]

Theoretically, automobile traffic could have dispersed evenly through the streets of the city, unlike trolley traffic, which had to follow fixed tracks, but some streets were more attractive than others for automobile traffic even before they had improved pavement. In Hartford these streets were straighter, broader, and longer, or headed more directly to important destinations—the downtown or the factory district. By no coincidence, they tended to be the same streets that the trolley companies had chosen as the most advantageous for track construction. Furthermore, the availability of trolley transportation had encouraged disproportionate residential development along the tracks while simultaneously encouraging the concentration of business and industry at points that were well served by converging lines. As a result, Hartford's land use patterns had been formed and reinforced in such a way that early automobile travel in the city necessarily followed the trolley routes, particularly on the radial avenues from the downtown to the rapidly growing residential and suburban areas. The radial avenues were used for long-distance as well as local travel. They were the routes recommended in the widely used motor guides, publications that included maps and directions for travelers.[21]

The state highway department encouraged and aided the paving of Hartford's radial avenues. The department contributed modest amounts of aid to local road-building projects in the late 1890s, and by 1900 it had begun planning a system of state highways. The department increased its funding of improvements to roads that could serve as either trunk lines or as tributaries in this system. Included as trunk lines were some of Hartford's major radial avenues—Wethersfield, Maple, Farmington, Albany, Bloomfield, and Windsor avenues. New Britain and Asylum avenues were designated connectors. The state funded and later supervised improvements to Newington, Blue Hills, and Asylum avenues, as well as the installation of concrete or asphalt paving on Albany, Bloomfield, and Maple avenues.[22] The Automobile Club of Hartford also encouraged the paving of the major avenues. In 1919, for example, the club petitioned the Common Council to pave Wethersfield Avenue, saying that its crumbling macadam surface damaged automobiles. In the following year the club deplored a decision to postpone the paving of Maple Avenue, the main connecting link between downtown and the Berlin Turnpike. "Every other main artery leading into Hartford has been taken care of," and Maple Avenue should as well, the club's monthly bulletin argued.[23]

But even though every major radial avenue in Hartford had durable paving by the time of the Depression, most side streets did not. Deterred

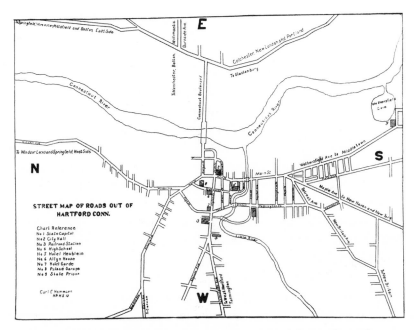

Roads out of Hartford, 1911. The rising use of the automobile, together with municipal paving policies, turned these radial avenues into major traffic routes by the 1920s. (ACH, *Bulletin*, November 1911)

by the cost, the city had covered only forty-three miles of all streets with such paving by early 1929. Another 117 miles of side streets were macadam, and there were even a few dirt streets left.[24] At the end of a decade of tremendous expansion in automobile use, downtown streets and the radial avenues were well paved, but most other streets still lacked surfaces designed for rapid transportation.

In the 1910s and 1920s the city widened some downtown streets and radial avenues, further encouraging the concentration of traffic on certain routes. Pearl Street was widened at a narrow spot in 1911 despite strong opposition from neighboring property owners. Jewell and Wells streets, beside Bushnell Park, were widened in 1913 and 1914. City officials hoped not only that the project would ease traffic flow but also that "the entire moral tone of the city will be lifted" by the destruction of nearby tenement houses. Other major projects widened all or parts of Church, Asylum, Park, Morgan, and Main streets, and Maple and

Asylum avenues, among others. But opposition succeeded in blocking proposed widenings of another part of Park Street and delayed plans to widen Church and High streets. Opponents of street-widening projects usually objected on the grounds that their buildings would be razed, but some, like the Capitol Avenue residents, opposed having the road in front of their homes turned into a busy thoroughfare.[25]

As winter driving increased in the late 1910s and the 1920s, snow-plowing patterns further confined traffic to a few major streets. At the turn of the century the city had removed snow from streets only during unusually heavy snowstorms. This practice did not become controversial until 1905, when a major fire, following a storm that had clogged the streets with deep snow, delayed the steam-powered fire engines. Issuing a radical proposal with defiant emphasis, the fire board president, Charles E. Parker, declared, "Yes sir, I'm in favor of every bit of snow being removed, down to the hardpan, the pavement," in the center of the city. Other prominent local men dismissed this proposal as ridiculously expensive, unnecessary, and disruptive to sleighing, but the idea eventually prevailed.[26]

At this time, most snowplowing was done by the street railroad company, which ran trolleys equipped with plows. The plows pushed the snow off the tracks but left it piled deeply in the street. Property owners dumped more snow in the street while shoveling their sidewalks. The street department would try to clear out the worst of the piles by hiring large numbers of day laborers to shovel the snow into wagons and dump it into the Park River. Crosswalks were also shoveled. The city did only limited clearing with horse-drawn snowplows.[27] Snow removal efforts in the 1900s and 1910s focused mainly on paved streets in the central business district. Motorists driving in other parts of the city after a heavy snowfall tended to follow in the trolley tracks, often causing delays for trolleys. After a 1920 blizzard, for instance, many motorists traveling along trolley lines stalled out in the trackside drifts as they attempted to turn into side streets. As pavement spread outward on the radial avenues, the city increased its amount of snow clearance, particularly after it mounted plows on trucks in 1921. Still, side streets continued to be neglected. "The majority of Hartford's side streets haven't seen a plow of any sort all winter," complained the *Automobiler*, the magazine of the

Automobile Club of Hartford, in 1923. "The snow has been packed down and there are now masses of bumps, ruts and holes." The neglect of macadamized side streets continued at least through the rest of the decade. In winter 1928–29, the city spent barely seven thousand dollars on clearing snow from the 115 miles of macadam streets, but more than three times that amount on the far smaller mileage of streets with improved paving.[28]

The funneling of traffic into major thoroughfares — encouraged by paving, widening, and snowplowing policies — was especially significant because the total volume of traffic continued to grow astronomically with the increase in private automobile ownership and the sudden appearance of jitneys. According to traffic counts by the street department, the number of motor vehicles on Hartford's streets quadrupled between 1914 and 1919, only to triple again by 1929.[29]

The Broad, Straight Streets

The increasing traffic had striking effects on the character of the neighborhoods along the major thoroughfares. Two of the most radically transformed streets had once been among the most prestigious addresses in the city: Washington Street and Farmington Avenue. Industrialists, insurance executives, political leaders, and other prominent and wealthy men had been building opulent homes along these semi-suburban streets since the mid-nineteenth century. Samuel Clemens, visiting the city in 1868 at the start of his literary success, was so impressed that he decided to settle in Hartford. Generalizing from his impressions of the wealthy areas he visited, particularly the Nook Farm enclave at Farmington Avenue and Forest Street, he described Hartford as a city

> composed almost entirely of dwelling houses — not shingle-shaped affairs, stood on end and packed together like a "deck" of cards, but massive private hotels, scattered along the broad straight streets, from fifty all the way up to two hundred yards apart. Each house sits in the midst of about an acre of green grass, or flower beds, or ornamental shrubbery, guarded on all sides by the trimmed hedges of arbor-vitae, and by files of huge forest trees that cast a shadow like a thunder-

cloud. . . . Everywhere the eye turns it is blessed with a vision of re-
freshing green. You do not know what beauty is if you have not been
here.[30]

Hartford was but one of many American cities in which the late
nineteenth-century elite had chosen grand, tree-lined avenues as the
ideal showplaces for mansions. Such avenues were in many cases the
main traveled roads from the city's center into the hinterland, and as such
were served by streetcar and utility lines. Wealthy residents did not often ride trolleys themselves, but they chose to build their homes on the
streets with the highest property values and most modern improvements.
The avenues underwent rapid change in the early twentieth century, as
most of the elite fled. Greatly increased traffic had combined with commercial and apartment development to make the avenues less desirable
as elite residential addresses, and more secluded suburban locations had
afforded an attractive alternative.[31] Like Cleveland's Euclid Avenue or
Detroit's Woodward Avenue, Hartford's premier residential avenues experienced the same dramatic rise and fall.

Hartford residents initially saw breadth and straightness as desirable
qualities in residential avenues, though by attracting traffic these features
ultimately contributed to the avenues' decline. Petitioners advocating
the straightening of a minor crook in Farmington Avenue in 1864 predicted that the project would help the street attain its destiny as "the
finest and most popular avenue leading out of the city . . . thickly studded
to West Hartford, with elegant dwellings." The petitioners said that wide,
straight streets laid out at right angles would make a pleasant change from
the "wild deformity" of the colonial street pattern in the neighborhoods
near the Connecticut River. "We require spacious streets and avenues to
invite men of wealth and influence to make pleasant homes with us." As
they had requested, the city straightened Farmington Avenue at its approach to the Park River around 1870, and Clemens soon built his osten-
tatious mansion at that very site.[32]

Though neighbors lost a battle to prevent the extension of horsecar
lines there, Farmington Avenue and the surrounding Asylum Hill neighborhood continued to attract men of wealth and influence through the
late nineteenth and early twentieth centuries. Farmington Avenue residents were heavily represented in the social register. Of all the streets in

the city, only nearby Asylum Avenue counted more listings in 1897. Farmington Avenue, however, had bigger homes and broader lawns.[33]

Unfortunately for the residents of the avenue, it was also the major link between the downtown and the rapidly developing affluent suburban areas in the West End and West Hartford. The city laid asphalt on the avenue in 1899 as far west as Woodland Avenue, by the Park River. The asphalt was extended to Tremont Street in 1910 despite neighborhood opposition, because city officials believed that "no suitable pavement except asphalt could be laid on Farmington Avenue which would stand the vast amount of traffic, both horse drawn and motor driven, over this trunk line thoroughfare." By 1911 the asphalt ran all the way to the city line. Traffic increased so much that, by 1920, the Automobile Club of Hartford urged relieving the congestion by widening Asylum Avenue so that it could serve as an alternate route.[34]

Developers built scattered apartment buildings along Farmington Avenue in the 1910s and added many more in the 1920s. Old homes were torn down or divided into lodging houses. Businesses also sprang up in the 1920s, including pharmacies, service stations, groceries, butcher shops, clothing stores, tailors, doctors' offices, barbershops, automobile dealerships and a movie theater. By 1928 Farmington Avenue was "practically a business thoroughfare," complained a woman who recalled its lost beauty. Still to come was the single most radical change: the construction in 1929–31 of the massive new headquarters of the Aetna Life Insurance Company.[35]

An even swifter transformation was seen on Washington Street, which ran along a low ridge stretching south from the capitol, with the factory district a short distance to the northwest and the downtown to the northeast. In the late nineteenth century, a carriage or two might be seen gliding down the street under overarching elms, but the clang of trolleys was never heard except at the far southern end. The owners of the Italianate and Classical Revival mansions were heavily represented in the blue book, and the street included so many prominent political figures that it was referred to as "Governors' Row."[36]

A long, wide, straight street without trolleys may have been an impressive setting for mansions; it was also attractive to automobile traffic. Early motorists' guidebooks recommended Washington Street as a north-south connector within Hartford, and as part of an alternate route to Meriden and New Haven. Signs (probably posted by the Automobile Club) also directed New Haven-bound motorists that way.[37]

Businesses alert to the flow of traffic began locating on Washington Street in the 1910s. By 1920 three car dealerships and an automotive supply store had been built. Homeowners were beginning to move out of the remaining houses, and formerly private homes were occupied by the Connecticut Humane Society and the Hebrew Old People's Home. Apartment buildings had been constructed just north of Retreat Avenue, where the trolley line from downtown entered the street. City officials decided in 1920 that Washington Street could go no longer without asphalt. "None could have foreseen the rapid deterioration of the macadam on Washington Street. It is without a doubt the worst in the city and is called on to carry a heavy traffic. An emergency has arisen," according to one report. Despite residents' opposition and an attempted veto by the mayor, the city laid asphalt there in 1921. After that, houses rapidly gave way to auto repair shops, apartment buildings, state offices, filling stations, the new county courthouse, and a supermarket. "Washington Street, the pride of Hartford, was desecrated by the inroads of trade," according to one 1928 observer.[38] Most of the elite had fled. Only twelve Washington Street addresses were listed in the blue book for 1929, compared with forty-seven in 1913 and sixty-four in 1909. The numerous listings in the 1929 blue book for addresses on West Hartford side streets clearly indicated the elite's preference for more secluded locations.[39]

Automobile versus Pedestrian

Paving, widening, and plowing policies helped turn a century-old road network into a modern traffic system and contributed toward some striking changes in land use patterns. But the creation of this traffic system depended on more than just physical improvements in the streets. In the early twentieth century, automobile owners, legislators, city officials, police and educators worked together to extend the customary and legal privileges of Hartford motorists. They cleared the way for high-speed travel by relaxing the speed limits, adopting regulations to ease traffic flow, and undertaking educational and legal efforts to control pedestrian behavior. Motorists' power continued to grow as their numbers exploded and as pedestrians learned to be wary of the increasingly dangerous streets. By the mid-1920s the major thoroughfares of the city were re-served almost exclusively for motor vehicles, and walkers who stepped off the curb did so at their own peril.

Until the early years of the new century, pedestrians, bicycles, trolleys, carriages, and wagons had mingled relatively easily on Hartford's streets. The congestion that had plagued Boston and New York for decades was virtually nonexistent in the smaller provincial capital. People commonly crossed the street without bothering to look both ways, and they crossed wherever they wanted to except when muddy seasons made it worth us-ing the stone crosswalk at the corner. Even the major intersections at City Hall Square were quiet enough that pedestrians could stand in the street conversing or waiting for trolleys without danger from the passing traf-fic.[40] Traffic accidents did occur from time to time and could even result in serious injuries or fatalities. Though horse-drawn vehicles generally moved slowly—Hartford's speed limit in the late nineteenth century was six miles per hour—heedless children and elderly people were some-times run over anyway. The greatest danger came from panicked horses, who would gallop through the streets as their terrified drivers pulled help-lessly at the reins. After electric streetcars were introduced in 1888, trol-leys sometimes collided with carriages and wagons. Nevertheless, such accidents were newsworthy aberrations in the era before widespread au-tomobile use.[41]

The automobile first entered Hartford's streets as a novelty that barely disturbed the mixture of other street uses. When the inventor Hiram Percy Maxim took what he claimed was the "historic first horseless-carriage ride in Hartford" in 1895, he drew a crowd of pedestrians into the roadway. Several dozen men and boys ran out into Park Street to follow the smelly machine as it clattered and coughed its way up the slope from the factory district. Maxim's early experimental drives always drew a flock of onlookers, some of whom would follow him on bicycle into the countryside. Even after Maxim's employer, Albert A. Pope, be-gan manufacturing them commercially in 1897, cars remained a curi-osity. When motoring enthusiasts met to form the Automobile Club of Hartford in 1902, there were only about eighty automobile owners in the area. Later that year, throngs of admiring spectators turned out to watch the arrival at the Allyn House of seventy dust-covered motorists on an endurance run from New York to Boston. So many people packed

Main Street in 1905, looking south from City Hall Square. In the years before widespread automobile use, different kinds of traffic shared the street with relatively little conflict. (Connecticut State Library)

Trumbull and Asylum streets that police could barely make way for the vehicles.[42]

Vehicular travel until the early twentieth century was given limited rights to the streets. In Hartford, as in other American cities, nineteenth century traffic regulations had given priority to the safety of all street users instead of to rapid traffic flow.[43] For example, Hartford officials, like their counterparts in a number of other cities, had been so leery of the new fad of bicycling that they banned it outright in 1879. The bans on bicycles were motivated by concerns about safety: bicycles traveled faster and more silently than horses and sometimes hit pedestrians.[44] Despite immediate petitions in Hartford for lifting the ban, it remained (unenforced) on the books until 1889, when city officials decided that pedestrians were adequately protected by the 6 mph speed limit already in place and by another ordinance that banned vehicles on sidewalks. The growing popularity of bicycles resulted in only limited changes in the traffic laws. The city raised the speed limit modestly in 1896, to 8 mph within half a mile of city hall and 10 mph in other parts of town.

This change was intended only to benefit bicyclists, but it applied to all vehicles.[45]

The primary goal of traffic regulation changed radically as the automobile gained popularity among the classes who made the laws. By the mid-1920s, when over more than twenty thousand automobiles were registered in Hartford, the laws clearly favored vehicular speed over pedestrian safety. The strict local speed limit came to an end in 1901, when the state legislature took away local authority to regulate the speed of motor vehicles and set a statewide limit of 12 mph within city limits and 15 mph elsewhere. (Police officers with stopwatches calculated motorists' speed by timing their travel along certain measured sections of roadway.)[46] Automobile manufacturers lobbied to have speed limits further increased in 1905 and tried to impress legislators by having them chauffeured through country roads in West Hartford at the breathtaking rate of 40 mph. The legislators were reportedly "astonished to find out how slow the legal speed limit of fifteen miles an hour seemed," and promptly raised it to 20 mph outside the city limits, annoying farmers, whose horses were panicked by speeding cars. The legislature raised speed limits again in 1909 and in 1917.[47] In 1927 speed limits were abolished altogether in Connecticut, and drivers were forbidden only to drive recklessly, dangerously, or "at a rate of speed greater than is reasonable."[48]

While the state was raising the speed limit, the city was adopting increasingly detailed traffic regulations to ease traffic flow. Under rules passed in 1911, Hartford began requiring slow-moving vehicles to keep to the right to allow faster ones to pass; it set rules for who had the right of way at intersections; it required signaling for turning, stopping, slowing, or backing; it banned stopping in the roadway; and it set a forty-minute parking limit in the heart of downtown. By 1921 the rules mandated one-way traffic on several major streets, banned certain left turns, and further restricted parking. The Automobile Club of Hartford supported most of these changes, explaining that it "is always in favor of any measure that will be beneficial to the motoring public."[49]

As the speed and number of automobiles increased, so did the number of pedestrians in the growing city, particularly in the dense commercial downtown. In 1917 an advertisement apparently placed by a real estate concern boasted that 10,800 people had passed through one downtown intersection in the space of a single hour.[50] The crowded conditions in working-class neighborhoods also meant that there were many children and other people on foot in the streets, playing, shopping, or talking.

The growth of two increasingly incompatible forms of street use resulted in alarmingly frequent collisions. Traffic accidents suddenly began killing dozens of Hartford residents in the 1910s. The Hartford Board of Health had reported that nobody was killed by vehicles or horses in 1902, and only one person in 1903. In contrast, the police department reported twenty-six people killed by automobiles in a twelve-month period in 1916 and 1917. The department's reports for the 1910s and early 1920s left it unclear whether any of these victims were themselves in automobiles, but a later statewide study by the Connecticut Department of Motor Vehicles indicated that the overwhelming majority were on foot. The department reported that thirty of the thirty-one people killed in automobile accidents in Hartford in 1925 were pedestrians. Police department figures show that, in addition to those killed, several hundred people every year were struck and injured by automobiles. In spring 1926, for instance, the police reported 573 such injuries in the preceding twelve months; another 132 people had been struck but not injured.[51]

Hartford pedestrians noticed the growing conflict with motorists as early as 1907, when several of them wrote letters of protest to the *Hartford Evening Post.* "Not a day goes by but lives are jeopardized by speed fiends," wrote one anonymous correspondent. Another urged that "the city fathers . . . take some steps to check the reckless speed that autoists drive their cars through the streets of this city. . . . When an auto dashes by a policeman at top speed he seems to be helpless to halt or check it, and stares in open-mouthed wonder at the fleeting car. I have witnessed a number of narrow escapes from running down pedestrians." Particularly frightening were the electric cars, which ran almost silently. Another writer reported, "Walking across Main Street, near Asylum, a noiseless machine came whistling by me about a half an inch from my nose . . . rushing through the streets on [its] way to a kill." Some motorists, noted the *Post,* "recognize no rights on the part of pedestrians, or even horse drivers, that they are in any way bound to respect."[52]

Other writers said that pedestrians were equally to blame. "Might we not walk in comparative safety if, before leaving the boundary of the curb for the street, we should glance to right and left? The simplest precaution surely, but one sadly neglected," wrote one pedestrian. "Again, the middle of the street is not the proper place to stand while waiting for a [trolley] car, yet this is a fixed habit with some. They stand absorbed in conversation, or their wits wandering in vacancy, only to be collected with a spasmodic jerk, which sends a possible 'victim' in the path of the anxiously advancing automobile."[53]

The Automobile Club of Hartford in 1911 printed a "Diary of a Hartford Motorist," intended humorously, in which an exasperated driver constantly encountered pedestrians intent on throwing themselves under his wheels. He narrowly missed a woman rushing out into traffic to catch a trolley, a child who "jumped out from ambush behind a trolley car," an Italian trying to learn to ride a bicycle, boys playing in traffic, and parochial school children running across the street to hear an organ-grinder. His biggest shock came when a five-year-old fell in his path but lay safely between the wheels as the car passed over. "No matter how you drive, the pedestrian will get you," concluded the motorist. "While you are figuring out what he is going to do another vehicle rams you. If people would only cross on the regular crossings and nowhere else it would be simply great."[54]

As the references to Italian bicyclists and Catholic students suggest, the conflict between motorists and pedestrians had ethnic and class overtones. Automobile ownership in the early twentieth century was limited primarily to members of the elite and of the upper middle class, and was sometimes derided as a "fad of the very rich." In Hartford, the Automobile Club initially attempted to maintain this elite image by screening out undesirable members. The club later recalled with amazement "the widespread feeling which existed against automobiles and automobilists. . . . Those who owned them were looked upon as snobs, as baby killers."[55] The growing use of the automobile produced greater class polarization than ever in the conflict over street use. Previous conflicts had sometimes seen spokesmen for the working class advocating traffic improvements against more affluent opposition, as in the examples of the Laurel Street extension through Pope Park and the proposed widening of Capitol Avenue. But by the 1910s, the advocates of traffic flow tended to be those who could afford automobiles.

The losers in this conflict were the poor and the young. Nationwide, the typical motor vehicle accident at this time was an encounter between a wealthier motorist and a poorer pedestrian, with the pedestrian receiving most of the injuries. Lower-class resentment was fueled by the fact that many of the victims were children. In Connecticut cities, most of the children killed by automobiles were "of foreign extraction," reported the motor vehicle commissioner, Robbins Stoeckel, in 1920. Stoeckel feared that the public was becoming hardened to frequent deaths and injuries among pedestrians. "There was a time, not so many years ago, when an automobile-pedestrian accident was a novelty," he wrote in 1926. "It attracted a large crowd, was talked about, was fully reported in newspapers and was discussed as to its causes and consequences. . . . But now it has become commonplace. Nobody, except the actual participant pays much attention to it." [56]

Stoeckel was exaggerating to make a point. Actually, the slaughter in the streets roused considerable alarm in the 1910s and 1920s and provoked a number of responses. The building of more playgrounds to give children alternative places in which to play was one response. Another kind of alternative space being built at this time was the "isle of safety," intended primarily to protect adult pedestrians. The isle of safety, which was common in other cities as well, was a raised concrete platform in a major intersection that served as a refuge for walkers who found themselves caught in the middle of traffic while attempting to cross the street. The island also forced traffic to follow well-defined paths. The first isle of safety in Hartford was built in 1910 at the downtown intersection of Trumbull and Pearl streets, where city officials and local reformers feared that people would be killed by speeding automobiles. The largest and most impressive isle was the one in the middle of State Street near its intersection with Main. It was designed as a waiting area for streetcar passengers who had previously annoyed motorists by standing in State Street next to the tracks or by rushing from the sidewalk across traffic as the trolley approached. "People have no sort of right to stand all over the street from Main to the post office — straggling like a flock of geese without a leader," one observer had fumed in 1911. "'Shoo' them on to the sidewalks, where they belong." The city accomplished this by building the safety isle, complete with a sixty-foot-long shelter, in 1913. The shelter, which was open to breezes in warm weather and glassed in during the winter, could hold up to two hundred people. People could board or

Traffic at the isle of safety, in the middle of State Street, 1924. The isle of safety offered trolley passengers a waiting area complete with tile-roofed shelter and allowed vehicular traffic to move with less interference than in the days when people had simply stood on the street. (The Connecticut Historical Society, Hartford)

dismount safely from trolleys there even while torrents of automobile traffic rushed by.[57]

But some other isles of safety were so small that they were not particularly safe; they were little more than bumps in the street with a single lamppost and a place for a few people to stand. City officials considered removing one such isle in 1917 after automobiles smashed into its lamppost six times, twice at such speeds that the post was completely demolished. Some "safety zones" for trolley passengers had no raised curb, but were separated from the rest of the roadway only by ropes or white lines painted on the pavement. At most intersections and trolley stops there were no safety isles at all, and pedestrians had to take their chances. "Crossing pedestrians may be frequently observed hugging the flashing beacon at Trumbull and Jewell streets, as they are overtaken by autos in crossing the street intersection," reported one observer in 1926. Of necessity, trolley passengers seeking to board or dismount at places without isles of safety continued to walk across traffic to the trolleys or stand waiting in the street.[58]

Clearly there was a limit to what a few isles of safety could accomplish. A more effective response to traffic accidents was the effort to teach both adults and children that the street was a place of dangerous high-speed traffic. Educational campaigns taught that pedestrians could cross safely only if they remained alert and followed special procedures.[59] Early traffic-safety lessons for adults took the form of traffic police yelling at jaywalkers. By 1918, reported Police Chief Garrett J. Farrell, "People [were] becoming more and more familiar in regard to the proper method of crossing the streets and obedience to the signals given by the Traffic Officers."[60] Other efforts included a 1918 advertising campaign, in which local businesses paid for the publication of full-page advertisements in the *Post* admonishing adults about the perils of traffic. One ad urged: *"Take Care on the Streets!* Think only of safely reaching the other side. . . . Leave off all conversations when you step off the curb. Don't look *back* — look where you're going! Keep your eyes *open* if you don't want them closed. And if you don't want to break a careful driver's heart, for Heaven's sake *you* be careful!" Another ad urged parents to teach their children never to cross streets except at the corners. In 1919 the Automobile Club further emphasized the importance of crossing at the corners by posting signs to that effect at major intersections.[61]

State officials and police chiefs throughout Connecticut organized a larger pedestrian safety campaign in 1921, employing propaganda techniques developed during World War I. Campaign leaders gave presentations at schools and "four minute" speeches at civic organizations. Ministers were asked to read the governor's proclamation about traffic safety from the pulpit. Automobile clubs distributed pamphlets and posters. To reach the immigrant working class, the state hired a director with experience in making wartime propaganda films to produce a movie entitled "Where Are Your Children?" This film, which was shown in a heavily attended open-air screening on the East Side, graphically showed the dangers of letting children play in the streets, as well as the dangers of jaywalking. The *Hartford Times* cooperated by printing a front page picture of a policeman with a stop sign, bearing the caption, "The guardian of your lives. Do as he signals."[62]

To ensure that pedestrians paid attention, the 1921 campaign was timed to coincide with the effective date of a new state law against jay-walking. This law, which had been strongly advocated by the Automobile Club of Hartford, levied a twenty-five-dollar fine on any pedestrian who ignored the directions of a traffic officer or who used the street "reck-lessly." As one police official put it, "The purpose of the law is to protect the automobilists against the careless pedestrian." The club had argued that without such a law, pedestrians would continue to cross the street wherever they wanted, ignoring the officers and the painted crossing lines that had cost the city good money.[63]

Even before the passage of the law, police had been trying with mixed success to force pedestrians to stay on the sidewalks until given permission to cross. The automobile club condescendingly reported "many amusing incidents" in which chastened jaywalkers were forced to return to the sidewalk.[64] Once the law took effect, jaywalkers were treated more harshly, as police would grab them and force them to retrace their steps. A pedestrian complained to the *Hartford Courant* about a policeman who was "laying violent hands upon different persons." One jaywalker, who had been ordered back to the curb at a time when the street was virtually empty of traffic, was arrested for objecting. "I looked up and down Pearl Street and Central Row and there wasn't a vehicle in sight," the man told the *Courant*. "I said to the policeman, in what I believe was a polite manner, 'You have no right to stop traffic when there are no vehicles in sight.' He stepped over to me and said 'You'll have a chance to talk that over in the police station — and you're going to ride there in the wagon.'" Most pedestrians were more compliant. Obeying police-men at the corner of Asylum and Main, "Herds of people in either direc-tion gathered every few minutes on either corner — fifty to seventy-five in each group. When the embargo was removed for a moment they hurried across in both directions like a flock of sheep," according to the *Courant* letter writer. "What I want to know is whether we are coming to be a lot of imbeciles, not knowing enough to take reasonable care of ourselves."[65]

Public opinion turned against pedestrians, blaming them for their own carelessness if they were struck by cars. "Many people, the other day on North Main Street, saw an amusing incident between a motorist and a careless pedestrian," reported the *Courant*, describing how the "sleep-walker" was hit and then dragged along the street, spilling the sack of sugar he was carrying. A 1929 report by the state Department of Motor Vehicles told of a "determined lady violator" who attempted to cross the street against the signal but was seized by a police officer and dragged back to the curb. "Judging by the laughter, the spectators were with the officer." Many drivers came to expect pedestrians to get out of the way and developed the habit of honking instead of slowing down when people walked in front of them, the Automobile Club admitted.[66]

Pedestrians seem to have learned their lesson and stayed out of the way. The annual death toll of automobile victims stabilized through the 1920s and 1930s at about twenty to twenty-five, despite continued increases in the number and speed of cars and in the population of the city. Some pedestrians continued to jaywalk even on busy downtown streets, but jaywalking never became more than an act of individual defiance. Only a few isolated voices complained about the loss of pedestrian rights. "How much longer must a patient public submit to the tyranny of the automobile?" asked an anonymous walker in a letter printed in the *Courant* in 1930. "Is not the man or woman on foot as valuable to the community as those who whiz through the streets in their own cars? . . . Why should the humble pedestrian be under a constant fear for his life, like a hunted animal?" Unlike motorists, pedestrians had no advocacy groups to defend their interests. Accepting the primacy of the automobile on major streets, herds of downtown pedestrians obediently waited on the corners and crossed on the crosswalks under the direction of policemen.[67]

The pedestrian safety campaigns, combined with the new traffic laws and the increased danger posed by high-speed automobiles, introduced sharper distinctions in the use of major thoroughfares. Such streets were now more exclusively the property of the automobile, and the confinement of pedestrians to the sidewalks was constantly reinforced. The change amounted to the monopolization of public space by a new form of transportation technology, but also, more subtly, by a social class. Automobilists' disregard for other street uses and their thinly concealed mockery of pedestrians reflected wealthier Hartford residents' attitude of superiority toward the poorer majority. Pedestrians might complain about reckless drivers, but their complaints neither slowed the pace of traffic nor prevented the adoption of new traffic laws encouraging even greater speeds. Less influential as individuals, and unorganized as a political force, walkers found their use of the major streets severely restricted by laws made in the interests of the more prominent and organized motorists.

Swan's Way

Regulation of street use proved a successful way to increase the efficiency of the evolving traffic system. City officials and planners seeking to ease congestion relied increasingly on regulation in the 1920s, as public opposition and prohibitively high costs blocked the taking of land for more street space.

By the late 1910s, it was obvious that physical improvements to the streets could not keep pace with the phenomenal increase in traffic. Mayor Frank A. Hagarty made a determined but limited attempt to widen and extend certain major streets in 1916 and 1917. Taking office in 1916, Hagarty argued that the streets were arteries for Hartford's lifeblood. "I am firmly convinced that our traffic problem is the most pressing of any which we have upon our hands at the present time, and that the prosperity of Hartford's future depends upon an early and wise solution of that problem," he declared. Hagarty attempted to act on a few of the ambitious street designs proposed in 1912 by the architectural firm of Carrère and Hastings, advisors to the Commission on the City Plan, but he was constrained by concerns about cost and by the need to secure voters' approval for major projects. With the backing of the commission and the Chamber of Commerce, Hagarty secured voters' approval in 1917 for a few street-widening and extension projects affecting Prospect and Church streets and part of Capitol Avenue, among others. But in 1918 his street projects were voted down — and he was voted out of office.[68]

Hagarty's accomplishments fell far short of what Carrère and Hastings had recommended, and downtown traffic jams continued to worsen in the 1920s despite some modest street improvements. As early as 1919, aldermen warned that the problem was becoming "unendurable" and that city must take drastic measures, such as an enormously expensive widening of Asylum Street starting at Main. The Asylum Street widening idea, which was strongly opposed by merchants, went nowhere, while the assembly lines of Detroit continued to pour automobiles into downtown Hartford. By 1929 there were more than thirty thousand cars registered in the city, not including those belonging to suburban commuters.[69] The Chamber of Commerce and the Automobile Club of Hartford continued to advocate ambitious street projects while recognizing the difficulty of overcoming the obstacles to them. During the 1920s, these organizations, as well as city officials, increasingly turned their attention to other ways to ease traffic flow. Among these alternatives were putting more policemen to work directing traffic, installing traffic signals, and adopting stricter parking regulations for downtown streets.[70]

Police in the late 1910s and 1920s devoted increasing amounts of time to enforcing traffic laws and directing traffic. By 1915 twelve officers were stationed at downtown intersections on every day but Sunday, whistling one stream of traffic to a halt and waving another on its way. By 1920 every police officer on duty during the morning and evening rush hours was assigned to direct traffic, supplementing the efforts of the continually growing traffic squad. The police chief persistently begged the city to let him hire even more officers, arguing that "the regulation of Traffic to-day is one of the most important functions of the Police Department," until the need for the more routine work was eased by the installation of mechanical traffic signals starting in the mid-1920s.[71]

While traffic flow could be made more efficient through regulation, parking problems were harder to solve. Unlike regulatory measures that choreographed street motion or favored motorists at the expense of other street users, limits on parking addressed an irreconcilable conflict between different uses of the automobile. In an era when more and more street space was needed, parking increasingly blocked what little there was. No-parking zones in congested areas could clear the street for moving traffic, but they created inconveniences for motorists with destinations in those areas. The imposition of parking bans also drew strong opposition from merchants, who feared losing customers.[72] The conflict was unavoidable by the 1920s, when parked cars lined the streets throughout the downtown and in nearby parts of the East Side. Motorists were frustrated both by the difficulty of finding empty parking spaces and by the snarling of traffic that parked cars caused. Seeking to resolve this quandary, the Automobile Club of Hartford urged the city to satisfy the car's voracious appetite for parking and street space at the expense of Bushnell Park. The club's secretary, Arthur Fifoot, called for extending Trumbull Street across the park and turning all the land east of the street into a parking lot, complete with corner filling stations. The proposal was never enacted, and parking problems continued to worsen. By the late 1920s, parked cars clogged downtown streets not only during working hours but through the evening theater hours as well. The problem had also spread to streets around the factory district.[73]

Better regulation could not solve all of Hartford's traffic problems, Mayor Norman C. Stevens warned in 1926:

There is a limit to increasing the traffic capacity of the streets merely by changing the traffic regulations, no matter how desirable these regulations may be in themselves. The prohibition of left-hand turns, the establishment of one-way streets, the installation of flashing beacons and electric automatic signals are all very good in themselves, but there are some things that they will not cure. They will not remedy defects in the street plan itself. Traffic can never be properly routed through improperly planned streets until corrective measures have been applied to the streets themselves.[74]

But regulation was far cheaper than changes in the street plan, so, despite its limitations, regulation drew considerable attention in the 1920s as a remedy for Hartford's congested traffic system. In 1926 a new consultant for the Commission on the City Plan issued a citywide traffic plan that emphasized regulation over physical improvements. The report, written by Herbert S. Swan of New York, did propose a number of major street expansion projects, but it seemed less than confident that the work would ever be done. "Because of the prohibitive expense of street improvements involving the taking of land in built-up sections, the remedy for congestion has to be found, as far as possible, in police regulations rather than in costly widenings and expansions." In contrast to Carrère and Hastings's grandiose plans for new parkways and boulevards, Swan wrote of Hartford's street system as a creaky old machine that could be tuned up using proper engineering principles. Swan included numerous charts, diagrams, and statistics to illustrate the turbulence problems in Hartford's traffic flow. Arguing that "promiscuously mixed traffic invariably results in congestion," he called for further separation of different forms of street use. Paint markings were needed to delineate travel lanes for faster and slower vehicles, and refuges for pedestrians in the middle of streets would also help to direct the routes of turning automobiles. Parking should be banned on more downtown streets to make way for moving traffic; in particular, it should be banned near intersections in order to clear space for additional travel lanes. Private parking garages would eventually ease the parking problem.[75]

Swan devoted considerable attention to the proper operation of a traffic signal system. Measuring travel times and delays to the tenth of a second, he proposed a configuration of synchronized traffic lights to ease travel through the downtown. He also called for an automatic traffic light system to speed the flow of automobiles down the major thoroughfares. He urged favoring the traffic flow on the major radial arteries, and forcing crossing traffic to stop. To avoid interrupting traffic flow, stoplights would be installed at only a few major intersections on each artery. Motorists could speed through the other intersections without having to yield the right of way.[76] "The automobile is in its very nature a high speed vehicle; to function properly it therefore should have a high speed thoroughfare," Swan explained. "A large part of the traffic problem in every city is to bring the automobile and the thoroughfare plan more nearly in tune with one another, to remove, to ameliorate or to control such obstructions in the thoroughfares as militate against the greatest usefulness of the automobile."[77]

Swan was more successful than Carrère and Hastings in gaining acceptance for his ideas. The city, which had begun installing automatic traffic signals in late 1925, created a coordinated system of traffic lights in and around the downtown in 1929. In 1930 Hartford finally adopted the through-street plan, letting automobiles speed down major arteries without having to yield the right of way to traffic on cross streets. Vehicles attempting to cross now had to wait for a break in traffic. Neighbors and merchants complained that high-speed traffic made it hard for pedestrians to cross the street, but they met with little sympathy.[78] The through-street plan put the final seal of official approval on a forty-year trend toward vehicular traffic's primacy on major thoroughfares.

The various efforts to create a modern street system in Hartford produced striking differences in traffic on different streets. By making physical and regulatory changes, the city government transformed the use of the long streets leading downtown and to the factory district. No longer protected as settings for the display of wealth, these streets became pipelines of constant high-speed traffic, integrating the economic machinery of the city and linking it to the evolving state highway network. Meanwhile, the city government allowed some streets to remain narrow, poorly paved, and unplowed, ensuring that their function in the traffic system would be limited to providing access to neighboring houses. Downtown, the intense regulation of street use further contributed to the differentiation of public space. The regulations ensured that pedestrianism, like children's play and street peddling, would be forced from major streets to alternative spaces — in this case, the sidewalks.

9

City Plans

In 1907, the man who would soon devise a city plan for Hartford spoke with regret about what had happened to American cities and streets. "In our cities, and in fact in our whole mode of life, we separate work from pleasure, the practical from the beautiful, instead of blending them as is so skillfully done by the older nations of the world," said John M. Carrère in an address to the Twentieth Century Club in Hartford. "A street is apt to be nothing but a thoroughfare, so that we must go and come and travel upon it without enjoyment, which we must seek elsewhere at given points laid aside for this particular purpose. . . . But there is no reason why our streets should not be thoroughfares and breathing spaces and pleasure grounds all in one." [1]

Carrère, a prominent New York architect, shared with Hartford's progressive reformers a belief in the potential of attractive environments to uplift people and enrich their lives, a belief that had shaped the local reform tradition since Horace Bushnell's efforts at civic improvement in the 1850s. In 1912 this common faith in environmental influence led Carrère's firm to devise a city plan that bore important similarities to Bushnell's own planning proposals. But Carrère's speech and city plan also showed how far students of city life had traveled from mid-nineteenth-century concerns about public space. Unlike Bushnell, Carrère and the Hartford progressives had come to care less about the environment's power to encourage social interaction than about its direct effect on the individual. Carrère bemoaned the streets' degeneration into traffic routes not because he was worried about the disappearance of play or commerce there, but because a traffic route did not offer individuals a healing encounter with beauty. "The beauty of a street induces beauty in buildings and adds beauty to life, whereas the confusion of streets and jumble of buildings that surround us in our American cities contribute nothing valuable to life," he told the Twentieth Century Club. "On the contrary, it sadly disturbs our peace of mind and destroys that repose within us which is the true basis of all contentment." [2] By treating public space as part functional and part artistic composition — and ignoring its value as what Bushnell had called "a social exchange" — Carrère's superficially similar planning proposals were subtly at odds with what Bushnell had intended. The pursuit of efficiency, refinement, and inner repose led Carrère to favor a more thoroughly differentiated system of public space that would actually further the trend toward segregating activities within the city, and thus separate different kinds of people. As his comment on the confusion of the streets indicates, he was happy with thoroughfares as long as they were beautiful and uncongested.

The 1912 city plan stood midway between Bushnell's city-planning proposals and the land use zoning of the 1920s. The old hope of uplifting city dwellers by improving their environment, still alive in the 1910s, withered away in 1920s Hartford. Instead, civic leaders embraced the empty shell of one of the two trends in the progressive reform of public space: segregation. No longer hoping to spread gentility throughout the city, no longer even so concerned with protecting or advancing it in certain areas, the men who controlled the reform of urban space in the 1920s were interested above all in separating conflicting activities for reasons of economic efficiency. They sought a traffic system that would speed the circulation of goods, employees, and customers within the city. Similarly, they sought a system of private land use that would prevent concerns about the quality of life from interfering with profitable real estate investment—a system that would encourage rapid and orderly development without destroying the neighborhoods where they made their homes. This system was based on zoning regulations, which divided the city into districts reserved for specific activities and imposed restrictions on the size, height, and placement of buildings. By making zoning the centerpiece of city planning, the civic leaders of the 1920s distorted the principle of segregated land use pioneered by Bushnell and applied by some progressive reformers to the use of parks and streets. Domesticity still had an influence on the use of urban space in the 1920s—in fact, it was now protected in certain legally defined residential neighborhoods—but it was no longer the model for citywide reform.

Municipal Art

Fifty years after Bushnell helped form the Society for Public Improvement and wrote "City Plans," issues of city planning returned to the forefront of the local reform agenda. At its formation in 1904, the Municipal Art Society declared that its object was "to conserve and enhance in every practicable way the beauty of the streets, buildings and public places of Hartford; to stimulate interest in the scenic, artistic and architectural development of the City; and to encourage a greater civic pride in the care and improvement of public and private property." It was a rather broad goal, and the diversity of the society's leadership opened the possibility for a wide variety of activities. The society's founding officers, directors, and committee chairmen were drawn from throughout the spectrum of elite and middle-class civic life in Hartford. The founding leadership included the artist Charles Noël Flagg; the state librarian, George S. Godard; the Civic Club president, Dotha Bushnell Hillyer; the city engineer, Frederick L. Ford; the attorneys Charles A. Goodwin and Walter S. Schutz; the future suffragist Josephine Bennett; the retired industrialist Louis R. Cheney; the Keney Park superintendent, George A. Parker; Mayor William F. Henney; and the Daughters of the American Revolution regent, Emily S. G. Holcombe.[3]

The society was held together by a common interest in beauty. In separate essays in the society's first publication, Flagg and Parker wrote of the need to preserve and enhance the city's beauty in the face of challenges created by what Flagg called "the spirit of commercialism." Parker added that part of the task was opening the eyes of the public to the beauty that was already there. "Mankind is apt to be art blind and to see only commercial values, when they might add much to their pleasure if they would see the aesthetic value and spiritual truths as impressed in material things; for after all art is but the expression of the spirit and mind of man." The sensitive souls who could feel the transcendent power of beauty had an obligation to provide beautiful surroundings for those dull plodders who could not, in the hope that at least the children could benefit. Flagg and Parker both linked the society's work with Bushnell's legacy, which neither defined very clearly. Flagg suggested that the society's efforts to beautify Hartford would extend "the good work already accomplished by . . . Dr. Horace Bushnell, and continued by our Park Board, the Civic Club, and various commissions and public and private enterprises."[4]

The society's rather hazy ideology allowed its leaders blithely to deny what others might consider significant distinctions. Parker argued that enlightened city planners would not have to choose between beauty and economic efficiency: "One definition of an engineer is a man who does something quickly, systematically, scientifically, and with the least expense . . . and a definition of an artist might be a man who can do all that the engineer does, but, in addition to it, he writes into the heart and soul of a man in loving sympathy with the higher life; and as it is the greatest economy for the city to employ the best engineer, so the investment that will pay the city the greatest dividend is Municipal Art." Further erasing the distinction between aesthetics and finances, William Henney declared in 1905, "The beauty of our city is an asset of commercial value, and money spent, within reasonable limits, in making it an attractive place of residence, is prudently spent. For it will draw to us people of wealth and refinement, seeking congenial homes, whose possessions will find their way into the grand list of the city."[5]

To some extent, the society's advocacy of street cleaning and billboard removal put it in harmony with the Civic Club and other groups seeking to purify the urban environment. But its ideology cannot be so narrowly defined, since the society's members also believed that beautifying the city went hand in hand with creating an efficient street system. Flagg urged Hartford reformers to follow the example of Baron Georges-Eugène Haussmann, the French city planner responsible for tearing new boulevards and avenues through Paris in the 1850s and 1860s. By creating "an intelligent lay-out of streets and avenues," Flagg wrote, Haussmann accomplished great things "for the proper sanitation and beautifying, as well as for the civic economy of Paris."[6]

The society's Committee on the City Plan added in a 1904 report that new transportation technologies made such changes more important than ever in early twentieth-century Hartford. This report, written by Parker, the committee's chairman, argued that Hartford should be seen as a unified organism, a living thing with a vital need for good circulation. "This unity is made up of composite parts within its borders the same as our body is made up of many organs and functions within our skin. This comparison could be carried still further. For instance, that the avenues are its arteries, the residential streets, [its] capillary system, homes, its corpuscles, and the parks its lungs. This comparison might be carried on until we find in the city a counterpart for every organ and function of the human life." The health of the city as a whole must take priority over the defense of petty private interests.[7]

It was not easy, Parker acknowledged, to discern this structure in the chaos of the modern city. The urban landscape had grown to such an extent that few individuals attempted to understand it in its totality; rather, they developed cognitive maps of the streets they used regularly. "How many do you suppose there are in Hartford that have passed even once through all these streets?" Parker asked, noting that there were 455 different streets in the city at that time. "Is it not true that with nine-tenths of the people, Hartford consists of simply a few streets, a few stores, a few shops and a few homes, that being the limit of their actual knowledge of the city?" Switching metaphors, Parker argued that the reformers on his committee had a responsibility to go beyond this fragmented understanding, for "what would you think of a housekeeper who . . . had been in only a few of the rooms of her house?"[8]

After spending a year studying Hartford's anatomy (or exploring its rooms), the committee reported in 1905 that the city's radial street plan was basically a good one. "Yet Hartford is growing so rapidly and the demands of travel will become so great that our present street plan will not meet them, and other main avenues should be provided," wrote Parker, during the growth spurt that was pushing the city's population from about 80,000 in 1900 to 138,000 in 1920. To ease the westward flow of traffic from the Connecticut River bridge then being built, he urged the creation of a new downtown street linking Morgan Street with Farmington Avenue. He also recommended the construction of a thoroughfare that would run along the Park River from the factory district to the railroad station and then bend to the northeast away from downtown. "These avenues would probably divert some of the through travel . . . from the center of the city, leaving that section freer for local business. It would seem as if some relief would have to be given to the fast growing congestion on Main street near the City Hall."[9] In 1906 Parker's committee further urged that narrow downtown streets be widened before the construction of new retail buildings made the cost prohibitive. The Municipal Art Society continued to urge street improvements until the end of its active existence in the late 1910s.[10]

A rationalized street system was not the only form of differentiated public space the Municipal Art Society sought. From its very beginning, the society called for the creation of a "civic center"—a beautiful cluster of impressive public buildings. City Beautiful reformers nationwide were showing a similar interest at this time, with works on the subject being written by Charles Mulford Robinson, Charles Zueblin, and (collaboratively) Daniel H. Burnham, John Carrère, and Arnold W. Brunner. The most impressive civic center plan was the one included in Burnham's 1909 *Plan of Chicago*, which proposed enormous administrative and cultural buildings along a boulevard west and south of the commercial district. "In this impressive reorientation of the city, the commercial district would occupy a decidedly secondary position," observes the historian Daniel Bluestone. "Much like the separate domestic realm anchored by parks, bolstered by churches and centered in residential enclaves and eventually suburbs, the proponents of a monumental civic center conceived of a separate realm for civic and cultural life."[11]

Civic centers nationwide were conceived as alternatives to the commercial hubbub and individual acquisitiveness typical of the business districts. For this reason, and because of their association with culture, refinement, and social harmony, they might seem to fall within the traditional gender dualism that Americans had long used for categorizing urban space. But the parallels with the feminized spaces of the home and nineteenth-century park should not be carried too far. Burnham and other early planners ascribed to civic centers the power to create a new form of social order. This power was not based on any friendly feeling that might be cultivated there by fleeting personal encounters between rich and poor. Rather, the splendor of the architecture was supposed to awe the viewer and instill a deep respect for the impersonal ideas of community and polity. In this way the civic centers were envisioned as having quite a different effect from the naturalized parks of the nineteenth century. They raised power above sentiment and abstractions above human warmth, so they were not so strongly rooted in "feminine" values. The central administration building proposed in his *Plan of Chicago*, Burnham wrote, would be "surmounted by a dome of impressive height, to be seen and felt by the people, to whom it should stand as the symbol of civic order and unity. Rising from the plain upon which Chicago rests, its effect may be compared to that of the dome of St. Peter's at Rome." The desire to raise the idea of the city to a level of moral and almost religious authority received intellectual justification during the Progressive Era from such works as Edward A. Ross's *Social Control* and Newton M. Hall's *Civic Righteousness and Civic Pride*. Progressive intellectuals shared with City Beautiful reformers a hope that this vague civic religion would provide a new basis for social order in a metropolis so riven by class and ethnic divisions that face-to-face relations had lost their power. The promotion of this abstract, impersonal faith reflected a larger trend during the Progressive Era and 1920s toward a reassertion of male cultural power—a trend embodied in such diverse examples as Theodore Roosevelt's celebration of masculine strength, the muscular Christianity of Billy Sunday and the Men and Religion Forward movement, the popularity of aggressive sports, the fixation on the androgynous flapper, and what the historian Ann Douglas has termed the "matricidal" swagger of 1920s modernist fiction.[12]

Somewhat like Burnham, Parker spoke of ways to promote what in 1910 he called "that immaterial, immeasurable, imponderable spirit of the city which in olden times might have been personified by a goddess or genii, but which our modern scientific age prevents us from naming." He feared that the spirit of Hartford was "in danger of being weakened by commercialism," and he warned also of the need to teach immigrants about Yankee traditions and institutions. "One of the most efficient ways for such a training is by monuments and memorials, which appeal to their sight," he wrote in 1911, urging that the Old State House (which served at that time as city hall) be preserved even after it ceased to house municipal offices. The half-apologetic way in which Parker sought to promote the civic religion, however, suggests that he may have been dimly aware of the hollowness of this artificial faith, which lacked the core of oppositional, feminine values that had given life to earlier environmental reform movements. He indicated in 1904 that a civic center should be placed apart from the business center not because separation would assert its superiority, but because "it must not interfere with that . . . which our modern cities represent, commercialism and industrialism. It must be subordinate to them." [13]

Parker may have been half-hearted in his promotion of the spirit of Hartford, but other city planning advocates treated the civic religion almost as an embarrassment. The Municipal Art Society chose to base its support for civic centers on arguments similar to later utilitarian rationales for zoning regulations. In an essay in the society's 1904 publication, *The Grouping of Public Buildings*, the city engineer, Frederick L. Ford, discussed both the economic and the aesthetic advantages of creating a civic center focused on the state capitol building at the west end of Bushnell Park. The purpose of the essay was to persuade the state to locate its proposed new armory on Capitol Avenue immediately west of the capitol, at a site then occupied by six tenement houses and an obsolete roundhouse owned by the Consolidated Railroad. At this time, in the decades around the turn of the century, impressive new armories were being built in cities throughout the United States to house volunteer militia units and to serve as deterrents to workers' uprisings. [14] If any such fear of class war influenced the Municipal Art Society's advocacy of an armory separating the factory district from the capitol, however, Ford chose not to mention it.

Ford wrote instead of the need to protect the value of the "prominent group of public and semi-public structures" around western Bushnell Park, specifically to protect the capitol "from the encroachment of private interests and objectionable surroundings," whose obnoxious influence already included tarnishing the capitol's exterior with soot. The capitol was protected on the north by the park, on the east by the construction of new insurance buildings, and on the south by the state's acquisition of land for the future Connecticut State Library. Only at the roundhouse site was it exposed. Ford argued, "The artistic grouping of public buildings in and around beautiful parks with harmonious surroundings, accomplishes more to bring a city nearer to the ideal than any other form of municipal development." Art made good financial sense, since "with all of the money which has been invested in public and semi-public buildings in and around Bushnell Park, I believe it would be an unpardonable mistake to neglect to take advantage of the opportunity which the roundhouse site offers." The clustering of state buildings would also make for more efficient state business, Ford argued. In response to the society's urging, the state built the armory at the roundhouse site instead of near the train station at the edge of downtown.[15]

The Municipal Art Society's proposals for street improvements and its arguments for civic centers reveal a stronger fascination with building rationalized systems than with beautifying the urban environment. The value of these systems was understood in financial terms: well-designed streets and civic centers would encourage the optimal growth of property values. Despite rhetorical flourishes about the inspiring influence of landscape beauty and fine architecture, the society chose to soft-pedal its initial noise about the conflict between commercial and spiritual matters. It sought to reassure property owners that increased municipal interference in property rights would end up working to their financial advantage. Beauty paid, whether in a system of beautiful streets or a system of beautiful land use. Everyone would benefit financially in the long run, and the spirit of Hartford would soar alongside the spirit of commercialism.

Parker edged toward open advocacy of zoning in his reports for the society's Committee on the City Plan. He mentioned in the 1905 report that the committee had studied "the subdivision of the city into natural neighborhoods of business, manufacturing, and social circles," and had "been deeply impressed with the need of pleasant and comfortable homes for people of small means, or of the earning power of workmen and mechanics in manufactures." A proper city plan should include some means of encouraging both the development of such homes and other forms of land use. "We should strive to have such a plan that will give to every foot of its territory the greatest use and value to its present owner, its future owner, and the city as a whole." Planning could benefit everyone. The 1906 report specifically stated that zoning rules would be a part of this effort. "The solution which seems promising is the creation within the territory of Hartford, [of] what is known in some cities as 'residential districts,' granting to such 'districts' certain privileges and imposing certain restrictions."[16]

Such a division of the city would have obvious parallels with Parker's division of parkland by function and by social class. Parker even explicitly stated that, by creating parks that appealed to the affluent, city governments could sort out urban residential patterns and maximize property values. Parks, he wrote, "have the effect of localizing certain classes and attracting near them a high-grade class of residences and thereby directly increase the valuation of land in their immediate neighborhood." Nevertheless, Parker did not see residential segregation as benefiting only the wealthy and swelling the tax rolls. In fact, he suggested in the 1906 report, the creation of residential districts would primarily benefit working-men in need of housing.[17]

There is little evidence, however, that Hartford's working classes felt much affection for the Municipal Art Society or shared its passion for landscape beauty and rising property values. The society's opposition to the public market proposed for Main Street stirred up strong class antagonisms. The armory proposal was not quite so explosive an issue, but it did provoke a blistering, if poorly spelled, denunciation from an elderly, self-styled "plebeian" named H. G. Loomis. "The Municipal Art Society may be beneficial to the millionaire's who should know to appreciate the value of money earned by Plebeians, who are compelled to pay all bills if they own anything more than a mortgage," Loomis wrote in a letter that was evidently sent to the society in 1904 or 1905. "The city was formerly conducted by practical men [who had] learned by experience to live within their means. The present time it is run by inexperienced juvenils matured verry young, who do not appreciate the differance between a small coin from a million dollars." The roundhouse, Loomis continued, "was considered a mark of great improvement for Hartford until someone smelled smoke. Then everything must be moved out of town, no shops to work in, no taxes to collect, no place for Plebeians to live. Freeholds to be converted into a jungle of wilderness for Parks, arrest and convict Plebeians as tramps should they be found thereon without work." Loomis ended by alluding vaguely to satanic corruption "practiced by Life Insurance Managers, Commissions etc. to deceive Plebeians without any recourse."[18]

The Commission on the City Plan

It took nearly twenty years for the city government to act on Parker's ideas about regulating land use. In the meantime, the current of city planning meandered along a different bureaucratic channel. In January 1907, shortly after Parker issued his call for zoning and increased city planning, a former Municipal Art Society president, Charles A. Goodwin, asked the city to form what was perhaps the first municipal planning commission in the United States. Goodwin explained in a short essay in the *Hartford Times* that such a commission was necessary in order "to aid in building up Hartford in an orderly fashion, to sift the good from the bad, the necessary from the impractical and generally to make the city's resources count to the uttermost." The commission could ensure efficient, wise, and cost-effective decisions about municipal projects, could lead a major urban renewal project in the East Side, and could devise a tentative planning map to guide Hartford's growth. Support for the idea came from Mayor William F. Henney, another member of the society, who predicted that the commission "would mean the development of the city in an orderly and systematic manner, having in view both utility and attractiveness and [would] have much to do with the appearance of the Hartford of 1950." Goodwin, who represented part of Asylum Hill in the Common Council, secured the council's backing for the necessary charter revision, which was approved by the legislature in March. The newly formed commission held its first meeting in May.[19]

Parker hoped that the commission could realize his dream of residential districts for workingmen. He further believed that it had the opportunity

> to help build up a most substantial City, one in which the weakest
> and least of its people shall have full opportunity in their own way to
> receive all of life, liberty, and happiness they are capable of absorbing, where the environments of everyone shall be such that whatever
> they have received from inheritance shall be strengthened and the

best development possible comes from it, where there shall be little or no poverty unless one deliberately chooses it, no sickness due to environments, where labor shall not be exhausted, and the joy of work and the spirit of life abound.[20]

Compared to these rosy visions, the real Commission on the City Plan was pretty drab. For one thing, although its high-powered membership included the mayor and other top city officials, the commission had only limited powers. The Common Council could direct the commission to carry out certain public improvements, and it was required to ask the commission's advice on all questions concerning the location of streets and public spaces. The commission could make maps showing advisable locations for public buildings, streets, and parks. Its greatest power was to appropriate private real estate for public improvements, including surplus land, which it could sell for a profit to fund the work. Commission members, however, acknowledged that this last provision was of dubious constitutionality and hesitated to use it. The commission's powers were soon expanded slightly by the requirement that developers secure its approval for all subdivisions of land before obtaining the city's approval for any new streets. This additional provision effectively gave the commission the right to determine street layouts, block size, and building lots in newly developing areas.[21]

The commission seemed to apologize for how little it accomplished. "It has felt that during the first year of its work it was best to proceed slowly and cautiously so as to gain the confidence of the public, without which it could hope to accomplish but little of real value to the city of Hartford. No attempt has been made to take advantage of the broad powers conferred upon the Commission by the charter amendments creating it," the commission explained in its first annual report. Evidently caution continued to be necessary, for the commission gave a similar explanation for its apparent inactivity in its third report.[22]

The bulk of the planning commission's work consisted of approving developers' proposed street layouts and advising the Board of Street Commissioners on street widenings and extensions. In this way, the commission continued the city government's established practice of influencing development by improving certain streets. The difference was that, instead of letting developers haphazardly plat streets to suit their own economic interests, the commission now took an active role in creating an orderly system. "Hartford like many American cities, has suffered from the destructive work of outside real estate speculators, who have purchased areas within the city limits and subdivided them with little or no reference to the layout of adjoining city streets or the customary or proper size of building lots," complained Ford. The planning commission's influence over street and subdivision plans, he said, would help "avoid this practice, which did more than anything else to injure the development of our street system along rational lines." Without such intervention, individual developers would supposedly make decisions that could result in short streets and a concomitant inefficient traffic flow. Examples of the effects of the new policy in the planning commission's first few years can be seen in the approval of street layouts and extensions that turned Greenfield Street and Tower Avenue into east-west arteries in the quickly developing North End. The commission also devised and secured the adoption of a street plan for what is now the Blue Hills neighborhood, which it declared to be superior to developers' plans that would otherwise have been enacted "without regard to . . . the convenience of the travelling public."[23]

Decisions about street layout did not have to be guided simply by a desire for rapid travel and lucrative real estate investment. Parker, who joined the planning commission in 1909, hoped these decisions would help achieve his ambitious reform goals. He believed that wise use of the commission's power would stop the creation of oversized blocks, which had encouraged landlords to build tenement houses in rear lots. He also supported a private developer's request that the city build a new thoroughfare to provide access to vacant land southwest of Pope Park, on the grounds that this would allow the construction of homes for workingmen.[24]

For the most part, however, the commission's idealistic and aesthetic side came out only in its advisory work. Among other recommendations, it called for the construction of public bathhouses and restrooms, the cleansing of the Park River, a continued ban on illuminated signs overhanging the sidewalks, and the extension of Bushnell Park to Main Street as a memorial to Horace Bushnell. The park extension would offer an attractive entrance from the business district, allow the construction of "a main artery from the south part of the city to the railroad station and the west," and let the city control and clean up both banks of the filthy Park River. It would be another way in which beauty, cleanliness, and traffic circulation could be promoted simultaneously.[25]

The commission placed its most ambitious hopes in the hands of Carrère and Hastings, the architects it hired in 1909 to prepare a city plan. The commission gave the architects a list of forty-three matters on which it wanted advice, including the design of the grounds around the Old State House, the armory, and the state library; the choice of sites for a new city hall, a new technical high school, a new train station, and new playgrounds; a plan for better downtown street lighting; the construction or improvement of numerous streets to ease travel in and around the downtown; the widening of major avenues; the extension of Bushnell Park to the Connecticut River; a plan for a railroad tunnel under Asylum Hill; methods of Park River pollution control; ways to limit fire hazards; ways to improve housing conditions; ways to regulate billboards, air pollution, and street noise; and "the advisability of dividing the city into zones for different uses and with possibly different restrictions regarding height of buildings, and the percentage of area which can be built upon, etc., following the practice which is being introduced in several German cities."[26]

Following three years of work, in 1912 the firm of Carrère and Hastings (John Carrère having died in the interim of injuries sustained in an automobile accident) issued a report that called for an almost utopian transformation of Hartford. The architects began by describing the general principles behind good urban planning, diagramming the structure and transportation systems of the ideal city. Eager to emphasize efficiency over aesthetics, they avoided the anatomical metaphor in favor of a mechanical one: "A city, in the light of modern civilization and modern science . . . must be considered as a great machine having a most intricate organism and a most complex function to perform, and it must be so well planned and put together and run, that as an engine it shall produce the maximum amount of efficiency in every direction and the least friction."[27]

The ideal urban machine displayed a radial structure, with an "industrial and manufacturing zone" and a separate "commercial zone" following the rail lines leading out from the administrative and financial center at the city's heart. Parks and parkways would also radiate from the center, or rather would bring the countryside in to meet the urban core. The parks and parkways would separate the industrial and commercial zones from two residential zones, one for working people and one for the well-to-do. Fortunately, the architects wrote, Hartford already had a rather efficient structure that reflected some aspects of the ideal plan, particularly the good park system and the radial avenues. Ideally the city would adopt zoning regulations to control the use of private land, but the architects regretfully supposed that Americans would not tolerate such interference with private property rights. Nearly as effective in producing a well-organized city, they said, would be the creation of a more efficient street system. "If the lines of traffic are the shortest in any direction and ample for all purposes, if the relation of width to length and purpose of the streets, avenues and parkways is well planned, the matter of developing the practical features of a city on this groundwork becomes a mere detail." [28]

For this reason the architects devoted most of their report to recommending changes in street patterns, which they claimed was the most important part of urban planning anyway. "Primarily a street is a means of circulation and as such should afford the most direct connection between any two given points," they wrote, adding that in the future this traffic would consist more and more of automobiles. But different streets had different functions and should be designed accordingly: Major arteries should be long, wide, and direct; secondary streets—particularly in residential neighborhoods—should be narrower, shorter, and curved. Residential streets should have macadam pavement to cut down on noise. New residential neighborhoods with short, curving streets would bring even workingmen into closer touch with nature and insulate them from the rush of traffic. To ease the flow of traffic through the city, the architects proposed opening new radial thoroughfares, building parkways along the Park River and its branches, widening existing downtown streets to ease the traffic on Asylum Street, and running new streets and parkways through Bushnell, Pope, Riverside, and Rocky Ridge parks and the South Green. One of the most important improvements, they urged, would be the construction of two concentric beltways. The inner one would embrace the downtown, the capitol area, and the most densely

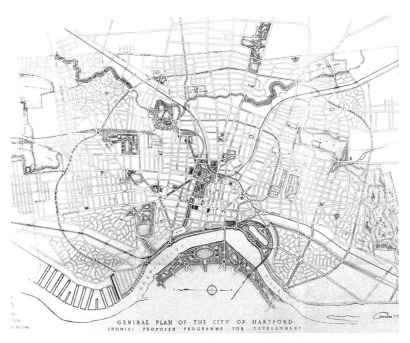

The Carrère and Hastings plan for Hartford, 1912, with new inner and outer boulevards, traffic circles at major intersections, and boulevards converging at the state capitol. Note the networks of crooked streets in Behind the Rocks (*upper left*), Blue Hills (*upper right*), and the North and South Meadows. Almost none of the changes proposed in this plan became realities.

developed part of the factory district. The outer one would arc out near the city line and link the more distant parks.[29]

Carrère and Hastings subordinated beauty and social welfare to transportation efficiency. They even made the peculiarly inaccurate claim that "throughout the report not a word has been mentioned about the beauty of the city and . . . particular stress has been laid throughout on organic and practical considerations." There was no conflict between the different goals anyway, the architects argued, since beauty as well as appropriate land use would result inevitably from improved street design. To impress this idea on the reader, they included pairs of photographs contrasting Hartford's streets unfavorably with those in European capitals. One of the most striking pairs juxtaposed a view of the Champs-Elysées with one of Morgan Street in the East Side slum. The architects designed their new avenues to end at points of visual interest as well as to provide convenient access. For instance, the street that would slice diagonally through Bushnell Park to the state capitol "would not only be an ornamentation to the park with the fine vista of the capitol that it would give, but would greatly increase and assist access to the southwest quarter of the city." The architects proposed taking another swath of land from Bushnell Park to create "a dignified Mall or Parkway" connecting the civic center at the state capitol with the planned new municipal building on Main Street. They further proposed the construction of numerous traffic circles at major intersections, where monuments could be placed for maximum visibility. Also included in the report were brief nods to some of the aesthetic and social issues that had already been pet projects of the Municipal Art Society and various other reformers: cleaning up the streets, building public restrooms, banning billboards, constructing playgrounds, suppressing unnecessary street noise, and strengthening traffic regulations.[30]

The claim that efficiency was the mother of beauty today seems disingenuous or even perverse, but the architects may well have been sincere. They thought that the experience of uninterrupted travel through a well-designed street system could expose the viewer to a series of pleasant sights. These would compensate for unavoidable urban eyesores and produce a favorable impression of the city as a whole. That was why it was so important to have the streets lead toward points of visual interest. "What should be aimed at, in the remodelling of our cities, is the creation of as many centers of interest throughout the city as possible," Carrère had said in 1907. "Certain sections of every city must of necessity be ugly and forbidding, and such centers are a refuge and a relief. We must then aim at an interesting and attractive and beautiful way of getting from any one important point in the city to the next point of interest, so that in whatever direction we may travel we may find recreation and rest." Similarly, the concentric beltways would be a way of physically integrating the diverse sections of the city. Like the parkways proposed earlier, they would allow the viewer to perceive the city as an attractive, coherent unit despite the contrasts in the passing landscape.[31]

The Carrère and Hastings plan shows both important similarities to and profound differences from what Bushnell had envisioned in writing

"City Plans." The similarities can be seen in the recommendations for public buildings and monuments at the intersections of major streets, for wide traffic thoroughfares, for curving and diagonal streets to break up the rectangular grid, and for major avenues along low valleys. Both Bushnell in the 1850s and Carrère and Hastings in the 1910s sought to create visual unity out of a seemingly chaotic landscape. They also minimized the conflict between aesthetic and functional considerations. The architects' status as trained experts may also seem to fulfill, in part, Bushnell's hope for a city-planning profession.

But the architects saw the purpose and effects of planning much differently from the way Bushnell had seen them. The theologian had hoped above all to unite different kinds of people and to give them a common sense of being gathered together into city life. He wanted to encourage "the sense of density and a crowding, rapid, all-to-do activity" in the streets, and "life and vivacity" in the parks. The parks were places through which rich and poor would stroll and "make acquaintance through the eyes." By the time Carrère and Hastings wrote their report, however, the city and its public spaces had been radically transformed. No longer the pleasant little town of the 1850s, Hartford had grown into a more diverse and industrialized city. Residents were now more likely to ride to work in a streetcar or an automobile than to walk. The parks where they took their pleasure were being divided into systems of recreational facilities that attracted people of different interests and class backgrounds. The bustling activity of the streets had remained confined to the central city while quiet residential neighborhoods sprawled out to the city line. Even in the central city, street activity was being moderated or displaced by crackdowns on peddlers, expressmen, prostitutes, and newsies. Progressive reformers and city officials shared Bushnell's faith in the power of the environment, but they had different goals. They wanted order, not social unity, and many of them were eager to split up urban space in order to achieve that order. Carrère and Hastings, like the Hartford progressives of the 1910s, said little about encouraging interclass encounters within public space. In fact, they said little about human interaction at all. They imagined citizens in their improved city riding in automobiles from one beautiful spot to another, soothed by the ease of travel and the well-designed vistas, unperturbed by the squalor

and ugliness of certain sections they passed. The problem with the un-
improved urban environment was not that it had a divisive effect on society, but that it was inefficient and could disturb one's inner peace.

The Carrère and Hastings plan certainly had its appeal at this time,
but even optimists acknowledged that "perhaps it might be called vision-
ary." Despite its wealth, Hartford could not possibly afford such an extensive reconstruction project. The Commission on the City Plan wrote,
"However idealistic these plans seem, whatever difficulties may interfere
with carrying them out in detail, however strongly they may be objected
to, they yet illustrate the important principles of city planning and afford
us a broader and clearer vision of what our city needs." The commission
supported its own modified grid design for the Blue Hills neighborhood
over the architects' unusual web of crooked streets. Parker claimed that
a private developer planned to follow the architects' similar plan for a
working-class neighborhood in the southern part of Behind the Rocks,
but this never materialized. All of the plan's recommendations were ignored except for a few relatively minor street improvements. "While the
desirability of all its features is recognized, the practicability of them has
been doubted, because of the expense to be incurred and the radical
destruction and reconstruction required," the *Hartford Daily Courant*
editorialized several years later.[32]

After issuing the plan, the commission gradually assumed a lower pro-
file. It continued to meet to consider developers' proposals for streets and
subdivisions and to make occasional planning recommendations, mainly
for easing traffic congestion. But the need for such work diminished as
the city reached its geographic limits without being able to annex suburban territory. The commission also focused more exclusively on the
traffic system, abandoning the attempt to balance efficiency with a supposedly complementary concern for beauty. This shift was in keeping
with national developments in city planning during the 1910s, often described as a change from the City Beautiful to the City Practical or the
City Functional. Advocates of the City Functional sought to base planning on such "facts" as traffic flow. Such an approach gave the movement an aura of scientific authority and enhanced the professional status
of city planners. "When the city planning movement was young, too
much emphasis was laid upon the usefulness of beauty," wrote a Hartford

commission member, W. A. Graham, in 1916. "Now-a-days the emphasis is laid on the beauty of usefulness."[33]

Zoning

Reform efforts slowed considerably in Hartford in the late 1910s and 1920s. Some of the major reform leaders—Dotha Hillyer, Mary Hall, Emily Holcombe, and George Parker—were winding down their activities because of age. The Municipal Art Society, already in decline by the time of its last publication in 1912, held no more annual meetings after the death of Charles Flagg in 1916. The society's directors continued to meet and found enough energy to protest the Main Street market plan in 1918 before beginning to discuss disbanding late in 1919. President William Honniss blamed the society's suspension of activities on "war conditions, the influenza epidemic, etc." The society survived in name only until its official dissolution in 1940.[34] The scarcity of new activists and new reform organizations was at least as damaging as the decline of the old ones.

The decline of the local reform spirit reflected a larger national trend after World War I. Many progressives were disillusioned and discouraged by Woodrow Wilson's exploitation of altruistic impulses during the war, by the suppression of pacifists and radicals, and by the powerful conservative reaction that followed the armistice. The unchecked conservative reaction did not overthrow the governmental powers exercised during the Progressive Era and the war, but only because businessmen recognized that the government could increase economic stability and ensure more reliable profits. Reformist businessmen ignored the utopian hopes that had shaped much of progressive reform and appropriated only those regulatory and administrative mechanisms that suited their purposes. Similarly, businessmen, real estate interests and bureaucrats gained greater power over city planning in the postprogressive years, shifting the purpose of planning more exclusively to supporting economic efficiency.[35]

City-planning efforts in Hartford in the late 1910s lagged as a result of the inactivity of the Municipal Art Society and the limited scope of the work done by the Commission on the City Plan. Without the energy of the progressive reformers, Hartford was no longer near the fore in American city planning. In 1924 Mayor Norman C. Stevens criticized the planning commission for having "lain dormant for fifteen years while over two hundred other cities and towns have created City Plan Commissions which are very active and have established their rights and duties." He proposed reviving the commission and assigning it to work on zoning, housing, and regional planning. "In my opinion Zoning is one of the greatest needs of Hartford today," he said, adding nothing further about housing or regional planning.[36]

Zoning, which meant very different things to different people, was gaining support throughout the United States in the late 1910s and 1920s. It appealed to a broad constituency that included conservative ideologues who wanted to segregate the classes, business leaders eager to ensure predictable growth in real estate values, efficiency-minded advocates of expanded governmental authority, and idealists seeking to improve slum conditions. Inspired largely by the example of German cities, Americans interested in city planning had begun promoting the idea energetically in 1909, with the publication of Benjamin Clarke Marsh's *Introduction to City Planning* and the convocation of the First National Conference on City Planning. At that conference, Henry Morgenthau of New York praised zoning as a way to mitigate the evils in the urban environment that he believed were sapping the vigor of the lower classes and breeding disease, depravity, and socialism. Other speakers supporting the idea included the younger Frederick Law Olmsted and Hartford's Frederick Ford. Ford described zoning as part of the effort to secure "healthful, orderly, and symmetrical development" and to prevent excessive population densities. He freely acknowledged that zoning meant unprecedented restrictions on the use of private property, but he argued that American city planners had only to look at the flawed development of older urban neighborhoods to see the need for efficient governmental control. "We should realize more than ever before that [new] development must be along radically different lines from the older work if we are to attain the highest ideals," he told the conference.[37]

In addition to producing improved housing and reducing density, the Municipal Art Society believed that zoning could help the community overcome individual greed and produce a more tasteful urban landscape.

In 1911 a group of Municipal Art Society members, including Flagg and Hillyer, asked the planning commission to seek an ordinance limiting the height of buildings facing parks, open spaces, and thoroughfares throughout the business district. The society was concerned that skyscrapers would destroy the beauty of the city's public spaces, particularly Bushnell Park. "Hartford is no longer a village," warned Hillyer. "The haphazard system of building is no longer possible for a city the size of Hartford."[38]

Zoning also had exclusionary implications that Hartford reformers did not discuss so openly. Parker wrote publicly of being inspired by German city planning, and he was undoubtedly guided by his own experience in dividing park space, but his private letters suggest that he was at least as influenced by the racial segregation laws of southern cities. As an official of the American Park and Outdoor Art Association and of the American Civic Association, he traveled extensively through the South in the first decade of the twentieth century, visiting numerous cities and their parks. Having once worked as an overseer of black farmhands on a Maryland plantation, he was sympathetic to the South's effort to maintain white supremacy, an effort that was aided by the Jim Crow laws being adopted and strengthened at this time. The Jim Crow laws rested on a broad base of political support among southern whites, ranging from progressives who believed legal segregation would produce a more harmonious racial order to radical racists motivated by hatred. Parker sympathized with both the reformers and the racists. In the course of his travels, he even befriended the savagely negrophobic U.S. senator, Benjamin R. Tillman, of South Carolina, advised Tillman on the landscaping of his home, and began a fawning correspondence with him.[39]

Parker favored zoning regulations as a way to apply the Jim Crow philosophy to the entire urban landscape, as he indicated in a 1906 letter to a fellow advocate of city planning. "Your method of segregating the white and colored population in units distributed over the city is all right," he wrote, referring to the other reformer's plan for Greenville, South Carolina. "But for some time I have been more and more impressed that it will become necessary for cities to have the right to set aside and designate certain parts of the city's territory for such purposes. For instance, designate a certain section, as the commercial or business section of the city, and one or more other sections for manufacturing, and especially to be able to designate certain sections as residential districts of the first, second, or third class."

Parker believed that it would not be necessary to write race into the zoning regulations explicitly. The regulations could "allow buildings of much cheaper construction in the residential districts of the third class and have the rate of taxation so low that naturally the colored people would be separated in sections designated for them." He thought that such methods were applicable to northern cities as well. "I look to the South to be leaders in the many lines of civic improvement which is hardly in the embryotic state at present. I have great faith in the South." [40] Parker was correct in thinking that southern cities would be innovators in city planning. Although Boston imposed height restrictions in 1891, and Los Angeles established industrial zones in 1909, southern cities took the lead in adopting zoning regulations in the 1910s. Baltimore enacted a racial zoning ordinance in 1910, inspiring imitations in Richmond, Atlanta, Birmingham, Louisville, and other southern cities. Housing reformers in Baltimore and Richmond provided crucial support for racial zoning campaigns. Throughout the South racial zoning drew support as a way to prevent the spread of housing blight, to prevent black encroachment on white neighborhoods, and to create an orderly system of differentiating and stabilizing the use of urban space. The racial zoning movement suffered an ultimately fatal injury when the U.S. Supreme Court struck down Louisville's ordinance in 1917, but additional cities, including Charleston, Dallas, Indianapolis, and New Orleans, continued to pass such ordinances for years. And zoning ordinances without racially specific language were used deliberately and quite effectively in promoting segregation. [41]

In Hartford, where in 1910 less than two percent of the population was black, class issues were more important than racial issues. Carrère and Hastings explicitly sought to promote class segregation by arguing that the ideal location of the "working people zone" was at the opposite side of town from the affluent "residential zone." Notwithstanding Parker's philanthropic advocacy of housing for skilled workers and the lower middle class, the Municipal Art Society was anxious to prevent the invasion of multifamily housing into Asylum Hill. In 1913 Flagg and other members of the society's board of directors discussed their fear that the spread of ugly apartment buildings was ruining the best residential districts and views.[42]

Though this peculiar mix of idealism, aestheticism, and snobbery lay behind Hartford reformers' early support for zoning, different motivations led to zoning's ultimate adoption. The business leaders and politicians who secured the passage of the necessary regulations in the 1920s sought to end the conflict between beauty and efficiency not by denying its existence, as the Municipal Art Society had done, but by segregating different land uses. In this way, they argued, they would make each neighborhood congenial for a specific use and protect real estate investments. "Among the results of 'zoning' are stabilizing of land values, protection of home neighborhoods, adequate and suitable space for industrial and commercial developments, relief of traffic congestion, improvement in conditions of health and morality, improved fire-fighting conditions, conservation of investment in public works, etc.," reported the planning commission in 1922. The commission made its report at a time when American business leaders and men of property were becoming reconciled to the idea of increased governmental intervention in economic life. Such intervention stifled some of the opportunities present when entrepreneurial competition was unrestricted, but at the same time it offered greater stability and safety for those already established in business or real estate. It benefited those who desired orderly economic development — at the expense of startup businesses. Mayor Norman C. Stevens told the Common Council in 1925, "Zoning is the scientifically planned development of a city. It brings order out of disorder, removes conditions which have become obstacles in the way of economic value, use and development of the City, and prevents desirable residential sections from being exploited by small business ventures."[43]

Other cities had adopted zoning regulations because of similar concerns about secure property values and the need to balance orderly development against quality of life. New York City enacted the first comprehensive zoning law in the United States in 1916, largely in response to Fifth Avenue property owners' concerns that the construction of industrial loft buildings would undermine the avenue's status as a prestigious shopping district. Zoning advocates did not try to stop the construction of skyscrapers in congested lower Manhattan even though these raised serious health and public safety issues. Instead, they devised a zoning map for the city that accepted much of the status quo. The zoning map and the accompanying regulations codified existing patterns of development considered beneficial to real estate investors, prohibiting those deemed threatening. They aimed to replace risky speculation with stability and to create a city in which developers could undertake construction projects with no fear that later, incompatible development would destroy the buildings' value. The New York zoning ordinance proved to be extremely influential both in its technical provisions and in its underlying philosophy. By the end of 1916 seven other American cities had enacted zoning ordinances, and by the end of the 1920s nearly eight hundred municipalities had done so. During this period of zoning's rapid expansion, however, the concept lost some of the reformist aura that had earlier surrounded it. It was transformed into the cause of business-minded men who believed that regulating development would be financially advantageous without threatening the quality of life.[44]

Perhaps fearing that the metaphors of the machine and of science would repel voters, later zoning advocates sought to explain their ideas by using the house as a metaphor. Unlike Bushnell, who had thought of the home as a place that drew people into warm interactions, such zoning advocates as Herbert S. Swan of New York thought in terms of the orderly differentiation of functions. "Just as we have a place for everything in a well-ordered home, so we should have a place for everything in a well ordered town," Swan wrote in a 1920 article in *American City* magazine, in which he emphasized order as an essential aspect of gentility. "What should we think of a housewife who insisted on keeping her gas range in the parlor and her piano in the kitchen? Yet anomalies like these have become commonplace in our community housekeeping." Swan's comments were quoted in a pro-zoning article issued by the U.S. Department of Commerce and reprinted in the Hartford Chamber of Commerce's *Hartford* magazine in 1922. The *Hartford* article went on to describe the unzoned city as a dirty and déclassé household "in which an undisciplined daughter makes fudge in the parlor, in which her sister leaves soiled clothes soaking in the bathtub, while father throws his muddy shoes on the stairs and little Johnny makes beautiful mud-pies on the front steps." Such a household was clearly not the home of the better sort of people, the article implied, and such a city would not project the image desired by the affluent members of the chamber of commerce. As the zoning advisor to Hartford in the mid-1920s, Swan undoubtedly had many opportunities to repeat this point.[45]

The zoning of the city could have been made part of a larger planning vision, a "subdivision of the city into natural neighborhoods," which, Parker had suggested, might promote a sense of community on a smaller scale. Indeed, the historians Zane L. Miller and Bruce Tucker suggest that a somewhat similar desire to promote neighborhood cohesion, ethnic community, and cultural pluralism influenced city planning in Cincinnati. But such a vision seems to have been lacking in Hartford in the 1920s. Following the disappearance of the progressive reformers, the vacuum in city planning was filled by the business-minded, Republican politicians who ran Hartford for most of the decade. The pattern of alternating party rule that had begun in the early 1890s ended in 1920. Except for a two-year interruption by the mayoralty of a conservative Democrat, Republicans controlled city hall throughout the 1920s, holding to a more narrowly probusiness agenda than had previous Republican mayors like William F. Henney and Louis R. Cheney, both members of the Municipal Art Society.[46]

The Republican Norman C. Stevens, a young Aetna Casualty and Surety executive who lived in the suburban West End, had made zoning his pet project even before his election as mayor in 1924. In 1923 he had persuaded fellow members of the Common Council to set up a committee to consider the matter. After assuming the mayoralty, he reorganized the Commission on the City Plan as a group of private citizens led by a local real estate agent, Herbert F. Fisher, and directed it to prepare a zoning ordinance. Swan assisted the commission in its work. A council subcommittee, headed by an alderman who worked as an attorney for Aetna Life Insurance, then presented the ordinance for public comment at a series of contentious hearings. Following some revisions, Mayor Stevens energetically sponsored this legislation to its passage by a vote of 28–0 in February 1926. Stevens and his supporters declared that zoning aimed to create a healthy environment both for home life and for real estate investment. In a debate on an interim zoning measure in 1925, one alderman argued, "If it is not passed our residential districts will suffer; if it is passed we will protect our residential districts." The editors of the *Times* added in 1926, "The purpose of zoning is to control the physical development of the city, insure against the erection of buildings where they do not belong and against the improper invasion of business and industry into residential districts. The purpose is to enhance property values and not to destroy them."[47]

The nearly interminable public disputes over the zoning ordinance in 1925 and early 1926 centered around how best to balance the goals of enhancing property values and establishing stable patterns of land use. They did not consider whether these goals were the appropriate focus of city planning. One point of controversy was whether to allow further business development on Asylum Avenue and Farmington Avenue, both major thoroughfares in Asylum Hill and the West End. Some Asylum Hill residents were anxious to preserve the residential character and fading grandeur of that area, while others thought that the character of their neighborhood was doomed anyway, and that Asylum Hill's brightest future lay in commercial development. "Asylum Avenue, if kept residential, will in the near future deteriorate into a cheap boarding house district," warned one man who wanted it zoned for business. Another controversial question was how strictly the city should limit the height of buildings. The early advocates of zoning had been particularly interested in restricting skyscraper construction, largely for aesthetic reasons, but some downtown property owners in the 1920s argued that Hartford should take pride in its rising skyline and do nothing to stop its growth. The few Hartford residents who were wholly opposed to zoning argued that it interfered with private property rights.[48]

The ordinance as finally adopted established a hierarchy of land use. The strictest protections were applied to the elite A residential zone, which was limited to the northern part of the West End, two small pieces of Asylum Hill, and some incompletely developed land in Blue Hills. Greater densities were permitted in the B and C residential zones, which included less prestigious areas of houses and multifamily buildings outside the core of the city. Most working-class and immigrant districts, however, were more leniently zoned for business or light industry. The ordinance was quite tolerant of new commercial development, as long as it followed established patterns of growth. By this time the concentration of traffic on certain streets had already encouraged intensive commercial development there. Recognizing the evolving pattern, the zoning map designated the radial thoroughfares as business streets, with the exceptions of Asylum Avenue, most of Blue Hills Avenue, and most of western New Britain Avenue. Washington Street was also zoned for business. The city officials who reached these decisions were not simply preserving the status quo. For example, before the adoption of the zoning rules, there were many houses and small tenements on Wethersfield Avenue, but few businesses; the city chose to zone the area for business anyway. Buildings as high as sixteen stories were permitted in an area extending from the South Green to Clay Hill and from the Connecticut River to eastern Asylum Hill, including nearly all the streets bordering Bushnell Park, even though skyscrapers could be found on only a few blocks in the downtown. Developers who felt too restricted by the height limit or any other clause in the ordinance could request an exemption from an appeals board.[49]

The preamble to the ordinance included a rhetorical acknowledgment of zoning's roots in progressive reform, declaring that zoning would help prevent overcrowding, ensure adequate light and air, and promote "the public health, comfort and general welfare in living and working conditions." But the ordinance itself undercut these stated goals by allowing housing densities as high as 140 families per acre throughout most of Hartford, as well as permitting continued construction of all but the most offensive heavy industries in many working-class areas. It gave businessmen a relatively free hand in developing much of the city—while protecting their own residential neighborhoods from commercial or industrial encroachments. There was little in the ordinance to indicate how zoning might help achieve Parker's vague dream of cottages for workingmen. Zoning, after all, could not tell property owners what should be built; it only told them what could not. It divided Hartford's private land into seven clearly defined grades analogous to the grades of a commodity like wheat. Zoning took some of the chance out of real estate investments and elevated the power of money, helping the buyer or developer ensure that he got more or less what he paid for. Workingmen could buy cottages in southwest Hartford if they had the money to do so, just as they could before zoning was adopted. The main difference was that they could now do so with greater confidence that poorer people and businesses would not follow. With zoning, neighborhoods would become and remain more homogeneous.[50]

In contrast to the planning proposals of Bushnell, the Olmsteds, and Carrère and Hastings, the new zoning ordinance and accompanying map did not seek to stem the fragmentation of Hartford. Zoning emphatically encouraged the ongoing segregation of the city by function and class, and it greatly enhanced central authority over urban development. The result was supposed to be a harmonious balance between diversity and unity. The city would remain a divided landscape — split into areas of poverty and wealth, production and consumption, masculinity and femininity — but its divisions would be controlled and codified under the unity imposed by municipal government. The theory was that zoning would manage diversity by arranging it spatially.

The coherence zoning provided was easier to see on a map than on the ground. Zoning thus marked a shift from the earlier goal of making the urban order visible. Even Carrère and Hastings, though favoring class segregation, had seen the need for greenbelts and scenic vistas to tie Hartford's disparate neighborhoods together; but there were no greenbelts, no parkways, and no vistas on the zoning map. Such aesthetic amenities were foreign to its purpose. Instead it served up a collection of neighborhoods and the same old radial thoroughfares (now frankly declared to be commercial strips), all centering on a commercial downtown. Discarding the reformist dream of teaching social unity, Stevens and the other city officials who devised the map sought primarily to impose administrative order on the patterns of growth that had been splitting Hartford since the late nineteenth century.

Nevertheless, they were not acquiescing helplessly in existing conditions. Their zoning map, by designating areas for uses that were not dominant at the time, was as much a value-laden blueprint for change as Carrère and Hastings's plan had been. It was innovative, even radical, in replacing the unbridled competition of the real estate market with a new, regulated system under municipal authority. It was also much more successful in effecting change than the previous plan had been, since it relied on the city government's police powers rather than its far more limited spending powers. Despite property owners' many requests for exceptions to and changes in the zoning rules, development in the next fifteen years generally followed the mandated patterns, and the configuration of land use in Hartford today shows striking similarities to the seventy-year-old zoning map.[51]

————————

Hartford city officials of the 1920s adopted a new planning philosophy that, while incorporating the familiar principle of segregating the use of space, transformed its meaning. Though the decision represented a major change, progressive reformers had been inching in that direction for some time. The segregation of the park system had established a precedent for dividing urban space into units reserved for specific social groups and functions. The city's role in creating a differentiated street system had also shown how government could segregate the use of public space and, in addition, influence private development. The Progressive Era shift toward segregating the use of space had been supported by reformers partly as a way to maintain order and preserve a cluster of values associated with the middle-class home, much as the shift toward stricter racial segregation had been viewed in the South.

Hartford reformers had forthrightly invoked values associated with gentility and Victorian womanhood in their campaigns to restrict newsgirls, expressmen, and peddlers; in their conflicts over the segregated vice district; and in the movement to reform play. They hoped to ensure that middle-class ideas of morality, order, courtesy, and self-restraint would be fostered by the environments in which Hartford's people lived. Reformers invoked the same ideas to justify the segregation of parks and the creation of a differentiated traffic system, but they gradually shifted their emphasis to efficiency, describing both the park and street systems as machines.

In applying the principle of segregated space to planning a modern city, reformers drifted ever further from Bushnell's concern for environmental influence. The Municipal Art Society had tried to have it both ways. It sought to minimize the distinction between sculpting a beautiful environment to nurture gentility, on the one hand, and engineering a physical setting for the efficient acquisition of wealth, on the other. Flagg and Parker at first seemed to acknowledge the difference but then retreated, perhaps fearing that beauty would lose in any direct confrontation with efficiency. They argued instead that the segregation of urban space would serve both purposes. The emphasis in Hartford's city planning gradually turned from the usefulness of beauty to the beauty of usefulness until the older values finally faded away. Following the decline of the Municipal Art Society and the Commission on the City Plan, the segregation of space was no longer used as a tool to better the influence of the environment on the community or the individual. Instead, in the hands of Herbert Swan and Norman Stevens, it became a way to balance conflicting impulses in order to protect both the residential neighborhoods and the investment interests of prosperous citizens. A beautiful environment became an amenity feasible only in neighborhoods with the proper zoning designation. Through zoning, Hartford's tradition of environmental reform was coopted by those who were preserving and managing the social divisions that Bushnell had tried to overcome.

10

Of Hartford Seen in a Different Light

For those who mourn the vitality and diversity of American streets, it is tempting to point an accusing finger at the public officials who facilitated automobile use. In parts of downtown Hartford, as in many other urban centers, one of the few signs of street life today is the engineered pulse of the traffic artery. Sidewalks are almost wholly abandoned to the derelict poor at the close of each workday, while torrents of automobiles surge past on their way to suburban safety. A pushcart peddler returning to sell tomatoes on Front Street would be flattened by thousands of tons of metal rushing down what is now called Columbus Boulevard.

Some of the most significant changes in the use of American streets took place in the Progressive Era, those energetic decades of reform around the turn of the century. Public officials transformed certain streets from multipurpose social spaces into transportation routes. City governments literally paved the way for increased automobile use as they restricted street activities that interfered with traffic. Mid-twentieth-century civic leaders, influenced by modernist planning theories, further promoted automobile traffic. Modernist architects like Le Corbusier bent their efforts toward facilitating driving; to them pedestrians' needs were of little interest.[1] In mid-twentieth-century Hartford, modernist planners displayed their contempt for street life by replacing much of the East Side with the sterile Constitution Plaza office complex and by leveling a retail and theater block for the concrete fortresses of Bushnell Plaza. Both these projects turned a cold shoulder to the surrounding streets. The alternative off-street spaces they produced have never been used as the designers intended.

It is tempting to blame the wastelands of modern American cities on the protraffic reformers and public officials of the Progressive Era. But such blame is neither entirely accurate nor entirely fair. It is inaccurate, first, because the desire to clear the way for traffic was but a small part of a reform effort to move social and commercial activity off the street—in a broader sense to segregate the use of urban space. As Hartford's example indicates, many of the changes in street use were produced or encouraged by reformers who believed that, by improving the urban environment, they could uplift the people of the city. They sought to get children off the streets into homes or playgrounds, and expressmen and peddlers off the streets into marketplaces or private buildings. They advocated these changes not simply—or even primarily—to make way for automobiles. Rather, they believed that the departure of these people would render the streets more orderly and that the people's relocation would be healthier in every respect. These environmental reformers believed that, by sorting out incompatible uses of space and creating appropriate spaces for each necessary activity, they could produce a better urban life, a life with fewer of the industrial city's perceived negative effects. Blaming protraffic reform for what has happened to late twentieth-century streets releases other reformers from their share of the responsibility.

Second, focusing the blame on the advocates of smooth traffic flow removes these people from the reform context, which shows them in a somewhat more favorable light. Progressive Era urban reformers cannot be divided so neatly into a group that idealistically sought to improve city life and another group eager to improve private transportation. For example, the Municipal Art Society advocated street projects that promoted better traffic flow, but its members sincerely considered these projects part of a broader campaign to beautify Hartford and produce a more refined citizenry. Although some of their work now seems misguided, the members of the society cared deeply about the quality of urban life. To interpret their efforts within the context of the time, while not freeing them from blame, at least allows us to see the effects of their work as unintended consequences.

It is tempting, too, when one is moved by righteous anger about the modern city, to view the starkest of the redesigned streets as somehow symbolic of all streets today. When the urban critic Mike Davis attacks the "sadistic street environments" of Los Angeles, he strikes a chord in readers who, seeing evidence of such brutal designs elsewhere, feel that he has said something fundamentally true about the American urban landscape. Many streets have indeed degenerated into "traffic sewers," but many others have not. Though relatively few now show the intricate "street ballet" of Jane Jacobs's idealized Greenwich Village,[2] there are many streets in residential areas where children still play or where an ice cream truck makes its evening rounds. The persistence of social and commercial uses on certain streets does not mean that one can dismiss the traffic sewers as aberrations. Both the hideously functional thoroughfare and the quiet residential side street are representative of American streets today—and the residential side street is quiet precisely because the busy thoroughfare channels traffic away. These two extreme types of streets exist not as signs of the future and the past, but as differing components of a system of urban space that arose from Progressive Era reforms.

This narrative has traced the evolution of that system in Hartford, where there was a strong tradition of environmental reform inspired in part by the mid-nineteenth-century innovations of Horace Bushnell. Bushnell, who developed the ideas of environmental influence that guided the work of Frederick Law Olmsted and thus much of the American park movement, had himself applied these ideas to urban design in the 1850s by creating a park to serve as an "outdoor parlor" in the center of Hartford. Bushnell hoped that the park would be a soothing, natural environment in which fleeting interclass contacts would produce some sense of social unity. The unity of an idealized past could be recaptured. Park construction and wise city planning could spread the feminine values associated with the home. In Bushnell's richly metaphoric understanding of urban space, the city would ultimately become like the park, which was like the middle-class home, which was like the "Puritan Arcadia" of preindustrial New England, which was a harmonious society of Christian love. Yet Bushnell's park also introduced striking contrasts in land use into the center of Hartford and promoted the idea of dividing the use of public space. The park project paralleled the growing distinction in middle-class thought and life between the corrupt public spaces of the city and the supposedly purer life of the home.

Bushnell left an ambiguous legacy for later reformers. Some Progressive Era reformers attempted to purify the entire city of Hartford. Drawing on the rhetoric of separate spheres that linked female domesticity with morality and order, women's groups from the 1890s through the early 1910s sought to extend the values of the middle-class home into the public sphere. Women's club members and suffragists undertook various "municipal housekeeping" projects to tidy up the city's public spaces and to suppress the most unsavory aspects of male-dominated street culture. Their greatest victory came in the campaign against Hartford's red-light district.

These women's groups focused greater public attention on the indecorous and immoral aspects of public space, but their hope of purifying the city was not shared by other Hartford reformers in the early twentieth century. Activists in the child labor reform, playground, and City Beautiful movements worked instead to separate the diverse activities found in public space. Child labor reformers, seeking to save children from moral contamination, won prohibitions against the employment of girls and young boys in street trades. Playground advocates succeeded in creating alternative recreational spaces for the children, though they failed to put an end to street play. City officials, irate homeowners, and members of the local City Beautiful group discouraged street peddling in residential neighborhoods. As a result of their pressures, and of unrelated changes in middle-class shopping habits, peddlers were segregated into a public market and a single street in the slums. Parks officials strengthened the trend toward segregating the use of public space by providing separate recreational facilities and, in some cases, entirely separate parks for different age groups, classes, and genders.

The efforts of this second group of activists and officials often—but not always—complemented the work of other prominent Hartford residents who saw the need for more efficient traffic circulation. Business leaders, wealthy motorists, and many city officials thought the city's prosperity and growth depended on smooth traffic flow. These men worked to turn the street grid into a modern traffic system and to remove obstacles created by alternative street uses. They passed laws allowing higher speeds of travel, and designated certain streets as "arteries" through which vehicles would be encouraged to flow. In the 1910s and 1920s, by widening these arteries, laying superior pavements, and building extensions to connect with other arteries, the city government directed traffic along certain routes. Side streets were allowed to remain quiet. City officials and the Automobile Club of Hartford also worked to control what they called the "reckless" pedestrian, who inconsiderately forced motorists to run him over. In response to complaints from motorists, police cracked down on jaywalking, and the schools and the automobile club promoted efforts to teach pedestrians how to cross the street. By the mid-1920s, pedestrians were finally learning that their place was on the sidewalks and crosswalks; pedestrian fatalities stabilized despite continuing increases in traffic flow and population. The dangers and disruptions posed by traffic also succeeded in forcing children's play off many streets.

In the first three decades of the twentieth century, environmental reformers and advocates of efficiency applied the concept of segregation to city planning. Some drew again on the metaphor of the house, but not in the same way as Bushnell and the advocates of municipal housekeeping had done. These men did not describe the home as a source of alternative values that could unite the city, but spoke instead of a physical space divided into different rooms for different functions. Increasingly, they valued the functional division of urban space for financial advantage rather than for social reform. In adopting zoning regulations in 1926, public officials turned away from the dying Bushnellian tradition of using urban space to uplift the community and the individual.

The wholesale segregation of urban space resulted from numerous piecemeal reform efforts and was strengthened by the unexpected explosion in automobile travel. It was not the result of any master plan to encourage private transportation. Though the reform campaigns were influenced by class tensions, the transformation of the street was not simply a triumph of elite reformers over recalcitrant lower classes. In some cases, such as the proposed extension of Laurel Street across Pope

Park, working-class people favored transportation improvements that members of the middle class fiercely opposed. Working-class advocates also supported some of the new spaces, notably the playgrounds, that were intended as alternatives to the street. Some nontransportation activities—street play, loitering, and peddling—survived in immigrant neighborhoods, at the margins of mainstream urban life. The persistence of such street uses allowed people with different cultural and economic backgrounds to preserve a measure of neighborhood autonomy without preventing reformers from bringing more order to the city's main public streets or seriously interfering with the creation of a traffic system. The segregation of public space can be seen in some ways as a compromise that allowed Hartford's diverse population to come to terms with the pluralism that Bushnell had feared.

In the long run, that solution exacted a heavy price. Space within metropolitan Hartford became increasingly segregated and narrowly defined for specific functions. Through the mid-twentieth century, downtown sidewalks maintained a false appearance of liveliness as throngs of pedestrians walked to shops and department stores. But these retail businesses, which had thrived when downtown Hartford was the hub of a regional streetcar system, have not in the longer run survived the shift to automobile transportation. Dying, they have taken with them the remaining life of downtown streets, revealing how limited street life has been for decades.[3] Downtown sidewalks had long since become routes of travel rather than multipurpose social spaces; now many are deserted altogether. The deeply divided metropolitan area, where class segregation is enforced by stringent zoning rules, lacks common public space that can adequately perform socially integrative functions. Interclass contact persists on downtown sidewalks and in Bushnell Park, but it takes the form primarily of uneasy encounters between well-dressed office workers on their way to lunch and vagrants seeking handouts or returnable cans. This is not what the reformers of the Progressive Era wanted, but it is what their well-meaning efforts helped produce.

Notes

The following abbreviations are used consistently in the notes, although the titles of volumes published annually and of newspapers can vary.

ACH   *Automobile Club of Hartford*
BH   *Annual Report of the Board of Health of the City of Hartford*
BPC   *Annual Report of the Board of Park Commissioners of the City of Hartford*
BSC   *Annual Report of the Board of Street Commissioners of the City of Hartford*
CHS   Connecticut Historical Society
CLC   Consumers' League of Connecticut Papers, Schlesinger Library, Radcliffe College, Cambridge, Mass.
Courant *Hartford Daily Courant* or *Hartford Courant*
CSL   Connecticut State Library, Hartford
GAPP   George A. Parker Papers, Connecticut Historical Society
HCH   Town and City Clerk's vault, Hartford City Hall
HD   *Geer's Hartford City Directory*
HPL   Hartford Collection, Hartford Public Library
JBA   *Journal of the Board of Aldermen of the City of Hartford*
JCCB   *Journal of the Common Council Board of the City of Hartford*
JCCC   *Journal of the Court of Common Council of the City of Hartford*
JHS   Jewish Historical Society of Greater Hartford, West Hartford
MAS   Municipal Art Society Papers, Connecticut State Library
MR   *Municipal Register of the City of Hartford*
NCLC   National Child Labor Committee
PDP   Parks Department Papers, Hartford Collection, Hartford Public Library
Post   *Hartford Post* or *Hartford Evening Post* or *Evening Post*
Times   *Hartford Daily Times* or *Hartford Times*
WPA   Works Progress Administration

Introduction

1. Joan W. Friedland and Wilson H. Faude, *Birthplace of Democracy* (Chester, Conn.: Globe Pequot Press, 1979). William S. Porter, "Hartford in 1640," map in F. Perry Close, *History of Hartford Streets* (Hartford: Connecticut Historical Society, 1969).*The Greater Hartford Directory* (Hartford: Hartford Printing, 1930), 1612, 1647–48, 1722–23, 1780–81. *Publications of the Municipal Art Society of Hartford, Connecticut*, bulletin no. 15, *The Old State House, Hartford: Why It Should Be Preserved* (Hartford: Municipal Art Society, 1911), 9.

2. "Arrest 25 Children for Roller Skating," *Courant*, 14 April 1916. Herbert S. Swan, *Traffic and Thoroughfare Plan, Hartford, Connecticut* (Hartford: Commission on the City Plan, 1926), 51–52. Photo looking south on Main Street from State House Square, mid-1920s, in Glenn Weaver, *Hartford: An Illustrated History of Connecticut's Capital* (Hartford: Connecticut Historical Society; Woodland Hills, Calif.: Windsor Publications, 1982), 110. Photo labeled "corner of Main & State St. (Harvey & Lewis Building), ca. 1934–36, negative no. 354, CHS.

3. Mike Davis, *City of Quartz: Excavating the Future in Los Angeles* (New York: Vintage Books, 1992 [1990]), 226. James Holston, *The Modernist City: An Anthropological Critique of Brasília* (Chicago: University of Chicago Press, 1989). Jane Jacobs, *The Death and Life of Great American Cities* (New York: Vintage Books, 1961). James Howard Kunstler, *The Geography of Nowhere: The Rise and Decline of America's Man-Made Landscape* (New York: Simon and Schuster, 1993). William H. Whyte, *The Social Life of Small Urban Spaces* (Washington: Conservation Foundation, 1980). See also Richard Ingersoll, "The Death of the Street: The Automobile and Houston," in *Roadside America: The Automobile in Design and Culture*, ed. Jan Jennings (Ames, Iowa: Iowa State University Press, 1990), 149–56. Ingersoll emphasizes the destructive influence of the automobile. Clay McShane, "Transforming the Use of Urban Space: A Look at the Revolution in Street Pavements, 1880–1924," *Journal of Urban History* 5/3 (1979): 279–307, at 283. Clay McShane, *Down the Asphalt Path: The Automobile and the American City* (New York: Columbia University Press, 1994). Andrew Brown-May, *The Highway of Civilisation and Common Sense: Street Regulation and the Transformation of Social Space in 19th and Early 20th Century Melbourne* (Canberra: Urban Research Program, 1995), at 42. See also Daniel M. Bluestone, "'The Pushcart Evil': Peddlers, Merchants and New York City's Streets, 1890–1940," *Journal of Urban History* 18/1 (1991): 68–92. John D. Fairfield, "The Scientific Management of Urban Space: Professional City Planning and the Legacy of Progressive Reform," *Journal of Urban History* 20/2 (1994): 179–204.

4. Linda Kerber has noted the importance of distinguishing "women's culture" from an ideological understanding of "women's sphere" that limited and spatially confined women. Linda K. Kerber, "Separate Spheres, Female Worlds, Woman's Place: The Rhetoric of Women's History," *Journal of American History* 75/1 (1988): 9–39. On women's culture, see Carroll Smith-Rosenberg, "The Female World of Love and Ritual," in Carroll Smith-Rosenberg, *Disorderly Conduct: Visions of Gender in Victorian America* (New York: Oxford University Press, 1985), 53–76. On the development of a female political culture in the nineteenth century, see Paula Baker, "The Domestication of Politics: Women and American Political Society, 1780–1920," *American Historical Review* 89 (1984): 620–47. See also Sheila M. Rothman, *Woman's Proper Place: A History of Changing Ideals and Practices, 1780 to the Present* (New York: Basic Books, 1978); Glenna Matthews, *The Rise of Public Woman: Woman's Power and Woman's Place in the United States, 1630–1970* (New York: Oxford University Press, 1992); and Josephine Donovan, *Feminist Theory: The Intellectual Traditions of American Feminism* (New York: Frederick Ungar, 1985).

5. A number of earlier studies of public space have taken this approach. See, for instance James Borchert, *Alley Life in Washington: Family, Community, Religion and Folklife in the City, 1850–1970* (Urbana: University of Illinois Press, 1980); Francis G. Couvares, *The Remaking of Pittsburgh: Class and Culture in an Industrializing City, 1877–1919* (Albany: State University of New York Press, 1984); Susan G. Davis, *Parades and Power: Street Theatre in Nineteenth-Century Philadelphia* (Philadelphia: Temple University Press, 1986); Peter G. Goheen, "Negotiating Access to Public Space in Mid-Nineteenth Century Toronto," *Journal of Historical Geography* 20/4 (1994): 430–49; Cary Goodman, *Choosing Sides: Playground and Street Life on the Lower East Side* (New York: Schocken, 1979); Kathy Peiss, *Cheap Amusements: Working Women and Leisure in Turn-of-the-Century New York* (Philadelphia: Temple University Press, 1986); Roy Rosenzweig, *Eight Hours for What We Will: Workers and Leisure in an Industrial City, 1870–1920* (Cambridge: Cambridge University Press, 1983); Christine Stansell, *City of Women: Sex and Class in New York, 1789–1860* (Urbana: University of Illinois Press, 1987); Maureen A. Flanagan, "The City Profitable, the City Livable: Environmental Policy, Gender, and Power in Chicago in the 1910s," *Journal of Urban History* 22/2 (1996): 163–90.

6. *Fifth Annual Report of the Juvenile Commission to the Mayor and Court of Common Council of the City of Hartford, Conn., for the Year Ending April 30, 1914* (Hartford: Bond Press, 1914), 93.

Chapter 1

1. "Fire," *Times*, 11 May 1853. Untitled news item, *Times*, 11 May 1853, p. 2. "Roman Catholic Church Burned," *Courant*, 12 May 1853. *HD* 16 (1853–54): 206–07, 256. Joseph W. Duffy, "Images of Hartford's Irish-Catholic Community: 1827–1867," *Connecticut History* 31 (1990): 26, 27.

2. *HD* 16 (1853–54): 48.

3. On Bushnell's devotion to park work in 1853 and 1854, see Mary Bushnell Cheney, *Life and Letters of Horace Bushnell* (New York: Harper and Brothers, 1880), 322–23. For an evaluation of his place in American theology, see Barbara M. Cross, *Horace Bushnell: Minister to a Changing America* (Chicago: University of Chicago Press, 1958) ix, 109–10, 156–68.

4. Cheney, *Life and Letters of Horace Bushnell*, 3–70, 423. Cross, *Horace Bushnell*, 4–12, 31–53, 109, 157–59. Horace Bushnell, *Prosperity Our Duty: A Discourse Delivered at the North Church, Hartford, Sabbath Evening, January 31, 1847* (Hartford: Case, Tiffany and Burnham, 1847).

5. Philip B. Eppard, introduction to Horace Bushnell, *Views of Christian Nurture and of Subjects Adjacent Thereto* (Delmar, N.Y.: Scholar's Facsimiles and Reprints, 1975), n.p. Bushnell, *Views of Christian Nurture*, 6, 16, 19, 191, 193. *Views of Christian Nurture* is the second 1847 edition, with additional material following what is in Bushnell's original *Discourses on Christian Nurture*. The text was revised considerably for the 1860 edition.

6. Bushnell, *Views of Christian Nurture*, 8, 40; see also 179.

7. Ann Douglas, *The Feminization of American Culture* (New York: Avon Books, 1977), 50–63. Barbara Welter, "The Cult of True Womanhood, 1820–1860," *American Quarterly* 18/2 (1966): 151–74. Kathryn Kish Sklar, *Catharine Beecher: A Study in American Domesticity* (New Haven: Yale University Press, 1973), 83–84, 153. Bushnell articulated these views more clearly in his 1860 revision, *Christian Nurture*. Describing a mother's love for her child, he wrote, "If she could sound her consciousness deeply enough, she would find a certain religiousness in it, measurable by no scale of mere earthly or temporal love. Here springs the secret of her maternity, and its semi-divine proportions. It is the call and equipment of God, for a work on the impressional and plastic age of a soul" (*Christian Nurture* [New York: Charles Scribner, 1861], 237; see also 405–06). Horace Bushnell, *Women's Suffrage: The Reform against Nature* (New York: Charles Scribner, 1869), 21, 51, 57. Catharine Beecher, who like Bushnell grew up in Litchfield County in the 1800s and 1810s, ran the Hartford Female Seminary from 1823 to 1831. She left the city more than a year before her contemporary's arrival (Sklar, *Catharine Beecher*, 3–27, 102–03).

8. Horace Bushnell, "The Age of Homespun," in *Work and Play; Or Liter-*

ary Varieties (New York: Charles Scribner, 1864), 368–402, at 376, 378–79, 382, 393.

9. Bushnell, "Age of Homespun," 400–01. Bushnell, *Prosperity Our Duty,* 7, 8, 9–10, 18, at 8, 23. On the canal project, see J. Eugene Smith, *One Hundred Years of Hartford's* Courant (New Haven: Yale University Press, 1949), 240.

10. Horace Bushnell, *Crisis of the Church* (Hartford: Daniel Burgess, 1835), 11. Bushnell, *Women's Suffrage,* 33–34.

11. Bushnell, *Views of Christian Nurture,* 18, 21, 183–84.

12. Ibid., 21–22. Horace Bushnell, "Unconscious Influence," *Sermons for the New Life* (New York: Charles Scribner, 1858), 186–205, at 194. Cheney, *Life and Letters of Horace Bushnell,* 162–63.

13. On Bushnell's concerns about slavery, see Bushnell, *Crisis of the Church,* 18–20. On changing class relations in early to mid-nineteenth-century American cities, see Paul E. Johnson, *A Shopkeeper's Millennium: Society and Revivals in Rochester, New York, 1815–1837* (New York: Hill and Wang, 1978), 38–48. On Bushnell family meals with farmhands, see Cross, *Horace Bushnell,* 1–2. The quotation on religious clannishness is from Bushnell, *Prosperity Our Duty,* 22.

14. On Bushnell's hostility to Catholicism, see Bushnell, *Crisis of the Church,* 22, 24, 25; Horace Bushnell, *Barbarism the First Danger: A Discourse for Home Missions* (New York: American Home Missionary Society and William Osborn, 1847), 24, 32. On common schools, Cheney, *Life and Letters of Horace Bushnell,* 298–303, at 300. On Mann, see John L. Thomas, "Romantic Reform in America, 1815–1865," *American Quarterly* 17/4 (1965), reprinted in *Ante-Bellum Reform,* ed. David Drion Davis (New York: Harper and Row, 1967), 166.

15. On the 1830s, see Charles Hopkins Clark, "Bushnell the Citizen," in *Bushnell Centenary: Minutes of the General Association of Connecticut at the One Hundred and Ninety-Third Annual Meeting Held in Hartford, June 17, 18, 1902* (Hartford: Case, Lockwood and Brainard, 1902), 63. On the start of planning see Bushnell to the mayor and Common Council of the city of Hartford, 26 September 1853 [marked "Communication from Horace Bushnell"], drawer marked "Parks: Tabulated Correspondence, 'A' to 'R,'" HCH.

16. Population figures for 1830 and 1840 are from HD 86 (1923–24): 1556. On the economy, see Smith, *One Hundred Years of Hartford's Courant,* 234–55. Cross, *Horace Bushnell,* 31–32, at 31.

17. Glenn Weaver, *Hartford: An Illustrated History of Connecticut's Capital* (Hartford: Windsor Publications and the Connecticut Historical Society, 1982), 75, 78, 85–88, 101. Smith, *One Hundred Years of Hartford's Courant,* 234, 240–42. Fredrika Bremer, *America of the Fifties: Letters of Fredrika Bremer* (New York: American-Scandinavian Foundation, 1924), 40–41. "Progress of Hartford," *Courant,* 18 September 1852. HD 86 (1923–24): 1556.

18. *Mayor's Address and City Government for 1879 and the Annual Reports of the Several Departments for the Municipal Year Ending April 1, 1879* (Hartford: Wiley, Waterman and Eaton, 1879), 37. Weaver, *Hartford*, 76, 78, 95. Duffy, "Images of Hartford's Irish-Catholic Community," 26. Smith, *One Hundred Years of Hartford's* Courant, 246, 253; for Bushnell's comments on brothels and gambling, see also Bushnell, *Prosperity Our Duty*, 9–10, 20. Hartford Architecture Conservancy, *Hartford Architecture*, vol. 3, *North and West Neighborhoods* (Hartford: Hartford Architecture Conservancy, 1980), 138; J. Weidenmann, *City of Hartford, Conn.*, 1864 bird's-eye view, CSL.

19. Weidenmann, *City of Hartford*. Elihu Geer, *Geer's New Map of the City of Hartford from the Latest Surveys*, 1854, CSL. Hartford Architecture Conservancy, *Hartford Architecture*, vol. 2, *South Neighborhoods* (Hartford: Hartford Architecture Conservancy, 1980), 17. *Hartford Architecture*, 3:137. Charles W. Burpee, *History of Hartford County, Connecticut, 1633–1928* (Chicago: S.J. Clarke, 1928), vol. 1, photograph opposite p. 314, showing East Side, ca. 1848. Charles Dickens, *American Notes and Pictures From Italy* (Oxford: Oxford University Press, 1957), 76, 73. Anthony Trollope, *North America* (New York: Knopf, 1951), 221. On the walking time, "The Proposed Park," *Courant*, 27 December 1853. On the beauty of the surrounding countryside, see also untitled editorial, *Courant*, 27 May 1859.

20. Horace Bushnell, letter from *Hearth and Home*, 6 February 1869, reprinted in *BPC* 48 (1908): 6–17. "Petition of Saml Tudor + Others," 12 April 1827, drawer marked "Park Department, Annual Reports, Miscellaneous, 1827 to 1874," HCH. Sherman W. Adams, "The Hartford Park System. I: Bushnell Park," *Connecticut Quarterly* 1 (1895): 70. W. A. Ayres, "Travel and Transportation," in *Memorial History of Hartford County, Connecticut, 1633–1884*, ed. J. Hammond Trumbull (Boston: Edward L. Osgood, 1886), 1:559; William A. Ayres, "Parks and Public Works," in Trumbull, *Hartford County*, 1:447. Untitled letter to the editor by "Cleane Lawne," *Courant*, 16 July 1853. "The Proposed Park," *Courant*, 27 December 1853. "Pet. de North Park +c," 22 May 1854, drawer marked "Park Department, Annual Reports, Miscellaneous, 1827 to 1874," HCH.

21. "The Proposed Park," anonymous letter in *Times*, 19 November 1853. Bushnell, letter in *Hearth and Home*, 9, 10–11. Map in Adams, "The Hartford Park System. I," 67. Ayres, "Parks and Public Works," 447.

22. Bruce Clouette, "Antebellum Urban Renewal: Hartford's Bushnell Park," *Connecticut History* 18 (Nov. 1976): 9–11.

23. George M. Fredrickson, *The Black Image in the White Mind: The Debate on Afro-American Character and Destiny, 1817–1914* (New York: Harper and Row, 1971; reprint with new introduction, Middletown, Conn.: Wesleyan Uni-

versity Press, 1987), 155–56. Cross, *Horace Bushnell*, 40–41. Ralph E. Luker, "Bushnell in Black and White: Evidences of the 'Racism' of Horace Bushnell," *New England Quarterly* 45/3 (1972): 408–16.

24. Bushnell, letter in *Hearth and Home*, 11. There are enough similarities between the park projects in New York and Hartford to support a suspicion that the simultaneous development of the two was more than coincidence. The mayor of New York made the unprecedented proposal in 1851 that a large park be laid out using public money, and the state senate authorized the city to take a site by eminent domain. Only in 1853 did Bushnell unveil his own proposal to take a park site by eminent domain and improve it with public money (Roy Rosenzweig and Elizabeth Blackmar, *The Park and the People: A History of Central Park* [Ithaca: Cornell University Press, 1992], 15–53). Controversies over New York's park site continued until January 1854, and the project received attention in the Hartford press. For example, the *Times* alluded to the proposals for a park in New York in a 28 July 1853 editorial on the need for a park in Hartford. Nevertheless, it is indisputable that Bushnell formulated his social philosophy for public parks four years before Olmsted even became involved in the Central Park project, let alone wrote his own rationales for the work. Contrary to some accounts, Bushnell's work on the Hartford park was done independently of Olmsted, who at the time was busy farming on Staten Island and then traveling as a journalist in England and the southern states. Claims that Bushnell and Olmsted collaborated on the project have been disproved in John Alexopoulos, "The Creator of Bushnell Park," *Connecticut Historical Society Bulletin* 47/3 (1982): 65–73. See also Robert L. Edwards, *Of Singular Genius, of Singular Grace: A Biography of Horace Bushnell* (Cleveland: Pilgrim Press, 1992), 180–82. On the beginnings of Olmsted's career, cf. Rosenzweig and Blackmar, *The Park and the People*, 127–28. On Olmsted's first articulation of a social philosophy for parks in 1858, David Schuyler, *The New Urban Landscape: The Redefinition of City Form in Nineteenth-Century America* (Baltimore: Johns Hopkins University Press, 1986), 94.

25. Bushnell, letter in *Hearth and Home*, 13. Edwards, *Of Singular Genius*, 174–75. "City Meeting," *Times*, 16 July 1853.

26. "Pet. of T.K. Brace + others for a Public Square between Washington + Lafayette Streets," 19 July 1853, drawer marked "Parks: Tabulated Correspondence 'S' to 'Z,' Miscellaneous Parks, Playgrounds," HCH; "Report on Public Square of Building near Trinity College–Lafayette St., 12 Sept. 1853," same drawer; "Common Council, Last Evening," *Times*, 13 September 1853; *HD* 16 (1853–54): 40, 52, 176, 177. "Pet. of Geo. Beach de New Park," 8 August 1853, drawer marked "Park Department, Annual Reports, Miscellaneous, 1827 to 1874," HCH; *HD* 16: 35. "Common Council," *Times*, 26 July 1853. "Com-

mon Council, Last Evening," *Times*, 23 August 1853; *HD* 16: 145. Anonymous letter by "H," *Times*, 28 September 1853.

27. Bushnell, letter in *Hearth and Home*, 9. Quotation from "Remarks of Dr. Bushnell," *Times*, 7 October 1853.

28. "Proposed New Park or Common," *Courant*, 7 October 1853.

29. "Remarks of Dr. Bushnell." At this time, Connecticut still had two capitals, Hartford and New Haven.

30. Ibid.; "Proposed New Park or Common"; Bushnell, letter in *Hearth and Home*, 12. Bushnell's map, a copy of which was once held by the Connecticut State Library, appears to have been lost.

31. Bushnell, letter in *Hearth and Home*, 13.

32. "The Proposed Park," *Courant*, 16 November 1853.

33. Katherine C. Grier, "The Decline of the Memory Palace: The Parlor after 1890," in *American Home Life, 1880–1930: A Social History of Spaces and Services*, ed. Jessica H. Foy and Thomas J. Schlereth (Knoxville: University of Tennessee Press, 1992), 49–74. Karen Halttunen, *Confidence Men and Painted Women: A Study of Middle-Class Culture in America, 1830–1870* (New Haven: Yale University Press, 1982), 58–60, at 60. John F. Kasson, *Rudeness and Civility: Manners in Nineteenth-Century Urban America* (New York: Hill and Wang, 1990), 173–76.

34. In recent years, a number of feminist geographers have examined the issue of how space is gendered both in buildings and in cities. See, for example, Lynn M. Appleton, "The Gender Regimes of American Cities," in *Gender in Urban Research*, Urban Affairs Annual Review, no. 42, ed. Judith A. Garber and Robyne S. Turner (Thousand Oaks, Calif.: Sage Publications, 1995), 44–59; Daphne Spain, *Gendered Spaces* (Chapel Hill: University of North Carolina Press, 1992); Linda McDowell, "City and Home: Urban Housing and the Sexual Division of Space," in *Sexual Divisions: Patterns and Processes*, ed. Mary Evans and Clare Ungerson (London: Tavistock Publications, 1983), 142–63; Susan Saegert, "Masculine Cities and Feminine Suburbs: Polarized Ideas, Contradictory Realities," in *Women and the American City*, ed. Catharine R. Stimpson et al. (Chicago: University of Chicago Press, 1980), 93–108. See also Dolores Hayden, *The Grand Domestic Revolution: A History of Feminist Designs for American Homes, Neighborhoods and Cities* (Cambridge: MIT Press, 1981).

35. Bushnell, "The Age of Homespun," 398–99.

36. "The Proposed Park," *Times*, 19 November 1853. "The Proposed Park," *Times*, 25 November 1853. "The Park," *Courant*, 5 January 1854.

37. Pet. of W. H. Green + Others de Public Square + Lafayette St.," 27 July 1853, drawer marked "Parks: Tabulated Correspondence 'S' to 'Z,' Miscellaneous Parks, Playgrounds," HCH; *HD* 16 (1853–54): 53, 89, 118, 135, 158.

Lydia Huntley Sigourney, "The Park," *Courant*, 21 November 1853; Cross, *Horace Bushnell*, 34–35; Sklar, *Catharine Beecher*, 61, 99. "And there, within that blissful glade / Glad troops of bright-eyed children play'd, / And invalids, no longer pale / Reviving drank the healthful gale, / While sons of wealth, and want, and care, / And weary toil found respite there," Sigourney wrote. Sigourney's piety, elitist sympathies, philanthropic inclinations, romantic aesthetics, and belief in female influence put her in ideological sympathy with Bushnell in such a project. Douglas, *The Feminization of American Culture*, 53–54, 87–88, 111–12. Sklar, *Catharine Beecher*, 88, 99. "The Proposed Park," *Courant*, 2 January 1854. "The Park Carried," *Courant*, 6 January 1854.

38. Clouette, "Antebellum Urban Renewal," 12. Bushnell, letter in *Hearth and Home*, 13–16. Sherman W. Adams, "The Hartford Park System. II. Bushnell Park," *Connecticut Quarterly* 1 (1895): 173–79. John Alexopoulos, *The Nineteenth Century Parks of Hartford: A Legacy to the Nation* (Hartford: Hartford Architecture Conservancy, 1983), 14–18. Frederick Law Olmsted, "Public Parks and the Enlargement of Towns," *Journal of Social Science* 3 (1871): 22, 23. Theodore Wirth to Charles E. Gross, 30 March 1904, gray binder of copies of letters from Wirth, marked "letters," PDP. George A. Parker, "Report on Widening of Jewell and Wells Streets," 7 October 1912, letterbox marked "1911–1912. Reports, Typewritten," PDP.

39. Weaver, *Hartford*, 94. "The Capitol Site," *Courant*, 8 January 1872.

40. On Olmsted's suburban designs, see Schuyler, *New Urban Landscape*, 162–66. Kenneth T. Jackson, *Crabgrass Frontier: The Suburbanization of the United States* (New York: Oxford University Press, 1985), 79–81. Quotation from Frederick Law Olmsted and J. J. R. Croes, "Preliminary Report of the Landscape Architect and the Civil and Topographical Engineer, upon the Laying Out of the Twenty-third and Twenty-fourth Wards," in *Landscape into Cityscape: Frederick Law Olmsted's Plans for a Greater New York City*, ed. Albert Fein (Ithaca: Cornell University Press, 1968), 352 (quoted in Schuyler, *New Urban Landscape*, 172).

41. Horace Bushnell, "Society for Public Improvement," *Courant*, 27 November 1854. Horace Bushnell, "City Plans," in *Work and Play; Or Literary Varieties* (New York: Charles Scribner, 1864), 308–09. Idem, untitled letter to the editor, *Courant*, 10 January 1855. Cheney, *Life and Letters of Horace Bushnell*, 345–48.

42. Bushnell, "City Plans," 312–14, 331, 333, at 313, 331, 314.

43. Katherine C. Grier, *Culture and Comfort: People, Parlors, and Upholstery, 1850–1930* (Rochester: Strong Museum; Amherst: University of Massachusetts Press, 1988), 1–17, 81–89. Robin Fleming, "Picturesque History and the Medieval in Nineteenth-Century America," *American Historical Review* 100/4 (1995): 1068, 1072.

44. Bushnell, "City Plans," 314–18, at 314.

45. Ibid., 321–24, 329–30, 334.

46. Ibid., 323.

47. Ibid., 335–36, at 336.

48. George M. Fredrickson, *The Inner Civil War: Northern Intellectuals and the Crisis of the Union* (New York: Harper and Row, 1965; reprinted with a new preface, Urbana: University of Illinois Press, 1993). R. Jackson Wilson, *In Quest of Community: Social Philosophy in the United States, 1860–1920* (New York: John Wiley and Sons, 1968), 26. Daniel Walker Howe, "The Social Science of Horace Bushnell," *Journal of American History* 70/2 (1983): 305–22.

Chapter 2

1. Population figures from *HD* 86 (1923–24): 1556. [Fred E. Dayton], "Hartford's Mauve Decade," *Times*, 16 March 1931.

2. On the depression of the 1870s, *City of Hartford: Mayor's Address and City Government for 1873* (Hartford: Geo. L. Coburn, 1873), 19; *City of Hartford: Mayor's Address and City Government for 1876* (Hartford: Wiley, Waterman and Eaton, 1876), 21; *City of Hartford: Mayor's Address and City Government for 1877* (Hartford: Wiley, Waterman and Eaton, 1877), 21; *MR* 1881, 19. On industry ca. 1890, Hartford Board of Trade, *Hartford, Conn., as a Manufacturing, Business and Commercial Center* (Hartford: Hartford Board of Trade, 1889), 92–151; *Hartford, Connecticut* (New York: Sanborn, 1885); *Board of Trade of the City of Hartford, Conn., Meeting of October 1st, 1888* (Hartford: Star Print [1888]); James J. Flink, *America Adopts the Automobile, 1895–1910* (Cambridge: MIT Press, 1970), 205; U.S. Department of the Interior, Census Office, *Report on Manufacturing Industries in the United States at the Eleventh Census, 1890. Part 2, Statistics of Cities* (Washington: Government Printing Office, 1895), 239.

3. On the nearby villages, Charles H. Clark, "The Charter Oak City," *Scribner's Monthly* 13/1 (1876): 6. J. H. Sutherland, *The City of Hartford and Vicinity and Their Resources* (Hartford: Evening Post Association, 1900), 5. On banks and insurance companies, Board of Trade, *Hartford, Conn.*, 20–74; at 20. Glenn Weaver, *Hartford: An Illustrated History of Connecticut's Capital* (Hartford: Connecticut Historical Society; Woodland Hills, Calif.: Windsor Publications, 1982), 84–89. Clark, "The Charter Oak City," 3–5.

4. Kenneth R. Andrews, *Nook Farm: Mark Twain's Hartford Circle* (Cambridge: Harvard University Press, 1950; Hamden, Conn.: Archon, 1967), 18–20. Clark, "The Charter Oak City," 2. Board of Trade, *Hartford, Conn.*, 84–85. "Mayor Henney Is Hopeful," *Courant*, 30 December 1907. Ellsworth Strong

Grant and Marion Hepburn Grant, *The City of Hartford, 1784–1984: An Illustrated History* (Hartford: Connecticut Historical Society, 1986), 50.

5. Henry A. Perkins, *Prospect Street in the "Eighties"* (Hartford: National Society of the Colonial Dames of America in the State of Connecticut, 1939), 1–2.

6. Daniel T. Rodgers, "In Search of Progressivism," *Reviews in American History* 10 (December 1982): 113–32.

7. Ibid.; John C. Burnham, "Essay," in John D. Buenker, John C. Burnham, and Robert M. Crunden, *Progressivism* (Rochester, Vt.: Schenkman Books, 1977), 3–29. Robert M. Crunden, "Essay," in Buenker, *Progressivism*, 71–103. The terms "Progressive Movement," "progressivism" and "Progressive Era" have been controversial in American historiography, particularly since the publication of Peter G. Filene's essay, "An Obituary for the Progressive Movement," *American Quarterly* 22 (1970): 20–34. Filene's essay did succeed in discouraging the use of the term "Progressive Movement." Nevertheless, as Rodgers observes, some historians have continued to find the term "progressivism" useful in the narrowly defined sense used above, namely, as a reference to a cluster of ideas and the associated rhetoric of discontent. More recently, Martin J. Sklar has argued that the term "Progressive Era" continues to serve as a useful designation of the period from about 1890 to about 1916. Sklar writes that there remains a scholarly consensus that these years "marked a distinct period in American history" characterized by the formation of some of the "basic social relations, institutions, outlooks, and movements of 20th-century American society" (Sklar, "Periodization and Historiography: Studying American Political Development in the Progressive Era, 1890s–1916," *Studies in American Political Development* 5 [Fall 1991]: 173–213, at 174, 175). In this book I use the term "Progressive Era" to designate the period in which progressivism was most prevalent—the decades of the 1890s, 1900s, and 1910s. "Progressive reform" refers to reform efforts in these years that were informed by progressivism, while "progressives" are those who held to progressive ideas.

8. "Due to Treachery," *Times*, 5 April 1904. "From Henney to Rankin: 25 Years of Municipal Politics," *Times*, 1 December 1931.

9. *7th Annual Meeting of the Hartford Board of Trade, January 8, 1895* (Hartford: Case, Lockwood and Brainard, 1895), 9.

10. Edward Bailey Eaton, "Inventions and Manufactures in Hartford," *Connecticut Magazine* 9/3 (1905): 643–58. Flink, *America Adopts the Automobile*, 205. Sutherland, *City of Hartford and Vicinity*, 6. *Hartford in 1912: Story of the Capitol City, Present and Prospective* (Hartford: Hartford Post, 1912), 185, 189, 191. Bureau of the Census, *Fourteenth Census of the United States, Manufactures, 1919: Connecticut* (Washington: Government Printing Office, 1922), 7,

38. Bureau of the Census, *Fifteenth Census of the United States, Manufactures: 1929*, vol. 3, *Reports by States: Statistics for Industrial Areas, Counties and Cities* (Washington: Government Printing Office, 1933), 100. Population figures are from *The Greater Hartford Directory, 1934* (Hartford: Price and Lee, 1934), 29.

11. *Art Work of Hartford: Published in Nine Parts* (Chicago: W.H. Parish, 1897), section 9, n.p.

12. Julius G. Rathbun, "Backward Glances at Hartford," *Connecticut Magazine* 5/1 (1899): 42–51.

13. "Busy Christmas Eve," *Courant*, 25 December 1896.

14. Alexander R. Merriam, *The Social Significance of the Smaller City* (Hartford: Hartford Seminary Press, 1903), 9. Robert W. DeForest and Lawrence Veiller, eds., *The Tenement House Problem: Including the Report of the New York State Tenement House Commission of 1900*, vol. 1 (New York: Macmillan, 1903), 155. *Atlas of the City of Hartford and the Town of West Hartford, Connecticut* (Springfield, Mass.: L.J. Richards, 1909). *Art Work of Hartford*.

15. Bruce Alan Clouette, "'Getting Their Share': Irish and Italian Immigrants in Hartford, Connecticut, 1850–1930" (Ph.D. diss., University of Connecticut, 1992), 92–96, 106–12, 159, 288–91. *Hartford in 1912*, 10. Grant and Grant, *The City of Hartford*, 66–68, 178. Bureau of the Census, *Social Statistics of Cities* (1886), 399; *Fourteenth Census of the United States Taken in the Year 1920*, vol. 3, *Populations 1920* (Washington: Government Printing Office, 1922), 158, 163; *Thirteenth Census of the United States Taken in the Year 1910: Statistics for Connecticut* (Washington: Government Printing Office, 1913), 595. Ward boundaries are from *HD* 64 (1901–02): 670–71; *HD* 82 (1919–20): 1483–84. [Graham Taylor, ed.], *A Religious Census of Hartford, Taken by the Connecticut Bible Society* (Hartford: Plimpton [1889]), 11. Sandra Hartwell Becker and Ralph L. Pearson, "The Jewish Community of Hartford, Connecticut, 1880–1929," *American Jewish Archives* 31/2 (1979): 196. Hartford Architecture Conservancy, *Hartford Architecture*, vol. 3, *North and West Neighborhoods* (Hartford: Hartford Architecture Conservancy, 1980), 21–22. "The Architecture of Hartford," clipping from the *Courant* dated December 1906, bundle of clippings marked "Circulars," box 5, MAS. "Hartford in 1907: How to Make It Bigger and Better," *Times*, 1 January 1907.

16. Clouette, "'Getting Their Share,'" 223–24, 262–63. Becker and Pearson, "The Jewish Community," 196. "Chinese Free Masons," *Courant*, 8 July 1895. "Three Raids on Chinese Resorts," *Courant*, 12 January 1912. "Dress Reform among Chinese," *Courant*, 21 January 1913. "Hartford's Chinatown a Place of Mystery," *Courant*, 14 December 1919. Armando Perretta, "A Walk on the East Side," *United Aircraft Quarterly Bee-Hive* 39 (Fall 1964), quoted in Clouette, "'Getting Their Share,'" 266–67.

17. Robert E. Pawlowski, *How the Other Half Lived: An Ethnic History of the Old East Side and South End of Hartford* (West Hartford: Northwest Catholic High School, 1973), 42–43. Clouette, "'Getting Their Share,'" 272–73. John J. McCook, "The Duty of a Hartford Citizen," speech to the Twentieth Century Club, 1893, in *The Social Reform Papers of John James McCook* (Hartford: Antiquarian and Landmarks Society of Connecticut, 1977), microfilm reel 1, item 16. Francis Goodwin II, "The Three Great Days," typescript, CHS. "Good Citizenship," *Courant*, 23 September 1895. MR 1899, 152. "A Walking Saloon," *Courant*, 25 September 1893. "When the Nightstick Was in Power," *Courant*, 1 November 1931. Photographs in folder marked "Vice Campaign," Connecticut Woman Suffrage Association papers, box 2, CSL. On prostitution, see chapter 3.

18. On contrasting views from the trolley, *Art Work of Hartford*, n.p. On the streetcar system, Weaver, *Hartford*, 97, 104.

19. *8th Annual Meeting of the Board of Trade, Hartford, January 14, 1896* (Hartford: Case, Lockwood and Brainard, 1896), 20.

20. William F. Henney, "Modern Factors in Municipal Progress," *Connecticut Magazine* 9/4 (1905): 816, 818. "A Hub Indeed," *Courant*, 16 June 1897. "Hartford, The Shopping Center of Connecticut," *Courant*, 23 May 1915. "Hartford's Great Volume of Trade from out of Town," *Courant*, 9 July 1916. "'Twas the Week before Christmas," *Courant*, 17 December 1916.

21. *Atlas of the City of Hartford Connecticut, Including, Also, the Town of West Hartford* (Springfield, Mass.: L.J. Richards, 1896). *Atlas of the City of Hartford, and the Town of West Hartford, Connecticut* (Springfield, Mass.: L.J. Richards, 1909). *Atlas of the City of Hartford and the Town of West Hartford, Connecticut* (New York: Sanborn, 1920). *Insurance Maps of Hartford Connecticut*, vol. 2 (New York: Sanborn, 1922). Carl Pitner, *Pitner's Map of Hartford, West Hartford, East Hartford and Environs* (Washington: Carl Pitner, n.d. [ca. 1930]). Hartford Architecture Conservancy, *Hartford Architecture*, vol. 2, *South Neighborhoods* (Hartford: Hartford Architecture Conservancy, 1980), 10, 48, 50, 102, 131, 134, 136, 169. Hartford Architecture Conservancy, *Hartford Architecture*, vol. 3, *North and West Neighborhoods* (Hartford: Hartford Architecture Conservancy, 1980), 10, 45, 77, 84–85, 177, 185. Kenneth T. Jackson, *The Crabgrass Frontier: The Suburbanization of the United States* (New York: Oxford University Press, 1985), 103–37. Sam Bass Warner, Jr., *Streetcar Suburbs: The Process of Growth in Boston, 1870–1900* (Cambridge: Harvard University Press, 1962).

22. Perkins, *Prospect Street in the "Eighties,"* 15. Fred E. Dayton, "Hartford's Mauve Decade, No. 243," *Times*, 26 December 1931. Conservancy, *Hartford Architecture*, 2:26, 102, 104, 131–39, 146, 169, 177. Conservancy, *Hartford Architecture*, 3:107–17, 138, 154, 171, 177, 185. *Atlas of the City of Hartford and the Town of West Hartford, Connecticut* (New York: Sanborn, 1920).

23. Hartford Board of Trade, *Hartford, Conn.*, 116. *Town and City Atlas of the State of Connecticut* (Boston: D.H. Hurd, 1893), 42. On direction of wind-blown smoke, *A Plan of the City of Hartford, Preliminary Report by Carrère and Hastings, Advisory Architects, to the Commission on the City Plan of the City of Hartford, Connecticut* (Hartford: Case, Lockwood and Brainard, 1912), 47. Hepburn anecdote from Christopher Andersen, *Young Kate* (New York: Henry Holt, 1988), 101.

24. On the middle class's loss of its monopoly on political and economic power, see Clouette, "'Getting Their Share,'"106–12, 209–12.

25. Angel Kwolek-Folland, *Engendering Business: Men and Women in the Corporate Office, 1870–1930* (Baltimore: Johns Hopkins University Press, 1994), 120, 123, 188, 191. See also E. Anthony Rotundo, *American Manhood: Transformations in Masculinity from the Revolution to the Modern Era* (New York: Basic Books, 1993), 250. The historian Daniel M. Bluestone argues that the corporate skyscraper functioned as an internalized and sanitized replacement for the street, one in which genteel decorum prevailed and from which the rowdy lower classes were excluded (Daniel M. Bluestone, "Landscape and Culture in Nineteenth-Century Chicago" [Ph.D. diss., University of Chicago, 1984], 234–35.)

26. *Memorial Service to Mrs. Dotha Bushnell Hillyer* (program dated 1 January 1933), CSL. Her rank in age can be determined from Mary Bushnell Cheney, *Life and Letters of Horace Bushnell* (New York: Harper and Brothers, 1880), 104, which indicates that in 1842 Bushnell already had two daughters (see also 175, 353); on Bushnell's views of his mother, see 26–34; on Bushnell as a father, 452–69. Quotations are from Cheney, *Life and Letters of Horace Bushnell,* 140–43.

27. "Mrs. A.R. Hillyer, Donor of Bushnell Memorial, Dies," *Courant,* 9 December 1932. "Sudden Death of A.R. Hillyer," *Courant,* 22 April 1915. *Atlas of the City of Hartford and the Town of West Hartford, Connecticut* (1909), plate 2. *Art Work of Hartford,* photographs with captions "View from YMCA Building Overlooking Bushnell Park," "YMCA Building," and "View from Dome of Capitol."

28. Photograph in *Tenth Anniversary Commemorative Booklet* (Hartford: Horace Bushnell Memorial Hall, [1940?]). William Douglas Mackenzie, "Dotha Bushnell Hillyer," *The Prompter* 3/4 (1933), photograph on 4. *HD* 60 (1897–98): 695. *HD* 61 (1898–99): 720. *HD* 62 (1899–1900): 720. *HD* 63 (1900–01): 784. *HD* 64 (1901–02): 886. *HD* 65 (1902–03): 887. *HD* 66 (1903–04): 951. *HD* 67 (1904–05): 951. *HD* 68 (1905–06): 950. *HD* 69 (1906–07): 950. *HD* 70 (1907–08): 950. *HD* 71 (1908–09): 1126. *HD* 72 (1909–10): 1126. *HD* 73 (1910–11): 1126. *HD* 74 (1911–12): 1127. *HD* 75 (1912–13): 1128. *HD* 76 (1913–14): 1384. *HD* 77 (1914–15): 1524. *HD* 78 (1915–16): 1524. *HD* 79

(1916–17): 1524. *HD* 80 (1917–18): 1524. *HD* 81 (1918–19): 1525. *HD* 82 (1919–20): 1527. *HD* 83 (1920–21): 1559. *Report of the Civic Club of Hartford, Conn., 1901–1905* (Hartford: Clark and Smith, 1905), 10–11. *Report of the Civic Club: School-Gardens, Household School, and Playground in Riverside Park, Hartford, Conn., June–September, 1905* (Hartford: Case, Lockwood and Brainard, 1905). *Report of the Juvenile Commission to the Mayor and Court of Common Council of the City of Hartford, Conn., 1926–1927* (Hartford: Pyne Printery, [1927]), n.p.

29. *BPC* 62 (1922): 105. "Mrs. Hillyer, Donor of Bushnell Memorial, Dies." Edwin Knox Mitchell, "Mrs. Hillyer: Dr. Mitchell Recalls Her Work for the Parks," *Courant*, 14 December 1932. (See also chapter 7.) *Publications of the Municipal Art Society of Hartford, Connecticut, no. 1, Officers, Directors, Standing Committees, Constitution, By-laws, and Members; What Is a Municipal Art Society?* (Hartford: Municipal Art Society, 1904), 2. "The Consumers' League of Hartford, Connecticut, Annual Report 1911," box 1, folder 3, CLC.

30. Andersen, *Young Kate*, 112, 117. Horace Bushnell, *Women's Suffrage: The Reform against Nature* (New York: Charles Scribner, 1869). Editorial titled "Mrs. Dotha Bushnell Hillyer," *Times*, 8 December 1932. *Tenth Anniversary Commemorative Booklet.*

31. Mackenzie, "Dotha Bushnell Hillyer," 3, 6. "The Civic Club: Writer Notes Mrs. Hillyer's Influence upon It," *Courant*, 31 December 1932. The club member quoted added: "It was Mrs. Hillyer who was the inspiration of the Club, and yet it was not a 'one woman' organization. There were committees on streets, health, schools, art and library, parks, domestic science, and for each of these there was an active chairman diligently working with her committee members to create public opinion and produce results based on intelligent understanding. Behind all these committees stood Mrs. Hillyer as friend and active helper. It was her custom to scan the leading newspapers and to make clippings bearing on the interests of the club. What enthusiasm resulted in a committee meeting when, with a handful of clippings, she would suggest new ideas or ways to get more light upon old ones! It was an unusual club. It held a remarkable position in the community. Its advice was sought because it was known that none would be given without study and proper appreciation of all the factors entering into a balanced judgment."

32. Dorothy Schneider and Carl J. Schneider, *American Women in the Progressive Era, 1890–1920* (New York: Doubleday, 1994; New York: Facts on File, 1993), 93–113. Mary Ritter Beard, *Woman's Work in Municipalities* (New York: D. Appleton, 1915). Suellen M. Hoy, "'Municipal Housekeeping': The Role of Women in Improving Urban Sanitation Practices, 1880–1917," in *Pollution and Reform in American Cities, 1870–1930*, ed. Martin V. Melosi (Austin: University

of Texas Press, 1980), 173–98. Suellen Hoy, *Chasing Dirt: The American Pursuit of Cleanliness* (New York: Oxford University Press, 1995), 59–86.

33. Daniel Eli Burnstein, "Clean Streets and the Pursuit of Progress: Urban Reform in New York City in the Progressive Era" (Ph.D. diss., Rutgers University, 1992), 67, 147. John Duffy, *The Sanitarians: A History of American Public Health* (Urbana: University of Illinois Press, 1990), 110–203. Barbara Gutmann Rosenkrantz, *Public Health and the State: Changing Views in Massachusetts, 1842–1936* (Cambridge: Harvard University Press, 1972), 103.

34. Marilyn Thornton Williams, *Washing the "Great Unwashed": Public Baths in Urban America, 1840–1920* (Columbus: Ohio State University Press, 1991), 1. Jacob A. Riis, *How the Other Half Lives: Studies among the Tenements of New York* (1890; reprint, with an introduction by Donald N. Bigelow, New York: Hill and Wang, 1957), 35. Burnstein, "Clean Streets and the Pursuit of Progress," ii, 68–70, 155. Hoy, *Chasing Dirt*, 16, 59. The historian Stanley K. Schultz has used the term "moral environmentalism" to describe this clustering of beliefs about cleanliness, environmental influence, and morality. Schultz, *Constructing Urban Culture: American Cities and City Planning, 1800–1920* (Philadelphia: Temple University Press, 1989), 113–14, 119.

35. Hoy, "'Municipal Housekeeping,'" 191. Maureen A. Flanagan, "The City Profitable, the City Livable: Environmental Policy, Gender, and Power in Chicago in the 1910s," *Journal of Urban History* 22/2 (1996): 163–90. Beard, *Woman's Work*, 84. Sheila M. Rothman, *Woman's Proper Place: A History of Changing Ideals and Practices, 1870 to the Present* (New York: Basic Books, 1978), 69.

36. Rothman, *Woman's Proper Place*, 93.

37. Burnstein, "Clean Streets," 214–26.

38. Barbara Finlay Donahue, "The Civic Club of Hartford, Connecticut: A Study of Women's Organizations in the Reform Era," (master's thesis, Trinity College [Hartford], 1992), 25. *Eighth Annual Meeting, Board of Trade, Hartford, Jan. 14, 1896*, 23. On women's charitable societies in Hartford, see chapters 3–5. On women's literary societies in Hartford, see Jane Cunningham Croly, *The History of the Woman's Club Movement in America* (New York: Henry G. Allen, 1898), 304, 312–14. For an analysis of how such clubs affected gender roles, see Karen J. Blair, *The Clubwoman as Feminist: True Womanhood Redefined, 1868–1914* (New York: Holmes and Meier, 1980). "The Civic Club," *Courant*, 25 January 1895. *Report of the Civic Club of Hartford Conn., 1895–1901* (Hartford: Case, Lockwood and Brainard, 1901), 5.

39. BSC 12 (for 1883): 9–10. BSC 13 (for 1884): viii. BSC 22 (for 1893): vii. BSC 24 (for 1895): viii. "In Favor of Clean Walks," *Times*, 14 March 1895. "Sunday Street Work," *Courant*, 9 May 1895. MR 1891, 28.

40. "Good Ideas for Hartford," *Times*, 11 April 1896. MR 1896, 284. As part of its effort to enlist public support for reform without making public declarations, the Civic Club regularly invited local and national reform figures to give speeches that were reported in detail in the press. Speakers in the 1890s and 1900s included George Waring, Jacob Riis, Robert DeForest, and Luther Gulick. *Report of the Civic Club of Hartford* (1901), 11–13. *Report of the Civic Club of Hartford* (1905), 11.

41. "Women Object to Reporters," *Courant*, 28 February 1895. *Report of the Civic Club* (1901), 11. "Civic Club Movements," *Courant*, 21 May 1895. "Observe the Laws," *Courant*, 5 October 1895. "In Favor of Clean Walks"; "Petition of the Civic Club," 22 April 1895, drawer marked "Ashes & Garbage," HCH. "Sunday Street Work," *Courant*, 9 May 1895. "Police Clean Streets," *Courant*, 20 November 1895.

42. "Mrs. Mumford on Civics," *Courant*, 7 December 1895. "More Waste Cans," *Courant*, 23 January 1896. "Converted Ash Barrels," *Courant*, 7 March 1896. *Eighth Annual Meeting, Board of Trade*, 23.

43. On white wings, "White or Blue 'Angels'," *Courant*, 14 December 1896; BSC 25 (for 1896): ix; BSC 30 (for 1901): xviii. On hopes for public cooperation, BSC 24 (for 1895): ix; BSC 31 (for 1902): 77; BSC 32 (for 1902): 51–52; BSC 33 (for 1903): 73. On health department's opinion, MR 1903–04, 432.

44. Untitled editorial, *Courant*, 18 January 1896. *Report of the Civic Club* (1901), 12. *Report of the Civic Club* (1905), 11. On spitting as a violation of middle-class norms, John F. Kasson, *Rudeness and Civility: Manners in Nineteenth-Century Urban America* (New York: Hill and Wang, 1990), 125–26. On concerns about tuberculosis, Hoy, *Chasing Dirt*, 133–34. On tuberculosis in Hartford, Sandra L. Wheeler, "Sanatorium Care for the Tubercular Poor in Hartford, 1900–1910," (master's thesis, Trinity College [Hartford], 1993), 78–79. On responses by the Board of Health, MR 1903–04, 400. On ordinance, JCCB 1906–07, 261. Quotation from MR 1905–06, 431. On continued spitting, "Anti-Spitting Law" and "Expectorating on Sidewalks," *Post*, 15 May and 14 June 1907; MR 1909–10, 533. On order to enforce, JBA 1910–11, 1064. On increased enforcement, BH 27 (1911): 48.

45. Burnstein, "Clean Streets," 198. Quotation from "Hartford in 1907: How to Make the City Bigger and Better," *Times*, 1 January 1907.

46. "Civic Club Meeting," *Courant*, 2 November 1895. MR 1905–06, 395. "Letters from the People: Hartford's Backyards and Alleyways," *Courant*, 26 April 1897.

47. Dotha Bushnell Hillyer, "Rousing Hartford to Housing Evils," *Survey* 30 (19 July 1913): 534–35, at 534.

48. *Report of the Civic Club* (1901), 13. "Tenement House Problem," *Cour-*

ant, 12 June 1896. "Tenement Houses," *Courant*, 2 May 1900. "Tenement Houses," *Courant*, 3 May 1900.

49. Fred Dayton, "Hartford's Mauve Decade, No. 102: Model House History," *Times*, 13 July 1931. "Block of 12 Houses," *Courant*, 29 March 1895. "Planning to Build Workingmen's Homes," *Courant*, 2 April 1912. George A. Parker to Frederick L. Olmsted, 9 May 1906, GAPP. *JCCB*, 1908–09, 26–30, at 27. George A. Parker to Benjamin C. Marsh, 24 February 1909, letterbox marked "Letter. 1910. Leaflet: XIII," PDP. George A. Parker, "Paper Read before the Manufacturer's Association," 19 February 1910, binder marked "Duplicates— 1909 + 1910," PDP. George A. Parker, "Housing Question," n.d., unpublished manuscript, box marked "Reports Typewritten. 1911–1912," PDP. *A Plan of the City of Hartford: Preliminary Report*, 48, 81. George A. Parker, "Housing," n.d., unpublished manuscript, letterbox marked "Letters. O.P., 1912–1924. Mr. Parker's Articles, Etc.," PDP. "Building Houses," *Hartford* 5/10 (1920): 6. Conservancy, *Hartford Architecture*, 2:171.

50. "Calls Tenements Loathesomely Dirty," *Courant*, 14 January 1907. Hillyer, "Rousing Hartford to Housing Evils," 534–35. "Bad Housing Conditions Found," *Courant*, 23 November 1911. "Tenements Are in Good Shape," *Courant*, 7 August 1913.

51. Hillyer, "Rousing Hartford to Housing Evils," 535. "Handbills Out for Clean-up Week," *Courant*, 4 April 1912. "Children in City Clean-up Work," *American City* 14/2 (February 1916): 157–58. By 1916 the leadership of the cleanup campaigns had passed to the Hartford Chamber of Commerce; "We're Cleaned Up for 1916," *Hartford* 1/8 (1916): 8.

52. "Every Day to be Clean-up Day," *Courant*, 28 March 1914. "East Side is 'Perking Up,'" *Courant*, 13 March 1921. David I. MacLeod, *Building Character in the American Boy: The Boy Scouts, YMCA, and their Forerunners, 1870–1920* (Madison: University of Wisconsin Press, 1983), xii, 3, 212–15. "The Boy Scout Movement in Hartford," *Courant*, 17 May 1914. "Boy Scout Day Here on May 23," *Times*, 13 May 1914. Quotation from "Letters from the People: The Triumph of the Scouts," *Courant*, 29 April 1912.

53. Armando T. Perretta, *Take a Number* (New York: William Morrow, 1957), 215.

54. Municipal Art Society, 1:5, 9–13, 17, 19. *Dau's Society Blue Book for Hartford, Conn.* (New York: Dau Publishing, 1905). William F. Henney, "Some Municipal Problems," in Municipal Art Society, *Publications of the Municipal Art Society of Hartford*, no. 4, *Proceedings of the Annual Meeting, October 17, 1905; Some Municipal Problems* (Hartford: Municipal Art Society, 1906), 22–23. Donahue, "The Civic Club," 75.

55. William H. Wilson, *The City Beautiful Movement* (Baltimore: Johns Hopkins University Press, 1989), 1–3, 305.

56. On street cleaning, minutes of 17 October 1905 meeting, in bound volume of minutes, 14 June 1904—17 October 1905, Municipal Art Society papers, CSL; Municipal Art Society, *Publications of the Municipal Art Society of Hartford, Connecticut*, no. 6, *Proceedings of the Annual Meeting, November 27, 1906. Officers, Members, Reports of Standing Committees* (Hartford: Municipal Art Society, 1907), 16. On houses of comfort, Municipal Art Society, 1:2 and 6:15; MR 1902–03, 482; MR 1908–09, 605; MR 1909–10, 533; *Fourth Annual Report of the Commission on the City Plan to the Mayor and Court of Common Council* (Hartford: Case, Lockwood and Brainard, 1911), 5; JBA 1913–14, 1007; JBA 1914–15, 829; "Report of Board of Park Commissioners and the Public Buildings Commission re Advisability of Erecting Additional Public Comfort Stations," 3 October 1919, drawer marked "House of Comfort," HCH. Other organizations had also advocated the construction of the house of comfort, including the City Club, the Woman's Christian Temperance Union, and the Central Labor Union (petitions in same drawer).

57. "Municipal Art Society: Outline of the Work of the Standing Committees," typescript, March 1908, box 1, MAS. William H. Wilson, "The Billboard: Bane of the City Beautiful," *Journal of Urban History* 13/4 (1987): 394–425. "Billboard Campaign in Hartford, Conn.," *Charities and the Commons*, 26 December 1908, 476–77. For one extreme example of a sign-covered building, see "Catlin Building at the Corner of Main and Asylum Streets," Taylor Collection (photographs), no. 8, CSL.

58. "Ordinance Committee," *Courant*, 7 March 1902. Edwin Knox Mitchell, *Hartford Council of Churches (Historical Sketch)* (n.p.: 1925), 5. Ethel Loomis Dickinson, "Civic Improvement: What Has Been Done in Hartford, Connecticut," *New England Magazine*, n.s. 41/1 (1909): 809.

59. Hartford Federation of Churches, minutes of 27 November 1905 meeting, in "Secretary's Book, Hartford, Conn., Federation of Churches," Capitol Region Council of Churches, Hartford. "War Against Billboards: Formulating Plan of Work," *Times*, 24 January 1908. "Billboard Campaign in Hartford," 477. Wilson, "The Billboard," 396. "Preparing for Campaign against the Billboards," *Hartford Times*, 10 April 1908. "Billboard Campaign in Hartford," 476–77. "Blacklist Is Asked of All the Billboards," *Times*, 23 May 1908. "For Regulation of Billboards," *Courant*, 23 May 1908.

60. "Hide Billboards at Certain Angles," *Courant*, 24 April 1908. Anonymous to H. Leonard Beadle, 8 June 1908, box 4, MAS. Dickinson, "Civic Improvement"; "War against Billboards"; MR 1911, 843–45. Minutes of 26 Oc-

tober 1911 meeting of board of directors of the Municipal Art Society, in minutes 1908–1933, box 1, MAS. "Ugly Signboard Raises Protest," *Post*, 28 April 1914.

Chapter 3

1. A. N. Brooks, "Segregation the Social Evil," *Times*, 8 January 1912. The city directory lists an Arthur N. Brooks, a traveling salesman; *HD* 75 (1912–13): 112. See also Michael J. Shay, "The Regulation of Vice: An Old Hack-Driver's Views on the Subject," *Courant*, 8 January 1908.

2. On the relationship between the separate-spheres ideology and the use of public space in the nineteenth century, see Mary P. Ryan, *Women in Public: Between Banners and Ballots, 1825–1880* (Baltimore: Johns Hopkins University Press, 1990), chapter 2. On the role of red-light districts, see Neil Larry Shumsky, "Tacit Acceptance: Respectable Americans and Segregated Prostitution, 1870–1910," *Journal of Social History* 19/4 (1986): 665–79.

3. "Evils May Exist, Say Officials," *Times*, 20 May 1907. "Believe Ministers Ignorant of Truth," *Post*, 21 May 1907.

4. The quotation is from *Report of the Hartford Vice Commission* (Hartford: Connecticut Woman Suffrage Association, 1913), 21.

5. [George B. Thayer], "Supplementary Report," *The Social Reform Papers of John James McCook* (Hartford: Antiquarian and Landmarks Society of Connecticut, 1977), microfilm reel 9. [Fred E. Dayton], "Hartford's Mauve Decade, No. 119: Shuttered Houses," *Times*, 1 August 1931.

6. Thayer, "Supplementary Report."

7. Anonymous manuscript dated "summer of 1901," included with material related to the Charity Organization Society in McCook Papers, reel 9. Hartford Federation of Churches to William F. Henney, n.d., evidently late 1906, CHS. *Report of the Hartford Vice Commission*, 21, 26. Eleven houses were closed by the mayor's order, and one had closed a month earlier by a judge's order; "Judge Orders Patsy's Resort Closed," *Courant*, 25 November 1911.

8. "Police News," *Courant*, 24 May 1880.

9. "Evils May Exist, Say Officials."

10. For examples of people released without penalties, "The Courts," *Courant*, 25 May 1880; "The Police Court," *Courant*, 16 June 1899. *Report of the Hartford Vice Commission*, 21. "The Connecticut State Farm for Women," *Suffrage News Bulletin* 6 (June–July 1920); this last quotation describes the situation in the years before 1913.

11. For a discussion of such "rescue homes" in a broader context, see Peggy Pascoe, *Relations of Rescue: The Search for Female Moral Authority in the American West, 1874–1939* (New York: Oxford University Press, 1990), chapter 2.

12. Barbara Meil Hobson, *Uneasy Virtue: The Politics of Prostitution and the American Reform Tradition* (New York: Basic Books, 1987; reprint, Chicago: University of Chicago Press, 1990), 53–55.

13. *Tenth Annual Report of the Woman's Aid Society of Hartford* (Hartford: Case, Lockwood and Brainard, 1888), 11, 12; *Fourth Annual Report, Woman's Aid Society of Hartford* (Hartford: Case, Lockwood and Brainard, 1882), 12–14. The middle-class character of the organization can be seen by comparing the membership listed in *Fourth Annual Report* against individual listings in HD 44 (1881).

14. *Seventh Annual Report of the Woman's Aid Society of Hartford* (Hartford: Case, Lockwood and Brainard, 1885), 11, 12. *Fourth Annual Report*, 14, 15.

15. *Fourth Annual Report*, 15. *Fifth Annual Report of the Woman's Aid Society of Hartford* (Hartford: Case, Lockwood and Brainard, 1883), 12. *Eighth Annual Report of the Woman's Aid Society of Hartford* (Hartford: Case, Lockwood and Brainard, 1886), 13–14. *Sixth Annual Report of the Woman's Aid Society of Hartford* (Hartford: Case, Lockwood and Brainard, 1884), 15. "Equal Rights Club," *Times*, 17 February 1890; "Equal Rights Club," *Times*, 20 April 1891. MR 1894, 37.

16. *Fifth Annual Report*, 11. *Sixth Annual Report*, 11, 15. *Seventh Annual Report*, 11. *Seventeenth Annual Report of the Woman's Aid Society of Hartford* (Hartford: Case, Lockwood and Brainard, 1894), 17, quotation at 11.

17. *Biennial Report, 1926–27, of the Woman's Aid Society of Hartford* (n.p.).

18. *The Shelter for Women, 1897* (n.p.). The generalization about the leadership is based on a comparison of names listed in this document against HD 60 (1897).

19. *Shelter for Women*. "The Police Court," *Courant*, 16 June 1899. That the shelter was slightly less condescending than the Woman's Aid Society can be seen from the reason it gave for charging nominal fees for lodging and clothing: to help clients maintain their self-respect. Such a goal was foreign to the Woman's Aid Society, which wanted prostitutes humbly to acknowledge their depravity as a step toward conversion. Compare *Shelter for Women* with *Ninth Annual Report of the Woman's Aid Society* (Hartford: Case, Lockwood and Brainard, 1887), 11.

20. Thomas S. Duggan, *The Catholic Church in Connecticut* (New York: States History, 1930), 143. "Sisters of Good Shepherd," *Catholic Transcript*, 18 December 1902. In early 1912 the house had 133 inmates, 77 committed by the courts; "The Good Shepherd Appeal Is Argued," *Courant*, 5 January 1912.

21. "Many Women on the Streets Last Night," *Courant*, 30 December 1911.

22. Petition of Andrew Heublein et al., presented 12 January 1880, drawer marked "Girard Avenue, Glendale Avenue, Gold Street," HCH. U.S. Census schedules for 1880 show a mix of Irish and black residents on Gold Street.

23. Helen Post Chapman, *My Hartford of the Nineteenth Century* (Hartford: Edwin Valentine Mitchell, 1928), 21. [Fred E. Dayton], "Hartford's Mauve Decade, No. 30: The Heublein's Hotel," *Times*, 18 April 1931. Emily S. G. Holcombe, *Restoration of the Ancient Burying-Ground of Hartford and the Widening of Gold Street* (Hartford: Ruth Wyllys Chapter of the Daughters of the American Revolution, 1904), 8. The description of soliciting appears in *Report of the Hartford Vice Commission*, 82.

24. "Mrs. J. M. Holcombe Dies Suddenly," *Times*, 28 March 1923. "Sudden Death of Mrs. Holcombe," *Courant*, 29 March 1923. "Mrs. Holcombe: A Tribute from a Friend," *Courant*, 30 March 1923. *Commemorative Biographical Record of Hartford County, Connecticut* (Chicago: J.H. Beers, 1901), 117–18. *Publications of the Municipal Art Society of Hartford, Connecticut, no. 1, Officers, Directors, Standing Committees, Constitution, By-laws, and Members; What Is a Municipal Art Society?* (Hartford: Municipal Art Society, 1904), 2. *Publications of the Municipal Art Society of Hartford, Connecticut, no. 6, Proceedings of the Annual Meeting, November 27, 1906. Officers, Members, Reports of Standing Committees* (Hartford: Municipal Art Society, 1907), 2. *Publications of the Municipal Art Society of Hartford, Connecticut, no. 11, Proceedings of the Annual Meeting, November 13, 1908. Officers, Members, Reports of Committees. Unnecessary Noises. The Billboard Question* (Hartford: Municipal Art Society, 1909), 2.

25. George Leon Walker, *Old Hartford Burying Ground* (Hartford: Case, Lockwood and Brainard, 1895), 28–30. The overwhelmingly middle-class character of the membership can be seen by checking the members' names given in Daughters of the American Revolution, Ruth Wyllys Chapter records, 1:51–74, CSL, against listings in *HD* 57 (1894).

26. Holcombe, *Restoration*, 5–15, at 5, 9–10, 15.

27. Holcombe, *Restoration*, 6, 73–77. Holcombe, "The Ancient Burying Ground of Hartford," *Connecticut Quarterly* 4/1 (1898): 78.

28. Holcombe, *Restoration*, 16–21. "Gold Street's Finish," *Post*, 22 April 1899.

29. *The Annual Report of the City Missionary to the City Missionary Society of Hartford, 1877–1878* (Hartford: Case, Lockwood and Brainard, 1878), 21. David J. Pivar, *Purity Crusade: Sexual Morality and Social Control, 1868–1900* (Westport, Conn.: Greenwood Press, 1973). Timothy J. Gilfoyle, *City of Eros: New York City, Prostitution and the Commercialization of Sex, 1790–1920*, (New York: W.W. Norton, 1992), chapters 9, 14.

30. Edwin Knox Mitchell, *Hartford Council of Churches (Historical Sketch)* (n.p., 1925). "Breach between Ministers and the Prosecutor," *Courant*, 27 May 1907. Federation of Churches to Henney.

31. Federation of Churches to Henney.

32. "From Henney to Rankin: 25 Years of Municipal Politics, No. 3," *Times*, December 3, 1931. See also chapter 9.

33. "Police Allies of Criminals?" *Times*, 20 May 1907.

34. "Police Board Calls Ministers," *Courant*, 21 May 1907. "Ministers Refuse to Tell; Subpoenas to Compel Them," *Courant*, 23 May 1907. "Pastors Submit Their Evidence," *Courant*, 25 May 1907.

35. "Breach between Ministers and the Prosecutor."

36. "Mr. Freeman and Mr. Peabody Confer," *Courant*, 28 May 1907. "Secretary's Book, Hartford, Conn., Federation of Churches, (Minutes, 1900–14), Capitol Region Council of Churches, Hartford," 167. "Honest Effort to Wipe out Vice," *Times*, 8 July 1907.

37. "Honest Effort to Wipe out Vice"; "Clear Evil Resorts From East Side," *Post*, 8 July 1907.

38. "Tidy Sum Netted to Police Funds by Sudden Raid," *Times*, 10 July 1909.

39. "Breach between Ministers and the Prosecutor."

40. On nightwalkers, MR 1893, 79; Barbara Meil Hobson, *Uneasy Virtue: The Politics of Prostitution and the American Reform Tradition* (New York: Basic Books, 1987; reprint, Chicago: University of Chicago Press, 1990), 32–33. On the moral associations of darkness, see also Mark J. Bouman, "The 'Good Lamp Is the Best Police' Metaphor and Ideologies of the Nineteenth-Century Urban Landscape," *American Studies* 32/2 (1991): 63–78. On the growth of commercial leisure and its link with improved street lighting, see David Nasaw, *Going Out: The Rise and Fall of Public Amusements* (New York: Basic Books, 1993), 3–9. On street lighting in Hartford, Harold J. Bingham, *History of Connecticut*, vol. 2 (New York: Lewis Historical Publishing, 1962), 728.

41. On programs at theaters, see advertisements in the *Courant*, 20 April 1907, 27 May 1907, 28 May 1907 (advertisement for concert and dance). On dancing and drinking, "Report of the Public Dance Hall Committee" (3 April 1914), attached to p. 332, "Secretary's Book. "What the Social Service Survey Did," *Courant*, 16 January 1912. On the presence and location of dozens of downtown and East Side saloons, HD 69 (1906–7). Dent and Kelsey were both anxious to limit the evil effects of commercial amusement. Dent, the pastor of the South Park Methodist Church, led a successful campaign around 1909 to prohibit the showing of movies on Sunday; "Both Merciful and Necessary," *Times*, 21 February 1914. Kelsey, the pastor of the Fourth (Congregational) Church, had led a similar attempt in 1905; "Secretary's Book," 105. (Kelsey had come to Fourth Church, which was devoted to serving the poor of Hartford's central neighborhoods, in 1888 as associate pastor under the Rev. Graham Taylor (Charles Trumbull Russ, "The Hartford Years of Graham Taylor, 1880–1892:

With Special Emphasis on His Association with the Fourth Church and the Hartford Theological Seminary" [master's thesis, Hartford Theological Seminary], 1960, 52).

42. "Breach between Ministers and the Prosecutor."

43. Kathy Peiss, *Cheap Amusements: Working Women and Leisure in Turn-of-the-Century New York* (Philadelphia: Temple University Press, 1986). *Report of the Hartford Vice Commission*, 56–64, at 62, 63.

44. "Breach between Ministers and the Prosecutor." On the increase in female employment in Hartford, see Tracey M. Wilson, "The 1911 Hartford Garment Workers Strike," *Connecticut Historical Society Bulletin* 50/1 (1984): 25, 27–28.

45. Hepburn was the mother of the famous actress.

46. Hepburn rejected the double standard of morality, but wanted men to be more chaste instead of women more sexual. Katharine Houghton Hepburn, letter in *Survey* 25 (1 October 1910): 79–80. Katharine Houghton Hepburn, *Woman Suffrage and the Social Evil* (New York: National Woman Suffrage Publishing, [1914]), 16.

47. The suffragists were part of a broad trend of feminist thought that has been called "cultural feminism," in which women sought victory over male values instead of greater access to male privileges. Josephine Donovan, *Feminist Theory: The Intellectual Traditions of American Feminism* (New York: Frederick Ungar, 1985), chapter 2.

48. On "outside housekeeping," see "Letters from the People: Votes for Women," *Times*, 2 April 1912. The historian Paula Baker describes this idea as part of the "domestication of politics" that helped women win the vote but ultimately cost them their special political culture. Baker, "The Domestication of Politics: Women and American Political Society, 1780–1920," *American Historical Review* 89 (1984): 620–47.

49. Smith's order followed demands for action from ministers, labor leaders, and a newspaper. (A heavily publicized trial of a federal agent investigating the white-slave traffic between New York and Hartford had exposed the friendly relations between the Hartford police and brothel-keepers.) The trial was of a federal agent investigating the "white slave" traffic between New York and Hartford. Police arrested the agent on a complaint from one of the suspected white slavers. The defense argued that the agent had been framed. "Pigniulo Trial Gets under Way," *Courant*, 20 December 1911. "Mayor Calls for Record in Fusco Case," *Courant*, 25 December 1911. "Jury Disagrees in Pigniulo Case," *Courant*, 25 December 1911. "Central Labor Union Demands an Investigation," *Courant*, 28 December 1911. "Turn on the Light," *Post*, 27 December 1911.

50. Barbara Leaming, *Katharine Hepburn* (New York: Crown, 1995), 5–164.

Thomas N. Hepburn, "Demand for an Open Change of Attitude towards the Social Evil," *Yale Medical Journal* 14/4 (1908): 167–73. *Report of the Annual Meeting of the Connecticut Society of Social Hygiene* (n.p., 1911), 3, 10. Allan M. Brandt, *No Magic Bullet: A Social History of Venereal Disease in the United States since 1880* (New York: Oxford University Press, 1985), 7–22. *Thirtieth Annual Report of the Woman's Aid Society of Hartford* (n.p., 1908), 3. Katharine Houghton Hepburn manuscript, n.d., box 6, folder 153, Florence Ledyard (Cross) Kitchelt Papers, Schlesinger Library, Radcliffe College. Connecticut Woman Suffrage Association (CWSA) records, box 1A, minutes 2:251, 255–56, CSL.

51. Leaming, 143–84, 264. Carole Nichols, *Votes and More for Women: Suffrage and After in Connecticut* (New York: Institute For Research in History and Haworth Press, 1983), 13–19. HD 76 (1913): 1387, 1390. CWSA records, box 2, Mrs. Thomas N. Hepburn to Executive Boards of CWSA, September 1917. The Equal Franchise League, apparently founded in 1909 or 1910, was initially called the Political Equality League (Katharine Houghton Hepburn, letter in *Survey* 24 [23 July 1910]: 637–38).

52. The Equal Franchise League's domination by prosperous Asylum Hill residents can be seen from the membership listed in HD 76 (1913): 1390. The Hepburn quotation is from her letter in *Survey* 24 (23 July 1910): 637 (despite her optimism, though, Hepburn was cautious enough to stop short of predicting prostitution's complete disappearance). On protective legislation, see also Katharine Houghton Hepburn, "Women of Wealth," and "Women in Industry," *New York Times*, 23 January and 16 March 1909. On class inequality, Hepburn, *Woman Suffrage and the Social Evil*, 7. On prostitutes' backgrounds, notebook labeled "Police Record—Women—Hartford Police Court 1910," in letterbox marked "Memorandums from 1911," PDP. *Report of the Hartford Vice Commission*, 45, 56–65.

53. *Official Program: Votes for Women Pageant and Parade, Hartford, Conn., May 2, 1914, 3 P.M.*, National American Woman Suffrage Association papers, container 51 (microfilm reel 34), LC. William Joseph Martin, ed., *Souvenir Book of the Municipal Building Dedication* (Hartford: Plimpton Press, 1915), 63.

54. Hepburn, *Woman Suffrage and the Social Evil*, 7.

55. Seth Koven and Sonya Michel, "Introduction: 'Mother Worlds,'" in *Mothers of a New World: Maternalist Politics and the Origins of Welfare States*, ed. Seth Koven and Sonya Michel (New York: Routledge, 1993), 1–42.

56. Hepburn, *Woman Suffrage and the Social Evil*, 4.

57. "Mayor Smith Opens Anti-Vice Crusade," *Courant*, 30 December 1911.

58. "As to Federation," *Times*, 30 December 1911. L. D. Fuller, "Letters from the People," *Times*, 30 December 1911. "As to Segregation, Etc.," *Times*, 8 Janu-

ary 1912. St. Louis had experimented with this form of regulated prostitution, on the European model, from 1870 to 1874, and San Francisco experimented with it from 1913 to 1915. Regulation was strongly opposed by most Progressive-Era antiprostitution reformers. Hobson, *Uneasy Virtue*, 147–48. Ruth Rosen, *The Lost Sisterhood: Prostitution in America, 1900–1918* (Baltimore: Johns Hopkins University Press, 1982), 16–17.

59. "Politicians Take Full Warning Now," *Times*, 26 December 1911. "'Blame No One City Official,'" *Times*, 29 December 1911. "Only Hope of Eliminating Social Evil Lies in Absolute Suppression Says Rev. Dr. White," *Post*, 8 January 1912. "Now Is Time to Attack White Slave Trade Says Rev. H. E. Brown," *Post*, 8 January 1912. "Plea Made for Support of Police Board," *Post*, 10 January 1912. Like the suffragists, members of the Federation of Churches wanted to attack prostitution at its roots, but they believed the most important root was personal immorality. The pastors helped an ecumenical religious organization, Men and Religion Forward, hold an eight-day revival campaign in January. "Old Fashioned Piety Needed to Cleane of [*sic*] Graft and Filth," *Post*, 16 January 1912. "Raymond Robins Talks on Fight on Social Evil," *Post*, 17 January 1912. "Campaign Ends; Forward Work But Just Begun," *Post*, 22 January 1912.

60. "Women Attack Black Plague," *Courant*, 9 January 1912. "Committee on White Slave Traffic," ibid. Joseph Mayer, "The Passing of the Red Light District—Vice Investigations and Results," *Social Hygiene* 4 (1918): 199. Mark Thomas Connelly, *The Response to Prostitution in the Progressive Era* (Chapel Hill: University of North Carolina Press, 1980), 92. Hepburn, *Woman Suffrage and the Social Evil*, 4–6 (Hepburn was president of the Hartford Equal Franchise League). "Committee of Fifteen Must Be Killed," *Courant*, 22 January 1912. "Circulars Are Rousing Protests," *Courant*, 17 January 1912. "A Nuisance," *Courant*, 17 January 1912. "Woman Faints at the Sight of Nauseous Pictures," *Courant*, 24 January 1912. On the white-slave scare and its basis in reality, see Rosen, *The Lost Sisterhood*, chapter 7. Explaining why female reformers emphasized "white slavery" when interpreting prostitution, Hobson writes: "To accept the notion that women actively sought sex with men in a casual way or sold their sexual services like any other commodity undercut the rationale for the women's movement. That would suggest that women, seeking political power to refashion the moral fabric of society, were not a class different in nature and values from men" Hobson, *Uneasy Virtue*, 174.

61. Hepburn, *Woman Suffrage and the Social Evil*, 6. "Woman Faints at the Sight of Nauseous Pictures."

62. "The Suffrage Sisters," *Times*, 25 March 1912. "Speaking for 'Votes For

Women,'" *Times*, 28 March 1912. Wilson, "The 1911 Hartford Garment Workers Strike," 33, 38.

63. "Candidates for Mayor on Fence," *Post*, 26 February 1912. "Suffragists Addressed by Dr. Anna K. Shaw," *Times*, 29 March 1912. "Stands on His Record: Senator Spellacy," *Times*, 28 March 1912. "To Delve into Vice Conditions in Hartford," *Times*, 3 May 1912. Hepburn, *Woman Suffrage and the Social Evil*, 9.

64. *Report of the Hartford Vice Commission*, 10–11, 14, 89–90. *JCCB* 1913–14, 406. "Vice Commission Now under Fire," *Courant*, 19 July 1913.

65. "Suffragists Sell Vice Report," *Courant*, 29 July 1913. "Everybody Step Up and Get One," *Times*, 28 July 1913. "Vice Crusaders and Suffragists," *Times*, 29 July 1913. Hepburn, *Woman Suffrage and the Social Evil*, 10–12.

66. *JCCB* 1913–14, 473, 540. On 11 August 1913, the Common Council Board voted 24 to 5 to postpone indefinitely a resolution praising the policy of suppressing vice. The five councilmen who voted against the resolution were solidly middle class. A slight majority of those voting for it were working class, even though middle class men held the majority of seats on the council. But it would be inaccurate to describe the vote as a class issue, as most middle-class men either favored the motion or abstained. The class composition of the board can be seen by comparing the roster of councilmen in *MR* 1914, 14–16, with listings in *HD* 76 (1913). Remember also that, as noted above, labor leaders supported the closing of the red light district.

67. "Votes for Women and Votes to Table the Hartford Vice Report," *Survey* 31 (18 October 1913): 73. This article includes a photograph of the signs. Hepburn, *Woman Suffrage and the Social Evil*, 12–14.

68. "Telling Just How Wicked Hartford Used to Be," *Times*, 4 December 1913. "Cheney in Favor of Vice Suppression," *Courant*, 20 March 1914. "Lawler Replies to the Women," *Courant*, 28 March 1914. "Blacklist For 'Unfaithful 17,'" *Courant*, 4 April 1914.

69. "Mayor's Stand on Law Enforcement," *Times*, 27 April 1914. "From Henney to Rankin: 25 Years of Municipal Politics, No. 12," *Times*, 14 December 1931. "From Henney to Rankin: 25 Years of Municipal Politics, No. 15," *Times*, 17 December 1931. "From Henney to Rankin: 25 Years of Municipal Politics, No. 28," *Times*, 2 January 1932. "From Henney to Rankin: 25 Years of Municipal Politics, No. 43," *Times*, 20 January 1932. Despite Spellacy's coolness to anti-prostitution reform, Hartford Democratic leaders in the early twentieth century were generally sympathetic to social reform campaigns, as the historian John D. Buenker has shown. They and their Democratic counterparts from other Connecticut cities formed the backbone of efforts at the state level to adopt such quintessentially progressive measures as electoral reforms, workplace safety reg-

ulations, child-labor reform laws, limits in working hours, and public utility regulations (John D. Buenker, "Progressivism in Connecticut: The Thrust of the Urban, New Stock Democrats," *Connecticut Historical Society Bulletin* 35/4 [1970]: 97–109). Hepburn, *Woman Suffrage and the Social Evil*, 15.

70. "Suffrage Parade Is Spectacular," *Times*, 2 May 1914. "Mrs. Hepburn's Denial," *Times*, 2 May 1914. "Crowd at Capitol to See Suffrage Parade," *Times*, 4 May 1914. *Official Program: Votes for Women Pageant and Parade*. For a discussion in a national context of suffragists' claim to public space, see Ellen Carol DuBois, "Marching toward Power: Woman Suffrage Parades, 1910–15," in *True Stories from the American Past*, ed. William Graebner (New York: McGraw-Hill, 1993). Margaret Finnegan, "'So Much Color and Dash': Commercial Culture, Woman Suffragists, and the Reordering of Public Space" (paper presented at the annual meeting of the Organization of American Historians, Washington, D.C., April 1995).

71. "'Lid On Tighter Than Ever,' Says Mayor Kinsella," *Courant*, 22 May 1918. Mitchell, *Hartford Council of Churches*, 6–7. Dayton, "Hartford's Mauve Decade, No. 119: Shuttered Houses."

72. Shumsky, "Tacit Acceptance," 665. Mayer, "The Passing of the Red Light District." Hobson, *Uneasy Virtue*, 157. Rosen, *The Lost Sisterhood*, 3. Gilfoyle, *City of Eros*, 306–15.

73. *Report of the Hartford Vice Commission*, 14–15, 48–51. On the seductive allure of Hartford's display windows, transcript of interview with Mrs. Samuel (Tillie) Neiditz, 26 January 1983, JHS. See also William Leach, *Land of Desire: Merchants, Power, and the Rise of a New American Culture* (New York: Random House, 1993; Vintage Books, 1994).

74. On the persistence of East Side prostitution, see *Report of the Hartford Vice Commission*, 11–13, 27–36; "Police in Various Raids Nab Offenders," *Times*, 21 October 1912; "Two Disorderly Houses Are Raided by Police," *Times*, 22 March 1913; "Police Court Cases," *Courant*, 24 March 1913; "Two Young Women Are Sent to Jail for Thirty Days," *Times*, 12 September 1913; "Violators of Liquor Law Are Punished," *Times*, 24 November 1913; " Jail for Offenders Taken in Police Raid," *Times*, 11 December 1913; "East Side Woman Said to Be a 'Roller,'" *Courant*, 28 March 1914; "Restaurant Men Are Prosecuted," *Courant*, 23 October 1915; "Lawyer Contends With Judge Steele," *Courant*, 18 February 1916; "Automobile Gang Appears in Court," *Courant*, 14 April 1916; "Many Sentenced in Criminal Court," *Courant*, 8 March 1917; "Get Colored Folks in State St. Raid," *Courant*, 31 March 1917; "Arrest Employees of Venetian Cafe," *Courant*, 19 July 1917.

On prostitution on the northern edge of downtown, see "Diving Girl and Bellboy in Raid," *Courant*, 25 August 1913; "Violators of Liquor Law Are Punished,"

Times, 24 November 1913; "Petrazzo Pleads Guilty, Bound Over," *Times,* 5 June 1914; "Gambling Joint Wasn't Eagan's," *Times,* 9 December 1915; "Threw Her Face Powder in the Street," *Courant,* 28 July 1916; "Another Chance Given 'Drunks,'" *Courant,* 8 May 1917; "Beer Peddlers Fined in Court," *Courant,* 10 December 1918; Hartford County Superior Court, Criminal Files, nos. 1677 (State *v.* Adelaide Young), 1858 (State *v.* Lottie Foster), 1896 (State *v.* Louis Bonin), 2019 (State *v.* Ullie B. Walker), 2058 (State *v.* Lillie O'Connor).

On prostitution on the southwestern fringe of downtown, see Criminal Files, nos. 1892 (State *v.* Anton Ullinsky), 3986 (State *v.* Isabelle Secor, 4051 (State *v.* Anna Mitchell). On prostitution in the heart of downtown, "Four Alleged Evil Resorts," *Times,* 23 July 1912; "Eight Are Fined Following Raid," *Times,* 24 January 1916. On all of the above, see the undated, unexpurgated draft of *Report of the Hartford Vice Commission,* labeled "Part II, Mr. Brainard," 117–20, 195–98, CHS.

75. On arrests in the southern half of Hartford, see "Mrs. Smith and Miss Conway Sent to Jail," *Times,* 31 March 1913; "Mother Forces Girl into Life of Shame," *Times,* 24 March 1914; "Police Raid House on Buckingham Street," *Courant,* 27 January 1919; "Vice Squad Makes Successful Raid," *Courant,* 24 July 1919; Criminal Court Files, nos. 1950 (State *v.* Ernestine Cooper), 3459 (State *v.* Milia Laskowska), 3616 (State *v.* May Leineweber et al.).

76. "Two Young Women Sent to Jail for Thirty Days," *Times,* 12 September 1913; "Judge Steele Scores Police," *Times,* 28 November 1916; "Walter E. Gard on Social Evil," *Courant,* 9 February 1914; "Gavin, Vice Squad Man Is Active," *Courant,* 30 July 1916; "Vice Squad Men Are Mentioned for Promotion," *Courant,* 5 June 1919.

77. MR 1908, 219–22. MR 1909, 265–69. MR 1910, 263–67. MR 1911, 249–53. MR 1912, 240–42. MR 1913, 250–52. MR 1914, 223–26. MR 1915, 214–16. MR 1916, 178–80. MR 1917, 226–28. MR 1918, 214–17, 34. MR 1919, 182–85. MR 1920, 166–69. (An unusually low number of prostitution-related arrests was made in 1911.) It would be a mistake to read the continuity in the arrest rate as evidence that there was absolutely no decline in prostitution, since arrest numbers reflect patterns of law enforcement as well as levels of crime.

Chapter 4

1. Transcript of interview with Anthony Tapogna, 22 March 1975, Peoples of Connecticut Oral History Project, Center for Oral History, University of Connecticut. On hours, see Lewis Hine, NCLC photographs, P & P lot 7480 (Microfilm Reel 3), captions 589, 657, Library of Congress. "Comments of Some

Hartford Newsboys on the License and the Badge," box 3, folder 36, CLC. On saloon sales, "Industry or Charity?" *Times*, 15 March 1895. On hopping trolleys, "Report of the CPP," box 2, folder 10, CLC. Newsgirls were uncommon in many other large cities; see untitled editorial, *Courant*, 11 May 1895. They were, however, found in some places, including Chicago, Detroit, Salt Lake City, Bridgeport, New Haven, Wilmington, Delaware, and Manchester, New Hampshire; testimony of W. O. Burr, n.d., "Stenographer's Notes of Public Hearings before the Joint Standing Committee on Education," General Assembly of the State of Connecticut, January Session 1909, 200, CSL; Edward N. Clopper, *Child Labor in City Streets* (New York: Macmillan, 1912), 65.

2. Howard P. Chudacoff, *How Old Are You? Age Consciousness in American Culture* (Princeton: Princeton University Press, 1989), 77–78.

3. David Nasaw, *Going Out: The Rise and Fall of Public Amusements* (New York: Basic Books, 1993), 169–70, 174–75.

4. Viviana A. Zelizer, *Pricing the Priceless Child: The Changing Social Value of Children* (New York: Basic Books, 1985), 57, 60–61.

5. On street sales, "New Headquarters of Boy Merchants," *Courant*, 24 July 1913; untitled editorial, *Courant*, 11 May 1895. On scavenging, "Early in the Morning Hartford's Little Wood Gatherers Get to Work," *Courant*, 12 August 1917; Armando T. Perretta, *Take a Number* (New York: William Morrow, 1957), 29, 81, 85; Michael Suisman, *Edward A. Suisman: On the Occasion of His Eightieth Birthday* (West Hartford: privately published, 1982), 11; JCCB 1907–08, 603. On messenger boys, NCLC, box 4 (1904–34), folder "Conn. 1914—Messengers," document headed "Investigation of the Messenger Service in Connecticut," Library of Congress; Hine, NCLC photo caption 592; testimony of E. W. Lord, 16 March 1909, "Stenographer's Notes," 55–56; Clopper, *Child Labor*, 101–03; O. R. Lovejoy, "Child Labor and the Night Messenger Service," *Survey* 24 (21 May 1910): 311–17. On bootblacks, MR 1881, 242; Hine, NCLC photo caption 4956; "Bootblacks' Troubles," *Courant*, 10 May 1902; Herbert Maynard Diamond, *Report of the Commission on Child Welfare to the Governor, Supplementary Number. Street Trading among Connecticut Grammar School Children* (Hartford: published by the State, 1921), 9.

6. *Third Annual Report of the Juvenile Commission to the Mayor and Court of Common Council of the City of Hartford, Conn., for the Year Ending April 30, 1912* (Hartford: Case, Lockwood and Brainard, 1912), 7. ("There are some older boys and girls who are still selling," the commission reported, but it did not provide a number.) Clopper, *Child Labor*, 52. In comparison to the more than six hundred newsies in Hartford in 1913, there were only about fifty boys selling chewing gum, for example. "New Headquarters of Boy Merchants," *Courant*, 24 July 1913. On young newsies, Hine, NCLC photo captions 599, 600, 601.

On the fact that most newsies obtained the required licenses, "Investigation of the Street-Sales-for-Children Ordinance" and "Report of the Committee on the Enforcement of the Street-trades Ordinance," box 3, folder 36, CLC; Christine J. Haas, president of the Council of Jewish Women, to Mary Cromwell Welles, 2 June 1914, box 3, folder 36, CLC.

7. Diamond, *Street Trading*, 19, 20, 45; Tapogna interview; transcript of interview with Moses Neiditz, 11 November 1974, Peoples of Connecticut Oral History Project. Transcript of interview with Informant No. 1 [Morton Tonken], Peoples of Connecticut Ethnic Heritage, WPA Writers' Project, box 61, folder 157: 1e ("Jews in Hartford: Interviews"), University of Connecticut Archives. On newsies buying candy and going to movies and vaudeville shows, testimony of C. L. Ames, 16 March 1909 hearing, "Stenographer's Notes," 73.

8. David Nasaw, *Children of the City: At Work and at Play* (New York: Oxford University Press, 1985), 63, 74–75. "They Have No Recognized Offices or Stores, Yet Hundreds Come to Them Each Day and Buy the Things They Sell," *Courant*, 19 January 1919.

9. On the entrepreneurial nature of the job, "Unlawful Exhibition or Employment of Children," *Hartford Times*, 11 May 1895; Nasaw, *Children of the City*, 67–68. On regular corners and customers, Clopper, *Child Labor*, 53; "Newsgirls Hearing," *Times*, 11 May 1895; testimony of H. P. Koppleman, 16 March 1909, "Stenographer's Notes," 86; "They Have No Recognized Offices or Stores." On swarming around customers, comments by Heinrich Radorn [?], small notebook kept by Mary C. Welles, box 3, folder 36, CLC. On aggressive salesmanship, "New Headquarters of Boy Merchants." The extended quotation is from Morton Tonken.

10. Hine, NCLC photo caption 595. Testimony of E. W. Lord, "Stenographer's Notes," 55. The "last paper" ruse was common in other cities as well; Clopper, *Child Labor*, 64. "Newsboys Out All Night," *Courant*, 27 August 1895.

11. On the first appearance of newsgirls, see "Facts in Case vs. Sentiment," *Times*, 9 February 1905. On the fact that most newsgirls were Jewish, see also testimony of Mary G. Jones, 16 March 1909, "Stenographer's Notes," 65; see also "'Times' Newsgirls," *Times*, 10 March 1894. On descriptions of newsgirl behavior: "Protect the Little Girls," *Courant*, 11 March 1895; "The Newsgirls," *Courant*, 10 May 1895; "The 'News'-Girls," *Courant*, 11 March 1895. Hine met one Hartford newsgirl who was reported to have an even fouler mouth than the newsboys; Hine, NCLC photo caption 597. On reasons for late-night sales, see untitled editorial, *Courant*, 11 May 1895.

12. "The 'News'-Girls," *Courant*, 11 March 1895. "The Newsgirls," *Courant*, 10 May 1895. Jon M. Kingsdale, "The 'Poor Man's Club': Social Functions of the Urban Working-Class Saloon," *American Quarterly* 25 (1973): 472–89.

Kathy Peiss, *Cheap Amusements: Working Women and Leisure in Turn-of-the-Century New York* (Philadelphia: Temple University Press, 1985), 27–28.

13. *JCCB* 1894–95, 359, 431–32. "Newsgirls," *Times*, 9 March 1895. "The Newsgirls," *Times*, 11 March 1895, 6. "Selling Newspapers" and "Newsgirls," *Times*, both 12 March 1895. See also Zelizer, *Pricing the Priceless Child*, 81. The newsgirls' presence on the streets had been controversial even before the Common Council began considering the matter. Warnings that they would fall into prostitution had been voiced as early as 1893. "Newsgirls and the Police," *Times*, 28 August 1893. "Poor Little Newsgirls," *Times*, 29 August 1893. "Newsgirls — An Important Question," *Times*, 1 September 1893.

14. Charles R. Hale Collection of Connecticut Headstone Inscriptions, vol. 70, section 117, p. 22, CSL. "Mary Hall of Good Will Club Dies," *Times*, 15 November 1927. *Commemorative Biographical Record of Hartford County, Connecticut* (Chicago: J.H. Beers, 1901), 1402–03. Charles W. Burpee, *History of Hartford County, Connecticut, 1633–1928*, vol. 1 (Chicago: S.J. Clarke, 1928), 487. "The Death of Ezra Hall," *Courant*, 5 November 1877. "The Late Ezra Hall," *Times*, 5 November 1877. HD 40 (1877–78): 90. Alice Felt Tyler, "Hooker, Isabella Beecher," in *Notable American Women,1607–1950: A Biographical Dictionary*, ed. Edward T. James et al., vol. 2 (Cambridge: Harvard University Press, 1971), 212–13. "Our Hartford Letter," undated news clipping in scrapbook no. 4, Mary Hall Papers, Stowe-Day Library, Hartford. John Hooker, *Some Reminiscences of a Long Life* (Hartford: Belknap and Warfield, 1899), 145–46. On the Wesleyan Academy at Wilbraham (also known as the Wilbraham Academy), see Carl F. Price, *Wesleyan's First Century: With an Account of the Centennial Celebration* (Middletown: Wesleyan University, 1932), 17. *Historical Sketch of the Good Will Club, 1880–1889: Annual Report for 1890* (Hartford: Case, Lockwood and Brainard, 1890), 6.

15. "Mary Hall of Good Will Club Dies." "Frances E. Burr, Woman's Rights Pioneer, Dead," *Times*, 9 February 1923. HD 48 (1885–86): 561. Emily P. Collins, "Miss Hall, A Public Benefactor," undated clipping from *Woman's Journal* (letter is dated 16 September 1898), in scrapbook no. 8, Mary Hall Papers. "Miss Mary Hall Put Out by Force," *Courant*, 2 June 1904. "Mary Hall," *Courant*, 9 March 1905.

16. [Mary Hall], untitled article, *Good Will Star* 10/2 (May 1913), in scrapbook no. 12, Mary Hall Papers. *Historical Sketch of the Good Will Club, 1880–1889*. For further information about the Good Will Club, see chapter 5.

17. "Facts in Case vs. Sentiment"; "'Times' Newsgirls," *Times*, 10 March 1894. Mary Hall, "A Word for the Newsgirls," *Times*, 2 September 1893. Hall to *Courant* (apparently never mailed), n.d., later marked 1894, in scrapbook no. 7, Mary Hall Papers.

18. "Newsgirls," *Times*, 9 March 1895.

19. "The Newsgirls," *Times*, 11 March 1895. "Give the Girls a Chance," *Times*, 11 March 1895. "Industry or Charity?" *Times*, 15 March 1895.

20. "Newsgirls," *Times*, 9 March 1895. "The Newsgirls," *Times*, 11 March 1895.

21. "Give the Girls a Chance"; "The Rev. Mr. Bristol Concerning the Newsgirls," *Times*, 12 March 1895. For similar comments by councilmen, see "Selling Newspapers," *Times*, 12 March 1895.

22. "A Plea for the Newsgirls," *Times*, 11 March 1895. "Give the Girls a Chance." "The Newsgirls Heard," *Post*, 11 May 1895.

23. Untitled editorial, *Times*, 11 March 1895. "A Plea for the Boy," *Times*, 13 March 1895. "Some Pointed Considerations," *Times*, 12 March 1895.

24. "Protect the Little Girls," *Courant*, 11 March 1895. "The Newsgirls," *Courant*, 18 March 1895.

25. "The 'News Girls': A Protest from Young Women Who See Facts," *Courant*, 15 March 1895.

26. "Newsgirls and Morals," *Courant*, 11 May 1895. Members of the Hartford Equal Rights Club, a woman suffrage organization, voted in favor of girls' being allowed to sell papers; "Not in Favor of Flogging," *Times*, 20 February 1895.

27. JCCB 1894–95, 431–32. JCCB 1895–96, 471, 525–26.

28. "Newsgirls on the Streets," *Courant*, 22 February 1905. Phelps was assisted in drafting the bill by the Rev. William DeLoss Love. On Phelps's mission, known as the Warburton Chapel, see Solon P. Davis, *The Warburton Chapel: Sunday School and Work, 1851–1901* (n.p.: 1901). Many of the members of the elite First Church of Christ (also known as Center Church) were active in civic affairs in the late nineteenth and early twentieth centuries. Among others were the Rev. George Leon Walker, the pastor emeritus who had initiated the fight to clean up Gold Street and who had argued against banning newsgirls in 1895; Walker's successor, the Rev. Rockwell Harmon Potter, who was active in the Federation of Churches' fight against prostitution in 1907 and 1912, and held leadership positions in the Consumers' League of Hartford, the Consumers' League of Connecticut, and the city's Juvenile Commission; and Emily Holcombe, the leader of the Gold Street campaign. Potter wrote that he owed his job in part to Holcombe, who had helped persuade her husband, a member of the pastoral search committee, to hire him in 1900. Rockwell Harmon Potter, *The Harvest of the Years*, taped and edited by Kendrick Strong (Janesville, Wis.: Hobby Press, 1962), 20–21.

29. "Facts in Case vs. Sentiment," *Times*, 9 February 1905. "Union Men Should Aid the Newsgirls," *Times*, 16 February 1905. *Report of the Civic Club of*

Hartford, Conn., 1901–1905 (Hartford: Clark and Smith, 1905), 10. Barbara Finlay Donahue, "The Civic Club of Hartford, Connecticut: A Study of Women's Organizations in the Reform Era," unpublished master's thesis, Trinity College, Hartford, 1992.

30. "Facts in Case vs. Sentiment." The *Times* denounced the calls for feminine seclusion as reflecting "what may be called the Mohammedan view of the presence of women on the streets." ("The Morbid View," *Times*, 22 February 1905).

31. "Facts in Case vs. Sentiment." *Journal of the Senate of the State of Connecticut*, January Session, 1905 (Hartford: Case, Lockwood and Brainard, 1905), 179, 563. "No 'Raines Law' For Connecticut," *Times*, 15 March 1905.

32. Clopper, *Child Labor*, 194–98, at 197–98.

33. Walter I. Trattner, *Crusade for Children: A History of the National Child Labor Committee and Child Labor Reform in America* (Chicago: Quadrangle Books, 1970), 109–14.

34. The Consumers' League of Hartford and the Consumers' League of Connecticut were separate but affiliated organizations, with some overlap in leadership. The statewide organization appears to have been dominated by Hartford residents. The Rev. Rockwell Harmon Potter of Center Church presided over the Hartford group from 1911 to 1913, then assumed the presidency of the statewide group. On the leadership of the Consumers' League of Hartford, see *HD* 73 (1910–11): 1128; *HD* 74 (1911–12): 1129; *HD* 75 (1912–13): 1129; *HD* 76 (1913–14): 1385; *HD* 77 (1914–15): 1526. For the leadership of the Consumers' League of Connecticut, see letterhead for 1910–19, box 2, folder 22, CLC. On the work that the CLC did on child labor and working conditions for women, see "Pioneer Work in Connecticut for Women and Children in Industry," n.d. [1924?], box 2, folder 9, CLC.

35. "Mary C. Welles Dies in Newington," *Times*, 2 January 1930. "Miss Welles Dies at Home in Newington," *Courant*, 3 January 1930. Sara M. Evans, *Born for Liberty: A History of Women in America* (New York: Free Press, 1989), 139, 147. "Death of Mary C. Welles," *Times*, 3 January 1930.

36. Hine, NCLC photo captions 589, 592, 595, 597, 599, 600, 601, 606, 657, 661, 662. Statements by Lewis Hine, 16 March 1909, "Stenographer's Notes," 57. "Child Labor in Connecticut," *Survey* 22 (1909): 675.

37. "Report of the Corresponding Secretary of the Consumers' League of Connecticut for the Quarter Ending Oct. 9, 1909," box 2, folder 10, CLC. "Report of the Corresponding Secretary" (9 January 1909), box 2, folder 10, CLC. Mary Graham Jones, Chairman [of Newsboys and Newsgirls Committee of the Consumers' League of Hartford] to George A. Parker, 24 December 1908, letterbox labeled "Letters, 1908—Mar. 1909," PDP. "The Consumers' League of

Connecticut: Report of the Corresponding Secretary for the Year Ending February 19, 1910," box 1, folder 3, CLC. *Journal of the Senate of the State of Connecticut,* January Session, 1909 (Hartford: published by the State, 1909), 196. Testimony of C. W. Gross, 16 March 1909, "Stenographer's Notes," 78. Testimony of John F. Gunshanan and Mary Hall, n.d., "Stenographer's Notes," 185–90. The Newsboys and Newsgirls Committee also included Phelps, the Civic Club's president, Dotha Bushnell Hillyer, and the reformist pastor Ernest Miel.

38. "Report of the Executive Committee for the Year 1910," 28 February 1911, box 1, folder 3, CLC.

39. "The Consumers' League of Connecticut: Report of the Executive Secretary for the year 1910" (28 February 1911), box 1, folder 3, CLC. "Hartford Regulates Street Trades," *Survey* 25 (31 December 1910): 511. MR 1912, 719–20. "Girls as Newsboys," *Survey* 25 (11 February 1911): 810.

40. *JCCB* 1910–11, 540, 728.

41. Clopper, *Child Labor,* 197–98.

42. *MR* 1881, 242. The Common Council passed an ordinance in 1888 requiring bootblacks, but not newsies, to obtain licenses from the police department. *JCCB* 1888–89, 193. MR 1889, 383–84.

43. Testimony of E. W. Lord, "Stenographer's Notes," 54.

44. Testimony of Mary Welles and Oscar Phelps, 16 March 1909, "Stenographer's Notes," 59, 62.

45. "Child Street Sales Permit," box 3, folder 36, CLC.

46. "Report of the General Secretary for the Quarter Ending January 19, 1912," box 2, folder 10, CLC.

47. "Report of the Ordinance Committee, June 1, 1912," box 2, folder 10, CLC.

48. "Comments of Some Hartford Newsboys on the License and the Badge," box 3, folder 36, CLC. Small notebook kept by Mary C. Welles, box 3, folder 36, CLC.

49. "Report of the CPP," box 2, folder 10, CLC. Minutes of meeting of Consumers' League of Hartford, 17 March 1914, box 1, folder 7, 54, CLC. Annie Fischer, manuscript dated 29 May 1914, box 3, folder 36, CLC. Christine J. Haas, president of the Council of Jewish Women, to Mary C. Welles, 2 June 1914, box 3, folder 36, CLC.

50. "Report of the General Secretary of the Consumers' League of Connecticut for the Quarter Ending Oct. 9, 1913," box 2, folder 11, CLC. "Report of the General Secretary for the Period Ending Oct. 24, 1914," box 2, folder 11, CLC. The Hartford Council on Child Welfare was an umbrella organization made up of representatives of twenty-eight local social-service groups.

51. "Report of the General Secretary for the Period Ending Oct. 24, 1914."

Sandra Hartwell Becker and Ralph L. Pearson, "The Jewish Community of Hartford, Connecticut, 1880–1929," *American Jewish Archives* 31/2 (1979): 204–05, 206–08. Morris Silverman, *Hartford Jews, 1659–1970* (Hartford: Connecticut Historical Society, 1970), 36. "Want Newsgirls Kept off Streets," *Times*, 20 November 1914.

52. "Report of the General Secretary for the Period Ending Oct. 24, 1914." "Report of the General Secretary for the Year Ending Jan. 29, 1915," box 1, folder 3, CLC. Minutes of 20 October 1914 meeting, box 1, folder 7, 65, CLC. *JBA* 1914–15, 523. "Want Newsgirls Kept off Streets"; "Blaze of Lights Packs Asylum St; Crowd of 20,000," *Courant*, 19 December 1911. Welles and Hall had also clashed over the issue of vocational education for poor children, which Welles favored and Hall opposed. (See "Mary Welles against [sic] Vocational Guidance," undated clipping from *Courant*, probably 1913, and "Miss Mary C. Welles for Vocational Guidance," undated correction from *Courant*, both in scrapbook no. 12, Mary Hall Papers.)

53. "Report of the General Secretary for the Year Ending Jan. 29, 1915." "Brief in favor of S.B. 518, concerning Newsgirls," n.d., box 3, folder 3, CLC. "Alleges Attack by Naked Man," *Post*, 4 December 1914.

54. "A Poor Family," *Times*, 7 December 1914.

55. "Report of the General Secretary for the Year Ending Jan. 29, 1915"; "Brief in favor of S.B. 518, Concerning Newsgirls." "Banish Newsgirls from City Streets: Council Raises Age Limit for Females to 16 Years," *Courant*, 15 December 1914. Becker and Pearson, "Jewish Community of Hartford," 208.

56. Minutes of executive committee meeting, 19 January 1915, box 1, folder 7, 68, CLC. The reformers attempted to secure state legislation that would impose even tighter restrictions on newsboys. "Fair Play for the Boy," *Courant*, 29 March 1915. "'Welfare' Bill Would Put 'Newsies' under 14 in Delinquent Class," *Courant*, 2 February 1923.

57. The Hartford Club for Child Welfare and the Juvenile Commission both advocated a curfew for children in the early 1910s. The city did impose a weak, partial curfew in 1924 that forbade children under fourteen from loitering on the streets or near theaters after 9 P.M. (but permitted them to be out later as long as they did not loiter). This anti-loitering measure received unanimous approval from the Common Council, drew little or no public comment, and was virtually ignored by the press. "Report of the Hartford Club for Child Welfare . . . to the Juvenile Commission, Jan. 1914" (letter from Bertha H. MacDonald to William S. Hamersley), in letterbox marked "Reports 1914," PDP. *Second Annual Report of the Juvenile Commission to the Mayor and Court of Common Council of the City of Hartford, Conn., for the Year Ending April 30, 1911* (Hartford: Case, Lock-

wood and Brainard, 1911), 13. *JCCC* 1923–24, 526, 614–15, 668. "Curfew May Yet Ring Again Here," *Courant*, 13 November 1923.

Chapter 5

1. George A. Parker, "To the Honorable Court of Common Council," n.d., letterbox marked "1911–1912. Reports typewritten," PDP. In another version of the same metaphor, Parker had the expert "taking in one hand the street urchin of the slums and in the other the over-burdened banker and business man." George A. Parker, "Greater Use of the Parks," n.d., ibid.

2. "Proposed New Park or Common," *Courant*, 7 October 1853. "The Proposed Park," *Courant*, 16 November 1853.

3. *City of Hartford Mayor's Address to the Court of Common Council; City Government and Reports* . . . (Hartford: Calhoun Printing, 1860), 10 (italics original).

4. "Park Commissioners Report to Common Council, April 5, 1864," drawer labeled "Park Department. Annual Reports, Miscellaneous, 1827 to 1874," HCH. Sherman W. Adams, "The Hartford Park System. II. Bushnell Park," *Connecticut Quarterly* 1 (1895): 176.

5. "Park Commissioners [illegible] Submitted April 2, 1861," drawer marked "Park Department, Annual Reports, Miscellaneous, 1827 to 1874," HCH.

6. On carriage ownership, Roy Rosenzweig and Elizabeth Blackmar, *The Park and the People* (Ithaca: Cornell University Press, 1992), 213–16. On the classism inherent in this view of contemplating nature, John F. Kasson, *Amusing the Million: Coney Island at the Turn of the Century* (New York: Hill and Wang, 1978), 11–16.

7. John Alexopoulos, *The Nineteenth Century Parks of Hartford: A Legacy to the Nation* (Hartford: Hartford Architecture Conservancy, 1983), 16–18. In creating the first version of the park, the city surveyor, Seth E. Marsh, also drew on plans by Gervaise Wheeler and Thomas D. McClunie; John Alexopoulos, "The Creator of Bushnell Park," *Connecticut Historical Society Bulletin* 47/3 (1982): 69–70. *City of Hartford Mayor's Address and City Government for 1866* (Hartford: Calhoun Printing, 1866), 29. Adams, "The Hartford Park System. II," 176–77, at 177 (italics original).

8. "Veto of Acting Mayor of Resolution, Granting Permission to Use Park for Public Mass Meeting," 18 August 1884, in drawer labeled "Parks: Tabulated Correspondence, 'A' to 'R,'" HCH. Though Kellogg's view later prevailed, the council in this instance overrode his veto ("Resolution: Mass Meeting Trades Union Bushnell Park," ibid.). "Report of the Park Commissioner upon the Petition of

George Sargent," 13 October 1884, drawer labeled "Park Department. Annual Reports, Miscellaneous, 1875 to 1905," HCH. See also "Petition of the Women's Christian Temperance Union for Leave to Hold Meetings on West Park," ibid.; *JCCB* 1891–92, 220.

9. *MR* 1889, 234.

10. "Report of the Board of Street Commissioners on Remonstrance of John Shortell et al. against proposed layout of South [*sic*] Front St. Park," 11 August 1873. Petition by John Shortell et al., to Court of Common Council, 29 March 1873. Petition by Anthony Donovan et al., 15 November 1873. Petition by John Shortell et al., 22 December 1873. "Petition for the Lay Out of North Front Street Park," 31 July 1876. "Report of the Park Commission on the Lay Out of North Front St. Park," 11 February 1878 (the original petition appears to be missing). All documents referred to are in the drawer labeled "Parks: Tabulated Correspondence, 'A' to 'R,'" HCH.

11. The historian Robin L. Einhorn, in a study of Chicago, has described a change in municipal polity in the post–Civil War era from ward-based, segmented government to the "new public interest," in which the city as a whole paid for improvements in individual neighborhoods. Initially this change worked mainly to the benefit of the elite, but it helped set up an infrastructure of general benefit and was the precursor to greater democratic control of the city (Einhorn, *Property Rules: Political Economy in Chicago, 1833–1872* [Chicago: University of Chicago Press, 1991]).

12. On the trolley system, *Town and City Atlas of the State of Connecticut* (Boston: D.H. Hurd, 1893), 42–43. Hartford's population reached 53,000 in 1890 and roughly 80,000 in 1900 (*HD* 86 [1923–24]: 1556). On the city's geographical expansion, *Atlas of the City of Hartford Connecticut, Including, Also, the Town of West Hartford* (Springfield, Mass.: L.J. Richards, 1896), e.g., plates 19, 28. On the effect of trolleys on geographical expansion in the 1890s, Hartford Architecture Conservancy, *Hartford Architecture*, vol. 2, *South Neighborhoods* (Hartford: Hartford Architecture Conservancy, 1980), 169.

13. Alexopoulos, *Nineteenth Century Parks of Hartford*, 23–27, 63. "Olmsted, John Charles," in *Dictionary of American Biography*, ed. Allen Jones (New York: Charles Scribner's Sons, 1929), 14:29–30.

14. David Schuyler, *The New Urban Landscape: The Redefinition of City Form in Nineteenth-Century America* (Baltimore: Johns Hopkins University Press, 1986), 126–46, at 130.

15. John C. Olmsted, "City's Park System," *Courant*, 10 July 1901.

16. Olmsted Brothers, "Pope Park: General Plan," 1 December 1898, in *BPC* 39 (1898–99): n.p. *The Picturesque Parks of Hartford* (Hartford: American Book Exchange, 1900), 45. On the Bushnell Park playground, *JCCB* 1886–87,

67. On the "common" area, *BPC* 35 (1895): 11–12. The historian Galen Cranz has noted that nineteenth-century parks with playing fields usually relegated them to the margins (Galen Cranz, *The Politics of Park Design: A History of Urban Parks in America* [Cambridge: MIT Press, 1982], 40).

17. *MR* 1894, 205 (see also 34–35); *MR* 1896, 44–45; *BPC* 37 (1896–97): 11; *BPC* 39 (1898–99): 19; *BPC* 40 (1899–1900): 33, 34, 36. Olmsted Brothers, "General Plan for Riverside Park," 1899, in *BPC* 40 (1899–1900): n.p. Fred E. Dayton, "Hartford's Mauve Decade, No. 98," *Times*, 8 July 1931. Alexopoulos, *Nineteenth Century Parks of Hartford*, 54.

18. On the nationwide trend in the late nineteenth century toward screening parks from their surroundings, see Cranz, *The Politics of Park Design*, 49. On the aesthetic goal of excluding sights of the city, see Schuyler, *The New Urban Landscape*, 88–93. Olmsted Brothers, "Pope Park General Plan." Theodore Wirth, "Elizabeth Park, General Plan," 1 March 1900, in *BPC* 40 (1900). Olmsted Brothers, "Goodwin Park, General Plan," 1900, in *BPC* 41 (1901). "Pope Park— Effective Border Plantation Screening Highway from Park," plate opposite p. 37 in *BPC* 43 (1903). *BPC* 65 (1925): 15–16. Alexopoulos, *Nineteenth Century Parks of Hartford*, 65. Theodore Wirth to Charles E. Gross, 30 March 1904, gray binder of copies of letters from Wirth, marked "Letters," PDP. Theodore Wirth, "Rocky Ridge Park, General Plan," 1903, box marked "Maps—Hartford (General) Box #1," PDP. Theodore Wirth, "The Report of May 5th to the Park Commissioners of Theodore Wirth, Superintendent of Parks, on the Proposed Plan for Laying Out Rocky Ridge Park West and South of Trinity College," *Trinity College Bulletin* 3/3 (1903): 19–24.

19. The Adams quotation is in *MR* 1890, 258. Board of Park Commissioners to Board of Aldermen, October 1907, in box marked "Copies: Board of Park Commrs. January 1 1907 to January 1 1908," PDP. On viewing scenery from a carriage, see "City's Park System"; *BPC* 65 (1925): 15. On pleasure driving in parks throughout the city, see "Parkway or Highway?" *Times*, 3 August 1905. On problems with vehicles, [Philander C. Royce], president of Board of Park Commissioners, to Pope Manufacturing, 13 August 1907, in box marked "Copies: Board of Park Commrs. January 1 1907 to January 1 1908," PDP. "Superintendent's Report—Automobiles in Goodwin Park," n.d., binder labeled "Park Papers—Hartford—1907," PDP. *BPC* 43 (1903): 42.

20. *BPC* 36 (1896): 8. *BPC* 37 (1897): 16–17. L. W. Burt, untitled map, 1896, later marked "Southern Parkway—Hartford," rolled up inside L. W. Burt, "Plan Preliminary to the Layout of a Parkway," 1896, box marked "Maps—Hartford (General)," PDP.

21. *BPC* 36 (1896): 8. *BPC* 37 (1897): 16–17. Minutes of the 10 May and 6 July 1897 meetings are in a binder labeled "Records Park Commission Vol. 2,"

87, 100, PDP. F. L. Olmsted and J. C. Olmsted, "Southern Parkway: Preliminary Plan," 14 May 1897, Olmsted Plan no. 808–9; L. W. Burt, "Plan of Land Near to and West of Park River between Farmington Ave. and Park Street, Prepared for the Laying out of a Park Way," August 1896, with later revisions, Olmsted Plan no. 811–5, part 1; and "Western Parkway, Hartford Conn., Sun Print of L.W. Burt's Plan with Revisions by Olmsted Brothers," November and December 1897, Olmsted Plan no. 811–8, plans and drawings collection, Frederick Law Olmsted National Historic Site, Brookline, Mass.

22. There appear to be few surviving records of this committee's work. Warner's personal papers at the Watkinson Library at Trinity College contain nothing on the subject. There is only limited material in the parks department papers. On one attempt by park officials to acquire land for the parkway, see anonymous to T. D. Owen, 17 February 1898, vertical file labeled "Letter Copies. 1898–1899," PDP. On lack of progress, BPC 38 (1898): 18. On using streets as parkways, BPC 39 (1899): 23–24. On continued hopes, BPC 40 (1900): 51; BPC 41 (1901): 52–53. The 1901 Wirth quotation is from Theodore Wirth to Francis Goodwin, 12 February 1901, binder with piece of paper identifying it as "Park Correspondence 1896–1902 by Theodore Wirth," 591, 595, PDP. On Scarborough Street and Westbourne Parkway, F. Percy Close, History of Hartford Streets (Hartford: Connecticut Historical Society, 1969), 98, 119; Hartford Architecture Conservancy, Hartford Architecture, vol. 3, North and West Neighborhoods (Hartford: Hartford Architecture Conservancy, 1980), 85, 103–04, 132–33, 197. On Wirth's views in 1905, Theodore Wirth to Andrew Wright Crawford, 8 February 1905, and Theodore Wirth to Olmsted Brothers, 11 July 1905, gray binder marked "Letters," PDP. Parker blamed both legal problems and land acquisition problems for preventing the creation of parkways. Parker to Cass Gilbert, 13 March 1906, folder marked "Keney Park—New York City," box marked "Keney Park, Outgoing Letters, 1900–1906, N–Z," GAPP; Parker to Andrew Wright Crawford, 12 February 1904, folder marked "Park Census, Philadelphia PA," box marked "American Park and Outdoor Art Association, Park Census, Outgoing Letters, 1901–1904, New York City–Z," GAPP.

23. "Expansionists on West Side," Courant, 26 October 1904. "Pope Park Cut Again Discussed," Courant, 15 June 1905. "How to Cross Pope Park," Courant, 19 November 1905. Publications of the Municipal Art Society of Hartford Connecticut, no. 3, Why Laurel Street Should Not Be Extended through Pope Park (Hartford: Municipal Art Society, 1905), 5–6.

24. J. C. Olmsted to William DeLoss Love, president of the park commissioners, 20 June 1905, letterbox marked "Copies, Board of Park Commrs. from Jan. 1 1905 to Jan. 1 1906," PDP.

25. "Pope Park Cut Again Discussed." *HD* 68 (1905): 107, 923. *Why Laurel Street Should Not Be Extended*, 3.

26. *Why Laurel Street Should Not Be Extended*, 4–6.

27. "Report of the Committee on Highways through Pope Park," in folder marked "Reports of Standing Committees," MAS.

28. *Why Laurel Street Should Not Be Extended*, 5–6. "Pope Park Cut Again Discussed." Minutes of 18 May 1905 meeting, in bound volume of minutes (14 June 1904–17 October 1905), box 1, 44–45, Municipal Art Society papers. "Statement of Mr. Theodore Wirth Sup't of Parks Re Proposed Highway through Pope Park. Prepared at Request of Meeting of May 31 1905," box 1, MAS.

29. "Highway across Pope Park," *Times*, 5 October 1905. "Against Highway through Pope Park," *Courant*, 27 December 1905. *Publications of the Municipal Art Society of Hartford Connecticut*, no. 6, *Proceedings of the Annual Meeting, November 27, 1906. Officers, Members, Reports of Standing Committees.* (Hartford: Municipal Art Society, 1907), 15–16. In this report, the society claimed to have consistently supported the indirect parkway idea, a claim contradicted by its own earlier publication, *Why Laurel Street Should Not Be Extended.* The compromise plan succeeded in keeping trolleys out of the park. See *Pitner's Map of Hartford, West Hartford, East Hartford and Environs* (Washington, D.C.: Carl Pitner, n.d., [ca. 1930]).

30. "No Roadway in Bushnell Park?" *Times*, 2 December 1913.

31. Arthur F. Eggleston to George A. Fairfield, 10 May 1897, binder marked "Park Papers—Hartford—1897," PDP. "Rowdies in Parks Cause Annoyances," *Courant*, 2 June 1914.

32. Charles E. Gross, president of the Board of Park Commissioners, to Cornelius Ryan, chief of police, 21 July 1904, in envelope marked "Bushnell Park," PDP. Charles E. Gross to J. G. Calhoun, prosecuting attorney, 14 July 1905, and Board of Park Commissioners to Court of Common Council, 3 August 1905, both in letterbox marked "Copies, Board of Park Commrs From Jan. 1 1905 to Jan. 1 1906," PDP. *BPC* 35 (1895): 11–12. H. G. Loomis, undated letter, in bound volume of minutes, 14 June 1904–17 October 1905, box 1, MAS.

33. *City of Hartford Mayor's Address and City Government for 1866; and the Annual Reports of the Several Departments of the City Government* (Hartford: Calhoun Printing, 1866), 29. *MR* 1885, 197. *MR* 1889, 234. On later vandalism at Bushnell Park, "A Resident" to George A. Parker, 3 February 1908, letterbox marked "Park letters, 1908," PDP.

34. *BPC* 51 (1911): 41. *BPC* 44 (1904): 42. "Hordes of Children Throng Pope Park," *Courant*, 14 July 1909. "Report of William E. Ball, Foreman at Pope

Park, on Recorded Vandalism in Pope Park for Year Ending Apr. 1, 1912," binder marked "Reports and Memorandums 1912," PDP.

35. Guy E. Beardsley to Franklin G. Whitmore, 5 October 1914, in letterbox marked "Letters, Board of Park Commissioners, January 1, 1912 to January 1, 1915," PDP. Minutes of 20 June 1901 and 1 July 1901 meetings, in volume of minutes from 1895 to 1902 marked "Records Park Commission Vol. II," 306, 309, PDP. Parker, "Memoranda for a Park Syllabus," binder marked "Duplicates—1906," PDP. Charles Welles Gross to Board of Police Commissioners, 6 July 1915, envelope marked "Misc. Correspondence 1920s/1930s," PDP. *BPC* 61 (1921): 55. Parker, "Memorandum, Friday, February 7, 1908," in letterbox marked "Misc. Notes, Letters, 1915–1922," PDP.

36. *BPC* 47 (1907): 29; *BPC* 48 (1908): 39; *BPC* 50 (1910): 35. Parker, "Parks," in letterbox marked "1911–1912, Reports Typewritten," PDP.

37. George A. Parker, "Report to Finance Committee, January 20, 1910," scrapbook marked "Papers—Park Affairs—1908," PDP. George A. Parker to Board of Park Commissioners, 1 April 1912, in binder marked "Reports and Memorandums," PDP.

38. *BPC* 42 (1902): 42–43. George A. Parker, "Address to Child Welfare," 25 December 1919, in manila envelope marked "Parks, general development, uses, etc." Olmsted Brothers, "General Plan for Riverside Park." *BPC* 44 (1904): 34–36.

39. Emma F. Ferguson to Lucius F. Robinson, 3 March 1900, manila folder marked "Gymnasiums (Outdoor)," PDP. Board of Park Commissioners to Mrs. Henry Ferguson, president, Civic Club, 9 March 1900, letterbox marked "Letters. Copies. Bd. of Park Commrs. from Jan. 1st 1900 to Jan. 1st 1905 inclusive," PDP. Minutes of 2 January 1900, 19 March 1900, and 7 April 1902 meetings, "Records of the Park Commission, Vol. II," 218, 222, 358–59. On the Turnverein movement, see Steven A. Riess, *City Games: The Evolution of American Urban Society and the Rise of Sports* (Urbana: University of Illinois Press, 1989), 23, 96–98.

40. Theodore Wirth to Henry Ferguson, 25 July 1905, in gray binder marked "Letters," PDP. *BPC* 50 (1910): 35. Parker to W. I. Twitchell, 30 September 1910, in binder marked "Duplicates—1909 + 1910," PDP.

41. "Petition for Base Ball Diamonds at Keney Park," 26 May 1913, and "Petition of James H. O'Leary for 3 Base-ball Diamonds Riverside Park," 3 May 1913, drawer marked "Parks: Tabulated Correspondence, 'A' to 'R,'" HCH. *JCCB* 1906–07, 110. "Nearly All Are for Colt Park," *Courant*, 4 November 1905. "An East Side Resident" to George A. Parker, 15 April 1911, letterbox marked "Letters. 1911," PDP. C. B. Whittlesey to George A. Parker, 5 February 1912,

letterbox marked "1911–1912. Letters—Received," PDP. George A. Parker, "Budget for 1911 and 1912," letterbox marked "1911–1912. Reports. Typewritten," PDP. "Bowling Green on Some City Park," *Courant*, 7 April 1908. On facilities, *BPC* 54 (1914): 60–62.

42. Henry Roberts to Board of Park Commissioners, 29 April 1903, letterbox marked "Letters to Board of Park Commissioners from 1900 to 1903, inclusive," PDP. Morgan Johnson et al. to George A. Parker, 17 July 1913, letterbox marked "Letters, File 3, 1913," PDP.

43. Mr. and Mrs. J. H. Adair to F. H. Whitmore, 15 June 1913, and John E. Zeiter to Thos. S. Weaver, 15 June 1913, both in letterbox marked "Letters, Board of Park Commissioners, January 1, 1912 to January 1, 1915," PDP. On the working-class desire for Sunday baseball, see *JCCB* 1901–02, 209–10.

44. *BPC* 50 (1910): 39; *BPC* 61 (1921): 60. Parker, "Budget for 1911 and 1912." George A. Parker, "Reasons for Pavilion at Colt Park," n.d., letterbox marked "1911–1912, Reports Typewritten," PDP.

45. George A. Parker to Grace E. J. Parker, Sec., Playground Association of America, 3 November 1910, greenish box marked "Playground Assn. 1910. Parker," PDP.

46. "G.A. Parker, 73, Dies of Heart Attack," *Courant*, 14 September 1926. *Fourth Annual Report of the Juvenile Commission to the Mayor and Court of Common Council of the City of Hartford, Conn., for the Year Ending April 30, 1913* (Hartford: Case, Lockwood and Brainard, 1913), 24. George A. Parker to Frederick Law Olmsted, Jr., 19 December 1903, folder marked "Park Census, Brookline Mass.," box marked "American Park and Outdoor Art Association, Park Census, Outgoing Letters, 1902–1904, A–F," GAPP. George A. Parker to Mrs. C. A. Woods, 22 February 1904, folder marked "Park Census, Marion S.C.," box marked "American Park and Outdoor Art Association, Park Census, Outgoing Letters, 1901–1904, G–New York City," GAPP. George A. Parker to J. Horace McFarland, 11 July 1904, folder marked "American Civic Association, Outgoing H's," box marked "American Civic Association, Park Dept., 1904–1905, Outgoing Letters A–M," GAPP. George A. Parker to Charles Zueblin, 25 October 1902, folder marked "Park Census Committee, Chicago Ill.," box marked "American Park and Outdoor Art Association, Park Census, Outgoing Letters, 1902–1904, A–F," GAPP. *Survey* 24 (18 June 1910): 491. George A. Parker to William S. Crandall, 29 January 1902, folder marked "Keney Park, Outgoing Letters, 1900–1906, N–Z," box marked "Keney Park, New York City," GAPP. George A. Parker to A. A. Hill, 23 June 1906, folder marked "Office Letters, NY City, Archibald A. Hill," box marked "Outgoing Letters, I–N," GAPP.

47. George A. Parker to Commission on Country Life, 4 December 1908,

letterbox marked "Letters 1908–Mar. 1909," PDP. George A. Parker, "The Human Scrap Heap," typescript, vertical file marked "1912" and "1912 R + M," PDP.

48. George A. Parker, "Memoranda for a Park Syllabus," typescript, binder marked "Duplicates—1906," PDP.

49. BPC 48 (1908): 48.

50. "How Hartford Makes Use of Its Parks," Hartford (official publication of the Hartford Chamber of Commerce) 1/2 (1915): 19.

51. George A. Parker, "Report of the Committee on Park Census, 1903," Reports of the Standing Committees at the Seventh Annual Meeting ([of the APOAA], Buffalo, 7–9 July 1903), 7/2 (Rochester: APOAA, 1903): 14, quoted in William H. Wilson, The City Beautiful Movement (Baltimore: Johns Hopkins University Press, 1989), 39. "How Hartford Makes Use of Its Parks," 1. BPC 55 (1915): 36.

52. "How Hartford Makes Use of Its Parks," 1, 19.

53. George A. Parker, "How Hartford Is Making Use of Its Public Parks as Play Centers," Hartford 4/11 (1919): 4. BPC 50 (1910): 42–43. On park segregation as a nationwide phenomenon in the Progressive Era, see Cranz, The Politics of Park Design, 61–99.

54. Hartford Street Railway, Hartford Parks and How to Reach Them by Trolley (Hartford: Hartford Street Railway, 1900). "'Day of Rest' Spent in Parks," Courant, 15 May 1911.

55. George A. Parker to Lewis Johnson, 26 December 1905, folder marked "Office Letters—New Orleans La.," box marked "Outgoing Letters, I–N," GAPP.

56. BPC 50 (1910): 43. See also BPC 54 (1914): 39.

57. On early comments on parks and streets, G. A. Parker, "The Trend of the Park Movement," Charities and the Commons 16/14 (7 July 1906): 407. The 1910 quotation is from BPC 50 (1910): 42. On children's play, George A. Parker, "Report Regarding Additional Playgrounds during July and August," 11 September 1912, vertical file marked "1912" and "1912 R + M," PDP; BPC 60 (1920): 44.

58. Robert H. Wiebe, The Search for Order, 1877–1920 (New York: Hill and Wang, 1967), 169–71. John C. Burnham, "Essay," in Progressivism, ed. John D. Buenker, John C. Burnham, and Robert M. Crunden (Rochester, Vt.: Schenkman Books, 1977), 13–14, 19–21. Howard P. Chudacoff and Judith E. Smith, The Evolution of American Urban Society, 4th ed. (Englewood Cliffs, N.J.: Prentice-Hall, 1994), 194–98. George A. Parker, "Child Life in Hartford," 7 January 1913, binder marked "Juvenile Commission, 1913," PDP; and see chapter 8. Parker hoped that recreation work would become "an exact science as

much so as medicine or engineering" (George A. Parker, "Greater Use of the Parks," letterbox marked "1911–1912, Reports Typewritten," PDP). The quotation about Parker's faith in the city is from George A. Parker, "Hartford and Recreation," 14 November 1911, letterbox marked "1911–1912," PDP.

59. "The Proposed Horse Railroad Extension," *Courant*, 22 September 1880. Henry A. Perkins, *Prospect Street in the "Eighties"* (Hartford: n.p., 1939), 1. "Sleigh Ride Parties," *Times*, 3 February 1894. "A Half-Hour with the Sleigh-Riders," *Courant*, 11 January 1896. "The Snow Track," *Times*, 13 January 1896. "The Good Old Days of Washington Street Racing," *Courant*, 3 June 1917.

60. On traffic on Washington Street, see chapter 8. *JCCB* 1908–09, 38, 178, 219–20; *JCCB* 1909–10, 539–40. "Petition of James H. O'Leary for 3 Base-ball Diamonds, Riverside Park," 3 May 1913, drawer labeled "Parks: Tabulated Correspondence, 'A' to 'R,'" HCH. "Snow Is Flying in the Speedway," *Courant*, 30 December 1909. "Inaugural Parade of the Hartford Road Drivers' Club," *Times*, 1 January 1910. "Horses of Quality Out for Parade and a Brush on the New Speedway in Riverside Park," *Courant*, 3 January 1910. "Road Drivers' Plan for Open Matinee," *Times*, 12 August 1913. "Road Drivers' Club Strives for Prizes," *Courant*, 5 July 1918. "The Good Old Days of Washington Street Racing"; *BPC* 58 (1917–18): 38.

61. "Dance Board—Colt Park—May 6, 1922," letterbox marked "Misc. Notes, Letters, 1915–1922," PDP. *BPC* 54 (1914): 63. "Conditions Governing Music for Dancing at Colt Park Pavilion for the Summer of 1919," letterbox marked "Misc. Notes, Letters, 1915–1922," PDP. "Dance Platform for Colt Park," *Times*, 11 July 1918. "Colt Park Pavilion, Where Young People of City Enjoy Outdoor Dancing," *Times*, 28 June 1919. "Larger Crowds at City's Parks," *Times*, 9 September 1919.

62. "Movies to Be Shown in Parks," *Courant*, 5 August 1919. "Free Movies Attract 4,000 to Colt Park," *Courant*, 18 August 1919.

63. On Potter, see chapter 6. Nannie Melvin, undated typescript, letterbox marked "1915. O–Z. March 1905 to February 1906." Parker, "Hartford and Recreation."

64. *BPC* 55 (1915): 37–38.

65. Frederick Law Olmsted, "Public Parks and the Enlargement of Towns," *Journal of Social Science* 3 (1871): 11, quoted in Thomas Bender, *Toward an Urban Vision: Ideas and Institutions in Nineteenth Century America* (Baltimore: Johns Hopkins University Press, 1975), 176.

66. Roy Rosenzweig has made a similar argument in his study of working-class leisure in Worcester, Massachusetts. Rosenzweig, *Eight Hours for What We Will: Workers and Leisure in an Industrial City, 1870–1920* (Cambridge: Cambridge University Press, 1983), 135.

Chapter 6

1. Informant No. 1 [Morton Tonken], Peoples of Connecticut Ethnic Heritage, WPA Writers' Project, University of Connecticut Archives, box 61, 157: 1e, "Jews in Hartford: Interviews."

2. Morris I. Davidson, *Growing Up in Hartford, Connecticut, 1908–1928* (Hartford: Andrew Mountain Press, 1987). Transcript of 15 September 1973 interview with Dr. Morris Cohen, JHS. "Streets as Playgrounds," ACH, *Monthly Bulletin* 11 (March 1919): 7. "Outdoor [*sic*] Calls Hartford People," *Courant,* 22 April 1916. [Fred E. Dayton], "Hartford's Mauve Decade, No. 224," *Times,* 3 December 1931. "Boys in the Street," *Courant,* 23 November 1911. "Letters from the People," *Courant,* 27 November 1911. "Letters from the People: Unseemly Street Conduct," *Times,* 15 December 1904. "Letters from the People: Protection against Snowballing," *Times,* 31 January 1907. "Warning to Bicycle Riders," *Courant,* 10 May 1890. Transcript of 11 November 1974 interview with Moses Neiditz, Peoples of Connecticut Oral History Project, Center For Oral History, University of Connecticut. Transcript of 30 August 1983 interview with Anna Tulin, JHS. "Hit Boy with Stone," *Courant,* 19 April 1895. "Hartford Gangs, Past and Present," *Courant,* 8 February 1914.

3. Henry A. Perkins, *Prospect Street in the "Eighties"* (Hartford: National Society of the Colonial Dames of America in the State of Connecticut, 1939), 2, 11. E. Anthony Rotundo, in his study of middle-class boys in the northern United States, describes them as forming an anarchic "boy culture" that thrived in the streets and open spaces of middle class neighborhoods. Boy culture, he writes, celebrated energy, aggression, noise, and violence—values diametrically opposed to those of the domestic, female world. Rotundo, *American Manhood: Transformations in Masculinity from the Revolution to the Modern Era* (New York: Basic Books, 1993), 31–55.

4. Steven A. Riess, *City Games: The Evolution of American Urban Society and the Rise of Sports* (Urbana: University of Illinois Press, 1989), 151.

5. Riess, *City Games,* 127. Dominick Cavallo, *Muscles and Morals: Organized Playgrounds and Urban Reform, 1880–1920* (Philadelphia: University of Pennsylvania Press, 1981), 3, 50–51. Jane Addams, *The Spirit of Youth and the City Streets* (New York: Macmillan, 1909), 27.

6. Historians have discussed play reform primarily in the context of reformers' attempts to impose social control or apply new ideas of child development. See Joseph F. Kett, *Rites of Passage: Adolescence in America, 1790 to the Present* (New York: Basic Books, 1977); Paul Boyer, *Urban Masses and Moral Order in America, 1820–1920* (Cambridge: Harvard University Press, 1978); Cavallo, *Muscles and Morals;* Donald J. Mrozek, "The Natural Limits of Unstructured

Play, 1880–1914," in *Hard at Play: Leisure in America, 1840–1940*, ed. Kathryn Grover (Amherst: University of Massachusetts Press, 1992), 210–26. These historiographical themes are analyzed in Stephen Hardy and Alan G. Ingham, "Games, Structures, and Agency: Historians on the American Play Movement," *Journal of Social History* 17 (1983): 285–301. Historians may have treated the geography of play as a matter of secondary importance, but they have not ignored it. Though Cary Goodman emphasizes a middle-class effort at social control, he considers the control of space as part of this effort (Cary Goodman, *Choosing Sides: Playground and Street Life on the Lower East Side* [New York: Schocken, 1979]). Boyer emphasizes that play reformers' attempts at social control were based on a belief in "positive environmentalism"—that by creating alternative play environments, they could manufacture better citizens. Two historians who assert that the working class successfully resisted this form of social control, Stephen Hardy and Roy Rosenzweig, describe the dispute over the playground movement as in part a struggle for the control of urban space (Stephen Hardy, *How Boston Played: Sport, Recreation, and Community* [Boston: Northeastern University Press, 1982]; Roy Rosenzweig, *Eight Hours for What We Will: Workers and Leisure in an Industrial City, 1870–1920* [Cambridge: Cambridge University Press, 1983]).

7. *The Good Will Club: Hartford, Conn., 1880–1910: Thirtieth Annual Report* (Hartford: Case, Lockwood and Brainard, 1910), 5. "Historical Sketch of the Boys' Clubs in Hartford, Conn.," *Good Will Star* 5/3 (1908), in scrapbook no. 11, Mary Hall Papers, Stowe-Day Library, Hartford. *First Annual Report of the Union For Home Work of Hartford (1872–73)* (Hartford: Case, Lockwood and Brainard, 1873). *Second Annual Report of the Union For Home Work of Hartford, 1873–1874* (Hartford: Case, Lockwood and Brainard, 1874), 38–41. *Sixth Annual Report of the Union For Home Work of Hartford* (1877–78) (Hartford: Case, Lockwood and Brainard, 1878), 19. Charles H. Clark, "The Charter Oak City," *Scribner's Monthly* 13/1 (1876): 21. *The Annual Report of the City Missionary to the City Missionary Society of Hartford, 1877–1878* (Hartford: Case, Lockwood and Brainard, 1878), 12–13. *The Annual Report of the City Missionary to the City Missionary Society of Hartford, 1878–1879* (Hartford: Case, Lockwood and Brainard, 1879), 9.

8. *The Good Will Club, Thirtieth Annual Report.* "Boys' Clubs in Hartford." *First Annual Report of the Union for Home Work of Hartford*, 33, 34.

9. *The Annual Report of the City Missionary to the City Missionary Society of Hartford, 1879–80* (Hartford: Case, Lockwood and Brainard, 1880), 7. Undated news clipping titled "The Boys' Club: The Wind Up for This Season" in scrapbook no. 4, Mary Hall Papers. *Historical Sketch of the Good Will Club, 1880–1889: Annual Report for 1890* (Hartford: Case, Lockwood and Brainard, 1890),

14. *The Annual Report of the City Missionary to the City Missionary Society of Hartford, 1884–85* (Hartford: Case, Lockwood and Brainard, 1886), 19. Robert Owen Decker, *Hartford Immigrants: A History of the Christian Activities Council (Congregational), 1850–1980* (New York: United Church Press, 1987), 136–39.

10. David I. MacLeod, *Building Character in the American Boy: The Boy Scouts, YMCA, and Their Forerunners, 1870–1920* (Madison: University of Wisconsin Press, 1983), 63, 64, 66.

11. *Historical Sketch of the Good Will Club, 1880–1889*, 4, 9, 28. *The Good Will Club, Thirtieth Annual Report*, 25.

12. *Historical Sketch of the Good Will Club, 1880–1889*, 3, 9, 13.

13. *Historical Sketch of the Good Will Club, 1880–1889*, 31. *Historical Sketch of the Good Will Club, 1880–1900: Annual Report for 1900* (Hartford: Case, Lockwood and Brainard, 1900), 34, 37, 39. *The Good Will Club: Hartford Conn., Thirtieth Annual Report*, 23, 43, 46–48. The Hall quotation is from "Children's Playgrounds," undated (ca. 1905) news clipping, in scrapbook no. 11, Mary Hall Papers.

14. [Mary Hall], untitled article, *Good Will Star* 10/2 (1913), in scrapbook no. 12, Mary Hall Papers. *Historical Sketch of the Good Will Club, 1880–1889*, 10–11. *The Good Will Club, Thirtieth Annual Report*, 7, 8. *The Good Will Club, Hartford Conn.,1880–1922: Forty-Second Annual Report*, 1923 (Hartford: Case, Lockwood and Brainard, 1923).

15. Morris N. Cohen, transcript of 30 May 1988 interview, JHS.

16. The Hartford YMCA provided similar physical education programs, including some for boys. The work, like that of the Good Will Club, aimed at building character along with muscles. The YMCA drew some Catholics and Jews as well as Protestants, but unlike the Good Will Club, it charged membership fees of several dollars a year, which may have discouraged attendance by poor children. The YMCA drew smaller numbers of boys than the Good Will Club. *Eleventh Annual Report of the Young Men's Christian Association of Hartford, Conn.* (Hartford: Star Printing, 1889), 28. *Twelfth Annual Report of the Young Men's Christian Association of Hartford, Connecticut* (Hartford: Peck and Prouty, 1890), 19. *Thirteenth Annual Report of the Young Men's Christian Association of Hartford, Connecticut* (Hartford: Peck and Prouty, 1891), 10. *20th Annual Report of the Board of Managers of the Young Men's Christian Association of Hartford, Conn.* (Hartford: Case, Lockwood and Brainard, 1898), 23, 39. "*Come On In*" [promotional brochure by YMCA] (n.p.: 1915).

17. *Atlas of Hartford City and County* (Hartford: Baker and Tilden, 1869), plates 21, 22, 24, 25.

18. *Atlas of the City of Hartford, and the Town of West Hartford, Connecticut* (Springfield: L.J. Richards, 1909). Views of the East Side marked "From Grand

Stand Boulevard Oct. 9—08," and "From Grand Stand, Oct. 9—08," small photograph album, HPL. "Wright's Panoramic View of Hartford, Conn.," ca. 1898, HPL. Hartford Architecture Conservancy, *Hartford Architecture*, vol. 2, *South Neighborhoods* (Hartford: Hartford Architecture Conservancy, 1980), 48–50. *Fifty-Third Annual Report of the Board of Park Commissioners* (Hartford: City Printing, 1913), 40.

19. *JCCB* 1886–87, 67. *MR* 1889, 234.

20. "Section of Charles St. looking north, 4/1/06, 10:15 A.M.," Thompson photographs of Hartford, no. 59H, CSL. "Commerce Street, South from State Street," Taylor Collection, no. 248, CSL. "Front St. north of Kilbourn, 4/1/06, 10:55 A.M.," Thompson photos, no. 63H. "Kilbourn St. west of Valley, 11/19/05," Thompson photos, no. 43H. "Market St. S. From Marsh Ct. Before Pav., Feb., 5 '14," photograph album marked "Dep't of Engineering 1914–1915. Photographs of street pavements. Paving Div. Book No. 2," HPL. "Marsh Ct. Market St. w. Feb. 28 1913," Ibid. Untitled, undated photo of Talcott Street, Taylor Collection No. 250. "Temple St., Front St. W. Before Pav., Mar., 31 '14," in "Dep't of Engineering 1914–1915." "Village St. North St. N. Before Pav.," Ibid. Reprinted photograph with caption, "This photograph of an unpaved Windsor Street was taken on March 31, 1914, by the City's Engineering Department," HPL. The concept of streets as rooms is borrowed from William C. Ellis, "The Spatial Structure of Streets," in *On Streets*, ed. Stanford Anderson (Cambridge: MIT Press, 1978), 115–31. Parks Superintendent George A. Parker also noted the enclosed character of the streets in a 1906 article, "The Trend of the Park Movement," *Charities and the Commons* 16/14 (1906): 407.

21. Morris Cohen interview, 15 September 1973. Davidson, *Growing Up in Hartford*. "The Whole Family the Whole Year, New Park Department Slogan," *Courant*, 14 January 1917. Dayton, "Hartford's Mauve Decade, No. 224." See also David Nasaw, *Children of the City: At Work and at Play* (New York: Doubleday, 1985), 21–22, 30. Amanda Dargan and Steven Zeitlin, *City Play* (New Brunswick: Rutgers University Press, 1990).

22. Raymond F. Wren et al. [to Louis R. Cheney, mayor], 16 July 1912, in vertical file marked "1912" and "P + A—Periodicals, Associations," PDP.

23. *JBA* 1891–92, 116, 182, 218–19. City officials in 1860 had forbidden ballplaying and kite-flying in every street in the city, a prohibition that, though not often enforced, is still on the books. *The Charter and Ordinances of the City of Hartford* (Hartford: Williams, Wiley and Waterman, 1864), 113, 114. *The Compiled Charter of the City of Hartford* (Hartford: n.p., 1931), 230, 231. *Municipal Code, City of Hartford, Connecticut* (Tallahassee, Fla.: Municipal Code Corporation [updated to February, 1995]), 1969.

24. *JCCB* 1892–93, 138. *HD* 55 (1892): 61.

25. John Alexopoulos, *The Nineteenth Century Parks of Hartford: A Legacy to the Nation* (Hartford: Hartford Architecture Conservancy, 1983), 54.

26. *Report of the Civic Club: School-Gardens, Household School, and Playground, in Riverside Park, Hartford, Conn., June–September 1905* (Hartford: Case, Lockwood and Brainard, 1905), 5–6.

27. "Vacation School Open," *Courant*, 29 June 1897. *MR* 1902, 721. "Nearly All Are for Colt Park," *Courant*, 4 November 1905. "Letters of Children," *Courant*, 6 August 1897. "Civic Club's Vacation School," *Times*, 28 June 1897.

28. "Vacation School Open"; *The Picturesque Parks of Hartford* (Hartford: American Book Exchange, 1900), 35.

29. "The Vacation School," *Courant*, 7 July 1897; "Letters of Children."

30. "Letters of Children"; "Vacation School Ends," *Courant*, 7 August 1897.

31. *Report of the Civic Club of Hartford, Conn., 1895–1901* (Hartford: Case, Lockwood and Brainard, 1901), 14–16. "Records Park Commission Vol. II" [volume of minutes from 1895 to 1902], 192, PDP.

32. *MR* 1902, 722, 724, 726, 735. "Records Park Commission Vol. II," 282–83. Civic Club members maintained their influence for a few years after the city took control by serving on the committee that supervised the program and by providing additional funds.

33. *MR* 1902, 723.

34. Ibid.

35. Goodman, *Choosing Sides*, 87–112. Herbert G. Gutman, "Work, Culture, and Society in Industrializing America, 1815–1919," in *Work, Culture, and Society in Industrializing America: Essays in American Working-Class and Social History* (New York: Random House, 1977), 3–78. Daniel T. Rodgers, *The Work Ethic in Industrial America, 1850–1920* (Chicago: University of Chicago Press, 1978).

36. *MR* 1902, 722–24, 726–27. Minutes of 1 July 1901 meeting in "Records Park Commission Vol. II," PDP. On Gunshanan, "J. F. Gunshanan Dies; Foe of Tuberculosis," *Courant*, 4 August 1930; "John F. Gunshanan," *Times*, 5 August 1930. Gunshanan, the son of a local expressman, was a leading advocate of antituberculosis measures and had established the Workingmen's Free Reading Room Association and the West Side Workingmen's Club. These organizations sought to improve interclass understanding and advocated such public improvements as public bathhouses, public comfort stations, and night trolley service.

37. *Annual Report of the Board of School Visitors of the Town of Hartford, March 31, 1905* (Hartford: Case, Lockwood and Brainard, 1905), 41. *MR* 1904, 735–36, 741.

38. *Annual Report, March 31, 1905*, 41–48. On Rood's regular job, *Annual*

Report of the Board of School Visitors of the Town of Hartford, March 31, 1907 (Hartford: Charles M. Gaines, 1907), 31.

39. *Annual Report of the Board of School Visitors of the Town of Hartford, March 31, 1906* (Hartford: Case, Lockwood and Brainard, 1906), 38, 40.

40. *Report of the Civic Club: School-Gardens; Annual Report, March 31, 1907,* 31–34. George A. Parker to Mr. Bolton Hall, 22 March 1910, binder marked "Letters—Park Business—1909. From Nov. 1st to April 20, 1910," PDP. MR 1902, 737–39. *Annual Report, March 31, 1906,* 35–36.

41. *Annual Report, March 31, 1907,* 31. *Annual Report of the Board of School Visitors of the Town of Hartford, March 31, 1908* (Hartford: Charles M. Gaines, 1908), 32–33. *Annual Report of the Board of School Visitors of the Town of Hartford. Year Ending July 14, 1912* (Hartford: Charles M. Gaines, 1912), 24. *Annual Report of the Board of School Visitors of the Town of Hartford. Year Ending July 14, 1913* (Hartford: City Printing, 1913), 18, 20. *Annual Report of the Board of School Visitors of the Town of Hartford. Year Ending July 14, 1914* ([Hartford:] n.p., [1914]), 19.

42. George A. Parker, text of speech to the Educational Club, 22 January 1909, in brown canvas-covered binder marked "Duplicates—1909 + 1910," PDP.

43. Howard P. Chudacoff, *How Old Are You? Age Consciousness in American Culture* (Princeton: Princeton University Press, 1989), 66–67, 73–74. Mrozek, "The Natural Limits of Unstructured Play," 211, 213. Benjamin G. Rader, *American Sports: From the Age of Folk Games to the Age of Spectators* (Englewood Cliffs, N.J.: Prentice-Hall, 1983), 155–56. R. Jackson Wilson, *In Quest of Community: Social Philosophy in the United States, 1860–1920* (New York: John Wiley and Sons, 1968), 116–17.

44. George A. Parker, "The City and Its Young People," 7 January 1913, binder marked "Juvenile Commission, 1913," PDP. BPC 63 (1922–23), 71–72. BPC 50 (1909–10), 37–38.

45. Parker, "Memorandum of Address Delivered at Colt Memorial, Evening of February 19, 1913," typescript, in vertical file marked "1912" and "1912 R + M," PDP. Parker, "Hartford and Recreation," 14 November 1911, typescript, letterbox marked "1911–1912. Reports typewritten," PDP. Parker, "The City and Its Young People." *Fifth Annual Report of the Juvenile Commission to the Mayor and Court of Common Council of the City of Hartford, Conn., for the Year Ending April 30, 1914* (Hartford: Bond Press, 1914), 93.

46. Parker, "Reasons for Pavilion at Colt Park and the Improvement of the Field for Athletic Sports," typescript, n.d. (ca. February 26, 1912), in letterbox marked "1911–1912, Reports typewritten," PDP.

47. Parker, text of speech to the Educational Club, 22 January 1909, in

brown canvas-covered binder marked "Duplicates—1909 + 1910," PDP. *Fourth Annual Report of the Juvenile Commission*, 20.

48. *Fifth Annual Report of the Juvenile Commission*, 89, 93. *Fourth Annual Report of the Juvenile Commission*, 25. Parker hoped that park and recreation officials would soon "formulate a science of Child Life in cities." He fumbled around for data and conceptual tools that might help, estimating available hours of leisure time in Hartford, calculating how they were spent, and hoping that his information would somehow help him develop "experience tables" that could better guide the provision of recreation (Parker, "The City and Its Young People" and "Memoranda for a Park Syllabus").

49. Parker, "The Trend of the Park Movement," 407–09.

50. "Children Dance at Keney Park," *Courant*, 16 May 1914. See also "Goodwin Park June Fete Is Fine Success," *Times*, 4 June 1913; "Seventeen Hundred School Children in May Day Fete in Keney Park," *Times*, 30 May 1913. "Maypole Dance of South District Girls at Goodwin Park," *Times*, 12 June 1919. In 1913 the North Street Settlement staged an even more organized, though smaller, pageant complete with costumes ("Park Transformed into Fairy Domain," *Courant*, 22 May 1913).

51. On the physical form of playgrounds, photograph album marked "Book 4," 90, 96, 98, HPL. On fences, see also BPC 57 (1916–17): 35; BPC 64 (1923–24): 72. "At the North Street Mission Playground," *Courant*, 7 September 1914. Public playground workers in Hartford were mainly women. "Playground Workers," *Times*, 23 June 1914.

52. Parker to Charles A. Whitte, 5 September 1906, folder marked "Office Letters—L's," box marked "Outgoing Letters I–N," GAPP. Parker, "Report Regarding Additional Playgrounds during July and August," typescript, 11 September 1912, vertical file marked "1912" and "1912 R + M," PDP. "Joy, Untrammeled and Supreme, in Children's Playgrounds," *Courant*, 22 July 1917. "'Breathing Place' on East Side," *Courant*, 30 June 1919. The quotation is from Parker, "How Hartford Is Making Use of Its Public Parks as Play Centers," *Hartford* 4/11 (1919): 5.

53. On school employees as supervisors, *Annual Report of the Hartford Board of Education* (Hartford: Case, Lockwood and Brainard, 1918), 7. "Plan Recreation for Hartford Women," *Courant*, 4 February 1919. In 1915, for instance, there were 143 paid employees at the playgrounds and recreation centers, not counting caretakers. Of the 143, 130 were school employees, all but four of them women ("Playground and Recreation Centers," typescript, letterbox marked "Minutes—City Plan Commission also letters + reports. Mr. Parker. Some General Correspondence," PDP). On directed play and free play, "Joy, Untrammeled and Supreme, in Children's Playgrounds"; "'Breathing Place' on East Side";

"Recreation and Play Grounds of Hartford," *Courant*, 5 October 1913. "Playground to Be Opened Today," *Courant*, 13 November 1916. "Playground Rules and Regulations—1920," typescript, letterbox marked "Misc. Notes, Letters, 1915–1922," PDP. On hours, see, e.g., *BPC* 61 (1920–21): 55; "Playground to Be Opened Today." Dominick Cavallo, remarking on the promotion of cooperative behavior and team sports, describes Progressive-Era playground advocates as seeking to train young people away from the extreme individualism that they associated with unregulated entrepreneurial capitalism. Instead they wished to inculcate behavioral patterns appropriate to a more organized, bureaucratic, and corporate society (Cavallo, *Muscles and Morals*, 3, 7–8).

54. Parker, "Report Regarding Additional Playgrounds during July and August"; *BPC* 55 (1914–15): 36; "School Gardens to Open Today"; "Playground to Be Opened Today"; *BPC* 52 (1911–12): 36.

55. *Fifth Annual Report of the Juvenile Commission*, 64. "Baseball. Rules and Regulations," letterbox marked "Memorandums From 1911," PDP. *BPC* 61 (1920–21): 56. "Charter Oak Playground Is Play Day Winner," *Courant*, 30 August 1919. *BPC* 69 (1928–29): 45.

56. "A East Side Resident" to George L. [*sic*] Parker, 15 April 1911, letterbox marked "Letters. 1911," PDP. *Summary of the Work of the Juvenile Commission to the Mayor and Court of Common Council of the City of Hartford, Conn., 1909–1925* (Hartford: Pyne Printery [1926?]), 5–7.

57. Horace Bushnell, *Christian Nurture* (New York: Charles Scribner, 1861), 338, 344. "Pastor Pleads for the Children," *Courant*, 10 June 1907.

58. *Third Annual Report of the Juvenile Commission to the Mayor and Court of Common Council of the City of Hartford, Conn., for the Year Ending April 30, 1912* (Hartford: Case, Lockwood and Brainard, 1912), 8. *Fourth Annual Report of the Juvenile Commission*, 7. Parker, "Report Regarding Additional Playgrounds during July and August." *JCCB* 1912–13, 139.

59. Parker, "Report Regarding Additional Playgrounds during July and August." [Parker], Superintendent, to W. Francis Hyde, Supervisor of Parks, Worcester, Mass., 23 January 1913, in vertical file marked "1912–1913 Park Letters," PDP. *BPC* 54 (1913–14): 70. *BPC* 55 (1914–15): 36. "'Breathing Place' on East Side." *Ninth Annual Report of the Juvenile Commission to the Mayor and Court of Common Council of the City of Hartford, Conn.* (Hartford: Case, Lockwood and Brainard, 1918), 9–10., 28. *BPC* 61 (1920–21): 55; *BPC* 63 (1922–23): 77; *BPC* 68 (1927–28): 40; *BPC* 70 (1929–30): 42. The two social settlements also opened playgrounds. See "Hartford Social Settlement Association" [annual report for 1915–16], letterbox marked "Letters, Associations, XI, 1916–1917," PDP; "Children Seesaw, Swing and Slide While Trains Thunder by New Spruce Street Playground," *Courant*, 23 August 1919.

60. Parker, "Report Regarding Additional Playgrounds during July and August." *BPC* 60 (1919–20): 44; *BPC* 55 (1914–15): 47; *BPC* 58 (1917–18): 38. S. Wales Dixon, Supervisor of Recreation, Department of Parks, to Eva Cohen, Secretary, Juvenile Comm., 16 December 1919, letterbox labeled "Reports 1919," PDP.

61. E. J. Ferguson to George A. Parker, 11 July [1913], orange-edged letterbox marked "Letters + Memos, Miscellaneous, 1913," PDP. "Folk Dances Shown in Goodwin Park," *Courant*, 11 June 1913. Francesca A. Henke, "Outdoor Recreation for Hartford Twenty Years Ago and Today," *Courant*, 20 August 1916. "Supervision of City Playgrounds," *Courant*, 8 November 1913. Parker, "Report Regarding Additional Playgrounds during July and August." "For Helping the City's Children," *Times*, 2 December 1913. *BPC* 60 (1919–20): 44.

62. W. J. Hamersley, undated and untitled speech, 1914, in letterbox labeled "Reports 1914," PDP. *BPC* 56 (1915–16): 43, 53.

63. Parker, speech to Education Club, 22 January 1909.

64. *Fifth Annual Report of the Juvenile Commission*, 94–95.

65. *BPC* 56 (1915–16): 44. "The Whole Family the Whole Year, New Park Recreation Slogan," *Courant*, 14 January 1917. Dixon believed more strongly than Parker did in the power of directed play; "Supervision of City Playgrounds."

66. See chapters 8 and 9. The quotation is from *Publications of the Municipal Art Society of Hartford Connecticut*, no. 4, *Proceedings of the Annual Meeting, October 17, 1905. Some Municipal Problems* (Hartford: Municipal Art Society, 1906), 21.

67. Transcript of 18 May 1975 interview with Rose Witkower, JHS. Ethel Usher, "Analysis of Automobile Accidents: A Summary, Classified by Towns, of the Conditions under Which the Motor Vehicle Accidents in Connecticut Occurred during 1925," *State of Connecticut Department of Motor Vehicles, Supplement to Bulletin No. 28*, 16 August 1926.

68. Ruth Cheney Goodwin to Fannie R. Karlson, 13 January 1913, vertical file marked "1912 Letters," PDP. "Joy, Untrammeled and Supreme." See also "Children without Playground Risk Life and Limb in Temple Street" (photo caption), *Courant*, 7 November 1921.

69. "Diary of a Hartford Motorist," ACH, *Bulletin* 1/1 (1911). "Diary of a Hartford Motorist," ACH, *Bulletin* 1/2 (Dec. 1911). "Streets as Playgrounds," ACH, *Monthly Bulletin* 11 (1919): 7. On Parker's membership, C. H. Gillette, Secretary, ACH, to Parker, 18 May 1912, binder marked "Letters, Dec. 1911 to May 1912," PDP. See also chapter 9.

70. "How the Police Protect School Children," *Courant*, 7 December 1913.

71. "Protection of Life Is Sought," *Times*, 27 March 1914. "'Safety First'

Takes Firm Hold," *Courant*, 26 April 1914. "Safety First School Talks," *Post*, 28 April 1914.

72. Robbins B. Stoeckel, *Report of the Commissioner of Motor Vehicles to His Excellency the Governor, for the Term Ended June 30, 1920* (Hartford: published by the State, 1920), 19. Viviana A. Zelizer, *Pricing the Priceless Child: The Changing Social Value of Children* (New York: Basic Books, 1985), 39–40.

73. Garrett J. Farrell, "Cooperation between Public School and Traffic Officials," *American City Magazine* 31/6 (1924): 551. Efforts to discipline child jay-walkers had begun earlier at the Washington Street School, where the principal in 1920 had begun using Boy Scouts to reprimand children who crossed in the middle of the block and to record their names for further punitive action by school authorities. "School Pupils Are Shown Dangers of 'Jay Walking,'" *Times*, 20 September 1921. (For the more cynical impressions of a child who experienced the safety education efforts, see Armando T. Perretta's semiautobiographical novel of life on the East Side, *Take a Number* [New York: William Morrow, 1957], 103.) More police were stationed as crossing guards at major intersections used by students going to and from school, but not every intersection could be watched, and children continued to be hit at unguarded crossings (Farrell, "Annual Report of Police Department for Year Ending March 31, 1924," drawer marked "Police Department, Annual and Quarterly Reports, 1915 to 1939," HCH). *Report of the Juvenile Commission to the Mayor and Court of Common Council of the City of Hartford, Conn., 1926–1927* (Hartford: Pyne Printery [1927]), 15–16.

74. Ethel Usher, "Connecticut Motor Vehicle Statistics for 1929," *State of Connecticut Department of Motor Vehicles*, bulletin no. 72 (1930). Zelizer, *Pricing the Priceless Child*, 35–36.

75. "The Italian People Who Live in Hartford," *Courant*, 29 August 1915. Morris Cohen interview, JHS. "Children without Playground Risk Life and Limb in Temple Street." (Temple Street was a short side street on the East Side and did not warrant such an alarmist caption.) Zelizer claims that the death rate nationally was brought under control only through the "the eviction of children" from the streets, and that "children lost the contest for public space." She argues that "saving child life meant changing the daily activities of city children, pushing them indoors into playrooms and schoolrooms or designing special 'child' public spaces such as playgrounds." The lethal power of the automobile had miraculously given victory to the reformers in the playground movement (Zelizer, *Pricing the Priceless Child*, 25, 35, 52, 53). Children's recollections of street play at later dates and continued concern among reformers indicate that this is an exaggeration.

Chapter 7

1. On the fact that the walk near the post office was particularly unpleasant for ladies because of carts and wagons, see *JBA* 1888–89, 426. On street musicians, "City Briefs," *Courant*, 30 May 1890; "Mayor's Two Vetoes," *Courant*, 9 July 1895; "The Crippled Musician," *Courant*, 15 October 1895; "The City Government," *Courant*, 27 April 1897. On knife-sharpening, "The Street Grindstone Man," *Courant*, 6 May 1917. On newsies, see chapter 4.

2. John R. Stilgoe, *Borderland: Origins of the American Suburb, 1820–1939* (New Haven: Yale University Press, 1988), 208. Peter Z. Grossman, *American Express: The Unofficial History of the People Who Built the Great Financial Empire* (New York: Crown, 1987), 38–40.

3. Photo with caption "Main Street. Conn. Mutual Building," in *Views. City of Hartford* (Boston: Nolman Photo, 1885). Photograph with caption "Main Street, Looking South from City Hall," in *Sunlight Pictures: Hartford. Artotypes by E. Bierstadt, N.Y., from Original Negatives by R.S. DeLamater* (Hartford: J.H. Eckhardt, 1892). "Petition from the Expressmen of the City of Hartford," 1 July 1886, in drawer marked "Expressmen: Stands, Licenses, etc.," HCH. "The Hackstand Question," *Times*, 22 November 1901. "May Not Move May 1," *Courant*, 30 April 1902.

4. *JBA* 1888–89, 425–26; *JCCB* 1889–90, 65.

5. "Hartford Lunch Carts That Are Nearly Gone," *Courant*, 27 May 1917. "Court of Common Council," *Times*, 23 March 1897. *JCCB* 1896–97, 761–63.

6. *JCCB* 1897–98, 754, 994. "Last Meeting of Council," *Times*, 29 March 1898. "Hartford Lunch Carts That Are Nearly Gone."

7. *JBA* 1901–02, 382, 450. "Petition re Removal of Hacks and Baggage Wagons from City Hall Square," 20 September 1901, drawer marked "Public Carriages—Hacks Stand, Jitneys," HCH. "Petition of Hackmen de Location of Public Hacks," 14 October 1901, same drawer. *HD* 64 (1901–02).

8. "Hacks and Express Wagons," *Times*, 21 November 1901. "Hackstand Question."

9. "City Hall Nuisance," *Courant*, 14 October 1901.

10. "Hack and Express Stands: Public Hearing before Street Board on Question of Their Removal," *Times*, 23 November 1901.

11. "Hack and Express Stands"; "Shall They Remain?" *Courant*, 23 November 1901. "Must Vacate May 1," *Times*, 5 December 1901.

12. "Still on Deck," *Times*, 1 May 1902. "Street Board Defied," *Courant*, 3 May 1902. "Hackman Arrested," *Times*, 3 May 1902. "Hackmen Are Defiant," *Courant*, 5 May 1902. "At the Old Stand," *Times*, 5 May 1902.

13. "Hackmen Are Defiant." "Another Step Taken," *Times*, 8 May 1902. "Pe-

tition from the Expressmen of the City of Hartford," 1 July 1886. "Mr. Buths Insulted," *Courant*, 8 May 1902. "Letters from the People: About the Street Board," *Times*, 13 May 1902. "Hackmen and Expressmen," 14 May 1902. "Favorable to Hackmen," *Times*, 15 May 1902. On Sullivan, see Bruce Alan Clouette, "'Getting Their Share': Irish and Italian Immigrants in Hartford, Connecticut, 1850–1930" (Ph.D. diss., University of Connecticut, 1992), 103, 211.

14. "Expressmen Will Move," *Courant*, 18 January 1906. "Expressmen Will Bargain with City," *Courant*, 23 January 1906. JCCB 1905–06, 830–31, 910–13, 931–33, 1084. For earlier protest about the Village and Windsor street site, see JCCB 1902–03, 27.

15. "Edward L. Smith, Ex-Mayor, Dies," *Courant*, 9 February 1923. MR 1911, 48. MR 1912, 885–89. "Expressmen Barred from Union Place," *Courant*, 23 January 1916.

16. Grossman, *American Express*, 148. William Leach, *Land of Desire: Merchants, Power and the Rise of a New American Culture* (New York: Random House, 1993), 184.

17. JCCC 1915–16, 524–25, 712. "Expressmen Barred from Union Place."

18. HD 35 (1872): 27, 30, 38, 80, 209, 213, 216. JCCB 1880–81, 121. "Thanksgiving Poultry," *Courant*, 27 November 1879. "Busy Christmas Eve," *Courant*, 25 December 1896.

19. "Petition Concerning Street Peddlers and Vendors of Produce," 24 August 1874, box marked "Ordinances to 1884," HCH. "Licensing Street Venders," *Times*, 30 August 1888. Grocers submitted further petitions calling for stricter regulation of peddlers in 1876, 1879, 1883, 1888, 1891, and 1893. "Partition [sic] for an Ordinance Compeling Vendors on Our Streets to Pay License," 28 August 1876, box marked "Ordinances to 1884." JCCB 1879–80, 66, 233; JCCB 1882–83, 232; JCCB 1888–89, 147, 196, 364; JCCB 1891–92, 227; JCCB 1893–94, 51. By 1911, there were more than three hundred produce peddlers in Hartford. BH 27 (1911): 46.

20. Richard F. Jones, "Hartford's Hill District, 1910–1920," typescript, CHS. See also Alice T. Enders, "Growing Up on Woodland Street," in *The Hartford Diaries of Mary Dudley Vaill Talcott (Mrs. Charles Hooker Talcott) from 1896–1919*, vol. 3 (Avon, Conn.: Alice Talcott Enders, 1990), 850. "Peddlers Protest at Wearing Badge," *Courant*, 16 September 1912.

21. Morris Cohen interview, 15 September 1973, JHS. Transcript of October 1968 interview with Louis Hyman, JHS. On the practice of following definite routes, JCCB 1911–12, 648. This practice was common in other cities as well; Padraic Burke, "Rolling Carts and Songs of Plenty: The Urban Food Vendor," *Journal of American Culture* 2/3 (1979): 483.

22. "Licensing Street Venders," *Times*, 30 August 1888. Transcript of 21 No-

vember 1974 interview with Samuel Hoffenberg, Peoples of Connecticut Oral History Project, Center for Oral History, University of Connecticut. James McManus, "In Favor of a Public Market Building at Temple Street and Boulevard," *Courant*, 24 September 1908. Max Neiditz interview, JHS.

23. Morris Cohen interview, 17 September 1973, JHS. Sandra Hartwell Becker and Ralph L. Pearson, "The Jewish Community of Hartford, Connecticut, 1880–1929," *American Jewish Archives* 31/2 (1979): 201. Alan M. Kraut, "The Butcher, the Baker, the Pushcart Peddler: Jewish Foodways and Entrepreneurial Opportunity in the East European Immigrant Community 1880–1940," *Journal of American Culture* 6/4 (1983): 76.

24. "Vegetables Fresh from Nearby Farms," *Courant*, 16 August 1913. "Where Hartford Gets Its Fruit," *Courant*, 9 November 1919. Morris Cohen interview, 17 September 1973. Louis Hyman interview, October 1968. Transcript of 22 March 1975 interview with Anthony Tapogna, Peoples of Connecticut Oral History Project, Center for Oral History, University of Connecticut. On the fact that peddlers were "living in nearly every case on the East Side," *JBA* 1914–15, 221. Pushcart peddlers, like peddlers who owned horses and wagons, typically followed daily routes.

25. *JCCB* 1888–89, 97, 197. "Many Matters of Interest," *Times*, 23 February 1894. *JCCB* 1893–94, 471, 493–94.

26. "Excessive Noise Made by Peddlers," *Courant*, 6 August 1913. "Hartford Noises," *New York Times*, 25 September 1915 (cited in Becker and Pearson, "The Jewish Community of Hartford," 202). "In re Loud Calling of Wares," 21 August 1922, drawer marked "Nuisances," HCH.

27. For example, "City News in Brief," *Courant*, 28 May 1909. "Too Much Noise Leads to Arrest," *Courant*, 12 May 1914.

28. Municipal Art Society, *Publications of the Municipal Art Society of Hartford, Connecticut*, no. 11, *Proceedings of the Annual Meeting, November 13, 1908. Officers, Members, Reports of Committees. Unnecessary Noises. The Billboard Question* (Hartford: Municipal Art Society, 1909), 34. "Hebrew Peddlers Unite: To Fight for Privilege of Yelling 'Banan' in the Streets," *Courant*, 7 June 1909 (cited in Morris Silverman, *Hartford Jews, 1659–1970* [Hartford: Connecticut Historical Society, 1970], 32, 112). WPA Writers' Project, "Hebrew Peddlers Association," in "Ethnic Groups Survey: Jews of Hartford (IX), Mutual Aid Societies (9)," box 59, folder 157: 1b, University of Connecticut Archives. *JCCB* 1913–14, 84. *JCCC* 1922–23, 247.

29. "Peddlers on Main Street," *Courant*, 15 March 1895. "The Licensing of Peddlers," *Courant*, 18 March 1895. "Wanted Hebrews to Stop Working Sunday," *Courant*, 10 June 1907.

30. *Second Annual Report of the Commission on the City Plan to the Mayor*

and Court of Common Council of the City of Hartford, Conn., for the Year Ending March 31, 1909 (Hartford: City Printing, 1909), 14. Frederick L. Ford, secretary, Commission on the City Plan, to Court of Common Council, 28 December 1908, drawer marked "Public Market, Mansion House, Pushcart Peddlers," HCH. "Petition of John H. McGuire et al. for Abatement of Nuisance of Farmers and Peddlers Making Main Street a Market Place," 6 August 1908, same drawer. *Twenty-Sixth Annual Report of the Board of Health of the City of Hartford for the Year Ending Feb. 28, 1911* (Hartford: Smith-Linsley, 1911) 44. "New Hucksters' Plaza Thronged with Farmers," *Times,* 22 July 1912.

    31. JCCB 1909–10, 588, 859. JCCB 1911–12, 133, 300–01, 356–60, 424–25, 443, 674–75. "New Hucksters' Plaza Thronged with Farmers." "Henmarket Open Thursday Morning," *Courant,* 23 July 1912. JCCC 1920–21, 79. On the persistence of the market, "$1,147,575 Business at Municipal Market," *Courant,* 14 January 1923 ("Municipal Market" was a later name for the marketplace, which was also called the "Farmers' Market"). "Idle to Start Apple Sale on Streets Here," *Courant,* 25 November 1930.

    32. "Killing Hens on Charles Street," *Courant,* 26 July 1912. "Vegetables Fresh from Nearby Farms." *Twenty-Eighth Annual Report of the Board of Health of the City of Hartford for the Year Ending Dec. 31, 1912* (Hartford: Smith-Linsley, 1913), 48. *Thirty-Fourth Annual Report of the Board of Health of the City of Hartford for the Year Ending December 31, 1918* (Hartford: Taylor and Greenough, 1919), 15.

    33. "Peddlers Protest at Wearing Badge"; "Peddlers Object to the Badge Ordinance," *Times,* 16 September 1912. Jacob Schwartz, David Nass, Frank Zuckerman, Hebrew Peddlers' Protective Association, to Court of Common Council, n.d., received 28 April 1913, drawer marked "Licenses," HCH. "Hard on the Farmers," *Times,* 26 July 1912. On wholesale produce dealers, "Waste Papers Occupy Street Board's Attention," *Times,* 28 July 1910. "Where Hartford Gets Its Fruit"; "Boulevard Market Strongly Opposed," *Courant,* 21 May 1915.

    34. JCCB 1906–07, 498, 849, 989; JCCB 1908–09, 335; JCCB 1909–10, 588, 859; JCCB 1912–13, 247, 683, 887, 1134–35; JCCB 1913–14, 1043; JCCC 1916–17, 773.

    35. "Public Hearing on Public Market," *Courant,* 14 December 1912. JCCB 1913–14, 1111. "What Cheney Has Done for Hartford," *Courant,* 4 April 1914. MR 1914, 41. On the old Market House, Melancthon W. Jacobus, "The City Hall and Market House in Hartford," *Connecticut Historical Society Bulletin* 35/1 (1970): 1–6; HD 48 (1885): 63; JCCB 1886–87, 206.

    36. JCCC 1917–18, 484–86. "Retail Curb Markets Play First Engagement," *Courant,* 5 September 1917. U.S. Department of Commerce, Bureau of the Census, *Municipal Markets in Cities Having a Population of Over 30,000: 1918*

(Washington: Government Printing Office, 1919), 32, 35, 48. Jane Pyle, "Farmers' Markets in the United States: Functional Anachronisms," *Geographical Review* 61/2 (1971): 179. *JCCC* 1919–20, 374–75.

37. "Park River Site for Public Market Given Up," *Courant*, 17 January 1919. "Market Location Denied Park River," *Times*, 17 January 1919.

38. "Hartford's Municipal Market as Proposed by Mayor for Park River Site," *Times*, 16 January 1919. "Public Market Plans Approved," *Courant*, 4 April 1919. *JCCC* 1919–20, 301. "Crowds of Buyers at Market Opening" and "New City Market Seen by Hundreds," both *Times*, 17 August 1920.

39. *JCCC* 1921–22, 632–34, 754, 842.

40. "New City Market Opens to Public," *Courant*, 16 August 1920. "New City Market Seen by Hundreds"; "Crowds of Buyers at Market Opening"; "Vote Abolishes Public Market," *Times*, 10 January 1922. "Order Marketmen to Vacate Stalls," *Courant*, 14 January 1922. "Discontinuance of City Market O.K.'d," *Courant*, 17 January 1922. *JCCC* 1921–22, 754, 842.

41. "The End of an Experiment," *Times*, 11 January 1922.

42. Ruth Schwartz Cowan, *More Work for Mother: The Ironies of Household Technology from the Open Hearth to the Microwave* (New York: Basic Books, 1983), 79–80. Numerous groceries in Hartford offered home delivery. *Hartford and Its Points of Interest: Illustrated from Original Photographs* (New York: Mercantile Illustrating, 1895), e.g., 81, 87, 92, 103.

43. James M. Mayo, *The American Grocery Store: The Business Evolution of an Architectural Space* (Westwood, Conn.: Greenwood Press, 1993), 86, 133. Richard Osborn Cummings, *The American and His Food: A History of Food Habits in the United States* (Chicago: University of Chicago Press, 1940), 104–08.

44. Lizabeth Cohen, *Making a New Deal: Industrial Workers in Chicago, 1919–1939* (New York: Cambridge University Press, 1990), 109–13. Cummings, *The American and His Food*, 104. Waverly Root and Richard de Rochemont, *Eating in America: A History* (New York: William Morrow, 1976), 239–40. Transcript of 30 May 1988 interview with Morris Cohen, JHS.

45. *HD* 1910, 965; *HD* 1920, 827, 1240, 1247. "To Clean Up Filth on the East Side," *Courant*, 17 December 1906. *Twenty-Third Annual Report of the Board of Health of the City of Hartford for the Year Ending February 29, 1908* (Hartford: Smith-Linsley, 1908), 36. *Twenty-Fourth Annual Report of the Board of Health of the City of Hartford for the Year Ending February 29, [sic] 1909* (Hartford: Smith-Linsley, 1909), 38. *Twenty-Sixth Annual Report of the Board of Health*, 43. *Twenty-Seventh Annual Report of the Board of Health of the City of Hartford for the Year Ending December 31, 1911* (Hartford: Smith-Linsley, 1912), 45. Armando T. Perretta, *Take a Number* (New York: William Morrow, 1957), 12.

46. *Twenty-Third Annual Report of the Board of Health*, 35. *Twenty-Fourth An-*

nual Report of the Board of Health, 37. Twenty-Fifth Annual Report of the Board of Health of the City of Hartford for the Year Ending February 28, 1910 (Hartford: Smith-Linsley, 1910), 40, 42. Twenty-Ninth Annual Report of the Board of Health, 15. "Huckster Methods Must Be Improved," Times, 26 July 1912.

47. JCCC 1922–23, 643.

48. "Pushcarts on Front St. Rozinsky's. Circa 1920," unlabeled box, section labeled "Business—Jewish owned—no people," JHS. In contrast, photographs from the 1900s and early 1910s show few if any peddlers, but unfortunately none of the photos appears to have been taken during the summer, when fresh produce was more abundant. For example, "Front Street south of Kilbourne," 19 November 1905, Thompson Photographs of Hartford (Picture Group 430), no. 42H, CSL; "J. Gorfine, groceries, Front St., 4/1/1906," and "Chas. Kramer Clothing Store, Front St., 4/8/1906," unlabeled box, section labeled "Business—Jewish owned—no people," JHS. Untitled photograph of the corner of Windsor and North streets, Engineering Dept. photo album marked "5 x 7 construction photos and other photos, 1912–1913, 1914. Hartford, Conn.," HPL.

49. Morris I. Davidson, Growing Up in Hartford. Robert E. Pawlowski, How the Other Half Lived: An Ethnic History of the Old East Side and South End of Hartford (West Hartford: Northwest Catholic High School, 1973), 44. Morris Cohen interviews, 15 and 17 September. Perretta, Take a Number, 13.

50. Morris Cohen interview, 15 September 1973. Pawlowski, How the Other Half Lived, 44. JCCC 1915–16, 396, 467–68. JCCC 1927–28, 512–13, 532–33, 637–38. "Pushcart Peddlers Have Hearing before Council Committees," Courant, 6 October 1927. JCCC 1928–29, 53. Theodore E. Buell, "Pallotti Wins Long Debate for Peddlers," Courant, 4 December 1929.

51. JCCC 1929, 255–56, 315. JCCC 1929–30, 34. Buell, "Pallotti Wins Long Debate." A 1926 ordinance forbade selling anything except newspapers on the sidewalks in the center of the city—including the downtown, most of the East Side, and parts of the South Green and Clay Hill neighborhoods, but this ordinance was aimed at controlling begging. It produced very little controversy and apparently had no effect on the pushcart peddlers, whose carts occupied the street itself rather than the sidewalk. JCCC 1926–27, 606–08, 654, 994.

52. On the decline of the peddling business and its concentration on Front Street, "Talk Eclipses Trade," Times, 28 August 1935. On the survival of the pushcarts until urban renewal, Pawlowski, How the Other Half Lived, 44, 49. On the continuation of peddling in the outlying neighborhoods into the 1940s, Irving Waltman, interviewed by Peter Baldwin, 28 September 1995. On peddling as an old man's business, WPA Writers' Project, "Hebrew Peddlers Association." On the horse and wagon as a form of upward mobility, Becker and Pearson, "The Jewish Community of Hartford," 201.

Chapter 8

1. *Art Work of Hartford: Published in Nine Parts* (Chicago: W.H. Parish, 1897), photograph marked "Capitol Street" [*sic*]. *Atlas of the City of Hartford, Connecticut, Including, Also, The Town of West Hartford* (Springfield, Mass.: L.J. Richards, 1896), plates 4, 8. *Atlas of the City of Hartford and the Town of West Hartford, Connecticut* (Springfield, Mass.: L.J. Richards, 1909), plates 1, 2. Bureau of the Census, *Thirteenth Census of the United States (1910)*, population schedules. Transcript of public hearing held 19 March 1914, drawer marked "Capitol Avenue, 1908 to 1929," HCH.

2. Public hearing, 19 March 1914.

3. Joint Standing Committee on Railroads to Court of Common Council, 8 August 1910, drawer marked "Capitol Avenue, 1908 to 1929." JBA 1906–07, 989; public hearing, 19 March 1914. "Asphalt Still Unpopular; Not Wanted in Paving," *Times*, 30 December 1909. "Remonstrance against Proposed Street Railway through Capitol Avenue from Trinity Street to Main Street," n.d., probably 1910, and "Report of the Jt. Spl. Committee in re Widening of Capitol Avenue from Main Street to Washington Street," 23 March 1914, both drawer marked "Capitol Avenue, 1908 to 1929." "Many against Cars on Capitol Avenue," *Courant*, 20 March 1914. McCook lived on Main Street directly across from the opening of Capitol.

4. Though neighborhood opposition to Capitol Avenue improvements diminished after 1914, the trolley company remained reluctant to install tracks there, and the city government found other places that needed asphalt more desperately. The street was not asphalted until 1929, and trolley tracks were never installed at the Main Street end, though the section west of Hudson Street became part of a bus line. "Report of the Board of Street Commissioners, recommending that Capitol Avenue from Whitman Court to Washington St. be paved with improved pavement during the season of 1917," 13 November 1916, and "Report of the Board of Street Commissioners on resolution in re relief of trolley congestion through Capitol Avenue, etc." 28 May 1917, both drawer marked "Capitol Avenue, 1908 to 1929." BSC 59 (1930–31): 8, 14. *New Map of Hartford and West Hartford, Conn.* (Hartford: Hartford Printing, 1928). *Pitner's Map of Hartford, West Hartford, East Hartford and Environs* (Washington: Carl Pitner, n.d. [ca. 1930]).

5. *Atlas of the City of Hartford* (1896). F. Perry Close, *History of Hartford Streets* (Hartford: Connecticut Historical Society, 1969), 2, 13, 42, 72, 119. *Atlas of Hartford and Tolland Counties* (Hartford: Baker and Tilden, 1869). "New Streets," *Courant*, 25 May 1880.

6. MR 1880, 85, 87. "Hartford's Paving Problems," *Hartford* 6 (March 1916):

4. Helen Post Chapman, *My Hartford of the Nineteenth Century* (Hartford: Edwin Valentine Mitchell, 1928), 15, 52. "Horse Stuck in the Mud," *Courant*, 11 April 1895. On macadamizing, BSC 4 (for 1875): 5. BSC 14 (for 1885): xii, xiii.

7. Clay McShane, *Down the Asphalt Path: The Automobile and the American City* (New York: Columbia University Press, 1994), 58. BSC 17 (for 1888): viii. Hiram Percy Maxim, *Horseless Carriage Days* (New York: Harper and Brothers, 1937), 49.

8. James J. Flink, *America Adopts the Automobile, 1895–1910* (Cambridge: MIT Press, 1970), 205. Albert A. Pope, *The Movement for Better Roads: An Address by Col. Albert A. Pope, of Boston, before the Board of Trade at Hartford, Conn., February 11, 1890* (Boston: Pope Manufacturing, 1892), 12, 15, 16. "Better Roads Needed," *Times*, 12 February 1890.

9. *MR* 1894, 31. BSC 22 (for 1893): ix, x. For an example of public clamor for asphalting, Hartford Equal Rights Club, records 1885–1919, meeting of 15 February 1890, vol. 2 (March 2 1889–June 23, 1894), 115.

10. McShane, *Down the Asphalt Path*, 63. *Report of the Board of Street Commissioners and Joint Special Committee of the Court of Common Council Concerning Improved Street Pavements, July 9, 1894* (Hartford: Waterman and Wright, 1894), 10. See also Robin L. Einhorn, *Property Rules: Political Economy in Chicago, 1833–1872* (Chicago: University of Chicago Press, 1991), 77. *Reports of the Majority and Minority of the Joint Special Committee Relative to Proposed Plan of Assessments for Street Improvements* (Hartford: n.p., 1874), 11, 13. BSC 4 (for 1875): 9.

11. *MR* 1893, 30. *MR* 1899, 650. For subsequent revisions of the law, *Special Acts and Resolutions Passed by the General Assembly of the State of Connecticut at the January Session, 1913* (Hartford: published by the State, 1913), 1021–22; *MR* 1915, 863–65; *MR* 1918, 794–795. The city began reducing the amount property owners were required to pay around 1920 and stopped all such assessments in 1936. Close, *History of Hartford Streets*, foreword.

12. *MR* 1894, 31. *Report Concerning Improved Street Pavements*, 6, 10. *MR* 1899, 650–52; HD 84 (1921): 1509.

13. G. A. Parker, "Report of the City Plan Committee," 18 October 1904, Municipal Art Society records, box 1, CSL. See also John B. Rae, *The Road and the Car in American Life* (Cambridge: MIT Press, 1971), 23, 205.

14. Clay McShane, "Transforming the Use of Urban Space: A Look at the Revolution in Street Pavements, 1880–1924," *Journal of Urban History* 5/3 (1979): 279–307. "Report of the Board of Street Commissioners Recommending an extra appropriation of $50,000 for paving Washington Street between Capitol Avenue and Vernon Street," drawer marked "Washington Street," HCH.

15. Bureau of the Census, *General Statistics of Cities: 1909* (Washington: Government Printing Office, 1913), 148–49. MR 1914, 289–90. Flink, *America Adopts the Automobile*, 301, 304–06.

16. Joel A. Tarr, "Urban Pollution—Many Long Years Ago," *American Heritage* 22/6 (1971): 65–69, 106. MR 1903, 446; MR 1904, 432; MR 1910, 533. City of Hartford, Department of Engineering, album marked "Photographs of Street Pavements, Paving. Div., Book No. 2," 1914–15, HPL.

17. For example, George H. Day, Electric Vehicle Company, to Board of Common Council, 22 September 1900, and Albert L. Pope, Manager, American Bicycle Company, Columbia Factory, to Court of Common Council, 24 September 1900, both drawer marked "Capitol Avenue, 1827 to 1907," HCH. *JBA* 1889–99, 313–14; *JBA* 1908–09, 887. "Asphalt Paving Board Hearing," *Times*, 18 November 1920.

18. "Report of the Board of Street Commissioners Recommending the Paving of Haynes Street, in 1898," 13 December 1897, drawer marked "Harper Street," HCH. "Petition de Paving of Hopkins St. with Sheet Asphalt," 4 October 1897; Laura C. and Lucy S. Williams, to Board of Street Commissioners, n.d.; and "Petition of John J. Dougherty et al. for the rescinding of order to pave Hopkins Street with Sheet Asphalt," 13 March 1899, all drawer marked "Holcomb Street," HCH. Bureau of the Census, *Twelfth Census of the United States (1900)*, population schedules. See also "Paving Church Street," *Courant*, 2 October 1895.

19. BSC 37 (1908–09): 22, 88: BSC 42 (1913–14): 5. "Inspection of Hartford's Street System: September 26th, 1912, at 3 P.M.," vertical file marked "1912," PDP.

20. "Street Construction," *Municipal Index 1924* (New York: American City Magazine, 1924), 209, 214–17. F. S. Besson, *City Pavements* (New York: McGraw-Hill, 1923), 33, 52, 60.

21. On the relation of land use patterns to trolley lines, see plates in *Atlas of the City of Hartford* (1909). Also, Hartford Architecture Conservancy, *Hartford Architecture*, vol. 2, *South Neighborhoods* (Hartford: Hartford Architecture Conservancy, 1980), 10; Hartford Architecture Conservancy, *Hartford Architecture*, vol. 3, *North and West Neighborhoods* (Hartford: Hartford Architecture Conservancy, 1980), 77. Sam Bass Warner, Jr., *Streetcar Suburbs: The Process of Growth in Boston (1870–1900)*, (Cambridge: Harvard University Press, 1962). For a discussion of the concentration of commercial and industrial activity at transportation nodes, Kenneth T. Jackson, *Crabgrass Frontier: The Suburbanization of the United States* (New York: Oxford University Press, 1985) 113–14. On routes taken by motorists, ACH, *Bulletin* 1/1 (1911), "Street Map of Roads out of Hartford, Conn."; *Automobile Blue Book*, vol. 2 (New York: Class Journal, 1908), 213;

Automobile Blue Book 1920, vol. 2 (New York: Automobile Blue Book Publishing, 1920), 301.

22. *Sixth Annual Report of the Highway Commissioner to the Governor for the Year Ended December 31, 1900* (Norwich: Bulletin Co., 1901), 107, 135, map opposite 200. *Biennial Report of the Highway Commissioner to the Governor, for the Years Ended December 31, 1907 and 1908* (Hartford: published by the State, 1909), plate between 222 and 223, and map titled "Connecticut: Showing System of 14 Main Trunk Lines and Subsidiary Connecting Highways as Proposed to Date." *Biennial Report of the Highway Commissioner to the Governor for the Term Beginning February 26, 1913, and Ending October 1, 1914* (Hartford: published by the State, 1914), 23, table titled "Roads Completed by the State Highway Department before October 1, 1914 and Paid For under State Aid or Trunk Line Appropriation since That Date." *Biennial Report of the Highway Commissioner to the Governor for the Term Beginning October 1, 1914, and Ending September 30, 1916* (Hartford: published by the State), table titled "Roads Completed by the Connecticut State Highway Department October 1, 1914, to September 30, 1916, Paid For from State Aid Repairs and Trunkline Repairs."

23. JCCC 1919–20, 25, 60–61. The council agreed to the 1919 request, citing the high cost of repairing macadam. "Maple Avenue Paving," ACH, *Monthly Bulletin* 22 (1920): 5. Wethersfield Ave. was the main route to Middletown, and Maple Ave. was the main route to New Haven and New York; ("Street Map of Roads out of Hartford, Conn.," ACH, *Bulletin* 1/1 [1911]: 22). For other advocacy of paving "main arteries," see "City Streets," ACH, *Monthly Bulletin* 25 (1920): 2; "Permanent Paving," ACH, *Monthly Bulletin* 29 (1920): 3; "Hartford Street Improvements," ACH, *Monthly Bulletin* 41 (1921): 6; "Hartford Streets," ACH, *Monthly Bulletin* 45 (April 1922): 2; and "Report of Traffic Committee," *Automobiler* 4/9 (1926): 28. A historical summary published by the ACH in 1944 noted lobbying for road improvements as a major part of its early work ("The Early Days," *Automobiler*, July–August 1944, 11).

24. MR 1920, 202. BSC 57 (1928–29): 7, 51, 55.

25. "First Part of Jewell Street Widening Nears Completion," *Courant*, 30 November 1913. BSC 40 (1911–12): 9; BSC 42 (1913–14): 8; BSC 44 (1915–16): 7; BSC 47 (1918–19): 9; BSC 48 (1919–20): 7–8; BSC 53 (1924–25): 7; BSC 54 (1925–26): 7; BSC 58 (1929–30): 7. "The North Main Street Widening," *Courant*, 23 March 1928. "Hartford's Streets Present Increasing Problems," *Hartford* 2/10 (1917): 2. "Many Kick against Park Street Widening," *Courant*, 6 June 1911.

26. On winter driving, "Hartford's Street—And the Winter Driver," *Automobiler* 1/9 (1923): 13. On snowplowing, BSC 27 (for 1898): xxi. "Clear Off Snow at Least to Sleighing Level," *Courant*, 3 February 1905.

27. "Trying to Solve the Snow Problem," *Courant*, 4 February 1905. "More Snow Sets City Back," *Courant*, 20 February 1914. A photograph of a trolley plow appears in *Courant*, 6 February 1920, p. 1. A photograph of the snow-dumping appears in "Turning Park River into Great White Way," *Courant*, 8 February 1920). On snow shoveling, see photos with caption "Shoveling Hartford Out from the Grip of a Snowstorm," *Times*, 16 February 1914; "Hundreds Are Given Work as City Digs From under Record Snowfall," *Times*, 21 February 1921.

28. Annual reports of the Board of Street Commissioners. In 1902, for example, the city spent $4,981 clearing downtown streets with permanent pavement and $4,828 clearing macadamized streets throughout the city. BSC 31 (for 1902): 55–56. "Blizzard Isolates Hartford as Rail Service Collapses," *Courant*, 6 February 1920. On first use of truck-mounted snowplows, BSC 50 (1921–22): 51. In that winter, the city spent $24,032 clearing paved streets and $7,052 clearing macadamized streets (BSC 50: 20–21)."Hartford's Streets—And the Winter Driver."

29. BSC 58 (1929–30): 58. "What It Means to Be a Hartford Traffic Policeman," *Courant*, 8 August 1915. Jitneys were automobiles that took passengers and charged a five-cent fare.

30. Quoted in Kenneth R. Andrews, *Nook Farm: Mark Twain's Hartford Circle* (Cambridge: Harvard University Press, 1950; Hamden, Conn.: Archon, 1967), 19–20.

31. Jan Cigliano, "Introduction," in *The Grand American Avenue, 1850–1920*, ed. Jan Cigliano and Sarah Bradford Landau (San Francisco: Pomegranate Artbooks, 1994), xi, xiv, xx–xxi.

32. *Petition to the Court of Common Council of Hartford, to Straighten Farmington Avenue, Lay Out Streets within the City Limits, and to Bring Connecticut River Water from Enfield* (Hartford: Case, Lockwood and Brainard, 1864), 3–4. *Atlas of Hartford and Tolland Counties* (1869). "Report of Highway Committee on Petition of E.C. Roberts et al. for Straightening and Widening Farmington Avenue," 27 July 1868, and "Report of the Board of Street Commissioners on Joint Resolution rel to Discontinuance of a Portion of Farmington Ave.," 23 September 1872, drawer marked "Farmington Avenue, 1855 to 1911 inclusive," HCH. Andrews, *Nook Farm*, 24.

33. "Remonstrance against Horse Rail Road on Farmington Ave.," May 1872, drawer marked "Farmington Avenue, 1855 to 1911 inclusive," HCH. *The City of Hartford Connecticut*, 1877 (bird's-eye view), n.p., CSL. Hartford Architecture Conservancy, *Hartford Architecture*, vol. 3, 138. *The Hartford Blue-Book: A Complete and Accurate List of Hartford's Society People* (Hartford: Fowler and Miller,

1897). *City Atlas of Hartford, Conn., Compiled, Drawn and Published from Actual Surveys* (Philadelphia: G.M. Hopkins, 1880), plates L, M, N, and O. *Atlas of the City of Hartford* (1896), plates 3, 5, 6, 18, 19, 20. Like its counterparts in other cities, Farmington Avenue was also chosen as the site for two major churches: St. Joseph's Cathedral and Immanuel Congregational Church.

34. On suburbanization in West Hartford, see *Atlas of the City of Hartford* (1909), plate 22; *Atlas of the City of Hartford and the Town of West Hartford, Connecticut (1920)* (New York: Sanborn, 1921). William H. Hall, *West Hartford* (Hartford: James A. Reid, 1930), 263. On paving, see BSC 28 (for 1899): x. "Asphalt Still Unpopular." Special Committee to Court of Common Council, 21 March 1910, drawer marked "Farmington Avenue, 1855 to 1911 inclusive," HCH. BSC 39 (1910–11): 6; BSC 40 (1911–12): 9. "Asylum Street [*sic*] Widening," ACH, *Monthly Bulletin* 29 (1920): 2.

35. *Atlas of the City of Hartford* (1909), plates 5, 15. *Atlas of the City of Hartford (1920)*, plates 3, 7, 8, 9. *Insurance Maps of Hartford Connecticut*, vol. 4 (New York: Sanborn, 1922 and revisions to 1941), plates 405, 408, 409. *Geer's Hartford, East Hartford, West Hartford Directory* (Hartford: Hartford Printing, 1929), 1665–68. "Westward Ho," *Hartford* 7/2 (1921): 6. Chapman, *My Hartford*, 24. Hartford Architecture Conservancy, *Hartford Architecture*, vol. 3, 152–54, 185.

36. "Suburbanism within a City," *Times*, 3 January 1942. Photographs in folder marked "Hartford—Streets—Washington Street," Hartford Collection (photographs), box 5, CSL. On lack of trolley lines, *Town and City Atlas of the State of Connecticut* (Boston: D.H. Hurd, 1893); one trolley line, in fact, made an odd detour down narrow Lafayette Street to bypass Washington Street. *Dau's Blue Book for Hartford, Conn.*, (New York: Dau Publishing, 1909).

37. *Automobile Blue Book* (1908), vol. 2, 213. *Automobile Blue Book*, vol. 2 (New York: Automobile Blue Book Publishing, 1911), 233. *Automobile Blue Book*, vol. 2 (Chicago: Automobile Blue Book Publishing, 1916), 207. *Automobile Blue Book 1920*, vol. 2 (New York: Automobile Blue Book Publishing, 1920), 301. Photograph by F. S. Berry ("Negative No. 30") in vertical file marked "Washington Street, east side" [*sic*], Samuel Taylor Collection, CHS. Louis R. Cheney, President, Automobile Club of Hartford, circular letter, 15 July 1912, vertical file marked "1912. P & A—Periodicals. Associations," PDP. "What Hartford's Auto Club Has Accomplished," *Courant*, 13 February 1916.

38. *Atlas of the City of Hartford* (1909), plates 2, 8. *Atlas of the City of Hartford* (1920), plates 1, 11. "Report of the Board of Street Commissioners, Recommending the paving of Washington St. from Capitol Ave. to Vernon St. with three-inch bituminous pavement laid on existing macadam," and "Minority Re-

port # 14 [of Board of Finance]," both drawer marked "Washington Street," HCH. BSC 50 (1921–22): 5. *Insurance Maps of Hartford, Connecticut* vol. 2, plates 216, 228, 229, 232, 233. HD 83 (1920): 1256, 1258, 1451–52. HD for 1929, 1791–92. Chapman, *My Hartford,* 24.

39. *Dau's Blue Book for Hartford, Conn.* (1909). *Dau's Blue Book for Hartford, Conn.* (New York: Dau Publishing, 1913). *The Hartford and Northern Connecticut Blue Book* (New York: Blue Books, 1929), 106.

40. On the quietness of the streets, see Fred E. Dayton, "Hartford's Mauve Decade, No. 89: As Life Was in the 90s," *Times,* 26 June 1931. Photograph dated May 6, 1899, in Dayton, "Hartford's Mauve Decade, No. 74," *Times,* 9 June 1931. Dayton, "Hartford's Mauve Decade, No. 76," *Times,* 11 June 1931. MR 1900, photograph with caption, "Main Street, Looking South from Asylum Street, 1900." Photographs: one dated February 1866, one labeled "Fourth Congregational Church and North Main Street (1885)," another "Htfd St.—Main St.—1896," and two labeled "Main Street from Mulberry Street, 1900," in folder marked "Hartford—Streets—Main Street," Hartford Collection photographs, CSL. Photograph labeled "State Street, from Main," (n.d. [ca. 1890]), in the same folder. Photographs with captions "Main Street. Conn Mutual Building," and "City Hall (Old State House)," *Views. City of Hartford* (Boston: Nolman Photo, 1885). Photographs with captions "Views on Farmington Avenue," "Farmington Avenue Showing Cathedral," "Scene on Wethersfield Avenue," "Washington Street," and "View on Main Street," *Art Work of Hartford.* "Main Street Looking South. In Left Distance the steeple of St. John's Episcopal Church. This photograph is dated 1905," photo no. 130, Taylor Collection Photographs, CSL. On the 1890s habit of crossing in the middle of the block, see also "Pedestrians at Crossings," *Automobiler* 4/7 (1926): 17. On larger cities, see Mark S. Foster, *From Streetcar to Superhighway: American City Planners and Urban Transportation, 1900–1940* (Philadelphia: Temple University Press, 1981), 37; Warner, *Streetcar Suburbs,* 25.

41. *The Charter and Revised Ordinances of the City of Hartford: With the Amendments and Other Acts Relating to the Charter, in Force January 1, 1884* (Hartford: Fowler and Miller, 1884), 245. The top speeds horse-drawn vehicles could reach—eight to fifteen miles per hour—were not much higher than Hartford's legal limit (Flink, *America Adopts the Automobile,* 180). Frances A. McCook, "Main Street—Now and Then," typescript, 9–10, CHS. Fred E. Dayton, "Hartford's Mauve Decade, No. 201," *Times,* 5 November 1931. "Runaways," *Courant,* 28 May 1880. "A Lively Runaway," 27 March 1889. "Boy Knocked Down," *Courant,* 24 January 1895. "Team Runs Away," *Courant,* 20 April 1895. "Woman Badly Injured," *Courant,* 19 June 1899. On the introduction of trol-

leys, see Glenn Weaver, *Hartford: An Illustrated History of Connecticut's Capital* (Woodland Hills, Calif.: Windsor Publications; Hartford: Connecticut Historical Society, 1982), 104. On trolley accidents, "Milk Wagon Upset," *Courant*, 12 May 1899; "His Life Crushed Out by a Trolley," *Times*, 27 June 1907. "Additional City News," *Times*, 14 December 1895. The situation in late nineteenth-century Hartford differed from that in larger and more densely developed cities like New York, where traffic fatalities were relatively common (McShane, *Down the Asphalt Path*, 49).

42. Maxim, *Horseless Carriage Days*, 43–45, 49. Hiram Percy Maxim, "Motoring Sixteen Years Ago," ACH, *Bulletin* 1/1 (1911): 4. Despite Maxim's claim, it is uncertain whether this really was the first time a self-propelled vehicle was driven in Hartford. Some historians have claimed that a local inventor, Apollos Kinsey, drove a steam-powered wagon nearly a century earlier, in 1797 (McShane, *Down the Asphalt Path*, 83). "Automobile Club," *Courant*, 22 February 1902. "Autos in Hartford," *Times*, 10 October 1902.

43. McShane, *Down the Asphalt Path*, 113. For a somewhat different interpretation, see Flink, "Regulating the Motor Vehicle," chapter 6 of *America Adopts the Automobile*.

44. "Report of the Ordinance Committee upon Petition de Goat Teams," 4 April 1879, and "An Ordinance Relating to Nuisances," 4 April 1879, both box marked "Ordinances to 1884," HCH. The banning of bicycles seems to have been an afterthought, a minor amendment to an ordinance banning the real menace: goat carts, which were children's toys but which sometimes panicked horses. On bicycles' growing popularity and cities' response, see McShane, *Down the Asphalt Path*, 54, 116. On the dangers of bicycles, see also untitled editorial, *Courant*, 11 May 1895.

45. On the bicycle ban, see "Petition of Goodwin Collier and Others for Repeal of Ordinance de Goat Teams," and "A.H. Olmsted and Others—Petition For Repeal of Ordinance," both box marked "Ordinances to 1884," HCH. JBA 1881–82, 108. JBA 1889–90, 109, 142–43, 160. On the 1896 change in the speed limit, JCCB 1896–97, 214–15.

46. "One Year's Damage Done by Autos," *Connecticut Department of Motor Vehicles Bulletin No. 17* (27 March 1925). *The General Statutes of Connecticut: Revision of 1902* (Hartford: Case, Lockwood & Brainard, 1902), 552–53. "Warrants for Eight Autoists," *Courant*, 11 June 1904.

47. "Legislators Ride 40 Miles an Hour!" *Times*, 11 May 1905. "The Auto Bills as Amended," *Courant*, 28 June 1905. "Farmers Criticize Highway Commissioner," *Courant*, 28 July 1905. During the 1900s and 1910s, the Automobile Club of Hartford also lobbied legislators in a successful attempt to shape legisla-

tion. "What Hartford's Auto Club Has Accomplished"; "Changes in Motor Vehicle Law," ACH, *Monthly Bulletin* 13 (1919): 6–7. *Laws Concerning Motor Vehicles, 1909*, (Hartford: Case Lockwood and Brainard for the Secretary of State, 1909). Office of Commissioner of Motor Vehicles, *Motor Vehicle Laws, State of Connecticut* (Hartford: Case, Lockwood and Brainard, [1917]).

48. Office of Commissioner of Motor Vehicles, *Connecticut Motor Vehicle Laws: Revised to July 1, 1927* (Hartford: L.E. Smith [1927]). "Proposed Automobile Legislation before General Assembly," *Department of Motor Vehicles Bulletin No. 41* (18 March 1927).

49. John J. Brouder, ed., *Hartford Municipal Yearbook* (Hartford: Calhoun Press, 1914), 163–67. "Many Discuss Traffic Rules," *Courant*, 10 November 1911. "Police Commissioners Unanimously Approve Traffic Regulations," *Courant*, 20 September 1921. "1911–1921," ACH, *Monthly Bulletin* 39 (1921): 2. By pairing the terms "motoring" and "public," the ACH was clearly attempting to conflate the interests of motorists with the general public good.

50. Advertisement entitled "Hartford's Business Center Developing around the New Municipal Building," *Courant*, 6 May 1917.

51. MR 1903, 459; MR 1904, 418; MR 1917, 230. Ethel Usher, "Analysis of Automobile Accidents: A Summary, Classified by Towns, of the Conditions under Which the Motor Vehicle Accidents in Connecticut Occurred during 1925," *Connecticut Department of Motor Vehicles, Supplement to Bulletin No. 28*, 16 August 1926. Garrett J. Farrell, "Annual Report of the Chief of Police for the Year Ending March 31st, 1926," drawer marked "Police Department, Annual and Quarterly Reports, 1915 to 1939," HCH.

52. "Speeding Motorists," *Post*, 29 May 1907. "Check on Autoists," *Post*, 17 May 1907. "Rights of the Road," *Post*, 11 June 1907. "Lights vs. Speed," *Post*, 27 June 1907. Untitled editorial, *Post*, 13 June 1907.

53. "A Timely Suggestion," *Post*, 6 June 1907. See also "A Curious Indifference," *Courant*, 24 November 1916.

54. "Diary of a Hartford Motorist," ACH, *Bulletin* 1/1 (1911): 12–15. "Diary of a Hartford Motorist," ACH, *Bulletin* 1/2 (1911): 13–14.

55. Flink, *America Adopts the Automobile*, 64–66, 73. McShane, *Down the Asphalt Path*, 174–77. G. K. Dustin, Secretary, ACH, to George W. Beach, 8 May 1906, ACH correspondence, volume containing correspondence from 24 April 1906 to 19 March 1908, ACH, West Hartford, Connecticut. "What Hartford's Auto Club Has Accomplished."

56. Viviana A. Zelizer, *Pricing the Priceless Child: The Changing Social Value of Children* (New York: Basic Books, 1985), 32–37, 45–49. Robbins B. Stoeckel, *Report of the Commissioner of Motor Vehicles to His Excellency the Governor, for the Term Ended June 30, 1920* (Hartford: published by the State, 1920), 20. Rob-

bins B. Stoeckel, "Accidents to Children," *State of Connecticut Department of Motor Vehicles Bulletin No. 32* (15 June 1926).

57. BSC 38 (1909–10): 11–12. On islands of safety in other cities, see Besson, *City Pavements*, 97–102. The Trumbull Street isle of safety had been strongly advocated by the Municipal Art Society (Municipal Art Society, *Publications of the Municipal Art Society of Hartford, Connecticut, no. 10, Competition for an Electrolier to Be Combined with an "Isle of Safety" at the Intersection of Trumbull and Pearl Streets* (Hartford: Municipal Art Society, 1908). "Letters from the People: Traffic Regulations," *Courant*, 16 November 1911. MR 1914, 305; Roscoe N. Clark, City Engineer, to Board of Street Commissioners, 27 August 1913, drawer marked "Illuminated Signs and Marquees, Isles of Safety," HCH. Photograph captioned "State St. Isle of Safety Looking East," ca. 1924, accession no. 1964-119-0, CHS.

58. Photograph labeled "Isle of Safety at Tunnel," 21 April 1915, album marked "Dep't of Engineering 1914–1915: Photographs of Street Pavements, Paving Div., Book No. 2," HPL. JCCC 1917–18, 622. Herbert S. Swan, *Traffic and Thoroughfare Plan, Hartford, Connecticut* (Hartford: Commission on the City Plan, 1926), 22. "Making Streets of Hartford Accident-Proof Latest Plan of Police," *Courant*, 14 July 1918. "A Dangerous Habit," ACH, *Monthly Bulletin* 10 (1919): 1. Richard F. Dow, letter in ACH, *Monthly Bulletin* 34 (1921): 6.

59. For discussions of the problem in a larger context, see McShane, *Down the Asphalt Path*, 176, 189, 201–02; Zelizer, *Pricing the Priceless Child*, 37–43.

60. MR 1918, 220.

61. Advertisements, *Post*, 4 May 1918, 8; *Post*, 1 June 1918, 6. "Pedestrian Signs," ACH, *Monthly Bulletin* 14 (1919): 3.

62. "Police Chiefs Called Together in Plan to Check Auto Accidents," *Courant*, 13 August 1921. "Police Chiefs Decide on Week of Sept. 19 for War on Accidents," *Courant*, 16 August 1921. "'For Safety's Sake,' Posters Will Mark One-Time Dangers," *Courant*, 18 September 1921. "5,000 see Accident Film," *Courant*, 27 September 1921. Graphic, *Times*, 24 September 1921, 1.

63. *Public Acts Passed by the General Assembly of the State of Connecticut in the Year 1921* (Hartford: published by the State, 1921), 3389. "Police Chiefs Decide on Week of Sept. 19 for War on Accidents"; "Traffic Laws For Pedestrians," ACH, *Monthly Bulletin* 19 (1919): 7. "Regulation of Pedestrian Traffic," ACH, *Monthly Bulletin* 22 (1920): 2.

64. "Pedestrian Regulations," ACH, *Monthly Bulletin* 26 (1920): 6; photograph, *Courant*, 31 October 1920, with caption "Although the new traffic signals have been installed on central street corners for many weeks, the police say that many persist in disregarding the signs." "Police Arrest Four in New Jay Walking Crusade on Main Street," *Courant*, 20 March 1921. Photographs, *Courant*,

20 March 1921, headed "How women who violated traffic rules were made to obey by police yesterday," and "Back, folks, back up and watch the signal." "Pedestrian Regulation," ACH, *Monthly Bulletin* 34 (1921): 8.

65. "One View of the Safety-First Rules," *Courant*, 20 September 1921. "'Cop' to Face Board for Arrest of Alleged 'Jay-Walker,'" *Courant*, 23 September 1921. For a similar letter, see "Dislikes 'Blue-Coated Czar,'" *Courant*, 21 September 1921. For another account of the privileges given to automobile over pedestrian traffic, see Ashleigh E. Brilliant, "Some Aspects of Mass Motorization in Southern California, 1919–1929," *Southern California Quarterly* 47/2 (1965): 191–208.

66. "Local Auto Notes," *Courant*, 6 May 1917. See also "Crossing the Street," *Courant*, 1 January 1919; "Stepped from Car in Front of Auto," *Courant*, 26 October 1920; and "Automobile Accidents," *Connecticut Hebrew Record*, 27 October 1922. Robbins B. Stoeckel, "The Pedestrian Question," *Department of Motor Vehicles Bulletin No. 69* ([16 December 1929]; this report did not specify the Connecticut city in which the incident took place). "Two Viewpoints on Automobile Accidents," *Automobiler* 1/10 (1923): 10.

67. "Tyranny of the Auto," *Courant*, 3 January 1930. Garrett J. Farrell, Chief of Police, annual reports for 1925–26, 1926–27, 1927–28, 1928–29, 1929–30, 1930–31, 1931–32, 1938–39, drawer marked "Police Department Annual and Quarterly Reports, 1915–1939," HCH. The stabilization of casualties was a statewide phenomenon (Ethel Usher, "Connecticut Motor Vehicles Statistics for 1930," *Department of Motor Vehicles Bulletin No. 79* (11 May 1931); "Connecticut Motor Vehicle Statistics for 1932," *Department of Motor Vehicles Bulletin No. 91* [15 February 1933]). Connecticut Motor Vehicle photograph captioned "Jaywalkers on Main Street, Hartford," *Department of Motor Vehicles Bulletin No. 8* (16 June 1924). "Safety Work for Motor Clubs," *Automobiler* 3/12 (1925): 5. Robbins B. Stoeckel, "The Pedestrian Question," *Department of Motor Vehicles Bulletin No. 69* (16 December 1929). Photograph labeled "Shopping District: Main St. looking south from near Morgan St. Christ Church Cathedral on the Right," n.d. (ca. 1922–24), folder marked "Main Street," Hartford Collection photographs, HPL. Photo looking south on Main Street from State House Square, mid-1920s, in Weaver, *Hartford*, 110. Photograph labeled "Corner of Main & State St. (Harvey & Lewis Building)," ca. 1934–36, negative no. 354, CHS. "Pedestrians at Crossings," *Automobiler* 4/7 (1926): 17.

68. MR 1916, 38. "Street Changes Urged and City Auditorium Suggested by Mayor," *Courant*, 28 November 1916. Carrère and Hastings, *A Plan of the City of Hartford: Preliminary Report* (Hartford: Case, Lockwood and Brainard for the Commission on the City Plan, 1912). "City Must Provide for Future Growth,"

Courant, 1 April 1917. "Street Money Voted," *Courant*, 4 April 1917. "Street Extension Plans Endorsed," *Hartford* 2/4 (1917): 9. "From Henney to Rankin: 25 Years of Municipal Politics, No. 59," *Times*, 8 February 1932.

69. "Traffic Changes," *Hartford* 5/10 (July 1920): 6. *JCCC* 1919–20, 705–07. *BSC* 58 (1929–30): 58 (The street department figures on automobiles apparently included trucks as well.) "Report of the Commission on the City Plan, 1920–1922," drawer marked "City Plan Commission, Communications, Reports, Etc.," HCH. "Connecticut Motor Vehicle Statistics for 1929," *Department of Motor Vehicles Bulletin No. 72* (18 June 1930).

70. "Chamber of Commerce Helping to Solve City's Traffic Problems," *Hartford* 5/11 (1920): 7. "Trumbull Street Cut-Off Advocated by Chamber's Municipal Affairs Committee," *Hartford* 6/5 (1921): 13. "Eventually, Why Not Now?" *Hartford* 7/12 (1922): 6. "Hartford Street Improvements," ACH, *Monthly Bulletin* 41 (1921): 6. "Traffic Committee Reports in Detail," *Automobiler* 1/8 (1923), 12. "Drastic Traffic Changes Adopted," *Automobiler* 3/8 (1925): 12–13. Arthur Fifoot, "Down Town Parking," *Automobiler* 3/11 (1925): 5–6, 17. "Annual Report of Chief of Police for Year Ending March 31st, 1923," and "Report of Chief of Police for Year Ending March 31st, 1927," both drawer marked "Police Department, Annual and Quarterly Reports, 1915 to 1939," HCH.

71. "What It Means to Be a Hartford Traffic Policeman," *Courant*, 8 August 1915. MR 1920, 172. "Annual Report of Chief of Police for Year Ending March 31st, 1923," and "Report from Chief of Police for Year Ending March 31, 1929," drawer marked "Police Department Annual and Quarterly Reports, 1915 to 1939," HCH. "Another Mechanical 'Cop' Installed," *Courant*, 3 December 1925.

72. "Where Shall We Park?" ACH, *Monthly Bulletin* 20 (1919): 6. Merchants had also objected to the adoption of one-way traffic regulations for downtown streets in the 1910s. Joint Committee on Ordinances by John E. Smith, Clerk, to Court of Common Council, 27 November 1911; "In Re Traffic Regulation of State Street: Petition," 25 May 1912; "Petition of Jerome E. Sage et al. Re 'One Way' For Pratt Street," 23 September 1914; "Petition de Removal of Traffic Restriction on Asylum Street," 13 April 1917, all four in drawer marked "Traffic: Signals, Policemen, Etc., 1896 to 1926," HCH.

73. "What Can Be Done about Parking Space?" ACH, *Monthly Bulletin* 18 (1919): 1–2. "Report of the Commission on the City Plan, 1920–22," drawer marked "City Plan Commission: Communications, Reports, Etc.," HCH. Swan, *Traffic and Thoroughfare Plan*, quotation on 56 and diagram on 57 ("Parked Cars, Downtown Hartford, July 24, 1925"). Fifoot, "Down Town Parking." "Report from Chief of Police for Year Ending March 31, 1929."

74. Norman C. Stevens, *Third Annual Message of Mayor Norman C. Stevens to the Court of Common Council of Hartford, Connecticut, May 10, 1926* (n.p., n.d.), 6–7.

75. Swan, *Traffic and Thoroughfare Plan*, 10, 22, 23, 26, 58, 60, 61.

76. Ibid., 29–34.

77. Ibid., 37.

78. "Traffic Signals" *Automobiler* 4/8 (1926): 17. "'Boulevard Stop' Plan to Start Feb. 24," *Courant*, 18 February 1930. "Annual Report from Police Department for Year Ending March 31, 1931," drawer marked "Police Department Annual and Quarterly Reports, 1915 to 1939," HCH. "Petition re 'Stop' and 'Go' lights at the intersection of Maple Ave., Adelaide and Kenneth Sts," 8 September 1930, drawer marked "Traffic: Signals, Policemen, Etc., 1927 to 1930," HCH.

Chapter 9

1. John M. Carrère, "City Improvement from the Artistic Standpoint," in *Publications of the Municipal Art Society of Hartford, Connecticut, no. 7, City Improvement from the Artistic Standpoint, an Address by John M. Carrère, New York* (Hartford: Municipal Art Society, 1908), 7.

2. Carrère, "City Improvement," 8.

3. *Publications of the Municipal Art Society of Hartford, Connecticut, no. 1, Officers, Directors, Standing Committees, Constitution, By-Laws, and Members. What Is a Municipal Art Society?* (Hartford: Municipal Art Society, 1904), 3–5. Biographical sketches of Henney, Flagg, and Godard in *Hartford in 1912: Story of the Capitol City, Present and Prospective* (Hartford: Hartford Post, 1912), 163, 173. On Schutz, see HD 67 (1904): 384. On Cheney, see *Hartford Bridge Souvenir Number* (East Hartford: American Enterprise, 1908). On Bennett, see Carole Nichols, *Votes and More for Women: Suffrage and After in Connecticut* (New York: Institute for Research in History and the Haworth Press, 1983), 13, and William Joseph Martin, *Souvenir Book of the Municipal Building Dedication* (Hartford: William Joseph Martin, 1915), 65.

4. *What Is a Municipal Art Society?* 17–24, at 17, 18, 23. On Bushnell's legacy, see also *Publications of the Municipal Art Society of Hartford, Connecticut, no. 2, The Grouping of Public Buildings* (Hartford: Municipal Art Society, 1904), 45–46.

5. *What Is a Municipal Art Society?* 23. *Publications of the Municipal Art Society of Hartford, Connecticut, no. 4, Proceedings of the Annual Meeting, October 17, 1905. Some Municipal Problems* (Hartford: Municipal Art Society, 1906), 23.

6. *What Is a Municipal Art Society?* 17.

7. "Report of the City Plan Committee," 18 October 1904, in envelope labeled "Reports of Standing Committees, 1904-5-6-8," box 1, MAS. On this anatomical metaphor for urban function, see Elizabeth Grosz, "Bodies-Cities," in *Sexuality & Space*, Princeton Papers on Architecture, vol. 1 (New York: Princeton Architectural Press, 1992), and Clay McShane, *Down the Asphalt Path: The Automobile and the American City* (New York: Columbia University Press, 1994), 65. On the Municipal Art Society's affection for Haussmann, *What Is a Municipal Art Society?* 17.

8. "Report of the City Plan Committee." On cognitive mapping, see also J. Douglas Porteous, *Environment and Behavior: Planning and Everyday Urban Life* (Reading, Mass.: Addison-Wesley, 1977).

9. Municipal Art Society, *Proceedings of the Annual Meeting, October 17, 1905*, 18–19. At this time, city hall was the building now known as the Old State House. *Publications of the Municipal Art Society of Hartford, Connecticut*, no. 6, *Proceedings of the Annual Meeting, November 27, 1906* (Hartford: Municipal Art Society, 1907), 32. Population figures are from HD 86 (1923–24): 1556.

10. *Publications of the Municipal Art Society of Hartford, Connecticut*, no. 14, *Proceedings of the Annual Meeting, November 22, 1910* (Hartford: Municipal Art Society, 1911), 17. Edwin Knox Mitchell to Walter S. Schutz, 28 April 1906, envelope marked "Reports of Standing Committees, 1904-5-6-8," MAS. Minutes of the annual meeting of 21 October 1913, in binder containing minutes from 1908 to 1933, MAS. William H. Honniss, President, and Leila A. Anderson, Secretary, to membership, 30 March 1917, box 2, MAS. In a 1906 letter, the Hartford Business Men's Association president, Normand F. Allen, spoke of the need to demolish buildings and widen streets partly to aid suburban commuting. "A Glance Ahead," *Times*, 1 January 1906.

11. William H. Wilson, *The City Beautiful Movement* (Baltimore: Johns Hopkins University Press, 1989), 91–92. Daniel Bluestone, *Constructing Chicago* (New Haven: Yale University Press, 1991), 183.

12. Daniel H. Burnham and Edward H. Bennett, *Plan of Chicago* (Chicago: Commercial Club, 1909), 116, quoted in Bluestone, *Constructing Chicago*, 195. Paul Boyer, *Urban Masses and Moral Order in America, 1820–1920* (Cambridge: Harvard University Press, 1978), 252–76. Ann Douglas, *The Feminization of American Culture* (New York: Avon Books, 1977), 397–99. Ann Douglas, *Terrible Honesty: Mongrel Manhattan in the 1920s* (New York: Noonday Press, 1995), 217–53. Gail Bederman, *Manliness and Civilization: A Cultural History of Gender and Race in the United States, 1880–1917* (Chicago: University of Chicago Press, 1995).

13. *Publications of the Municipal Art Society of Hartford, Connecticut*, no. 13, *Proceedings of the Annual Meeting, February 25, 1910. Officers, Committees,*

Reports of Standing Committees, "What We Can Do to Improve Hartford" (Hartford: Municipal Art Society, 1911), 21–22. Publications of the Municipal Art Society of Hartford, Connecticut, no. 15, The Old State House, Hartford: Why It Should Be Preserved (Hartford: Municipal Art Society, 1911), 9. The Grouping of Public Buildings, 62. On the uplifting power of the Old State House, see also "Common Council Petition of Prominent Citizens," submitted by the Civic Club in February 1906, in Publications of the Municipal Art Society of Hartford, Connecticut, no. 5, Preservation and Restoration of City Hall (Hartford: Municipal Art Society, 1906), 15. In pleading for the preservation of the Old State House, the society emphasized the building as an architectural and artistic form connected with a presumably admirable Yankee past. Reverent nostalgia served to conceal the building's more problematic — indeed, nearly treasonous — history as the site of the Hartford Convention of 1814.

14. Robert M. Fogelson, America's Armories: Architecture, Society and Public Order (Cambridge: Harvard University Press, 1989), 182–84.

15. The Grouping of Public Buildings, 7–20, at 7, 14. Municipal Art Society, Proceedings of the Annual Meeting, October 17, 1905, 28–30.

16. Municipal Art Society, Proceedings of the Annual Meeting, October 17, 1905, 19–21. Municipal Art Society, Proceedings of the Annual Meeting, November 27, 1906, 31–32.

17. George A. Parker to J. Horace McFarland, 4 May 1905, folder marked "American Civic Assn, Outgoing H's," box marked "American Civic Association, Park Dept., 1904–1905, Outgoing Letters A–M," GAPP. Municipal Art Society, Proceedings of the Annual Meeting, November 27, 1906, 31–32.

18. H. G. Loomis, undated handwritten letter, inside bound volume of minutes, 14 June 1904 — 17 Oct. 1905, box 1, MAS.

19. "John M. Holcombe Chosen President," Courant, 10 December 1906. Mel Scott, American City Planning since 1890 (Berkeley: University of California Press, 1969), 80–81. "Hartford in 1907: How to Make the City Bigger and Better," Times, 1 January 1907. HD 69 (1906–07): 209. "Legislation for the City of Hartford," Courant, 12 January 1907. "Changes in the City Government," Courant, 15 January 1907. Publications of the Municipal Art Society of Hartford, Connecticut, no. 8, Proceedings of the Annual Meeting, January 25, 1908. Officers, Members, Reports of Standing Committees (Hartford: Municipal Art Society, 1908), 22–23. First Annual Report of the Commission on the City Plan to the Mayor and Court of Common Council of the City of Hartford, Conn., for the Year Ending March 31, 1908 (Hartford: Case, Lockwood and Brainard, 1908), 6.

20. George A. Parker to R. N. Clark, Secretary, City Plan Commission, 22 August 1912, in vertical file marked "1912. R + M. Reports," PDP.

21. Municipal Art Society, *Proceedings of the Annual Meeting, January 25, 1908*, 22–23. *Second Annual Report of the Commission on the City Plan to the Mayor and Court of Common Council of the City of Hartford, Conn., for the Year Ending March 31, 1909* (Hartford: City Printing, 1909), 7–8. Frederick L. Ford, "The Commission on the City Plan at Hartford," *American City* 3/5 (1910): 237–39.

22. *First Annual Report of the Commission on the City Plan*, 16. *Third Annual Report of the Commission on the City Plan to the Mayor and Court of Common Council* (Hartford: Case, Lockwood and Brainard, 1910), 22–23.

23. [George A. Parker], "Suggestions Regarding a Report on Allen Boulevard," n.d. (probably late 1909), unlabeled black binder, PDP. Ford, "The Commission on the City Plan," 238–39. *Second Annual Report of the Commission on the City Plan*, 7, 9. *Fifth Annual Report of the Commission on City Plan to the Mayor and Court of Common Council* (Hartford: Case, Lockwood and Brainard, 1912), 16 and accompanying map. *Sixth Annual Report of the Commission on the City Plan to the Mayor and Court of Common Council, City of Hartford, Connecticut, Year Ending March 31, 1913* (n.p., n.d.), 5–6.

24. Parker to Clark, 22 August 1912. [George A. Parker], "Report Regarding the So-Called 'Allen Boulevard,'" 17 December 1909, unlabeled black binder, PDP. *Second Annual Report of the Commission on the City Plan*, 8. MR 1909, 22. MR 1910, 22.

25. *Second Annual Report of the Commission on the City Plan*, 9, 15–18. *Fifth Annual Report of the Commission on the City Plan*, 7–16.

26. *Second Annual Report of the Commission on the City Plan*, 19–24.

27. Carrère and Hastings, *A Plan of the City of Hartford: Preliminary Report* (Hartford: Case, Lockwood and Brainard for the Commission on the City Plan, 1912), 7–8. On the Progressive-Era metaphor of the city as a machine, see John D. Fairfield, "The Scientific Management of Urban Space: Professional City Planning and the Legacy of Progressive Reform," *Journal of Urban History* 20/2 (1994): 179–204. Lewis Mumford described the machine metaphor for the city as emphasizing quantitative matters such as "expansion, extension, progress, mechanical multiplication, power," and the organism metaphor as emphasizing qualitative issues of "growth, norms, shapes, inter-relationships, implications, associations, and societies. [By understanding the city in these terms,] we realize that the aim of the social process is not to make men more powerful, but to make them more completely developed, more human, more capable of carrying on the specifically human attributes of culture" (Lewis Mumford, *The Culture of Cities* [New York: Harcourt, Brace, 1938], 303). See also Kevin Lynch, *Good City Form* (Cambridge: MIT Press, 1992), 81–98. On the death of Carrère, see "Car-

rère, John Merven," in *Dictionary of American Biography*, vol. 3 (New York: Charles Scribner's Sons, 1929), 518–20.

28. Carrère and Hastings, *Plan of the City of Hartford*, 9, 10, 13–15.

29. Ibid., 37–38, 48, 77, map facing 14.

30. Ibid., 14–15, 32, 59, 72, 75, 76, 78, 84, map facing 14, photos opposite 40.

31. Carrère, "City Improvement," 8.

32. *Hartford in 1912*, 18. *Fifth Annual Report of the Commission on the City Plan*, 6. George A. Parker to *Springfield Republican*, 30 July 1912, vertical file marked "1912 Park Business. Park Letter," PDP. Carrère and Hastings, *A Plan of the City of Hartford*, map opposite 14. "Choosing a Market Site," *Courant*, 19 August 1918.

33. *JCCC* 1917–18, 19–20; *JCCC* 1924–25, 11. "Report by Commission on City Plan in Re New Railroad Station," 11 May 1914, "Report of the Commission on the City Plan on Petition of J.H. Clarkin for new streets between Wethersfield Avenue and Franklin Avenue," 15 August 1921, and "Report of the Commission on the City Plan, 1920–1922," 24 April 1922, all three in drawer marked "City Plan Commission. Communications, Reports, Etc.," HCH. "Chamber of Commerce Authorizes 'Greater Hartford' Committee," *Hartford* 7/ 12 (1922): 7. "Annexation Bill Bitterly Opposed," *Courant*, 22 April 1925. Wilson, *The City Beautiful Movement*, 2, 285–90. Scott, *American City Planning*, 117–25. Blaine A. Brownell, "Urban Planning, the Planning Profession, and the Motor Vehicle in Early Twentieth-Century America," in *Shaping an Urban World*, ed. Gordon E. Cherry (New York: St. Martin's Press, 1977), 59–77. W. A. Graham, "Emphasis upon Beauty of Usefulness," *Hartford* 1/8 (1916): 1.

34. *Publications of the Municipal Art Society of Hartford, Connecticut*, no. 16, *Proceedings of the Seventh Annual Meeting, December 4, 1911. Officers, Members and Reports of Standing Committees* (Hartford: Municipal Art Society, 1912), 14. "The Municipal Art Society of Hartford: Minutes of Latest Meetings of the Society and of the Directors," 2 February 1928, folder 8, box 4, MAS. Minutes of directors' meeting, 6 November 1919, binder containing minutes of meetings, 15 December 1908 – 29 June 1933, box 1, MAS. Edwin Knox Mitchell to William H. Honniss, 4 May 1933, folder 8, box 4, MAS. Certification by State of Connecticut, Office of the Secretary, 1 July 1940, folder no. 9, box 4, MAS.

35. David M. Kennedy, *Over Here: The First World War and American Society* (Oxford: Oxford University Press, 1980), 92, 250, 287, 292. Robert H. Wiebe, *The Search for Order, 1877–1920* (New York: Hill and Wang, 1967), 293–302. M. Christine Boyer, *Dreaming the Rational City: The Myth of American City Planning* (Cambridge: MIT Press, 1983), 61–66, 153–55.

36. *JCCC* 1924–25, 10–11.

37. Seymour I. Toll, *Zoned American* (New York: Grossman, 1969), 123–29. Garrett Power, "The Advent of Zoning," *Planning Perspectives* 4 (1989): 1–13. Frederick L. Ford, "The Scope of City Planning in the United States," in *City Planning: Hearing before the Committee on the District of Columbia, United States Senate, on the Subject of City Planning* (Washington: Government Printing Office, 1910), 70–73.

38. Commission on the City Plan, minutes of 9 May 1911 meeting, in unlabeled black binder, PDP. See also "Against Sky Scrapers, Municipal Art Society," *Times*, 28 November 1906.

39. On Parker's Southern travel, e.g., George A. Parker to Richard M. Venable, 15 September 1905, folder marked "American Civic Assn, Outgoing B's," box marked "American Civic Association, Park Dept., 1904–1905. Outgoing Letters A–M," GAPP; Parker to Belle Williams, 29 November 1905, folder marked "Keney Park C's," box marked "Keney Park Outgoing Letters, 1900–1906, A–M," GAPP. On Parker's plantation job and his racism, Parker to Mrs. C. A. Woods, 22 February 1904, folder marked "Park Census, Marion S.C.," box marked "American Park and Outdoor Art Association, Park Census, Outgoing Letters, 1901–1904, G–New York City," GAPP. On Jim Crow laws and progressive support for them, C. Vann Woodward, *The Strange Career of Jim Crow* 3d ed. (New York: Oxford University Press, 1974), 97–102; William A. Link, *The Paradox of Southern Progressivism, 1880–1930* (Chapel Hill: University of North Carolina Press, 1992), 61–63, 68; Dewey W. Grantham, *Southern Progressivism: The Reconciliation of Progress and Tradition* (Knoxville: University of Tennessee Press, 1983), xix, 125; John W. Cell, *The Highest Stage of White Supremacy: The Origins of Segregation in South Africa and the American South* (Cambridge: Cambridge University Press, 1982), x, 18–19. On Parker's friendship with Tillman and its influence on him, Parker to Tillman, 27 August 1904, folder marked "American Civic Assn., Outgoing T's," box marked "American Civic Association, Park Dept. 1904–1905. Outgoing Letters N–Z," GAPP; Parker to Tillman, 22 March 1905, same folder; Tillman to Parker, 4 July 1904, folder marked "T," box marked "Incoming Letters, South Manchester, Conn.–W," GAPP; Parker to C. C. Newman, 30 August 1904, folder marked "American Civic Assn., Outgoing C's," box marked "American Civic Association, Park Dept. 1904–1905. Outgoing Letters A–M," GAPP; Parker to Frederick A. Ober, 15 August 1904, folder marked "American Civic Assn., Outgoing H's," same box.

40. On segregation, George A. Parker to Harlan P. Kelsey, 18 December 1906, folder marked "Office Letters—Salem Mass., Harlan P. Kelsey," box marked "Outgoing Letters O–Z," GAPP. On the "Southern question" and the South's destiny of national leadership, Parker to E. G. Routzhan, 22 March 1905, folder marked "American Civic Assn., Outgoing C's," box marked "American

Civic Association, Park Dept. 1904–1905, Outgoing Letters A–M," GAPP. On housing, *Publications of the Municipal Art Society of Hartford, Connecticut, no. 11, Proceedings of the Annual Meeting. November 13, 1908. Officers, Members, Reports of Committees. Unnecessary Noises, The Housing Question, The Billboard Campaign* (Hartford: Municipal Art Society, 1909), 41. JCCB 1908–09, 26–30. On housing problems of blacks, see also "Helping the Negro," *Hartford* 2/11 (1917): 6.

41. Christopher Silver, "The Racial Origins of Zoning: Southern Cities from 1910–40," *Planning Perspectives* 6 (1991): 189–205. See also Boyer, *Dreaming the Rational City*, 166–67. On Boston, Michael Holleran, "Boston's 'Sacred Sky Line': From Prohibiting to Sculpting Skyscrapers, 1891–1928," *Journal of Urban History* 22/5 (1996): 552. On Los Angeles, Boyer, *Dreaming the Rational City*, 94.

42. Minutes of Board of Directors' meeting, 2 June 1913, binder containing minutes of meetings, 15 December 1908–29 June 1933, MAS. The society was just one of many organizations nationwide that sought to block the spread of apartments; see Kenneth Baar, "The National Movement to Halt the Spread of Multifamily Housing, 1890–1926," *Journal of the American Planning Association* 58/1 (1992): 39–48.

43. "Report of the Commission on the City Plan, 1920–1922," 24 April 1922, drawer marked "City Plan Commission, Communications, Reports, Etc.," HCH. Robert H. Wiebe, *Businessmen and Reform: A Study of the Progressive Movement* (Cambridge: Harvard University Press, 1962). James Weinstein, *The Corporate Ideal in the Liberal State, 1900–1918* (Boston: Beacon Press, 1968). JCCC 1924–25, 10.

44. Toll, *Zoned American*, 143–87, 193, at 188.

45. Herbert S. Swan, "Does Your City Keep Its Gas Range in the Parlor and Its Piano in the Kitchen?" *American City* 22/4 (1920): 339. "Some Advantages of the So-Called Zoning System for Building Regulation," *Hartford* 7/9 (1922): 2. Parker, too, was fond of the building metaphor for city planning, writing of the need for "an architect of cities" who would plan the "location of its different functions" (George A. Parker to James Draper, 7 January 1902, folder marked "Keney Park, Worcester, Mass.," box marked "Keney Park, Outgoing Letters, 1900–1906, N–Z," GAPP). See also Toll, *Zoned American*, 239, 240.

46. Zane L. Miller and Bruce Tucker, *Changing Plans for America's Inner Cities: Cincinnati's Over-the-Rhine and Twentieth-Century Urbanism* (Columbus: Ohio State University Press, 1998). "From Henney to Rankin: 25 Years of Municipal Politics, No. 1," *Times*, 1 December 1931. "From Henney to Rankin: 25 Years of Municipal Politics, No. 81," *Times*, 22 February 1932.

47. "Ex-Mayor Stevens Dies Suddenly," *Courant*, 13 November 1932. "Reso-

lution de Zoning Plan," 25 June 1923, in drawer marked "City Plan Commission, Communications, Reports, Etc.," HCH. *JCCC* 1924–25, 10–11, 215–16. *Third Annual Message of Mayor Norman C. Stevens to the Court of Common Council of Hartford, Connecticut, May 10, 1926* (n.p., n.d. [1926]), 3. *JCCC* 1925–26, 252–53, 683–84, 825–26. On Fisher, *HD* 88 (1925–26): 88 (among the other members of the commission were an attorney, an insurance executive, and another real estate agent). Swan's role is noted in "Swan to Address Public Meeting," *Times*, 3 February 1926. The council's zoning committee was headed by Robert E. Hall (*JCCC* 1925–26, 1028; *HD* 88 [1925–26]: 383). The process also included obtaining enabling legislation from the state (*JCCC* 1924–25, 738–43). On the passage of the ordinance, see "Zoning Ordinance Passes Council, Soon Effective," *Courant*, 9 February 1926. During the preparation of the zoning ordinance, the council passed an interim ordinance in April 1925 ("Zoning Ordinance to Be Submitted," *Courant*, 12 April 1925; "Zoning Ordinance Passed by Council, May Go to Courts," *Courant*, 28 April 1925). "A Legitimate Complaint," *Times*, 6 February 1926.

48. "Interim Zone Law Flayed by Butler," *Courant*, 26 April 1925. "Zoning Ordinance Passed by Council, May Go to Courts." "Garage Zone Rules Made Less Strict," *Courant*, 1 January 1926. "Allow Business Buildings on Farmington Av.," *Times*, 2 January 1926. "Calls Lawrence St. 'Bootleggers' Row'," *Courant*, 3 February 1926. "New Zoning Plan Attacked Again," *Times*, 3 February 1926. "A Legitimate Complaint."

49. *JCCC* 1925–26, 883–99. "Building Zone Map, Hartford, Connecticut," in *JCCC* 1925–26, following 898. *Insurance Maps of Hartford, Connecticut*, vol. 2 (New York: Sanborn, 1922, with revisions to 1941).

50. *JCCC* 1925–26, 883–99, at 883.

51. For numerous examples of requested changes to zoning rules, see, for example, *JCCC* 1926–27, index, 204–08. On development to 1941, "Building Zone Map, Hartford, Connecticut," compared against *Insurance Maps of Hartford, Connecticut*. On present land use, personal observation. On zoning as a blueprint for change, see also Patricia Burgess, *Planning for the Private Interest: Land Use Controls and Residential Patterns in Columbus, Ohio, 1900–1970* (Columbus: Ohio State University Press, 1994), 100.

Chapter 10

1. Clay McShane, *Down the Asphalt Path: The Automobile and the American City* (New York: Columbia University Press, 1994), 209.

2. Jane Jacobs, *The Death and Life of Great American Cities* (New York: Random House, 1961), 50–54.

3. The sterility of downtown public space was obvious long before the collapse of downtown retailing in the late 1980s and early 1990s. It was one of the main issues explored by the Project for Public Spaces in 1980 in its federally funded study, "Downtown Hartford: Managing for Change," file marked "Community Development," vertical files collection, HPL.

Index

Adams, Sherman, 119, 123–24
African Americans, 19, 21–22, 72, 74
Albany, N.Y., 18
Americanization efforts, 148, 151, 158, 236–37
Ames, Charles, 107
armories, 237–38
Arnold, Herbert, 182
Arsenal neighborhood, 42, 153
Asylum Hill neighborhood: affluence of, 45, 212–13; development of, 19, 153, 252, 256–57; as home of reformers and political leaders, 45, 81, 86, 240; proposed rail tunnel under, 243; reform of public space in, 53, 62; use of public space in, 62, 134, 186. *See also* Farmington Avenue
athletics: facilities, 117, 122–23, 133–37, 142, 148, 155, 161; in parks, 118, 123, 130, 134, 145, 167–68, 170; separation from other park uses, 123, 137–39; in streets, 154–55; supervision of, 133, 151–52, 158–61, 167–68; viewed as aiding child development, 148, 152, 158–60, 163; viewed as alternative to misbehavior, 144, 148, 159, 163, 170; viewed as disruptions of parks, 119–20, 134, 136–37

Automobile Club of Hartford, 173–74, 208–11, 213–15, 217, 219, 222–24, 226, 265
automobiles, 213–28, 244, 247, 261–62, 265–66; effect on other uses of public space, 4–6, 149, 175–76, 220, 226, 228–29; effect on real estate development, 202, 213–14; effect on street surfaces, 206–8, 213–14; local manufacturing of, 39, 125; in parks, 125, 128–29; patterns of travel, 207–11; presence in streets, 1, 3–4, 172, 174, 184, 202, 205, 211, 215–17, 225–29; as threat to pedestrians and children, 172–76, 214–15, 218–24; use by elite, 219–20; use for prostitution, 90; use for shopping, 184, 194–95, 199. *See also* drives; parking; traffic

Baltimore, 204, 252
banking industry, 1, 18, 35, 46
Barry Square neighborhood, 36
bathhouses, 242
Beecher, Catharine, 15
Behind the Rocks neighborhood, 127–29, 245, 248
Bennett, Edward, 181
Bennett, Josephine, 232
Besson, Frank, 207

bicycles, 129, 140, 148, 204–5, 215–17, 219

billboards, 6, 50, 60–62, 243, 246

Bishoff, Annie, 158

Blacks. *See* African Americans

Blue Hills neighborhood, 45, 242, 245, 248, 256

bootblacks, 95, 177

Boston, 18, 69, 107, 121–22, 215, 252

Boys' Club, 149–50

boys' clubs, 101, 149–53, 156

Boy Scouts, 57–58

Boys' Reading Room Association, 149–50

Brainard, Leverett, 155, 204

Bristol, Cornelius, 102–3

Brooks, A. N., 64

Brunner, Arnold, 235

Buffalo, N.Y., 121–22

Bulkeley, Morgan, 47, 180

Burnham, Daniel, 235–36

Burr, Alfred, 101, 152

Burr, Frances, 101

Bushnell, Horace: biographical information, 13–14, 29, 42; and Bushnell Park, 12, 18, 20–29, 32, 116–19, 121, 125, 145; desire for social order, 12–13, 15–18, 24–25, 28–29, 32, 34, 260; distaste for social diversity, 12, 17, 22; ideas of child development, 14, 16, 168; ideas of city planning, 12, 29–33, 60, 231–32, 246–47, 258–60, 263–65; ideas of domesticity and women, 5, 12–16, 26, 29–32, 47–48, 254; ideas of public space, 5, 9, 12–13, 24–26, 28–33, 117, 121, 125–26, 145–46, 164, 168, 230–32; legacy for later reformers, 12, 32–33, 37–39, 48, 115, 125–26,

136, 139, 146, 164, 230, 233, 242, 264–65. *See also* "unconscious influence"

Bushnell Park: Bushnell's hopes for, 12, 18, 24–26, 28–29, 32, 121, 145; construction, 28; efforts to preserve, 62, 118, 129, 251; landscaping, 28, 117–19; legacy for later reformers, 46, 48, 264; naming of, 29; planning, 22–25, 27–28; in proposal for civic center, 237–38; proposals for changes to, 226, 242–44, 246; site, 20–22, 24; use of, 28–29, 117–20, 122–24, 129–30, 138, 145, 153–54, 266; zoning of adjacent land, 251, 257

Bushnell Plaza, 262

Carlin, Joseph, 183

Carrère, John, 230–31, 235, 243, 246

Carrère and Hastings (architectural firm), 225, 227–28, 231, 243–48, 252, 258

Catholics, 11–12, 17, 88, 106, 151, 224

Central Park, New York City, 22, 28, 124

Chamber of Commerce, 56, 225–26, 254–55

Chapman, Charles, 119

Charity Organization Society, 56, 66

Charter Oak neighborhood, 19, 45

Cheney, Louis, 87, 127–28, 192, 232, 255

Chicago, 85, 236

child development, ideas about, 14, 79, 94, 115, 132, 136, 148, 156–57, 159, 162–65, 168, 175–76

child labor, 94–96, 100, 107–8, 110, 264. *See also* newsboys

Child Labor Commission of New England, 108, 110

children in public space, attitudes toward, 78–79, 83–84, 93–94, 100, 102–15, 132–33, 148, 152, 156–57, 159, 168, 171–76. *See also* play; playgrounds

churches, 11–14, 16–17, 21–22, 60, 144, 235. *See also* clergy; Hartford Federation of Churches

Cincinnati, 255

City Beautiful movement, 59–60, 248, 264

City Hall Square. *See* State House Square

City Missionary Society, 75

City Plan Commission. *See* Commission on the City Plan

civic centers, 235–38, 246

Civic Club: advocacy of Juvenile Commission, 168; cleanliness campaigns, 33, 52–58, 62, 233; and female role in urban reform, 49, 51–52, 63; goals, 48; housing reform efforts, 55–57; membership, 51, 59; participation in billboard campaign, 61; participation in newsgirl campaign, 106; play reform efforts, 133, 156–59, 161

civic religion, 236–37

Clark, Roscoe, 206

class relations, 263, 265–66; and automobiles, 219–20, 224; and children's use of public space, 102, 104–5, 148, 151, 164, 220; ideas about, 12, 15–17, 25–26, 33, 46–47, 82–84, 91, 102, 104–5, 236, 247, 250, 263; and park space, 25–29, 46, 117–20, 125–27, 133–34, 137–39, 145–46; and peddlers, 177, 182, 187, 193–95, 200; and "progressive" reform, 37–38; and prostitution, 69–71, 82–84, 87; and residential development, 19, 28, 33, 45–46; and street improvements, 125–27; working-class participation in reform campaigns, 27, 86, 104–6, 133–34, 160, 265–66; working-class resistance to reform campaigns, 8, 58, 71, 107–8, 182–83, 193–95, 239, 265. *See also* labor unions; segregation of public space; strikes

Clay Hill neighborhood, 42, 257

Clemens, Samuel, 211–12

clergy, in reform campaigns, 60, 65–66, 69, 75–80, 85, 91, 102, 106, 129, 134, 149, 151, 168–69, 222. *See also* Bushnell, Horace

Clopper, Edward, 110

Cohen, Morris, 152, 175

Colt, Samuel, 121

Colt Park, 121, 138, 142–43, 155, 162, 169

Commission on the City Plan: Carrère and Hastings work for, 225, 243–48, 258; decisions on street layouts, 242, 248; formation, 240; and housing reform, 56, 240–41; lack of accomplishments, 241, 248–50, 260; powers of, 241; and public restrooms, 59; reformist goals, 242–43, 248–49; reorganization, 255; supervision of developers by, 241–42; Swan report for, 227–28; and zoning, 250

commuters, 93, 96

Connecticut River, 1, 18–19, 125

Connecticut Society for Social Hygiene, 81

Connecticut Woman Suffrage
Association, 81, 85, 87–88, 156
Constitution Plaza, 262
Consumers' League of Connecticut,
107–8, 111–12
Consumers' League of Hartford, 48,
106–8
Council of Jewish Women, 112–13
curfews, 104, 115

dancing, 50, 79, 112, 142–43, 145
Dashaway Club, 149–50
Daughters of the American
Revolution, 33, 61, 72–74
Davidson, Morris, 197
Davis, Mike, 4, 263
Day, Alice, 51, 53
DeForest, Robert, 41
Deming, Henry, 117
Dent, Elmer, 77–80, 115
department stores. *See* retail stores
Dickens, Charles, 20
dirt, ideas about, 50–51, 53, 58
Dixon, S. Wales, 142–43, 170–71
domesticity, ideas about, 5, 7, 12, 15–
16, 26, 32–33, 39, 47, 50–52, 56,
65, 69–70, 78, 80, 83, 92, 103–4,
106, 115, 149–50, 232, 254, 259,
263–64
Douglas, Ann, 236
drinking, 16, 38, 44, 70, 75–76, 79,
98, 130–31, 150–51, 183, 189
drives, in parks, 25, 28, 118, 124–25,
127–29, 139–40
Dwight, Henry, 52, 155

East Side neighborhood: children's
play in, 156–57, 171–73;
cleanliness campaigns in, 56–58;
described, 19–20, 41–44; dirtiness

of, 54–58, 62, 206; drinking in, 44,
79; effect on children debated,
103–5, 156–57; housing conditions
in, 20, 41–42, 56, 153; immigrants
in, 19–20, 41–44, 106–7, 187;
peddlers, grocers, and markets,
177–78, 187, 189–90, 194–99;
poverty in, 19–20, 44, 106; prostitution in, 44, 64, 66–68, 77–79,
89–91, 115; recreation facilities
for, 123, 142, 155–56, 173;
redevelopment of, 262; traffic safety
effort in, 222
East Side Push-Cart Peddlers'
Association, 198
economy of Hartford, 18, 34, 37
Eliot, Charles, 124
Elizabeth Park, 121–22, 124–26,
135–39, 169
expressmen, 3, 177–85, 199–200,
247, 259, 262

factory district: description, 40;
development, 19, 35; parking, 227;
proximity to residential areas, 45,
213; relationship with Pope Park,
121, 138; and street system, 206–8,
229, 245; working-class desire for
better access to, 127–29, 201
farmers, 181, 185–87, 189–94
Farmington Avenue, 211–13, 256
Farrell, Garrett, 174, 222
Farrell, Robert, 54
Fifoot, Arthur, 226
Fisher, Herbert, 255
Flagg, Charles, 58, 232–34, 249,
251–52, 259
Ford, Frederick, 61, 232, 237–38,
242, 250
Freeman, Harrison, 77

Frog Hollow neighborhood, 128,
153–55, 160, 193

gambling, 16, 19, 66, 75–76, 97, 108
gardening, 161–62
Garvan, Patrick, 126
gender, ideas about, 5–8, 14–15, 26,
33, 38–39, 46–49, 51, 58, 62–63,
65–66, 69, 75, 79–80, 83–84, 91–
92, 94, 99, 101–4, 107, 115, 117,
200, 236–37, 259
gentility, ideas about, 6–7, 26, 33,
46–47, 117–18, 231, 254, 259
Gleason, Dennis, 106
Godard, George, 232
Goddard, H. P., 149–50
Gold Street, 71–74, 91
"Good Roads" movement, 204
Good Will Club, 101, 150–53, 175
Goodwin, Charles, 183, 232, 240
Goodwin, Francis, 121
Goodwin Park, 121–22, 125–26,
138–39
Graham, W. A., 249
Greenville, S.C., 251
grocers, 43, 111, 147–48, 185–86,
192, 194–98
Gross, Charles, 123, 125, 131
Gulick, Luther, 163
Gunn, William, 66, 68–69, 77
Gunshanan, John, 107–8, 160, 182

hacks, 179–83
Hagarty, Frank, 192–93, 225
Hall, G. Stanley, 163
Hall, Mary: biographical information,
100–102, 108, 249; and Good Will
Club, 101, 150–53; ideas about
public space, 102, 105, 114–15,
152–53, 175; and newsgirls, 101–2,

105–7, 113–15; woman suffrage
efforts, 101, 100–102, 105–8, 113–
15, 150–53, 175, 249
Hall, Newton, 236
Halttunen, Karen, 26
Hamersley, W. J., 170
Hansling, Philip, Jr., 54
Hartford Board of Trade, 35, 39
Hartford Equal Franchise League, 33,
48, 63, 80–81, 86–87
Hartford Equal Rights Club, 70, 81,
101
Hartford Federation of Churches, 60–
61, 75–76, 106, 168
Hartford Home Building Association,
56
Hartford Turnerbund, 133
Hartford Vice Commission, 83, 85–
88, 90
Haussmann, Baron Georges-Eugène,
234
health officials, 54, 57–58, 190, 196,
206
Hebrew Peddlers' Association, 189,
191
Henney, William, 45, 59, 75–76, 107,
232–33, 240, 255
Hepburn, Katharine: anti-prostitution
efforts, 80–89, 92, 102, 114–15;
biographical information, 81;
maternalist views, 83–84, 89, 102;
views on gender, 80–84, 86, 89,
102; views on public space, 80, 84,
89, 92, 102, 114–15; views on
working class, 45–46, 83–84, 86;
woman suffrage efforts, 80–84
Hepburn, Thomas, 81
Hillyer, Dotha: biographical information, 47–49, 249; in city
planning efforts, 59, 232, 251;

Hillyer, Dotha (*continued*)
in cleanliness campaigns, 6, 48, 53,
63; in housing reform, 48, 57; other
reform activities, 48–49; and parks,
48, 129, 142; in play reform, 48,
157–58, 168, 175
Hine, Lewis, 97, 99, 108–9
Hobson, Barbara Meil, 90
Holcombe, Emily: biographical information, 72–73, 249; Gold Street
campaign, 72–74; in Municipal Art
Society, 232; reform strategy, 74, 91
Holcombe, John, 73
Holston, James, 4
home, as model for public space, 5,
7, 12, 16, 25–26, 29–33, 39, 46–
47, 50–51, 59, 92, 115, 128, 139,
145, 234, 236, 254, 259, 263–65.
See also domesticity; municipal
housekeeping
homosexuality, 68, 131
Honniss, William, 249
Hooker, John, 101
Hooker, Isabella Beecher, 101
horses: presence in parks, 125, 142;
presence on streets, 40, 44, 178,
181–84, 207, 213, 215; racing,
141–42; as sanitation problem, 52,
181–83, 200; and traffic safety, 157,
172–73, 215; use in peddling, 187,
199
hotels, 3, 75–76, 90
House of the Good Shepherd, 71
housing conditions: descriptions, 21–
22, 41–42; growth of slums, 19, 24,
41–42; middle-class reactions to,
19, 21–22, 42, 55; reform efforts,
38–39, 48, 55–58, 62, 72, 74, 196,
242–43, 252, 257

housing development: and class
segregation, 19, 28, 45, 238–39,
244, 252; middle-class districts, 19,
28, 45, 203, 244, 252; model
tenement plans, 56; proposed
workingmen's homes, 56, 240, 248,
252, 257; and racial segregation,
252; regulation by city, 241–42,
248; upper-class districts, 211–13;
working-class districts, 19, 45, 127,
153, 244, 252–53; and zoning, 232,
243, 252, 257. *See also* housing
conditions

immigrants: adjustment to
industrialization, 160; and child
labor, 95–96, 98; children's play,
147–48; differing use of public space, 43–44, 55, 177, 188,
199, 266; housing conditions
of, 55; neighborhoods, 42–43;
participation in reform activities,
86, 133; as targets of reform efforts,
55–56, 58, 112–13, 164, 187–88,
222, 236–37; as victims of traffic
accidents, 220; Yankee concern
about, 37, 42, 55, 81, 134, 148,
160, 188. *See also* Americanization
efforts; Irish Americans; Italian
Americans; Jews; nativism and
racism
immigration, 7, 33, 37, 42, 148
industrialization, 7, 13, 15, 33–34, 37.
See also manufacturing
infanticide, 131
insurance industry, 1, 18, 35, 46–47,
55, 57, 183, 213, 238, 240
interior decorating, 26, 29–30
Irish Americans, 11, 19, 22, 42, 120

isles of safety, 220–22
Italian Americans, 42–43, 95, 106, 187, 191, 197, 219

Jacobs, Jane, 4
jaywalking, 215, 222–24, 265
Jews, 19, 43, 86, 88, 98, 106–7, 112–13, 151, 187, 189, 191, 197
Jones, Mary, 168
Juvenile Commission, Hartford, 48, 95, 109, 168–69, 174
juvenile delinquency, 135, 148, 152, 163, 170. *See also* child development; vandalism

Kellogg, Frank, 119
Kelsey, Henry, 77
Keney Park, 121–22, 124–26, 135, 139, 165
Kinsella, Richard, 89, 91
Kunstler, James, 4

labor unions, 35–36, 104, 106, 119, 182, 192–93
landscaping in parks, 24–25, 28, 118–19, 124, 127, 132–33, 135, 137
law enforcement: against children, 3; against drunks, 44; against jaywalkers, 222–24; against litterers, 53, 55; against loiterers, 130; against newsboys, 114; against peddlers, 198; against prostitutes and brothelkeepers, 3, 65–71, 76–78, 90–91; against slumlords, 57; against speeders, 217; against spitters, 54; in traffic, 226; against vandals, 119, 132. *See also* police
Lawler, Joseph, 88–89

Le Corbusier, 261
littering, 51–55. *See also* street cleaning; trash disposal
Little River. *See* Park River
Loomis, H. G., 239–40
Lord, E. W., 110
Los Angeles, 252
lunch wagons, 179–80, 200

Manee, James, 193
Mann, Horace, 17
manufacturers: advocacy of street improvements, 204; opposition to child labor laws, 108; opposition to speed limits, 217
manufacturing: districts, plans for, 243, 252–53, 256; growth of, 18–19, 34–35, 37; pollution, 45. *See also* factory district
markets: chicken market, 190–91; curb markets, 189, 192–93, 197–200, 264; Hucksters' Market, 5, 169, 187, 189–92, 194; Market House, 185; Public Market, 192–95, 239, 249; in State House Square, 1, 186
Marsh, Benjamin, 250
Marsh, Seth, 27
Mason, Philip, 194
Maxim, Hiram, 215
Mayer, Henry, 106–7
McCook, Anson, 202
McCook, John, 44, 55, 193
McDowell, Mary, 51
Melvin, Nannie, 144
messenger boys, 95
Morganthau, Henry, 250
motherhood, ideas of, 9, 15, 70, 82–84, 102, 164

movies, 50, 79, 94, 96, 111, 143, 222
Municipal Art Society: billboard
    campaign, 60–62; city planning
    efforts, 232–35, 237–40, 249–53,
    259–60, 262–63; goals of, 59,
    232–34, 262–63; membership,
    232; and parks, 117, 127, 129;
    participation in cleanliness
    campaigns, 58–60; and Public
    Market, 193; suppression of noise,
    188–89, 199
municipal housekeeping, 33, 47–63,
    115, 264–65

National American Woman Suffrage
    Association, 82
National Child Labor Committee,
    107–8, 110
National Safety Council, 174
National Woman's Party, 82
nativism and racism, 12, 19, 22, 42,
    55, 148, 251–52
nature, ideas about, 26, 117–18, 140
New Haven, 18, 20, 31, 95
newsboys and newsgirls: demography,
    95–96; descriptions of work, 93,
    96–100; girls and boys viewed
    differently, 6, 94, 99–115, 259;
    presence in streets, 3, 93, 95, 112,
    114, 177; subculture, 97–99; as
    targets of reform campaigns, 3, 6,
    93–95, 100–115, 247, 259
newspapers: business, 96–97, 101;
    intervention in reform campaigns,
    76, 86–87, 99–104, 113, 218, 222
New York City: anti-prostitution
    efforts in, 69, 75; boys' clubs in,
    151; child labor reform in, 107;
    cleanliness campaigns in, 51, 54;
    economic relations with, 18; park

development in, 22, 28; providing
    models for local reform, 22, 31, 51,
    53–54; traffic in, 215; use of public
    space in, 263; zoning, 253–54
nightlife, 78–79, 115
noise ordinances, 188–89, 243, 246
North Meadows, 36, 245

office buildings, 1, 35, 40, 42, 99, 238,
    262. See also skyscrapers
Old Burying Ground, 72–75
Old State House, 1–3, 73, 237
Olmsted, Frederick, Jr., 250
Olmsted, Frederick Law: and Horace
    Bushnell, 22, 263; and Bushnell
    Park, 119; ideas on segregated
    space, 28–29, 146, 258; park
    designs, 22, 28, 121–22; remarks
    about crowded streets, 144–45
Olmsted, John: design of Hartford
    parks, 121–26, 132–33; opposition
    to traffic in parks, 127–28, 140;
    views on function of parks, 122,
    128–29, 137, 139, 146

packaged food, 195–96
pageants, 165–66, 176
Pallotti, Rocco, 198
Pankhurst, Emmeline, 81, 86–87
parades, 89, 117–18
Parker, Charles, 210
Parker, George: biographical
    information, 135, 249; and city
    planning, 9, 141, 172, 232–42,
    251–52; comments on importance
    of streets, 205; and housing reform,
    56, 248, 252, 257; ideas about child
    development, 132, 135–36, 162–
    67; ideas about segregated space,
    116, 127–29, 137–39, 145–46,

167, 171–72, 175–76; racial
attitudes, 251–52; and reform of
parks, 132–33, 135–41, 143–46,
168–70; and vandalism, 130–32
parking, 194, 198, 226–28
Park River, 19–22, 28, 35, 42, 122,
126–27, 193–94, 210, 235, 242–
44
parks: and children's play, 117–20,
122–23, 149, 155–56, 159–61,
164–69; complaints about
insufficient park space, 20, 120,
155; as components of urban
system, 5, 140–41, 244; design
philosophies, 24–25, 28, 31, 116–
19, 121–25, 127–29, 132–33, 135–
39, 145–46, 246; misbehavior in,
129–32; as model for reform of
public space, 39, 251, 259; as part
of trend toward segregation, 115–
16, 123, 126, 128, 137, 139, 145–
46; systems of, 116–17, 120–22,
125–26, 139–40; views of proper
use, 24–26, 31–32, 116–20, 122–
25, 127–29, 132–45; views of
social function, 12, 18, 22, 24–26,
29, 31–32, 39, 116, 125–26, 131–
32, 135, 145–46, 163–65, 236,
247, 263–64. *See also* athletics;
gardening; playgrounds; vacation
schools; *and individual parks by
name*
Parkville neighborhood, 134
parkways and boulevards, 59, 121,
125, 129, 244–46, 258
parlors, 25–26, 149
Paul, Alice, 82
paving. *See under* street improvements
Peabody, Harry, 76–78
peddlers: clientele, 52, 185–87, 191,

195–97, 199; conflicts with
children, 147–48; conflicts with
grocers, 185–86, 197–98, 200;
descriptions of work, 43, 186–88,
197–99; efforts to regulate, 3, 115,
177–78, 185, 187–89, 192, 196–
98, 247, 259, 264; immigrants as,
187–88, 199; middle-class dislike
of, 177, 188–89, 200; reactions to
Hucksters' Market, 191; segregation
of, 3, 177–78, 185, 187, 189, 197–
200, 229, 262, 264, 266. *See also*
East Side Push-Cart Peddlers'
Association; Hebrew Peddlers'
Association; markets
pedestrians: efforts to regulate, 3, 115,
203, 222–25, 229, 265; experience
described, 144–45; incovenienced
by peddlers, 189, 192; in parks,
125; in streets, 214–15, 219–24,
227–29; as victims of accidents,
215–16, 218–20, 222–24, 265;
walking to work, 201. *See also* isles
of safety; jaywalking; traffic safety
campaigns
Phelps, Oscar, 106, 111
Philadelphia, 204
picnicking, 44, 122, 135, 137, 139–
40, 158
play, in streets, 3, 52, 134, 147–49,
152, 154–57, 164, 166, 168–76,
229, 263, 265–66. *See also* boys'
clubs; child development; children
in public space; parks; playgrounds;
traffic accidents; traffic safety
campaigns; vacation schools
playgrounds: construction of, 159–61,
168–69; description, 166; as form
of segregation, 116, 149, 176, 264;
motivations for construction of, 3,

playgrounds (*continued*)
133, 148, 155–57, 159–60, 162–
65, 168–70, 262; in parks, 116,
133, 136, 160; supervision of, 148–
49, 160, 165–67, 169, 171; use of,
133, 170, 172; working-class
support for, 160, 266
police: assistance to homes for
prostitutes, 70–71; conflict with
East Side residents, 44; corruption,
64, 76–77; and expressmen, 184;
female officers, 87; interference
with street play, 154–55, 166; and
newsies, 110, 114; and peddlers,
192, 197–98; policy toward prostitution, 66, 68–69, 77, 83, 91;
traffic and crossing duties, 173–74,
216–18, 222–24, 226. *See also* law
enforcement
politics, 39, 63, 87–89, 119, 182, 255
Pope, Albert, 121, 204, 215
Pope Park, 121–23, 125–34, 137–38,
155, 160, 167, 219, 242, 244, 265
population, 18–19, 34, 39, 121
Potter, Rockwell H., 143–44, 168–69
profanity, 98, 130, 147, 181–82
"progressive" reform, 37–38, 82, 141,
148, 236, 249, 259
Prohibition, 59
prostitution: in automobiles, 90;
background of prostitutes, 79, 83;
clientele, 81, 83; and concern
about newsgirls, 100, 102–4;
defense of segregated prostitution,
64, 68–69; geography, 3, 19, 44,
66–68, 71–72, 77–78, 89–92, 155;
law enforcement against, 3, 65–71,
76–78, 90–91; messenger boys
and, 95; in parks, 131; police
corruption and, 64, 76–77; police

policies toward, 66, 68–69, 77, 83,
91; reform efforts against, 3, 6, 38–
39, 63, 65–66, 69–92, 112, 114–
15, 184, 247, 259, 264
purification of public space, 6–8, 12,
33, 39, 47, 62–63, 65–66, 74, 78,
88, 92, 104, 115, 196, 231, 264

racism. *See* nativism and racism
railroads, 18–22, 24, 40, 90, 97, 124,
130, 237–38, 243
railroad stations, 20, 22, 25, 90, 97,
179, 184, 205, 243
refrigerators, 195, 199
religious beliefs, influence on reform,
8, 12, 14–16, 38, 55, 58, 65, 69–70,
80, 136, 149, 151–52, 200, 264
religious conflict, 12, 17
restaurants, 1, 76, 90, 99, 144, 179
restrooms, 59, 131, 242, 246
retail stores, 1, 40–41, 44–45, 79, 87,
90, 108, 144, 154, 174, 178, 266
Riis, Jacob, 50
Riverside Park, 121–23, 131–33, 138,
142, 155, 159–61, 244
Roberts, Henry, 134
Robinson, Charles, 235
Rocky Ridge Park, 124–25, 244
Rood, Stanley, 160–61
Roosevelt, Theodore, 236
Root, Edward, 52
Ross, Edward, 236
Rothman, Sheila, 51

saloons, 19, 44, 59, 75–76, 85, 90,
98–100, 102–3, 108, 135, 144, 150,
179. *See also* drinking
schools, 17, 57, 61, 94, 106, 110–11,
114, 157, 159–62, 166, 169, 174
Schutz, Walter, 232

segregation, racial, 251–52, 259
segregation of public space, 5–8, 12,
  32–33, 38, 46–47, 64–65, 69, 78,
  84–85, 91–92, 104, 115–18, 122–
  23, 128–29, 137, 139, 141, 145–
  46, 149, 152, 167, 172, 175, 227,
  229, 231, 239, 247, 251–53, 258–
  60, 262, 264–66
settlement houses, 37, 106, 168
sex crimes, 113–14, 131. *See also*
  prostitution
sexual harassment, 3, 130, 144, 182,
  200
sexuality, 65, 79–80, 83–84, 114,
  131–32. *See also* homosexuality;
  prostitution; sex crimes
Shelter for Women, 70–71
shopping, 41, 44–45, 52, 87, 90, 104,
  144, 194–200, 266
Sigourney, Lydia, 27
Sigourney Square, 134
Sixth Ward Temperance Society,
  149–50
skyscrapers, 251, 256–57
slum clearance, 28, 72, 74, 209
Smith, Edward, 81, 84, 86, 88,
  184–85
snow removal, 210–11, 214, 229
Society for Public Improvement, 29
South End neighborhood, 90
South Green, 20, 120, 244, 257
South Green neighborhood, 19, 45
South Meadows, 36, 245
Spellacy, Thomas, 87–89
spitting, 54–55
Springfield, Mass., 18
state capitol, 24, 237, 246
State House Square (City Hall
  Square), 1–4, 36, 40, 59–60, 93,
  97, 111, 177–86, 199, 205

Stevens, Norman, 227, 250, 253, 255,
  258, 260
Stoeckel, Robbins, 174, 220
streetcars, 3–5, 40–41, 44–45, 54,
  93, 97, 111, 121, 128–29, 139–41,
  147, 157, 178, 181, 201–3, 205,
  207–8, 210, 212–13, 215, 219–22,
  247, 266
street cleaning, 37, 39, 48, 50–55,
  57–59, 196
street improvements: effect on
  development, 4–6, 202, 208, 212–
  14; effect on traffic patterns, 4–6,
  202–3, 207–9, 211, 213, 228–29;
  extensions, 225, 227, 235, 241–42,
  244–45, 265; limitations of, 226–
  27; method of financing, 204–5;
  opposition to, 202–3, 205–7, 210,
  212–13, 219; paving, 4, 59, 115,
  181, 202–11, 213–14, 229, 244,
  261, 265; straightening, 212;
  widening, 32, 71–72, 202, 206,
  209, 213, 225, 227, 235, 241, 244,
  265. *See also* isles of safety; traffic
  signals
street lighting, 78, 113, 132, 140, 144,
  180
streetscapes, 30–31, 154, 231, 263
strikes, 35–36, 87
suburbs, 4, 35, 44–45, 93, 213, 235, 261
suffragists, 6, 8, 63, 65–66, 80–89,
  91–92, 101–2, 114, 169, 264
Sullivan, Ignatius, 182–84
Sunday, Billy, 236
Swan, Herbert, 227–28, 254–55, 260

telephones, 181–82, 199
Thayer, George, 66–68
theaters, 75–76, 79, 90, 98, 111, 144–
  45, 227. *See also* movies

Tillman, Benjamin, 251
Todd, Robert, 56
Tonken, Morton, 147–48
traffic, 1, 3–7, 32, 141, 149, 155–57,
    171–76, 178, 180–81, 184–85,
    192–93, 199–200, 202–3, 206–29,
    231, 244, 253, 256, 259, 261–66
traffic accidents, 172–75, 218–24,
    229, 265
traffic laws, 203, 214, 216–17, 223–
    24, 227–29, 246, 265
traffic safety campaigns, 173–75,
    222–24, 265
traffic signals, 3, 226–28
tramps, 44, 123, 130–31, 261, 266
trash disposal, 52–55, 57–59
trolleys. *See* streetcars
Trollope, Anthony, 20
Tunnel Park, 130
Twain, Mark, 211–12

"unconscious influence," 16, 24, 26,
    38, 136, 139, 164
Union Station. *See* railroad stations
Upper Albany neighborhood, 36

vacation schools, 48, 133, 151–52,
    157–63, 165, 168, 175
vandalism, 130–33, 145, 148
Vaux, Calvert, 121
Veiller, Lawrence, 41, 56–57
venereal disease, 80–81, 84, 92, 113
vice district. *See* prostitution
vistas, 24–25, 28, 30–31, 246–47,
    258

Walker, George, 73, 102–3, 106
Waring, George, Jr., 51, 54
Warner, Charles, 126
Washington, D.C., 31, 107
Washington Street, 19, 28, 45–46,
    134, 141–42, 211, 213–14, 257
Weidenmann, Jacob, 28, 119
Weinstein, Yetta, 111
Welles, Mary, 107–8, 110–14
West End neighborhood, 45, 71, 153,
    255–56
Whyte, William, 4
Wilson, Woodrow, 249
Wirth, Theodore, 123–24, 126, 128–
    29, 133, 139, 146
Witkower, Rose, 172
Woman's Aid Society, 69–71, 144
Women: in paid workforce, 46–47,
    67, 79–80, 82–83, 86, 102, 104–5;
    in reform movements, 7–8, 49–51,
    58, 63, 65, 69–70, 86, 91–92, 114–
    15, 264. *See also* domesticity;
    gender
World War I, 39, 112, 142, 193, 224,
    249

Young Men's Christian Association,
    48, 151

Zeiter, John, 134
zoning, 6, 202, 231–32, 238–40,
    243–44, 250–58, 260, 265–66
Zueblin, Charles, 235

Urban Life and Urban Landscape Series
Zane L. Miller, General Editor

The series examines the history of urban life and the development of the urban landscape through works that place social, economic, and political issues in the intellectual and cultural context of their times.

Cincinnati, Queen City of the West: 1819–1838
  Daniel Aaron

Proportional Representation and Election Reform in Ohio
  Kathleen L. Barber

Fragments of Cities: The New American Downtowns and Neighborhoods
  Larry Bennett

The Lost Dream: Businessmen and City Planning on the Pacific Coast,
1890–1920
  Mansel G. Blackford

Planning for the Private Interest: Land Use Controls and Residential Patterns
in Columbus, Ohio, 1900–1970
  Patricia Burgess

Cincinnati Observed: Architecture and History
  John Clubbe

Suburb in the City: Chestnut Hill, Philadelphia, 1850–1990
  David R. Contosta

Main Street Blues: The Decline of Small-Town America
  Richard O. Davies

The Mysteries of the Great City: The Politics of Urban Design, 1877–1937
  John D. Fairfield

The Poetics of Cities: Designing Neighborhoods That Work
  Mike Greenberg

History in Urban Places: The Historic Districts of the United States
  David Hamer

Getting Around *Brown*: Desegregation, Development, and the Columbus
Public Schools
  Gregory S. Jacobs

Building Chicago: Suburban Developers and the Creation of a Divided
Metropolis
  Ann Durkin Keating

Silent City on a Hill: Landscapes of Memory and Boston's Mount Auburn
Cemetery
  Blanche Linden-Ward

Plague of Strangers: Social Groups and the Origins of City Services
in Cincinnati, 1819–1870
  Alan I Marcus

Changing Plans for America's Inner Cities: Cinannati's Over-The-Rhine
and Twentieth-Century Urbanism
  Zane L. Miller and Bruce Tucker

Polish Immigrants and Industrial Chicago: Workers on the South Side,
1880–1922
  Dominic A. Pacyga

The New York Approach: Robert Moses, Urban Liberals, and Redevelopment
of the Inner City
  Joel Schwartz

Designing Modern America: The Regional Planning Association and Its
Members
  Edward K. Spann

Hopedale: From Commune to Company Town, 1840–1920
  Edward K. Spann

Visions of Eden: Environmentalism, Urban Planning, and City Building
in St. Petersburg, Florida, 1900–1995
  R. Bruce Stephenson

Welcome to Heights High: The Crippling Politics of Restructuring America's
Public Schools
  Diana Tittle

Washing "The Great Unwashed": Public Baths in Urban America, 1840–1920
  Marilyn Thornton Williams